Awareness ✦ Technology ✦ Spina Bifida ✦
Injury ✦ Tourette Syndrome ✦ Traumatic
Visual Impairments ✦ Hearing ✦ Autism ✦ Attention
Deficit Disorders ✦ Pervasive Developmental Disorders
✦ Cerebral Palsy ✦ Education ✦ Deafness ✦ Cleft Palate ✦
Facial Differences ✦ Blindness ✦ Mental Illness ✦ Down

The Special-Needs ReadingList

Syndrome ✦ Technology ✦ Physical Disabilities ✦ Rare
Disorders ✦ Education ✦ Hydrocephalus ✦ Speech and
Language Disorders ✦ Traumatic Brain Injury ✦ Hearing
Loss ✦ Fragile X Syndrome ✦ Disability Awareness ✦
Blindness ✦ Autism ✦ Sensory Integration Disorder
✦ Alternative Communication ✦ Tourette Syndrome ✦ Visual
Impairments ✦ Cleft Palate ✦ Mental Illness ✦ Cerebral
Palsy ✦ Epilepsy ✦ Technology ✦ Health Care ✦ Fetal
Alcohol Syndrome ✦ Learning Disabilities ✦ Mental
Retardation ✦ Muscular Dystrophy ✦ Physical Disabilities
✦ Education ✦ Rare Disorders ✦ Sensory Integration
Disorders ✦ Speech and Language Disorders ✦ Disability
Awareness ✦ Autism ✦ Blindness ✦ Visual Impairments ✦

The
Special-Needs
ReadingList

◆ An Annotated Guide to the Best Publications
for Parents and Professionals ◆

◆ Wilma K. Sweeney ◆

◆ Foreword by Ann Turnbull ◆

Woodbine House
1998

Library of Congress Cataloging-in-Publication Data

Sweeney, Wilma K.
    The special-needs reading list : an annotated guide to the best publications for parents & professionals / by Wilma K. Sweeney.
       p.   cm.
    Includes indexes.
    ISBN 0-933149-74-3 (pbk.)
    1. Handicapped children—Bibliography. 2. Parents of handicapped children—Books and reading. 3. Best books. I. Title.
Z5814.C52S84 1998
[HV888]   97-52803
016.3624'083--dc21   CIP

Manufactured in the United States of America

10 9 8 7 6 5 4 3 2 1

This resource guide is dedicated to my very special resources,

Daniel, Chris, and Jeff.

I love you,
Mom

Table

of Contents

PART ONE: ALL DISABILITIES

Acknowledgements

No one can ever write a book without help and I have had plenty.

First, I have to say "Thank you" and "I love you" to my husband and resident Ph.D., cook, bottle washer, and kid raiser, Ray. For three years, he put up with my obsessive-compulsive drive to complete this resource guide for all of you.

Special "Thanks" to Dr. Michal Clark at Kern Regional Center in Bakersfield, California, for keeping those shelves in the HEARTS Connection Family Resource Center Library full of publications and videos for *all* the families in Kern County. The women at HEARTS have my sincere thanks for putting up with my many calls and inquiries, and my use of their resources.

Research is a true art and requires an incredibly talented person who attacks the process like a dog attacks the mail carrier. Linda Beatty is truly a researcher with incredible tenacity and devotion . . . not only to this project, but also to her friends.

The main reason that you can find anything in this book is because of the expertise of speech pathologist and very special friend, Ellen Jakubowski. Ellen organized and cross-referenced everything as the manuscript grew. Thank you for sharing one of your many talents with me.

God has blessed me by providing a church family who kept heart and soul together by feeding us; calling the organizations listed in the book and making sure they were still in operation; checking the 800 numbers listed; and organizing files and typing the manuscript. Thank you, Kelly Miller, Gretta Stevens, Gloria and George Hassemer, Ann Feehan, and Betty and Grady Moore. A special thanks to Kathy Brown, who typed every word I submitted to Woodbine House. Thank you, Tehachapi Valley United Methodist Church.

The computer was a "must" to complete this project. Thanks to colleague Darleen Jehnsen, who made my computer a reality just when I needed one.

Support groups are mentioned a lot in this book, but mine has been extra special. The folks at the Beach Center at the University of Kansas in Lawrence have been there for me throughout this process.

Thanks and hugs for Ann Turnbull, Martha Blue-Banning, and Opal. Thanks also to Cindy Higgins for that final review.

Thank you, Susan Stokes, Woodbine House editor. Your expertise, patience, and guidance have been invaluable.

Additionally, thank you, Janeen Adil, Beth Binns, Joyce Glenner, Deidre Hayden, Joan Medlen, Don Meyer, Craig Schulze, Sue Schwartz, and Romayne Smith, who all offered their time and expertise to read, review, and add to the manuscript. I am especially indebted to Mary Seward at the Fragile X Association of Southern California, Salie Farber at the Orange County Fragile X Resource Center, and Katherine Clapp at the FRAXA Research Foundation for helping me put together the resources in the section on fragile X syndrome.

Finally, thank you to Hod Gray at Special Needs Project World Wide for sending me books to review, providing me with "you can do it" phone calls, and being such a good long-distance friend.

Foreword

"We are drowning in information but starving for knowledge."
—Rutherford Rogers

All of us who seek information in the disability field have experienced the explosion of new publications over the last decade. On top of this print publication explosion has been the increasing presence of the World Wide Web, which has added an almost infinite expansion of information. In the midst of it all, however, we, as parents and professionals, can continue to *starve for knowledge while we drown in the information.*

It is precisely for this reason that I wholeheartedly endorse ***The Special-Needs Reading List: An Annotated Guide to the Best Publications for Parents and Professionals***. Wilma Sweeney has done an incredible job of identifying useful and practical information that answers priority questions. In reviewing Wilma's selections, I found many "favorites" of my own, as well as information of which I have been unaware that seems highly pertinent to both my parental and professional needs.

What difference will it make when our starvation for knowledge is satisfied? As Wilma reminds us, knowledge is power. When we are highly informed about our needs, strengths, preferences, and legal rights, we can then most effectively advocate for our children, our families, and others with disabilities. In our work at the Beach Center on Families and Disability, we study factors that contribute to empowerment—being able to get our wants and needs met. Through both our research and our ongoing relationships with countless families across the country, it is clear that knowledge is a key component of empowerment. Thus, ***The Special-Needs Reading List*** can enable each of us as readers—whether parents or professionals—to enhance our individual empowerment and the collective empowerment of those with whom we share this information.

I would be remiss in writing this Foreword if I didn't comment on Wilma Sweeney herself. I've had the pleasure of knowing Wilma for four or five years and communicating with her on a regular basis.

The first time I talked with Wilma on the telephone, I knew she was one of those empowered individuals brimming with knowledge, energy, and great expectations for the future. This has been confirmed to me over and over again throughout all of our interactions. I have tremendous trust in Wilma's judgment in reviewing, selecting, and highlighting key literature in the field. It's important to note that Wilma is the parent of sons with a disability. Her own experiences as a parent inform her judgment about the relevance of publications. Also as a consummate professional, Wilma has had a long career in supporting families and is highly sensitive to issues of diversity related to parental preferences. Thus, Wilma's double-pronged expertise adds to the richness of ***The Special-Needs Reading List.***

In sum, I am grateful to Wilma and to Woodbine House for preventing us as parents and professionals from *drowning in information* and for *satisfying our craving for knowledge.*

Any P. Turnbull
Beach Center on Families and Disability
The University of Kansas

Introduction

You hold in your hand the key to opening the doors marked "Help" and "Hope" for families of children with disabilites. This book is meant to guide you to publications that can empower you with the knowledge needed to achieve the most healthy, fulfilling lives possible for your child with disabilities and your family.

Included in this guide are books and periodicals available from commercial sources, as well as booklets, fact sheets, newsletters, and other print materials available from national, state, and local organizations and federal agencies. All materials were selected with an eye toward listing the most useful materials for *parents* of children with disabilities.

The books and periodicals (magazines, journals, newsletters) included here were chosen because they are:

- up-to-date;
- acccurate;
- written in parent-friendly language;
- written with a parent's information or support needs in mind;
- generally affordable;
- and, in the case of older books that might not represent the most current thinking on a subject, considered a classic.

Publications written primarily for professionals were included only when: 1) less technical publications on the subject were not available; or 2) the information contained in the publications would be extremely interesting and useful to parents despite the more technical language.

Most books listed were in print at the time they were reviewed. In a few instances, books known to be out of print were included because they were judged to be exceptionally useful or were on a subject about which little is currently available for parents. When more than one edition of a book was available, we listed the least expensive edition.

Organizations that are listed here were included primarily because they offer materials—books, booklets, fact sheets, newsletters, videos, reading lists, etc.—that satisfy the same criteria given above for books and periodicals. Where space permitted, we included information about other types of support and information provided by these organizations. Except in a few instances, organizations that disseminate information solely through web sites were not listed, although we made every effort to include e-mail addresses and web site addresses for organizations that offer information via web sites as well as print materials.

■ HOW TO USE THIS BOOK

The Special-Needs Reading List is organized into two major sections. Part I, All Disabilities, contains topically organized reviews of books and other publications on subjects of interest to families of children with a wide range of disabilities. For example, under the "Family Life" subject heading, you will find publications that are as useful for siblings of children with visual impairments as they are for siblings of children with cerebral palsy. Likewise, under the "Education" heading, you will discover publications with information relevant to any child who may be eligible for special education services. Publications related to Family Life or Education for children with *specific* disabilities, however, are listed in the second major section of the book, Part II. The majority of publications in Part I are for a parent audience, with the exception of the "Disability Awareness" category. In this section are listed publications that parents, teachers, or other professionals can use to acquaint children with issues such as differing abilities, disability etiquette, and what it is like to have a disability.

Part II, Specific Disabilities, provides reviews of publications about several dozen of the most common mental, physical, and emotional disabilities of childhood. Once again, the majority of publications included are for parents. However, we also included a sampling of books that parents might read with their children or recommend to older siblings or children with disabilities in each section. Parents who have read the section on their child's specific disability and are still looking for more information might browse the titles under other disabilities. For example, information on Mental Retardation in general might be helpful to parents of children with other types of developmental disabilities, and the information on children with a diagnosis of "speech and language disorder" might be useful to parents of children whose disability includes a communication delay. In particular, parents might want to check the organizations listed under each section for publications and other services that might be of use to them.

To locate publications on a particular topic, you can skim the subject headings in the Table of Contents or check the subject index in the back of the book if you want to ensure you do not overlook any relevant publications. Additional indexes allow you to look up publications by author or title, and to find all entries for particular organizations, many of which are listed in more than one section of the book.

■ HOW TO GET THE PUBLICATIONS YOU NEED

Buying Books

If you read a review of a book that you would like to get your hands on, there are several ways to proceed, depending on whether you would like to buy or borrow a copy of the book.

If you want to buy a book you read about in this work, you may first want to check on the price and availability of the book, depending on how many years have passed since publication of this volume. To do so, look up the book in a current edition of *Books in Print* at your public library or local bookstore, or ask a librarian or bookseller to check for you. You can also contact the publisher of the book directly, at the address and phone number listed at the back of this book. (In the publication data given for books reviewed here, the publisher's name appears after the city and state—or province—of publication.)

To order a copy of the book, it helps to know the ISBN (International Standard Book Number). This is the ten-digit number given at the very end of the publication data for each book. If you know the ISBN and the publisher's name, most bookstores will "special order" a book for you. This process, however, may take weeks or even months. A quicker way to obtain the book may be to call the publisher directly and ask whether you can place an order with them, with or without pre-payment. You will have to pay shipping and handling for the book, but you will not have to wait for your bookstore to order the book from a middle-man book distributor, which may or may not have the book in stock.

There are also bookshops that specialize in books about disabilities. They may have a book that interests you in stock, or may be able to track down a copy for you. Several of the more established bookshops are:

Books on Special Children (BOSC)
P.O. Box 305
Congers, NY 10920
(914) 638-1236; (914) 638-0847 FAX
E-mail: bosc@j51.com
> BOSC has an annotated list of books and articles on special-needs topics.

Disability Bookshop (Twin Peaks Press)
P.O. Box 129
Vancouver, WA 98666
(360) 694-2462; (360) 696-3210 FAX
E-mail: 73743.2634@Compuserve.com
> The Disability Bookshop will try hard to find any special-needs book a customer is looking for. The Bookshop's catalog is $5.00.

Special Needs Project
"Good Books about Disabilities"
3463 State St., Suite 282
Santa Barbara, CA 93105
(800) 333-6867; (805) 683-2341 FAX
E-mail: Books@specialneeds.com
> Special Needs Project has an extensive "Master Catalog" of books for adults and children on disability issues, and will also attempt to locate specific books a customer is seeking.

There are also Internet "bookstores" that list virtually every book in print on their "shelves." Although they do not have physical copies of every book in their warehouses, they can often ship your order to you within a matter of days. Although you have to pay shipping and handling costs, book prices are often discounted, so you may end up spending less, or only slightly more, than you would pay for the same book at a traditional bookstore. The two major Internet bookstores are:

1. Amazon Booksellers
> Sells both new and out-of-print titles. Inquire at: http://www.amazon.com

2. Barnes & Noble
> Inquire at: http://www.barnesandnoble.com

Borrowing Books

If a book is out of print or you would like to read without buying, try the obvious first—the public library. Check in the card file or computer indexing system. If your public library system does not own a copy of the book you are looking for, ask the librarian about borrowing it from another library through inter-library loan.

Remember to check with special-needs organizations near you. There well may be private collections held by chapters of the ARC or March of Dimes, parents' groups, or public or private schools or universities near your home. These are good places to find ephemeral, costly, or out-of-print material.

You may also be able to borrow books via the Southeast Kansas Education Service Center. This center "houses all of the materials that have been produced or obtained through various state grants and mails them anywhere in the world on loan"! The user pays return postage. Topics covered by their library include: assessment, communication, community-based instruction, deaf-blind integration, medical/health, parents/family, supported work, technology, early childhood, children's books, and general information. For further information, contact:

Southeast Kansas Education Service Center
P.O. Box 189
Girard, KS 66743-0189
(800) 531-3685; (316) 724-6281; (316) 724-6284 FAX
ATTN: Peggy A. Malicoat-Gentry, Coordinator PIN
(Professional Information Network)

Obtaining Organizational Publications

In this book, publications available from organizations are listed two different ways, depending on their length. The titles of newsletters, books, and booklets of approximately 50 pages or more are in bold-face type. The titles of publications shorter than 50 pages are enclosed in quotation marks.

If an organization produces a variety of materials of interest to you, you may wish to call to request a publications catalog to check on price and availability of titles. If you are just interested in one publication, it is wise to call and check on its price and availability before sending any money through the mail.

If you have Internet access, by all means, check out an organization's web site before placing an order for materials. The publication you are interested in may be available to download for free. Many organizations post their current newsletter on their web site, and others make a variety of fact sheets and other informational materials available.

■ KEEPING UP WITH THE INFORMATION EXPLOSION

In 1990, the publisher of this book published a bibliography called *A Reader's Guide for Parents of Children with Mental, Physical, or Emotional Disabilities.* This book, the predecessor to *The Special-Needs Reading List,* contained descriptions of approximately 1,000 publications of interest to parents of children with disabilities, and the author was reasonably certain that she had tracked down most publications in print that were useful to parents.

Whether fortunately or unfortunately, such comprehensiveness is no longer possible. Today, there is an information explosion in the disabilities field. More and more publishing companies are publishing books in this area, new organizations are continually being formed, and fresh Internet sites are springing up daily. These days, it would be impossible to put together a directory of *every* publication of interest to parents of children with disabilities—unless that directory was posted on a web site and updated every couple of days.

Since *The Special-Needs Reading List* could not be comprehensive, it is selective instead. It is intended to guide you to some of the very best publications available on a variety of disability-related topics. It represents what the author (and, in some case, advisors in different subject areas) deemed to be the most useful publications they came across. If a particular publication or organization does *not* appear in these pages, it does not mean that it was not judged to be worthy of parents' attention. It may have been inadvertently overlooked, or be on a topic that is already well-represented in the book. In addition, the following types of materials were deliberately excluded from the book:

- Publications that are not easily obtainable in the United States. Since readers in the U.S. can easily order print materials from Canadian organizations and web sites, you will find many Canadian organizations listed together with the U.S. organizations. Canadian books, however, are not routinely sold in the U.S.; hence the majority of books listed were published by U.S. publishers.

- Publications that deal exclusively with issues affecting *adults* with disabilities. To do justice to adult issues would require another volume, so this book focuses on issues affecting children (school age and under) and issues affecting all ages.

- Publications about chronic illnesses as opposed to disabilities. Although chronic illnesses can sometimes be disabling, because of space limitations this book concentrates on the conditions that most frequently qualify children for special education services.

- Publications from organizations that did not respond to our requests for information or copies of their materials. Although several organizations useful to parents were excluded in this manner, we did not wish to include organizations that might ignore parents' requests for information.

Within these parameters, *The Special-Needs Reading List* is as up-to-date and accurate as we could make it. It is inevitable, however, that some of the publications listed here will go out of print during the lifetime of this book. If you happen upon an out-of-print title that you feel you have to read, try the suggestions given above under "Borrowing Books," check your Yellow Pages under "Book Search Services," or ask a second-hand bookdealer to help you locate a copy.

Remember, knowledge *is* power. We hope this book will help you obtain the knowledge you need to help you and your family live life to the fullest.

Part 1
AllDisabilities

1.

General Interest and Reference

■ BOOKS AND PERIODICALS

Accardo, Pasquale J., and Barbara Y. Whitman. *Dictionary of Developmental Disabilities Terminology.* Baltimore, MD: Paul H. Brookes, 1996. 348 pp. $35.00. ISBN 1-55766-112-X.
> This dictionary defines over 3,000 terms related to developmental disabilities. Included are terms related to specific disabilities; assessment and treatment; disability-related legislation; and medical problems.

Accent on Living. Cheever Publishing, Inc., P.O. Box 700, Bloomington, IL 61702. (800) 787-8444.
> For over 40 years, this quarterly magazine has been providing information and resources for people with disabilities and their families. It publishes articles about independent living, resources, ideas, and personal accounts of individuals and families coping with disabilities. A one year subscription is $12.00. The magazine also publishes an annual *Buyers' Guide* ($15.00), which offers information about everything from automobile controls to publications. Products, sources, organizations, and dealers of equipment, supplies are all cross indexed for easy reference.

Batshaw, Mark L. *Children wih Disabilities.* 4th ed. Baltimore, MD: Paul H. Brookes, 1997. 992 pp. $49.95. ISBN 1-55766-293-2.
> For parents of children with disabilities, this readable, one-stop reference book offers much of value. It covers many common causes of disabilities in children, including prematurity, substance abuse, Down syndrome, fragile X syndrome, metabolic disorders, mental retardation, learning disabilities, vision and hearing problems, language disorders, autism and PDD, cerebral palsy, neural tube de-

fects, seizures, and traumatic brain injury. The author is careful to provide all the background needed to understand how conditions result in a disability, and therefore thoroughly explains information on genetics, fetal development, how the brain and nervous system work, and more. Daily care issues such as nutrition and feeding, dental care, coping emotionally, and behavior management are also addressed. An appendix new to this edition describes properties and uses of drugs and medicines.

Disability Resources Monthly. Disability Resources, Inc., 4 Glatter Lane, Centereach, NY 11720-1032. (516) 585-0290.

> This newsletter was designed to keep people with disabilities, their family members, and professionals informed about the most current and useful resources. It features reviews and notices about disability-related books, pamphlets, videos, software, and databases. A must for parents who want to keep abreast of developments in a broad range of disability issues. A one-year subscription is $30 ($40 outside the U.S.). Disability Resources also operates "Disability Resources on the Internet," which is profiled under "Internet Resources" in this book.

Exceptional Parent. P.O. Box 3000, Dept. EP, Denville, NJ 07834. (800) 562-1973. Web site: http://www.familyeducation.com

> This glossy monthly magazine is for parents of children and young adults with any disability. It offers articles on a wide range of issues of interest to parents, including education, laws and benefits, daily care, family life, resources, technology, and medical concerns. In a monthly column called "Search and Respond," readers can ask for help from other readers--whether it be information about their child's rare or undiagnosed condition, tips on coping with daily care or behavior problems, or requests for networking. An annual subscription is $32.00 in the U.S.; $43.00 in Canada.

Impact. Institute on Community Integration, 109 Pattee Hall, 150 Pillsbury Dr. SE, University of Minnesota, Minneapolis, MN 55455. (612) 624-4512.

> This quarterly newsletter is for parents, educators, service providers, and others interested in the well-being of persons with developmental disabilities. Each issue takes an in-depth look at a different topic and is targeted for a specific audience. Recent issues have focused on Inclusion and School Restructuring; Supporting Diversity; and Inclusive Recreation and Families. One copy of each issue is free; additional copies are $2 each.

Mackenzie, Leslie, and Amy Lignor, eds. *The Complete Directory for People with Disabilities.* Lakeville, CT: Grey House Publishing, 1994. 749 pp. $120.00. ISBN 0-939300-53-2.

> Although too expensive for the average parent, this comprehensive directory would be a great addition to any resource library. Included are sources for, and descriptions of, products, resources, books, and services for individuals with disabilities.

NARIC. *Directory of National Information Sources on Disabilities.* Silver Spring, MD: NARIC, 1994. 719 pp. $15.00.

> The two volumes in this set list hundreds of organizations and databases in the United States that provide information, referral, and direct services on a nationwide basis. The entries for each organization cover disabilities served, users served, description of the organization, and information services, including publications.

NARIC. *Guide to Disability & Rehabilitation Periodicals.* Silver Spring, MD: NARIC, 1994. 172 pp. $15.00.

> This useful directory includes descriptions and ordering information for more than 400 journals, magazines, and newsletters that cover disability and rehabilitation issues. Included are many periodicals available in braille or on cassette.

Pickett, Olivia K., Eileen M. Clark, and Laura D. Kavanagh, eds. ***Reaching Out: A Directory of National Organizations Related to Maternal and Child Health.*** Arlington, VA: National Center for Education in Maternal and Child Health, 1994. 190 pp. Free. ISBN 1-57285-001-9.

> This user-friendly directory lists nonprofit organizations that provide information and respond to questions from the public and health care professionals; national information centers funded by the Maternal and Child Health Bureau; and professional organizations that provide training to health professionals. It includes approximately 50 pages of listings devoted to organizations that focus on specific chronic illnesses and disabilities. Also included are organizations related to health and development issues in infants, children, adolescents, and women; nutrition; services for children with special-health care needs; and others. One copy of the directory is available free of charge from the National Maternal and Child Health Clearinghouse, listed under "Organizations" below.

Resources for Families and People Who Work with Families. Lawrence, KS: Beach Center on Families and Disability, updated twice yearly. $3.00.

> Hundreds of resources helpful to families of children with disabilities are listed in this directory. It includes up-to-date listings of useful publications, publishing companies, information and support services, Internet resources, and research and training centers.

Webb-Mitchell, Brett. ***God Plays Piano, Too: The Spiritual Lives of Disabled Children.*** New York, NY: Crossroad Publishing, 1993. 200 pp. $21.95. ISBN 0-8245-1374-6.

> The author's interest in the "religious imagination" of people with developmental disabilities was the impetus for this book. In it, he explores the religious beliefs of Christians and Jews with disabilities, and discusses what these beliefs mean about the nature of God, religion, and our society, which often discounts the spirituality of people with disabilities. His narratives are based both on spontaneous conversations, experiences, and encounters he has had with children and adults with disabilities and also on structured interviews with young people about their religious beliefs--including the nature of God, Satan, faith, and death.

■ ORGANIZATIONS

Alliance of Genetic Support Groups
35 Wisconsin Circle, Ste. 440
Chevy Chase, MD 20815-7015
E-mail: alliance@capaccess.org
Web site: http://medhelp.org/www/agsg.htm

> PURPOSE: A network of people with genetic conditions, parents, and professionals with an interest in the "consumer" approach toward genetics.
> PUBLICATIONS: ***Health Insurance Resource Guide*** ($10.00; free to members); *"Starting a Support Group"* (No charge); *"Informed Consent: Participation in Genetic Research Studies"* ($1.00).

March of Dimes
Resource Center
1275 Mamaroneck Ave.
White Plains, NY 10605
(888) MODIMES; (914) 997-4764 TTY; (914) 997-4763 FAX
Web site: http://www.modimes.org

> PURPOSE: The Resource Center of the March of Dimes provides information to the public about birth defects, pregnancy, and children's health issues.

PUBLICATIONS: Has free fact sheets on disabilities such as achondroplasia, cleft lip and palate, Down syndrome, neurofibromatosis, PKU, and spina bifida, as well as on genetic testing.

National Center for Youth with Disabilities
University of Minnesota, Box 721
420 Delaware St., SE
Minneapolis, MN 55455-0392
(612) 626-2825; (800) 333-6293; (612) 624-3939 TDD
E-mail: ncyd@gold.tc.umn.edu
Web site: http://www.peds.umn.edu/Centers/ncyd

PURPOSE: "An information and resource center focusing on adolescents with chronic illnesses and disabilities."

SERVICES: Operates a National Resource Library which collects information on adolescents, disability, and transition and is accessible to the public through a toll-free number.

PUBLICATIONS: Offers a number of *Cydline Reviews,* annotated bibliographies on selected topics related to youths with chronic illnesses or disabilities. Topics include: *"Promoting Decision-Making Skills by Youth with Disabilities"*; *"Issues in Sexuality for Adolescents with Chronic Illnesses and Disabilities"*; *"Issues in Nutrition for Adolescents with Chronic Illnesses and Disabilities"*; *"Developing Social Skills."* Costs range from $4.00-$6.50.

NIH Neurology Institute
National Institute of Neurological Disorders and Stroke
P.O. Box 5801
Bethesda, MD 20824
(800) 352-9424; (301) 402-2186 FAX
Web site: http://www.ninds.nih.gov

PURPOSE: Supports research into brain and nervous system disorders.

PUBLICATIONS: Free publications include: *Neurological Disorders: Voluntary Health Agencies and Other Patient Resources* (a directory); *"Know Your Brain"* (fact sheet on anatomy and function); fact sheets on a variety of neurological disorders, including autism, the dystonias, Friedreich's ataxia, Joseph Disease, Lipid Storage Diseases, the Neurofibromatoses, progressive supranuclear palsy, Tourette syndrome, and tuberous sclerosis.

National Information Center for Children and Youth with Disabilities (NICHCY)
P.O. Box 1492
Washington, DC 20013-1492
(800) 695-0285; (202) 884-8441 FAX
E-mail: nichcy@aed.org
Web site: http://www.nichcy.org

PURPOSE: A clearinghouse that provides information on disabilities and disability-related issues, with an emphasis on children and young people birth to age 22.

SERVICES: Personal responses to questions on disability issues; referrals to other organizations and agencies; database searches; technical assistance to parent and professional groups.

PUBLICATIONS: *"State Resource Sheets"* for each state and territory in the U.S. (free); *"National Resources"* (free); *"Parenting a Child with Special Needs: A Guide to Readings and Resources"* (free); *"A Parent's Guide: Accessing the ERIC Resource Collection"* ($2.00). Many others, especially on educational issues.

National Maternal and Child Health Clearinghouse

2070 Chain Bridge Rd., Ste. 450
Vienna, VA 22182-2536
(703) 356-1964; (703) 821-2098 FAX
E-mail: nmchc@circsol.com
Web site: http://www.circsol.com/mch

> PURPOSE: "Disseminates state-of-the-art information about maternal and child health." Most of the publications distributed were developed through programs funded by grants from the Maternal and Child Health Bureau.
>
> SERVICES: Clearinghouse staff respond to requests for information or refer callers to other information agencies and sources.
>
> PUBLICATIONS: Include *Understanding DNA Testing: A Basic Guide for Families* (#D088, no charge); *National Survey of Treatment Programs for PKU and Selected Other Inherited Metabolic Diseases* (#C049, no charge); *The Open Door: Parent Participation in State Policymaking about Children with Special Health Needs* (#B339, no charge). Most publications are free. Request a publications catalog.

National Organization on Disability

910 16th St., NW
Washington, DC 20006
(202) 293-5960; (202) 293-5968 TTY; (202) 293-7999 FAX
Web site: http://www.nod.org

> PURPOSE: A national network organization concerned with all disabilities, all age groups, and all disability issues. Promotes the full and equal participation of Americans with disabilities in all walks of life.
>
> SERVICES: Has a number of programs. Through its Community Partnership Program, responds to community requests and provides advice and ideas to expand the participation of individuals with disabilities in their communities. Its Religion and Disability Program aims to remove barriers to the full participation of persons with disabilities in religious life.
>
> PUBLICATIONS: Include *That All May Worship,* to assist religious groups in welcoming persons with disabilities ($10); *From Barriers to Bridges,* to foster dialog between people with disabilities, religious leaders, and the community ($10); *"Guide to Organizing a Community Partnership Program"* (free).

The National Rehabilitation Information Center (NARIC)

8455 Colesville Rd.
Suite 935
Silver Spring, MD 20910-3319
(800) 346-2742; (301) 588-9284
Web site: http://www.naric.com/naric

> PURPOSE: A library and information center on disability and rehabilitation. NARIC collects and distributes the results of federally funded research projects, as well as commercially published materials.
>
> SERVICES: Offers free quick reference and referral services by phone. For a nominal fee, an information specialist will search NARIC's bibliographic database (REHABDATA) and provide a printout of all the documents available on a particular topic. These documents can be ordered through NARIC.
>
> PUBLICATIONS: In addition to several publications described above, publications include directories of disability research, resource guides on specific disabilities and topics, disability statistics, *NARIC Calendar of Events* (monthly listing of disability-related conferences and other events). Many publications available online. Request a publications list.

2.

Disability Awareness

Included in this section are: 1) books that can help children understand how people with and without disabilities are similar and alike; and 2) books that can help adults choose appropriate books and activities to increase children's understanding of disability issues. Children's books on specific disabilities are included in *Part Two*.

■ BOOKS

For Adults

Bunch, Gary. *Kids, Disabilities, and Regular Classrooms: An Annotated Bibliography of Selected Children's Literature on Disability.* Toronto: Inclusion Press, 1996. 111 pp. $15.00.
> The purpose of this fine guide is to direct educators and children to children's literature that presents people with disabilities in a positive light. Brief descriptions of about 150 children's stories are provided.

Friedberg, Joan Brest, June B. Mullins, and Adelaide Weir Sukiennik. *Portraying Persons with Disabilities: An Annotated Bibliography of Nonfiction for Children and Teenagers.* 2nd ed. New Providence, NJ: R.R. Bowker, 1992. 385 pp. $39.95. ISBN 0-8352-3022-8.
> The focus of this bibliography is on nonfiction books that are meant to "foster constructive attitudes toward human differences." More specifically, the books listed generally deal with disabling conditions that affect younger people and last throughout life. Included are reference books on

disabilities; books dealing with physical problems; sensory problems; cognitive and behavior problems; multiple/severe disabilities. For each book, a synopsis is provided, followed by the authors' analysis about how useful, current, and unbiased the content of the book is. Reading levels, from preschool through young adult, are given as well as citations to help readers locate additional reviews of the book. Most books reviewed were published since 1984.

Getskow, Veronica, and Dee Konczal. *Kids with Special Needs: Information and Activities to Promote Awareness and Understanding.* Santa Barbara, CA: The Learning Works, 1996. 200 pp. $16.95. ISBN 0-88160-244-2.

> This is an awareness manual for parents, teachers, and kids. After reviewing the grief cycle, laws, and what's available in your community for kids with special needs, the book explains how to create awareness activities that can be helpful in *any* classroom. There's a class survey, activities, a disability myth game, and much more. The resource sections are especially valuable.

Robertson, Debra. *Portraying Persons with Disabilities: An Annotated Bibliography of Fiction for Children and Teenagers.* 3rd ed. New Providence, NJ: R.R. Bowker, 1992. 482 pp. $39.95. 0-8352-3023-6.

> This bibliography reviews more than 650 fiction titles for young people that promote acceptance and understanding of people with disabilities. A synopsis of each book is given, along with the author's analysis about how realistic, current, and unbiased the work is. Books appropriate for preschool children through young adults are included.

Vaughn, Sharon, and Liz Rothlein. *Read It Again! Books to Prepare Children for Inclusion.* Glenview, IL: GoodYearBooks/Scott, Foresman, 1994. 124 pp. $9.95. ISBN 0-673-36082-2.

> Although designed primarily for classroom teachers, this book also includes home activities for parents to do with their children. It recommends specific picture books that the authors feel will help children in grades kindergarten to third grade understand classmates with various physical, mental, and emotional disabilities. Lists of discussion questions and activities for each book are included.

For Children

FICTION

Derby, Janice. *Are You My Friend?* Scottdale, PA: Herald Press, 1993. 40 pp. $12.95. ISBN 0-8361-3609-8.

> We are more alike than different is the message of this children's book. Every page talks about differences and challenges *and* the strengths of the individual. It sets the stage for making friends and understanding feelings.

Kraus, Robert. *Leo the Late Bloomer.* New York, NY: HarperCollins, 1971. 32 pp. $16.00. ISBN 0-87807-042-7. (Other editions available.)

> Leo is a tiger cub who just can't keep up with what the other animals are doing. He can't read, write, or speak, and he is a sloppy eater. His mother is sure that Leo is simply a late bloomer, and she turns out to be right. A good book to help young children understand that everyone develops at their own rate.

O'Shaughnessy, Ellen. *Somebody Called Me a Retard Today . . . and My Heart Felt Sad.* New York: Walker and Company, 1992. 20 pp. $14.85. ISBN 0-8027-8197-7.

> This very simply worded book is designed to help nondisabled children understand that children with disabilities have feelings too. Suitable for older preschool and elementary school children.

Pinkwater, Daniel Manus. *The Big Orange Splot.* New York: Scholastic, 1977. 32 pp. $3.95. ISBN 0-590-44510-3.

> All the houses on Mr. Plumbean's street are the same until a seagull drops a bucket of paint on his house. This event eventually helps both Mr. Plumbean and his neighbors realize that being different is not necessarily a bad thing.

Schwier, Karen Melberg. *Keith Edward's Different Day.* San Luis Obispo, CA: Impact Publishers. 27 pp. $4.95. ISBN 0-915166-74-7.

> Join Keith Edward as he meets a variety of people with differences, including Down syndrome and physical differences, and learns that being different is OK. A discussion guide for parents and teachers is included. The book would be appropriate for preschool or lower elementary grades.

Schwier, Karin Melberg. *Idea Man.* Eastman, Quebec: Diverse City Press, 1997. 43 pp. $10.00. ISBN 1-896230-09-1.

> Erin is angry when her parents leave her overnight with family friends. The family's older son, Jim, is in the "dummy class" at school and better known as the Dork. Erin's worst fears are realized when two girls from her seventh grade class witness Jim giving her a hug. After Jim helps Erin with a creative writing homework assignment, however, she begins to see her mistake in judging Jim based on what others say. A good book to get middle schoolers thinking about the importance of being sensitive to others' feelings and looking beneath surface differences. Although Jim apparently has Down syndrome, no labels are used, making this a useful jumping off point for understanding people with a variety of developmental disabilities.

NONFICTION

Bunnett, Rochelle, and Carl Sahlhoff. *Friends in the Park.* New York, NY: Checkerboard Press, 1992. 37 pp. $7.95. ISBN 1-56288-347-X.

> Eye-catching, candid color photographs illustrate this story about preschoolers playing together in the park. Children with and without disabilities are shown swinging, sliding, playing ball, blowing bubbles, riding trikes, and, in general, enjoying each other's company. The disabilities are not pointed out in the text, but short biographical notes at the end of the book identify the children's interests and their disabilities, if any. Appropriate for ages 4-8.

Exley, Helen, ed. *What It's Like to Be Me.* New York, NY: Friendship Press, 1984. 127 pp. $10.95. ISBN 0-377-00144-9.

> You will rarely find a book that is more candid than this one. Children from all over the world write about themselves and their disabilities. They tell us how they see themselves and how they want to be seen. For instance, one ten-year-old boy contributes, "I'm not unhappy with my situation as I could have been born a duck or a chicken." All of the illustrations are created by the children and are priceless. Selections include both poetry and prose.

Kent, Deborah, and Kathryn A. Quinlan. *Extraordinary People with Disabilities.* Danbury, CT: Children's Press, 1996. 288 pp. $15.95. ISBN 0-516-26074-X (paperback).

> Nearly 50 men and women with mental or physical disabilities are profiled in this collection for students in grades 5-10. There is a good mix of historical and contemporary, well-known and lesser-known, male and female individuals of all races, with both acquired and congenital disabilities. Among those profiled are: a champion wheelchair marathoner with spina bifida, a partially blind ballet dancer, a photographer with polio, a deaf author and book reviewer, an Indian chief with muscular dystrophy, and an activist and psychotherapist with cerebral palsy, as well as such well-known figures as Thomas Edison, Ludwig van Beethoven, Harriet Tubman, Tom Cruise, Chris Burke, and Robert Dole. The book is illustrated with black and white photographs.

McCarthy-Tucker, Sherri. ***Coping with Special-Needs Classmates.*** New York, NY: Rosen, 1993. $15.95. ISBN 0-8239-1598-0.

> In this young adult text, the author provides descriptions of a number of disabilities, then offers examples of how children themselves view disabilities. Strategies for teaching awareness and guidelines to use with children who are learning about disabilities are included, as is a chapter about understanding your own personal feelings regarding challenges and people who live with them. A brief list of resources and a good glossary complete this well-written book.

McConnell, Nancy P. ***Different and Alike.*** 3rd ed. Colorado Springs: Current, 1993. 40 pp. $5.50. ISBN 0-944943-32-2.

> The message of this children's book is "being different is just another way of being you." Colorful pictures, smiling faces, and information about "some differences called disabilities" are important parts of this delightful book. Each section has suggestions about accommodating and befriending people with different disabilities. In the section on hearing loss, pudgy little fingers illustrate the alphabet in sign. An example of Braille is provided in the section on visual disabilities. This is a wonderful awareness book. Children will love the pictures and the discussion and the exercises as they learn a little about what it may feel like to have a disability and how they can make friends with people with differences.

Smith, Sally L. ***Different Is Not Bad, Different Is the World.*** Longmont, CO: Sopris West. 30 pp. $7.50.

> This illustrated book for children in grades 2-6 is designed to help children with and without disabilities reach a better understanding of cognitive and physical disabilities and children who have them. The emphasis is on the value of all people. Included is information about well-known, successful people with disabilities.

Stein, Sara Bonnett. ***About Handicaps: An Open Family Book for Parents and Children Together.*** New York, NY: Walker and Co., 1991. 48 pp. $14.95 (Hardcover) ISBN 080-2772-250. $8.95 (Paperback) ISBN 080-2761-747.

> This book focuses on the relationship between two boys, one with cerebral palsy. It provides a family, a daycare provider, or a teacher with a knowledge base about disabilities. Although it was originally written in 1974, its message is timeless. There is small print for the adult to read and large print for the child to read. This approach *requires* interaction between adult and child. The book is a great resource for discussion about inclusion and all the challenges that go along with it. Many black and white photographs are included.

Westridge Young Writers Workshop. ***Kids Explore the Gifts of Children with Special Needs.*** Santa Fe, NM: John Muir Publications, 1994. 115 pp. $9.95. ISBN 1-56261-156-9.

> Part of the "Kids Explore" series, this slim paperback is meant to help readers learn to respect all people. The authors are students in the third through sixth grades who got to know fellow students with disabilities and then wrote short biographical essays about them. The students profiled have fetal alcohol syndrome, cerebral palsy, dyslexia, osteogenesis imperfecta, ADHD, Down syndrome, hemophilia, hearing loss, blindness, and dwarfism. The essays answer questions commonly asked about each disability, and also offer glimpses into how the students get along at school, in their families, and in the community. Many black and white photographs are included.

■ ORGANIZATIONS

National Easter Seal Society
230 W. Monroe St., Ste. 1800
Chicago, IL 60606-4802
(312) 726-6200; (312) 726-1494 FAX
Web site: http://www.seals.com

> PURPOSE: To help people with disabilities achieve independence.
>
> SERVICES: Operates nearly 500 direct service sites providing therapy and other needed services for children and adults with disabilities throughout the U.S. and Puerto Rico. Also sponsors public education campaigns, advocates for needed legislation and programs, and promotes use of assistive technology.
>
> PUBLICATIONS: *Friends Who Care Teachers Kit* ($25.00) is a curriculum to help teachers help students understand what it is like to have a disability. Includes a teacher's guide, activity sheets, posters, and video.

United Cerebral Palsy (UCP)
1660 L St., N.W., Ste. 700
Washington, DC 20036
(800) 872-5827; (202) 776-0414 FAX; (202) 973-7197 TTY
Web site: http//www.ucpa.org

> PURPOSE: "To advance the independence, productivity and full citizenship of people with cerebral palsy and other disabilities, through our commitment to the principles of independence, inclusion, and self-determination."
>
> SERVICES: Include a toll-free information and referral line, for information on disability issues in general, as well as on cerebral palsy. Local affiliates provide direct services to people with disabilities and their families, including therapy, assistive technology training, advocacy, and employment assistance.
>
> PUBLICATIONS: *Walk with Me* ($6) was written by a boy with cerebral palsy to help other children understand what it is like to have a disability. UCP also distributes a "Basic Bookshelf," a catalog of print materials on a variety of disability topics published by a variety of publishers.

3.

Infants and Toddlers

■ BOOKS AND PERIODICALS

Basic Information

Auckett, Amelia. ***Baby Massage-Parent-Child Bonding Through Touch.*** New York, NY: Newmarket Press, 1982. 127 pp. $10.95. ISBN 1-55704-022-2.

> This book teaches loving and nurturing your baby through massage. The author shares her personal views about the positive aspects of massage throughout the book. She believes that both mother and father can receive the benefits of this loving experience along with their baby. Although the techniques described are illustrated, the book is best used as support with a hands-on course in infant message.

FIRST START Program. ***Handbook for the Care of Infants & Toddlers with Disabilities & Chronic Conditions.*** Lawrence, KS: Learner Designs, Inc., 1991. 284 pp. $34.95 ISBN 0-9622675-1-1.

> One of the best training manuals around. The manual describes a variety of specific disabilities, as well as common considerations such as skin care, nutrition, and selecting and using adaptive equipment. This is an excellent resource for day care centers, preschool centers, aides, technicians, and teachers, as well as parents.

Growing Child. Dunn & Hargitt, Inc., 22 N. 2nd St., Lafayette, IN 47902. (317) 423-2624.

> While the focus of this quarterly newsletter is on the typically developing young child, it is important to remember that children with special needs are often more typical than atypical. Each issue provides suggestions for age-appropriate toys, as well as information about issues

such as social adjustment for infants and toddlers and common areas of parental concerns. Subscriptions are $15.00 yearly.

Manginello, Frank P., and Theresa F. DiGeronimo. *Your Premature Baby: Everything You Need to Know about the Childbirth, Treatment, and Parenting of Premature Infants.* New York, NY: John Wiley & Sons, 1991. 296 pp. ISBN 0-471-53587-7.

> This guide for parents of premature babies covers what to expect in terms of appearance, behavior, feeding, and respiratory problems for babies born at gestational ages between 25 and 37 weeks. The authors include a thorough discussion of possible medical complications of premature birth, as well as treatments. Several parents have contributed detailed stories about the birth and early days of their premature babies. A new edition of this book is to be released in 1998 (ISBN 0-471-23996-8).

Segal, Marilyn. *In Time and with Love: Caring for the Special Needs Baby.* New York, NY: New Market Press, 1988. 191 pp. $12.95. ISBN 0-937858-96-X.

> This author provides information for parents and caretakers of children born pre-term and those with delays. Emotions, day-to-day interactions, using play activities to teach, and building parent/ professional collaboration are focal points.

Child Care

Rab, Victoria Youcha, and Karren Ikeda Wood. *Child Care and the ADA.* Baltimore, MD: Paul H. Brookes, 1995. 240 pp. $25.95. ISBN 1-55766-185-5.

> This is a guide for child care providers, early interventionists, and preschool teachers who are including children with special needs in their programs. The authors explain the Americans with Disabilities Act and how it affects programs for children birth to 5 years old. Sample Individual Family Services Plans are included.

Roeher Institute. *Quality Childcare for All: A Guide to Integration.* North York, Ontario: Roeher Institute, 1992. 81 pp. $18.00. ISBN 1-895070-06-0.

> This manual for parents and daycare providers offers suggestions for creating an inclusive program. Included are forms for taking an inventory of the children's needs and a checklist for determining the degree of parent involvement. This is a great resource for identifying a good daycare program.

Searl, Julia. *Serving Children with Special Needs in Your Child Care Facility.* Syracuse, NY: Center on Human Policy, 1996. 46 pp. $6.95.

> Although targeted at child care providers, this short manual may prove useful to parents seeking an inclusive child care center. It covers the benefits of inclusion, strategies for family involvement, and methods for fostering staff attitudes and skills necessary for successful inclusion of children with disabilities in child care facilities.

Early Intervention & Preschool

Beckman, Paula J., and Gayle Beckman Boyes. *Deciphering the System: A Guide for Families of Young Children with Disabilities.* Cambridge, MA: Brookline, 1993. 180 pp. $21.95. ISBN 0-914797-87-5.

> This book was written specifically to guide parents of children with disabilities aged birth to five through the educational system. There are checklists and guides for developing IFSP/IEPs and for planning transitions, and an exceptional explanation of assessment and assessment tools (tests). Many suggestions are provided to help parents work collaboratively with professionals. Appendices include a glossary, an extensive reference list, and a list of state contacts.

Bricker, Diane, and Juliann J. Woods Cripe. ***An Activity-Based Approach to Early Intervention.*** Baltimore, MD: Paul H. Brookes, 1992. 240 pp. $27.00. ISBN 1-55766-087-5.

> The focus of this manual is on learning to use naturally occuring events to teach infants and toddlers. Although intended for teachers and therapists, parents might find it useful when working with professionals to develop their child's IFSP or IEP.

Coleman, Jeanine G. ***The Early Intervention Dictionary.*** Bethesda, MD: Woodbine House, 1993. 337 pp. $16.95. ISBN 0-933149-62-X.

> In easy-to-understand language, this book offers definitions for hundreds of terms relating to early intervention. Entries include words and abbreviations from the fields of pediatric medicine, child development, early intervention and special education, physical, occupational, and speech-language therapy, audiology, and education of the deaf and visally impaired. Growth charts, APGAR scoring charts, immunization schedules, and nutritional and feeding positions are included.

Hanson, Marci J., and Eleanor W. Lynch. ***Early Intervention: Implementing Child and Family Devices for Infants and Toddlers Who Are at Risk or Disabled.*** Austin, TX: PRO ED, 1989. 449 pp. $42.50. ISBN 0-89079-198-8.

> Although this guide was written for implementers of early intervention services, it also provides an enormous amount of information for parents, who are the most important part of the implementation team. There are references, selected readings, and best practice information at the end of each chapter. The parent questionnaire and the best practice questions provide excellent program evaluation tools.

Johnson, Lawrence, R.J. Gallagher, M.J. La Montagne, June B. Jordan, James J. Gallagher, Patricia L. Hutinger, and Merle B. Karnes. ***Meeting Early Intervention Challenges: Issues from Birth to Three.*** 2nd ed. Baltimore, MD: Paul H. Brookes, 1994.297 pp. $30.00. ISBN 1-55766-131-6.

> Parents who are peer-counselors, professionals working with families of young children, and parents who want to research the "why" and "how" of early intervention may be interested in this text. It was written by leaders in the field of early intervention. The authors carefully examine theories and then identify the challenges to providing early intervention services to families and children. This text is rich with resources, ideas, and information. A long list of references is provided at the end of each chapter.

Jordan, June B., James J. Gallagher, Patricia L. Hutinger, and Merle B. Karnes, eds. ***Early Childhood Special Education: Birth to Three.*** Reston, VA: The Council for Exceptional Children, 1990. 257 pp. $27.00. ISBN 0-86586-179-X.

> This book is a comprehensive referenced approach to defining, structuring, and maintaining early intervention programs. While written for professionals, parents may find this text informative because it illustrates the foundation for professional learning and philosophy as they relate to early intervention. One particular emphasis is on the kind of professionals with expertise in a variety of areas who are and will be working with young children and their families. This is a fine, information-packed publication.

Weber, Jayne Dixon. ***Transitioning "Special" Children Into Elementary School.*** Boulder, CA: Books Beyond Borders, Inc., 1994. 56 pp. $8.50. ISBN 1-883862-04-3.

> This short book is useful for parents, although written to help infant development and preschool programs help parents and caretakers plan for the move to Kindergarten. The author offers numerous steps, strategies, and points to think about. Personal accounts lend a parent-to-parent touch. Throughout, the author emphasizes the importance of teamwork in accomplishing a successful transition.

Zipper, I.N., C. Hinton, M. Weil, and K. Rounds. *Family Centered Service Coordination: A Manual for Parents.* Chapel Hill, NC: University of North Carolina, 1992. 33 pp. $3.00.

> This is a brief but thorough explanation of early intervention for parents—from federal mandate to transition planning. A parent checklist and reference section are included.

For Children

Collins, Pat Lowery. *Waiting for Baby Joe.* Niles, IL: Albert Whitman & Co., 1990. 40 pp. $12.95. ISBN 0-8075-8625-0.

> When Missy's brother, Joe, is born two months early, he weighs just over three pounds. On her first visit to the NICU, Missy thinks that Joe looks like a "scary frog" and is afraid to touch him. Once she gets over her fears, she begins to resent all the attention the baby is getting from her parents. Eventually, however, Missy begins to feel better about the situation when she judges that Joe is finally ready for a big sister. Because Baby Joe has medical problems including jaundice and a heart defect and needs to be on an apnea monitor when he comes home, this book would be useful to young siblings of babies hospitalized for a variety of reasons, not just prematurity. The black and white photos capture the expressions of Missy—who appears five or six years old--especially well.

■ ORGANIZATIONS

ADA Disabilities Information Line
U.S. Department of Justice
Civil Rights Division
Disabilities Rights Section
Box 66730
Washington, DC 20035-66738
800-514-0301; 800-514-0383 (TDD)
202-514-6193 (electronic modem)
Web site: http://www.usdoj.gov/crt/ada/

> PURPOSE: The Dept. of Justice is responsible for enforcing Titles II and III (Public Services and Public Accommodations) of the ADA and for disseminating information about the act.
> SERVICES: By calling ADA Information Line, callers can listen to an overview of the ADA and complaint process, obtain information on Titles II and III, order materials in print and alternative format on the ADA, and be referred to other agencies for additional assistance.
> PUBLICATION: A booklet, *"Commonly Asked Questions about Child Care Centers and the ADA,"* is free of charge.

Association for the Care of Children's Health
7910 Woodmont Ave., Ste. 300
Bethesda, MD 20814
800/808-2224; 301/654-6549
E-mail: acch@clark.net
Web site: http://www.acch.org

> PURPOSE: A multidisciplinary membership organization that strives to improve the quality of care for children and their families through education, dissemination of resources, research, and advocacy.
> PUBLICATIONS: ***Bringing Your Baby Home: A Guide to Discharge Planning from Neonatal Intensive Care*** ($5.50); ***Guiding Your Child Through Preterm Development*** ($6.00). Members of ACCH receive a substantial discount on publications.

Beach Center on Families and Disability
University of Kansas
3111 Haworth Hall
Lawrence, KS 66045
(785) 864-7600 voice & TDD; (785) 864-7605 FAX
E-mail: beach@dole.lsi.ukans.edu
Web site: http://www.lsi.ukans.edu/beach/beachhp.htm
> PURPOSE: Conducts research on training and disability issues affecting families, sponsors conferences, publishes and disseminates a wide range of publications on family issues.
> PUBLICATIONS: *"Get a Family-Friendly IFSP"* ($.50); ***Handbook for the Development of a Family-Friendly Individualized Family Service Plan*** ($7.00); ***Parent Handbook for Individualized Family Service Plans*** ($5.00).

Child Care Law Center
22 2nd St., 5th Floor
San Francisco, CA 94105
(415) 495-5498; (415) 495-6734
> PURPOSE: a nonprofit legal services organization dedicated to fostering the development of high quality, affordable child care.
> PUBLICATIONS: ***Child Care and the ADA: Highlights for Parents of Children with Disabilities*** ($5); *"Assistance of a Personal Nature under the ADA"* ($1.50).

Illinois State Board of Education
Education Board for Midwestern United States
1124 Rosemont
Chicago, IL 60660
(773) 262-0533
> PUBLICATION: *"Special Children, Special Care: Early Childhood Education for Children with Disabilities"* is a free booklet that covers developing strategies, monitoring progress, and developing an educational process that focuses on your child's strengths and needs. The information is not specific to Illinois.

La Leche League International
P.O. Box 4079
Schaumburg, IL 60168-4079
(847) 519-7730; (847) 519-0035 FAX
E-mail (orders only): OrderDepartment@llli.org
Web site: http://www.lalecheleague.org/
> PURPOSE: To provide education, information, support, and encouragement to women interested in breastfeeding.
> PUBLICATIONS: Has a variety of books, booklets, and fact sheets on breastfeeding in general, as well as on "Special Situations" such as breastfeeding a baby who is premature, chronically ill, or has Down syndrome or a cleft lip or palate. Request a publications catalog.

National Center for Clinical Infant Programs
733 Fifteenth St., NW
Washington, DC 20005
(202) 347-0308
> PURPOSE: Dedicated to the sound health, mental health, and development of infants and toddlers.
> SERVICES: Information sharing.

PUBLICATIONS: *"Four Critical Junctures: Support for Parents of Children with Special Needs,"* a brochure that makes a great handout for parent/professional trainings. Also, ***Zero to Three,*** a newsletter published three times a year. It provides information about new publications, videos, and current topics for early intervention professionals. Publications are free.

National Information Center for Children and Youth with Disabilities (NICHCY)

P.O. Box 1492
Washington, DC 20013-1492
(800) 695-0285; (202) 884-8441 FAX
E-mail: nichcy@aed.org   Web site: http://www.nichcy.org
> PURPOSE: A clearinghouse that provides information on disabilities and disability-related issues, with an emphasis on children and young people birth to age 22.
>
> SERVICES: personal responses to questions on disability issues; referrals to other organizations and agencies; database searches; technical assistance to parent and professional groups. Information and referral for parents of children with special needs.
>
> PUBLICATIONS: Information from NICHCY is available on many subjects that relate to disabilities. For parents of infants and toddlers, there are publications on writing IFSPs, legal issues, coping, and *"A Parent's Guide: Assessing Programs for Infants, Toddlers and Preschoolers with Disabilities."* There is a small charge for most print items, or they can be downloaded free of charge from the Internet.

National Library Service for the Blind and Physically Handicapped

Library of Congress
1291 Taylor St., NW
Washington, DC 20542
(800) 424-8567
E-mail: nls@loc.gov   Web site: http://www.loc.gov/nls
> PURPOSE: Distributes reading materials in alternate formats (braille, audiotape) to U.S. citizens who are blind or have a physical impairment that prevents them from using ordinary printed materials.
>
> PUBLICATION: Reference circular no. 92-1, "Parent's Guide to the Development of Preschool Children with Disabilities: Resources and Services" lists special-format materials, educational games, toys and play equipment, a selected bibliography and national organizations concerned with infants, toddlers, and preschool children with disabilities. Free.

The Roeher Institute

Kinsmen Building
York University
4700 Keele St.
North York, Ontario
Canada M3J 1P3
(416) 661-2023 Voice/TDD; (416) 661-5701 FAX
Web site: http://indie.ca/roeher/intro.html
> PURPOSE: "Promotes the equality, participation, and self-determination of people with intellectual and other disabilities."
>
> SERVICES: Information services include reference and referral information, customized responses to questions, the development of information packages on specific topics, and operation of an extensive library. Also conducts research and public policy analysis and social development and training.
>
> PUBLICATIONS: Include ***Quality Child Care for All: A Guide to Integration*** ($18.00) and ***Literature Review of Early Intervention*** ($10.00).

4.

Daily Care

■ BOOKS AND PERIODICALS

Independence-Building Skills

Baker, Bruce L., and Alan J. Brightman. *Steps to Independence: Teaching Everyday Skills to Children with Special Needs.* 3rd ed. Baltimore: Paul H. Brookes, 1997. 392 pp. $26.00. ISBN 1-55766-268-1.

> True to its title, this indispensible and practical guide explains, step-by-step, how to help children with disabilities master everyday skills. The authors explain strategies to use in teaching skills to children in general, and also discuss teaching specific skills, including toilet training, dressing, household chores, play skills, and more. A helpful section on managing behavior problems at home is included, as well as using technology to enhance children's learning.

Briggs, Freda. *Developing Personal Safety Skills in Children with Disabilities.* Baltimore: Paul H. Brookes, 1995. 226 pp. $34.00. ISBN 1-55766-184-7.

> This handbook for parents and professionals explains why teaching personal safety skills to children with disabilities is so crucial and discusses self-esteem and assertiveness as foundations to safety skills. The author also covers specific safety skills, such as dealing with strangers, what to do when lost, and avoiding sexual abuse.

Mannix, Darlene. *Life Skills Activities for Special Children.* West Nyack, NY: Center for Applied Research in Education, 1992. $27.95. ISBN 0-87628-547-7.

> Included in this collection of lesson plans are dozens of activities designed to help teach "life skills" to children with disabilities. The skills are organized into four sections: 1) Basic Survival Skills (personal information about oneself, telephone skills, using money, time concepts, etc.); 2) Personal Independence (dressing, grooming, food and eating, etc.); 3) Community Independence

(community places such as restaurants and movie theaters, getting around, reading a map or schedule, etc.); 4) Getting Along with Others (recognizing diversity, cooperating with others, understanding others, good manners). The activities are designed primarily to be used by teachers with students in upper elementary grades, but might also be useful at home.

Mannix, Darlene. *Social Skills Activities for Special Children.* West Nyack, NY: Center for Applied Research in Education, 1993. $27.95. ISBN 0-87628-868-9.

> Primarily a practical manual for teachers, this book includes ready-to-use lesson plans for teaching a variety of social skills to children with special needs in upper elementary grades and beyond. Topics covered include: Accepting Rules and Authority at School; Relating to Peers; and Developing Positive Social Skills. Skills are taught within the context of real-life activities and sections are clearly organized and full of reproducibles. Many of the lessons in this book could be applied to home and recreational planning for children with and without special needs.

Mealtimes

Horsley, Janet. *Nutrition Management of Handicapped and Chronically Ill School Age Children: A Resource Manual for School Personnel, Families and Health Professionals.* Richmond, VA: Virginia Dept. of Health & Virginia Dept. of Education, 1996. 93 pp. No charge.

> This loose-leaf manual is intended to help school personnel and parents manage dietary and special feeding problems at school. It covers practical interventions during the school day for food-related problems that often accompany disabilities, including overweight, underweight, constipation, and feeding problems. It also provides a several-page overview of dietary considerations related to specific disabilities and chronic illnesses. A helpful section on the Individualized Education Plan and 504 Accomodation Plan explains, with examples for various disabilities, how nutrition goals and objectives can be incorporated into a child's educational plan. One copy of the book (pub. #I113) is available free from the National Maternal and Child Health Clearinghouse, at the address listed in the Publisher's section at the back of the book.

Klein, Marsha Dunn, and Tracy A. Delaney. *Feeding and Nutrition for the Child with Special Needs: Handouts for Parents.* San Antonio, TX: Therapy Skill Builders, 1994. 601 pp. $97.00. ISBN 0-7616-4332X.

> The 195 reproducible articles in this manual are intended to be used by therapists as handouts for parents. They cover feeding and nutrition issues of concern to families of children with specific disabilities, as well as concerns of a more general nature. Some of the broad topics covered include Nutrition Guidelines, Tube Feedings, Breast and Bottle Feeding, Introducing Food from a Spoon, and Family Mealtime Interactions/Communication. Families of children with significant feeding difficulties may want to invest in this publication; others may want to ask their children's therapist to share information in the book that is of interest to them.

Nutrition Focus. CHDD-University of Washington, Box 357920, Seattle, WA 98195-7920. (206) 685-7990.

> A publication of the Nutrition Section at the Center on Human Development and Disability, this newsletter focuses on nutritional concerns of children with special health care needs. Articles cover special concerns related to children with specific disabilities such as cerebral palsy or Down syndrome, as well as information useful to children with many different illnesses or disabilities, such as strategies for helping underweight children gain weight or dental care concerns. The newsletter is published six times a year. Subscriptions are $30.00 annually.

Satter, Ellyn. *How to Get Your Kid to Eat . . . But Not Too Much.* Palo Alto, CA: Bull Publishing, 1987. 396 pp. $16.95. ISBN 0-915950-83-9.

> In this wonderfully delightful and practical book, the author provides insight into feeding a child from birth through adolescence. Most of the book is written for parents of all children, but one chapter is devoted to issues related to feeding children who were premature or who have developmental disabilities, critical illnesses, or life-threatening diseases.

Toilet Training

Foxx, Richard M., and Nathan H. Azrin. *Toilet Training Persons with Developmental Disabilities: A Rapid Program for Day & Nighttime Independent Toileting.* Champaign, IL: Research Press, 1983. 156 pp. $9.95. ISBN 0-87822-025-9.

> Step by step, the authors outline a program for teaching children and adults with mental retardation to use the toilet independently. Their techniques involve working intensely on toileting skills over a period of time, offering plenty of drinks so that there are many opportunities to practice, and providing rewards immediately to reinforce progress.

Gilpin, Michelle, and Dorothy Harris. *Toilet Teaching with Your Special Child.* 2nd ed. London, Ontario: Thames Valley Children's Centre, 1996. 40 pp. $9.95. ISBN 0-9680545-0-1. (Distributed by Devinjer House.)

> Rather than explaining step-by-step how to toilet train a child with disabilities, this spiral-bound book offers general guidelines to bear in mind when training a child with physical or developmental disabilities. There is useful information about how constipation can affect toilet training and how to reduce constipation. The authors also cover such general concerns as how to decide whether a child is ready; choosing a potty seat; motivating the child; switching from diapers to underwear; and night-time dryness.

Sleep

Durand, V. Mark. *Sleep Better! A Guide to Improving Sleep for Children with Special Needs.* Baltimore: Paul H. Brookes, 1998. 288 pp. $21.95. ISBN 1-55766-315-7.

> This practical guide describes techniques successfully used to treat sleep disorders in children with a variety of special needs. Case stories of real families who have solved their children's sleep problems enliven the book. Also included are a sleep diary, behavior log, and lists of resources such as support groups and sleep centers.

■ ORGANIZATIONS

La Leche League International
P.O. Box 4079
Schaumburg, IL 60168-4079
(847) 519-7730; (847) 519-0035 FAX
E-mail (orders only): OrderDepartment@llli.org
Web site: http://www.lalecheleague.org/

> PURPOSE: To provide education, information, support, and encouragement to women interested in breastfeeding.
> PUBLICATIONS: Has a variety of books, booklets, and fact sheets on breastfeeding in general, as well as on "Special Situations" such as breastfeeding a baby who is premature, chronically ill, or has Down syndrome or a cleft lip or palate. Request a publications catalog.

National Association for Continence
P.O. Box 8310
Spartanburg, SC 29305
(800) 252-3337; (864) 579-7902
Web site: http://www.nafc.org

> PURPOSE: Strives to be "the leading source of education, advocacy, and support to the public and to the health professional about the causes, prevention, diagnosis, treatments, and management alternatives for incontinence."
>
> PUBLICATIONS: Publications available include: *"Seeking Treatment for Incontinence"* ($5.00); *"Let's Get Things Moving,"* a book about causes of and treatments for constipation ($9.95); *"Dry All Night,"* an illustrated book designed for parents and children to use together ($15.95). Fact sheets on a variety of topics are available for $1.00 each. Members receive a quarterly newsletter and a *"Resource Guide"* listing products and services for incontinence (also available for purchase, $10.00).

UCP of Birmingham
2430 11th Ave. North
Birmingham, AL 35234

> **Publications:** Offers a series of pamphlets written by a dietitian about nutrition-related problems in children with disabilities: *"Oral-Motor Development and Feeding Techniques"; "Promoting Weight Gain"; "Management of Constipation"; "Weight Control for the Overweight Child"; "Meal Planning for the Childhood Years."* Pamphlets are $1.00 each.

5.

Family Life

■ BOOKS AND PERIODICALS

Basic Information

Batshaw, Mark L. *Your Child Has a Disability.* Boston, MA: Little, Brown, 1991. 345 pp. $18.95. ISBN 0-316-083682.

> This is a terrific reference book for parents. The author describes the effect that a disability may have on the entire family. He discusses the grieving process and how families may cope with it. Many aspects of decision making prior to and during the diagnosis period are discussed. Personal, medical, and genetic planning are included. A special part of this book is the question and answer section at the end of each chapter. Dr. Batshaw addresses commonly asked questions ("Why me?", "Why my child?"), treatment approaches, accessibility issues, and planning for the future. He provides the kind of information parents need to make informed decisions. Real-life examples are used, adding a personal touch.

Duffy, Susan, Kathy McGlynn, Jan Mariska, and Jeannie Murphy. *Acceptance Is Only the First Battle.* 2nd ed. Missoula, MT: Montana University Affiliated Rural Inst. on Disabilities, 1990. 45 pp. $4.00 (includes S&H).

> This brief, empathetic guide to coping with the changes that having a child with a disability bring was written by four mothers who met in a parent support group. The chapter on "Being a Medical Detective" would be extremely helpful to parents still seeking a diagnosis, as it lists specific steps to take in trying to figure out a baffling problem. Another chapter includes a checklist of factors to consider when given conflicting professional advice. The chapter called "Things Some Professionals Did That Drove Us Nuts and Made Us Crazy" will hit home with many parents and help empower them to persist in going after what is right for their child. For new parents, there is an excellent account of the coping strategies one mother used that helped her survive emotionally the first three years after her daughter's birth with Down syndrome.

Exceptional Parent. P.O. Box 3000, Dept. EP, Denville, NJ 07834. (800) 562-1973. Web site: http://www.familyeducation.com

This glossy monthly magazine is for parents of children and young adults with any disability. It offers articles on a wide range of issues of interest to parents, including education, laws and benefits, daily care, family life, resources, technology, and medical concerns. A major emphasis is on providing information from parents and professionals to help in coping with the lifelong challenges of raising a child with disabilities. In a monthly column called "Search and Respond," readers can ask for help from other readers--whether it be information about their child's rare or undiagnosed condition, tips on coping with daily care or behavior problems, or requests for networking. A one-year subscription is $32 in the U.S.; $43 in Canada.

Families and Disability Newsletter. Beach Center on Families and Disability, University of Kansas, 3111 Haworth Hall, Lawrence, KS 66045. (785) 864-7600 voice & TDD; (785) 864-7605 FAX.

This newsletter includes stories of how real-life families are coping with the challenges and joys of raising children with disabilities, updates on research, and practical advice for parents. Subscriptions to the newsletter, published three times a year, are free.

Gill, Barbara. *Changed by a Child: Companion Notes for Parents of a Child with a Disability.* New York, NY: Doubleday, 1997. 314 pp. $19.95. ISBN 0-385-48242-6.

The author, the mother of a child with Down syndrome, assembled this collection of very brief essays to reassure and uplift other parents of children with disabilities. She uses personal experiences, anecdotes that other parents have related to her, and brief excerpts from others' writings as jumping off points to explore difficult issues or to pose points to ponder related to raising a child with disabilities. Examples of topics discussed include: "Sorrow," "Fate," "Rage," "Potential," "Dreams," "Complaining," "Grandparents," "Fatigue," "Hope," "Lighten Up," "Patience," "Tiger Mothers," "Risk," "Siblings," "Losing It," "School Meetings," "Empowerment," "To Fight or Not to Fight." Because of its topical organization, the book does not have to be read from front to back; it invites parents to skip around to find a topic that will speak to them and help them put troubling aspects of their lives into perspective.

Goldfarb, Lori, Mary Jane Brotherson, Jean Ann Summers, and Ann P. Turnbull. *Meeting the Challenge of Disability or Chronic Illness: A Family Guide.* Baltimore: Paul H. Brookes, 1986. 181 pp. ISBN 0-933716-55-9. Out of print.

These authors identify the effects of having a child or family member with a disability. They describe how everyone is affected, feels the strain and frustrations, and copes. This book guides the family as they look at their value systems, philosophies, strengths, and needs. Issues such as communication problems and balancing the needs of family members are addressed and strategies for smoothing out these potential rough spots are included.

Miller, Nancy B. *Nobody's Perfect: Living & Growing with Children Who Have Special Needs.* Baltimore: Paul H. Brookes, 1994. 307 pp. $21.00. ISBN 1-55766-143-X.

Parents of children with special needs have to do what *they* think is best for their children, according to the author of this supportive book. Typically, parents' perceptions of what is right change as they progress through the four stages of adaptation: surviving, searching, settling in, and separating. To help parents make the right decisions and feel good about themselves and their families at every stage, this book first examines common emotions, coping strategies, and goals in the life of a family. Afterwards, the book looks at the many different relationships needed for successful adaptation (between husband and wife, siblings, friends, and professionals) and provides practical suggestions to help make these relationships work. An especially useful chapter focuses on preserving the emotional health of parents, offering many strategies for recognizing and reducing stress. Throughout the book are numerous quotations from four mothers of children with special needs—spina bifida, autism, Pierre Robin sequence, and a chromosomal abnormality similar to Prader-Willi syndrome. These quotations underscore the author's belief that there are many "right" ways to cope with raising a child with special needs and many "right" ways to achieve a satisfying life for everyone in the family.

Satir, Virginia. *The New Peoplemaking.* Mt. View, CA: Science and Behavior Books, 1988. 393 pp. $19.95. ISBN 0-8341-0070-6.

> Although this self-help book was not written specifically for parents of children with disabilities, it offers much of value. Chapters focus on family dynamics and what can go awry. The author writes knowledgeably about miscommunications that can and do occur in family situations, then describes how to handle them.

Simons, Robin. *After the Tears: Parents Talk about Raising a Child with a Disability.* Orlando, FL: Harcourt Brace, 1987. 89 pp. $7.95. ISBN 0-15-602900-6.

> This slim volume takes an intimate look at how a child with disabilities affects the emotional life of the family. Quotations and anecdotes from parents are interwoven with the author's comments about typical stages of adjustment and suggestions for coping. Although the book does not shy away from difficult issues such as marital stresses and parental anger at the child with disabilities, the overall tone is upbeat: "Instead of looking at all the ways you *can't* operate in the world, look at all the ways you *can.*"

Tuesday's Child. P.O. Box 270046, Ft. Collins, CO 80527. (970) 416-7416. E-mail: tueskid@frii.com.

> This glossy, illustrated magazine was launched in 1997. It features informative, supportive articles on issues of interest to all parents of children with disabilities, as well as articles on issues unique to children with specific disabilities. Articles generally incorporate one or more families' experiences into the story and include resources for further information. Some articles take a look at alternative and/or controversial approaches. The magazine includes product reviews and a "Family Piazza" feature where parents share questions and comments with other families. A yearly subscription (6 issues) is $24.00 in the U.S., and $26.00 elsewhere.

Weinhouse, Don, and Marilyn Weinhouse. *Little Children, Big Needs: Parents Discuss Raising Children with Exceptional Needs.* Niwot, CO: University Press of Colorado, 1994. 256 pp. $14.95. ISBN 0-87081-338-2.

> The authors of this book interviewed fifty families with young children with disabilities (age six and under) about their concerns and experiences. They then organized the questions and concerns into topical chapters, and provided answers for the questions, illustrating them with quotations from the parents about their experiences. Topics covered include: First Concerns and Reactions; Services for Young Children; Stress; Parents as Case Managers; Support Networks; The Future: Fears and Anxieties, Goals and Hopes.

Fathers

May, James. *Fathers of Children with Special Needs: New Horizons.* 2nd ed. Bethesda, MD: ACCH, 1997. 51 pp. No charge.

> Although written for professionals, this brief monograph is of interest to parents as well. It provides a succinct overview of research related to fathers of children with disabilities; discusses reasons and strategies for increasing the involvement of fathers in the service delivery system;

and offers information on establishing a support group for fathers. Many photos of fathers and children and parent quotations are included. Other publications for and about fathers are listed at the end. One copy of this publication (#J057) is available free from the National Maternal and Child Health Clearinghouse, listed in the Publisher's section at the back of this book.

May, James. *Circles of Care and Understanding: Support Programs for Fathers of Children with Special Needs.* Bethesda, MD: Association for the Care of Children's Health, 1992. 85 pp. $6.95. ISBN 0-937821-86-1.

> This book explores the emotions that fathers have when faced with the challenges of raising a child with a disability. It includes a step-by-step guide for the creation of a successful father's support group, covering everything from recruiting fathers to leadership skills development.

Meyer, Donald J., ed. *Uncommon Fathers: Reflections on Raising a Child with a Disability.* Bethesda, MD: Woodbine House, 1995. 206 pp. $14.95. ISBN 0-933149-68-9.

> Nineteen fathers contributed essays to this thoughtful collection. Their children range in age from four to twenty-eight, and have a variety of disabilities, including autism, cerebral palsy, Down syndrome, hydrocephalus, mental retardation, multiple disabilities, and neuromuscular disease. In discussing their experiences raising a child with special needs, the fathers muse on philosophical issues (Why me? why my child?); emotional issues (continuing anger at doctors; grief; pride) and practical issues (settling on the best education; preserving "normal" family life). So many perspectives and experiences are represented that this book should provide food for thought for any father of a child with disabilities, as well as for anyone else who would like to understand what it is like to be a father.

First Person Perspectives

Featherstone, Helen. *A Difference in the Family: Life with a Disabled Child.* New York, NY: Viking-Penguin, 1980. 262 pp. $13.95. ISBN 0-1400-5941-5.

> The word "classic" is overused, but applies fully to this exceptional book written in loving terms by the mother of a child with severe disabilities. In gripping terms, Featherstone traces her emotional and philosophical journey to acceptance and understanding of her son. Her perspectives are unique, yet touch the thoughts and struggles of every parent of a child with a disability. This book is particularly useful for parents of newly diagnosed children who seek validation of the feelings they confront.

Marsh, Jayne D.B., ed. *From the Heart: On Being the Mother of a Child with Special Needs.* Bethesda, MD: Woodbine House, 1995. 149 pp. $14.95. ISBN 0-933149-79-4.

> Nine mothers who participated in a parent support group in Maine contributed memories, anecdotes, and reflections about what it is like to raise a child with disabilities. Topics covered include coping, family life, school issues, and relationships with professionals, family, and friends, as well as specific challenges they have confronted in dealing with their child's disabilities, which include autism, Down syndrome, ADD, complications of prematurity, and multiple disabilities. As none of the parents' contributions are more than a couple of pages long, this is a book that is easy to read in bits and pieces.

Spiegle, Jan A., and Richard A. van den Pol. **Making Changes: Family Voices on Living with Disabilities.** Cambridge, MA: Brookline, 1993. 175 pp. $19.95. ISBN 0-914797-93-X.

> Parents, teachers, therapists, medical professionals, and siblings talk honestly about raising, living with, and working with children who have disabilities. Each chapter reflects on the thoughts, perceptions, and actions of people dealing day-to-day with people with exceptional needs. Special

care has been taken to structure this book so it can be used as a text, a basis for discussion in support groups, and an awareness tool. The book includes a topical index that would be useful for parent group facilitators.

Sullivan, Tom. ***Special Parent, Special Child.*** New York, NY: G.P. Putnam's Sons, 1995. 239 pp. $21.95. ISBN 0-87477-782-8.

> This book was conceived with the idea of allowing "parents to speak openly, intimately, and in depth about their feelings and experiences" raising a child with special needs. The author, who is blind, interviewed six couples and then wove into a narrative their insights and experiences dealing with professionals, their emotions, their family, the system, and socialization of their child. The parents interviewed have children with cerebral palsy, visual impairment, leukemia, deafness, ADD, and Down syndrome.

Turnbull, H.R. III, and Ann P. Turnbull. ***Parents Speak Out: Then and Now.*** 2nd ed. New York: MacMillan, 1985. 304 pp. $40.00. ISBN 0-675-20404-6.

> The authors of the chapters are parents of children with mental retardation who also happen to be professionals working in the field of disabilities. They look at their lives in the 1970s and report their status in the 1980s. This book presents a picture of how a variety of families cope and make decisions and how having a child with a disability affects the lives of everyone in the family.

Siblings

FOR PARENTS

Lobato, Debra J. ***Brothers, Sisters, and Special Needs: Information and Activities for Helping Young Siblings of Children with Chronic Illnesses and Developmental Disabilities.*** Baltimore, Paul H. Brookes, 1990. 224 pp. $30.00. ISBN 1-55766-043-3.

> This book aims to help parents and professionals understand how having a brother or sister with a disability is similar to and different from having a sibling without a disability. It covers typical emotional reactions of siblings of different ages, and discusses what researchers have learned about the effects of growing up with a sibling with special needs. Most of the suggested activities for helping young children adjust to having a sibling with a disability are best done in a group setting (discussion group, workshop) rather than within the family. There is, however, a short chapter with helpful guidelines for discussing the disability within the family, including suggestions of what to say when explaining about a disability to a young child.

Meyer, Donald J., and Patricia F. Vadasy. ***Sibshops: Workshops for Siblings of Children with Special Needs.*** 2nd ed. Baltimore: Paul H. Brookes, 1994. 256 pp. $32.00. ISBN 1-55766-169-3.

> This book explains how to plan and run a sibshop--an event for brothers and sisters of children with disabilities aimed at helping them understand their sibling's disability, discuss their concerns, explore ways of handling troublesome situations, and learn how to tell their parents about their concerns. The ideas for games, activities, and discussions are appropriate for siblings from eight to thirteen years of age, and some can be adapted for home use.

Powell, Thomas H., and Peggy Ahrenhold Ogle. ***Brothers & Sisters: A Special Part of Exceptional Families.*** Baltimore, MD: Paul H. Brookes, 1993. 2nd ed. 320 pp. $23.00. ISBN 1-55766-110-3.

> This volume mixes research about the sibling relationship with words from siblings themselves to examine the experience of growing up with a brother or sister with a disability. The authors offer information on siblings' needs and methods of coping, and also include practical suggestions to help parents improve relationships between siblings with and without disabilities.

Siegel, Bryna, and Stuart Silverstein. **What about Me? Growing Up with a Developmentally Disabled Sibling.** New York, NY: Plenum, 1994. 296 pp. $24.95. ISBN 0-306-44650-2.

> This book was written for parents and for professionals who counsel families. One of the authors, Stu Silverstein, writes from personal experience. In the first chapter, he describes what it was like for him and his sister to grow up with a brother who has autism. Later chapters look at families from a clinical point of view. Feelings, adjustments, and coping strategies are discussed, and ideas for support are offered. There are a number of questionnaires that can provide the catalyst for expression during support group meetings and counseling sessions.

FOR CHILDREN

Listed in this section are books written specifically for or about siblings of children with special needs. Other children's books that may be helpful for siblings may be found under **"Disability Awareness"** *(p. 9) and in the sections in Part II on individual disabilities.*

Collins, Pat Lowery. *Waiting for Baby Joe.* Niles, IL: Albert Whitman & Co., 1990. 40 pp. $12.95. 0-8075-8625-0.

> When Missy's brother, Joe, is born two months early, he weighs just over three pounds. On her first visit to the NICU, Missy thinks that Joe looks like a "scary frog" and is afraid to touch him. Once she gets over her fears that Joe will die, she begins to resent all the attention the baby is getting from her parents. Eventually, however, Missy begins to feel better about the situation when she judges that Joe is finally ready for a big sister. Because Baby Joe has medical problems including jaundice and a heart defect and needs to be on an apnea monitor when he comes home, this book would be useful to young siblings of babies hospitalized for a variety of reasons, not just prematurity. The black and white photos capture the expressions of Missy—who appears five or six years old—especially well.

Duncan, Debbie. *When Molly Was in the Hospital: A Book for Brothers and Sisters of Hospitalized Children.* Windsor, CA: Rayve Productions, 1994. 38 pp. $12.95. ISBN 1-877810-44-4.

> Anna's little sister must go to the hospital for an operation due to an unnamed problem that makes her cry and lose interest in everything. Although Anna initially resents the extra attention Molly gets, she is also scared that her sister will not get better, and that it might be her fault that her sister is sick. This sensitively told story, illustrated with black-and-white line drawings, would be helpful for elementary school-aged children coping with the hospitalization of a sibling.

Meyer, Donald, and Patricia F. Vadasy. *Living with a Brother or Sister with Special Needs: A Book for Sibs.* 2nd ed. Seattle WA: University of Washington Press, 1996. 139 pp. ISBN: 0-295-97547-4. $14.95.

> The authors wrote this book to address the many questions and concerns that brothers and sisters of individuals with disabilities have and may never have expressed. It validates their feelings of jealousy, resentment, embarrassment, loneliness, and concern for the family, and suggests positive strategies for coping with emotions. The book also provides information on the causes and effects of the most common disabilities and on laws, programs, and services that can benefit people with disabilities and their families. This book wisely, realistically, and with great compassion reaches out to parents and children as it guides and supports all members of the family. Numerous illustrations and anecdotes about real families make this a very kid-friendly book for children from about grade 3 on.

Meyer, Donald J. **Views from Our Shoes: Growing Up with a Brother or Sister with Special Needs.** 114 pp. $14.95. Bethesda, MD: Woodbine House, 1997.

> Nearly fifty children and teenagers, ranging in age from four to nineteen, contributed their insights about living with a brother or sister with a disability to this book. Their frank essays cover

the good, not-so-good, and in-between aspects of their family lives. Their siblings have a variety of disabilities, including autism, mental retardation, seizures, hearing loss, heart defects, blindness, and Tourette, Down, and fragile X syndromes. Whimsical line illustrations enhance the appeal of this collection, which should be an eye-opener not only for siblings but also for parents and professionals. The book would be appropriate for children from about third through seventh grades.

Thompson, Mary. *My Brother, Matthew.* Bethesda, MD: Woodbine House, 1992. 32 pp. $14.95 ISBN 0-933149-47-6

> Matthew moves and talks differently than other children and also has more trouble learning. His older brother, David, loves him, but also is bothered by the fact that his parents often seem to overlook his feelings and needs. Although the primary audience of this beautifully illustrated book is children in grades K-5, it will also help parents discover and validate sibs' special insight about their brother or sister with special needs.

■ ORGANIZATIONS

Beach Center on Families and Disability
University of Kansas
3111 Haworth Hall
Lawrence, KS 66045
(785) 864-7600 voice & TDD; (785) 864-7605 FAX
E-mail: beach@dole.lsi.ukans.edu
Web site: http://www.lsi.ukans.edu/Beach/Beachhp.htm

> PURPOSE: Conducts research on training and disability issues affecting families, sponsors conferences, publishes and disseminates a wide range of publications on family issues.
> PUBLICATIONS: Include a *"Parent to Parent Information Packet"* ($3.00) and the fact sheet *"Start Your Own Parent to Parent Program"* ($.50). Also, *Families and Disability* newsletter (no charge), reviewed above.

National Father's Network
The Kindering Center
16120 NE Eighth Ave.
Bellevue, WA 98008
(425) 747-4004; (425) 282-1334

> PURPOSE: Bringing fathers of children with special needs together.
> SERVICES: Networking and mutual support.
> PUBLICATION: Quarterly newsletter.

Sibling Information Network
University of Connecticut
A.J. Pappanikou Center
249 Glenbrook Rd., U-64
Storrs, CT 06269-2064
(860) 486-4985

> PUBLICATIONS: Publishes two quarterly newsletters: *Sibling Information Network Newsletter* ($8.50 per year), filled with information and resources for and about siblings (of all ages) who have a brother or sister with a disability; and *Kaleidoscope: A Spectrum of Articles Focusing on Families* ($7 per year), which includes reviews, information, and resources for all members of families which include a person with a disability.

Sibling Support Project
Children's Hospital and Medical Center
P.O. Box 5371, CL-09
Seattle, WA 98105
(206) 368-4911; (206) 368-4816 FAX
E-mail: dmeyer@chmc.org
Web site: http://www.chmc.org/departmt/sibsupp
> PURPOSE: "A national program dedicated to the interests of brothers and sisters of people with special health and developmental needs. The Project's primary goal is to increase the availability of peer support and education programs for brothers and sisters of people with special health and developmental needs."
> SERVICES: Conducts workshops on issues confronting siblings and on how to start a Sibshop; maintains a database of sibling programs across the U.S. Operates the SibNet Listserv, a bulletin board for siblings of all ages (visit the web page above or contact the Sibling Support Project for a free subscription).
> PUBLICATIONS: Publishes *The National Association of Sibling Programs Newsletter.*

Specialized Training of Military Parents (STOMP)
12208 Pacific Highway SW
Tacoma, WA 98499
(253) 588-1741; (253) 984-7520 FAX
> PURPOSE: Provides training and support to military parents in the U.S. and overseas.
> PUBLICATIONS: A newsletter, information on DoD schools, brochures.

6.

Discipline and Behavioral Concerns

■ BOOKS AND PERIODICALS

Blechman, Elaine A. *Solving Child Behavior Problems at Home and at School.* Champaign, IL: Research Press, 1985. 296 pp. $18.95. ISBN 0-87822-247-2.

> This manual includes step-by-step suggestions for improving behaviors of children and adults. Behaviors covered include difficulties with routines and responsibilities, trouble handling emotions, and antisocial behaviors. The manual is meant to help parents and teachers achieve real change in communication, problem-solving, and behavior management skills.

Carr, Edward G., et al. *Communication-Based Intervention for Problem Behavior: A User's Guide for Producing Positive Change.* Baltimore: Paul H. Brookes, 1994. 288 pp. $25.00. ISBN 1-55766-159-6.

> At the core of this manual are two premises: 1) that problem behavior typically serves a specific purpose for people with developmental disabilities; and 2) that intervention should take place in the community. Included is information on conducting functional assessments (to determine the purpose of the behavior); communication-based intervention strategies; strategies for assisting in generalization; and procedures for managing crises.

Denkmeyer, Don, Gary D. McKay, and James S. Denkmeyer. *Parenting Young Children: Using the Systematic Training for Effective Parenting (STEP).* Circle Pines, MN: AGS, 1989. 156 pp. $10.80. ISBN 0-88671-356-0.

> This important book provides parents with basic and practical information about raising any child. The authors explain how the child's environment affects him, his self-esteem, and potential. Ac-

tivities and points to remember keep parents on target; a positive approach toward parenting. The *Just for You* section helps parents remember that they are human and what to do when life feels out of control.

Meyer, Luanna H., and Ian M. Evans. ***Nonaversive Intervention for Behavior Problems: A Manual for Home and Community.*** Baltimore: Paul H. Brookes, 1989. 224 pp. $27.00. ISBN 1-55766-018-2.

> This book written for a professional audience focuses on identifying the reasons behind challenging behaviors and then teaching more acceptable behaviors in their place. Problem behaviors both at home and in the community are analyzed.

The Positive Behavioral Change Bulletin. Positive Behavioral Supports, University Affiliated Program, Rhode Island College, 600 Mt. Pleasant Ave., Providence, RI 02908. (401) 456-8072.

> The purpose of this newsletter is to help parents and professionals assess the function that challenging behavior serves for an individual and to provide information on appropriate skills or behaviors to teach the individual instead. Each newsletter includes a profile of an adult or child with a challenging behavior; information on positive approaches to changing behavior; information on research; and resources.

Rhode, Ginger, William R. Jenson, and H. Kenton Reavis. ***The Tough Kid Book: Practical Classroom Management Strategies.*** Longmont, CO: Sopris West, 1995. 120 pp. $19.50.

> Written primarily for regular and special education teachers, this nontechnical book focuses on research-tested strategies for reducing disruptive behavior in the classroom. Helpful resources for more information are included.

Schwartz, Linda. ***Monkey See, Monkey Do.*** Santa Barbara, CA: The Learning Works, 1991. 32 pp. $4.95. ISBN 0-88160-187-X.

> Kids will be attracted to the colorful pages in this story about choices and using good judgment to make them. A good book on being an individual and not following the crowd.

■ ORGANIZATIONS

Beach Center on Families and Disability
University of Kansas
3111 Haworth Hall
Lawrence, KS 66045
(785) 864-7600 voice & TDD; (785) 864-7605 FAX
E-mail: beach@dole.lsi.ukans.edu
Web site: http://www.lsi.ukans.edu/beach/beachhp.htm

> PUBLICATIONS: *"Positive Behavioral Support as a Means to Enhance Successful Inclusion for Persons with Challenging Behavior"* ($4.50) is designed to help families deal with difficulties that hinder inclusion. *"Why Does Samantha Act Like That? A Positive Behavioral Support Story of One Family's Success"* ($5.25) explains how family, friends, and professionals worked to understand and develop a support plan for one girl's behavioral problems. Also available: *"Functional Assessement Questionnaire"* ($3.00), a form that helps pinpoint and understand problem behaviors, and a video ($30.00) that accompanies the story of Samantha, above.

Council for Exceptional Children (CEC)

1920 Association Dr.

Reston, VA 22091

(703) 620-3660; (703) 264-9494 FAX

Web site: http://www.cec.sped.org

PURPOSE: "To improve educational outcomes for individuals with exceptionalities."

SERVICES: A nonprofit membership organization for professionals and students that focuses on 17 different areas of Special Education. Learning disabilities, mental retardation, early childhood education, and communication disorders are just a few of the areas of focus.

PUBLICATIONS: Offers several booklets on behavior management in the classroom, including "Disruptive Behavior: Three Techniques to Use in Your Classroom" ($8.90) and "Non-Compliance: Four Strategies That Work" ($8.90).

7.

Education

■ BOOKS AND PERIODICALS

Basic Information

This section describes comprehensive works about special education issues in the United States. For publications that focus on specific laws relating to special education, see **"Advocacy and Legal Rights"** (p. 53). For publications dealing solely with early intervention, see the section on **"Infants and Toddlers"** (p. 15).

Anderson, Winifred, Stephen Chitwood, and Deidre Hayden. ***Negotiating the Special Education Maze: A Guide for Parents and Teachers.*** 3rd ed. Bethesda, MD: Woodbine House, 1997. $16.95. ISBN 0-933149-72-7.

> This book provides the foundation that parents need to take charge of their child's special education. It walks the reader through every step involved in obtaining and maintaining an appropriate education for a child with disabilities, from evaluation and eligibility, to creating and monitoring the Individualized Education Program (IEP), to placement in the least restrictive environment and monitoring to make sure the child's program is properly implemented. There are separate chapters on early intervention for parents of children under 3 and on making the transition out of high school. The emphasis is on rights and requirements under the Individuals with Disabilities Education Act (IDEA), but there is also a chapter on how Section 503 of the Rehabilitation Act of 1973 and the Americans with Disability Act (ADA) pertain to special education. This book may be used as a text for parent/professional training or for parents as they prepare to work as advocates for their child.

Bateman, Barbara D. ***Better IEPs: How to Develop Legally Correct and Educationally Useful Programs.*** 2nd ed. Longmont, CO: Sopris West. 194 pp. $19.50.

> This guide is intended to help both parents and educators understand, write, and implement effective Individualized Education Programs (IEPs). The emphasis is on creating truly individual-

ized IEPs through a step-by-step process. Information about relevant features of the Individuals with Disabilities Education Act is included.

Beckman, Paula J., and Gayle Beckman Boyes. ***Deciphering the System: A Guide for Families of Young Children with Disabilities.*** Cambridge, MA: Brookline, 1993. 180 pp. $21.95. ISBN 0-914797-87-5.

> Two sisters have written this book for parents of young children with special needs. The book guides parents gently through every aspect of the educational system. There are checklists and guides for developing IFSP/IEPs and for planning transitions, and an exceptional explanation of assessment and assessment tools (tests). Many suggestions are provided to help parents work collaboratively with professionals. Appendices include a glossary, an extensive reference list, and a list of state contacts.

Cutler, Barbara Coyne. ***You, Your Child, and "Special" Education: A Guide to Making the System Work.*** Baltimore: Paul H. Brookes, 1993. 249 pp. $22.00. ISBN 1-55766-115-4.

> The author of this guide takes the viewpoint that most parents will encounter at least some problems in obtaining an appropriate IEP for their child or making sure that it is followed. She discusses "good guys" vs. "bad guys" in special education, as well as common, illegal "snow jobs" used to deny services. With the goal of helping parents become effective negotiators, she provides many examples of what to do, say, or write in specific situations. The major emphasis is not on what the laws say, but on empowering parents to obtain what their children are entitled to under the laws.

Gorn, Susan. ***What Do I Do When . . . The Answer Book on Individualized Education Programs.*** Horsham, PA: LRP Publications, 1997. 120 pp. $32.50. ISBN 1-57834-003-9.

> In question-and-answer format, this volume takes an indepth look at the process of developing, revising, and monitoring an IEP. Topics include developing an appropriate IEP; parental rights during IEP meetings; resolving disagreements between parents and the school district's about the IEP.

Pierangelo, Roger, and Robert Jacoby. ***Parents' Complete Special Education Guide.*** West Nyack, NY: Center for Applied Research in Research in Education, 1996. 332 pp. $27.95. 0-87628-614-7.

> Although this book sets out to be a comprehensive guide to special education issues for all parents, it would be especially useful to parents of children who are uncertain whether their child needs any special education services. The authors offer guidance on normal child development milestones, problems that might indicate a disability, school screening procedures for suspected disabilities, and when and how to refer your child for services. There are also sections on the special education process, the IEP, related services, and making the transition to adult life. Checklists, a glossary, information about tests used in special education, and a guide to publications and organizations round out the book.

SPEAK OUT. PEAK Parent Center, Inc., 6055 Lehman Dr., Ste. 101, Colorado Springs, CO 80918. (719) 531-9400; (719) 531-9452 FAX.

> This family-friendly newsletter is full of suggestions and strategies for successful educational advocacy. It is an excellent resource for information about special education laws and parents' rights and responsibilities. Legislative updates are also provided. Subscriptions are $9.00 per year (3 issues).

Stainback, William, and Susan Stainback. ***Controversial Issues Confronting Special Education: Divergent Perspectives.*** 2nd ed. Needham Heights, MA: Allyn & Bacon, 1996. 384 pp. $53.00. ISBN 0-205-18266-6.

> In this thought-provoking collection for educators, different writers examine the pros and cons of a variety of controversial issues in special education. Topics addressed include the pros and cons

of: inclusion for all students; labeling; different assessment methods; different methods of instruction; different classroom management strategies; different methods of preparing teachers to instruct students with disabilities; and more. Although the writing is technical at times, parents who want to understand both sides of an issue will find this text valuable.

Vergason, Glenn A., and M.L. Anderegg. ***Dictionary of Special Education and Rehabilitation.*** 4th ed. Denver, CO: Love Publishing, 1997. 210 pp. $19.95. ISBN 0-89108-243-3.

Over 2,000 terms related to special education and rehabilitation are defined in this dictionary. Also included are listings of professional organizations in the disability field.

Weber, Jayne Dixon. ***Transitioning "Special" Children Into Elementary School.*** Boulder, CA: Books Beyond Borders, Inc., 1994. 56 pp. $8.50. ISBN 1-883862-04-3.

This short book is useful for parents, although written to help infant development and preschool programs help parents and caretakers plan for the move to Kindergarten. The author offers numerous steps, strategies, and points to think about. Personal accounts lend a parent-to-parent touch. Throughout, the author emphasizes the importance of teamwork in accomplishing a successful transition.

Wehman, Paul. ***Life Beyond the Classroom: Transition Strategies for Young People with Disabilities.*** 2nd ed. Baltimore: Paul H. Brookes, 1996. 533 pp. $55.00. ISBN 1-55766-248-7.

This text focuses on ways to help young adults with disabilities "adjust to the challenges of adulthood"—and, in particular, the workplace." The emphasis is on carefully planning and then implementing individualized life-skills training at school by the age of 14 or 16. Because it is written for professionals, the book talks about parents, rather than to them, and is not an easy read. Parents of older children may find it worthwhile, however, to read the overview chapter on developing an Individualized Transition Plan (ITP), with its many examples of goals for employment, vocational education/training, financial/income needs, independent living, transportation/mobility, social relationships, recreation/leisure, health/safety, and self-advocacy. There are also separate chapters on developing ITPs for students with mild mental retardation, severe disabilities, sensory impairments, learning disabilities, behavior disorders, orthopedic and other health impairments, and traumatic brain injury. Parents whose children have already left high school may be interested in the chapters on finding jobs, vocational placements, and independent living.

Wilson, Nancy O. ***Optimizing Special Education: How Parents Can Make a Difference.*** New York, NY: Plenum, 1992. 300 pp. $26.50. ISBN 0-306-44323-6.

This is a combination advocacy and support book. The laws as they relate to education and how they affect children and families are explained. Parents also share their feelings and experiences in coping with the trials and frustrations of raising a child with special needs. What has worked and will not work within the educational system are discussed. There is an emphasis on parent/professional partnerships and on taking things a day at a time when working with the educational system. An extensive glossary, bibliography, and resource section are included.

Inclusion

The publications in this section focus on resources for adult readers that deal with philosophies and practical approaches to inclusion within the classroom. For information on other aspects of inclusion, see the section on **"Community Integration and Friendship"** *(p.81). For resources to help children in inclusive classrooms better understand classmates with disabilities, see the section on* **"Disability Awareness"** *(p. 9).*

Blenk, Katie, and Doris Landau Fine. ***Making School Inclusion Work: A Guide to Everyday Practices.*** Cambridge, MA: Brookline, 1995. $24.95. ISBN 0-914797-4.

> This book offers a practical guide for parents and professionals who want inclusion to work for the children they are raising and teaching. The authors acknowledge in the very beginning that inclusion is not universally accepted by parents, *or* professionals. The strategies suggested are those developed at the Kids are People School, "an urban educational program in Boston, Massachusetts." There is a frank discussion regarding who should and should not be included. Special points are made about the importance of communication, the environment, the curriculum, and evaluations. A wonderfully written chapter entitled "From Segregation to Inclusion" gives a historical perspective. Checklists are provided that give an excellent idea of what should be taught and when. In the end, parents and children tell their own stories about inclusion. Resources include a reference section, glossary, a "Sample Evaluation Checklist" of daily living skills, and an exceptional list of "Resources for the Classroom."

Chandler, Phyllis A. ***A Place for Me: Including Children with Special Needs—Early Care and Education Setting***. Washington, DC: National Association for the Education of Young Children, 1994. $4.50. ISBN 0-935989-59-5.

> This book explains to parents and professionals how to create a successful inclusion experience. Emphasis is placed on the emotions that accompany the process of inclusion. Strategies for preparing the inclusion team—parents, professionals, and the child—are described. A great resource section is included.

Duncan, Janet, and Kathy Hulgin, compilers. ***Resources on Inclusive Education***. Syracuse, NY: Center on Human Policy, 1993. 99 pp. $5.20.

> This information packet consists of reprints of articles and chapters on inclusive education, sample case studies of children receiving inclusive educations, and an extensive bibliography of publications and videos on inclusive education. A good place to start for parents and educators wishing to learn about inclusive educational practices.

Hammeken, Peggy A. ***Inclusion: 450 Strategies for Success—A Practical Guide for All Educators Who Teach Students with Disabilities.*** Minnetonka, MN: Peytral Publications, 1995. 138 pp. $19.95. ISBN 0-9644271-7-6.

> Written for special education and general education teachers, this easy-to-use guide is helpful to parents as well. The first section offers information on setting up, expanding, or improving an inclusionary program at school. The second section lists hundreds of short tips for modifying the curriculum and teaching strategies for a variety of different subjects and for children with different learning needs. For example, there are suggestions for modifying textbooks, giving directions, teaching students in a large group, and for modifying spelling, reading, and mathematics instruction and requirements.

Inclusion News. Inclusion Press International, 24 Thome Crescent, Toronto, Ontario, Canada M6H 2S5. (416) 658-5363; (416) 658-5067 FAX. Web site: http://www.inclusion.com

> The focus of this free newsletter is inclusion in all aspects of life. It is published "occasionally" by a privately funded source. Articles are inspiring and offer suggestions to make inclusion work. Anecdotes, personal messages, poetry, and resources are sprinkled throughout this publication.

Lehr, Donna H., and Fredda Brown. ***People with Disabilities Who Challenge the System.*** Baltimore: Paul H. Brookes, 1996. 469 pp. $34.00.

> In this professional text, the authors and their colleagues have written about the dramatic changes in the service delivery system for children with the most severe disabilities—deaf-blindness,

severe to profound mental or physical disabilities, multiple disabilities. While the laws support these changes, whether the family experiences these changes is dependent on several factors, which the authors explore. The authors also describe the types of supports that can enable individuals with severe disabilities to be fully included in the classroom, the community, and the workplace. Real-life accounts of inclusion experiences are reported.

Moon, M. Sherril, ed. *Making School and Community Recreation Fun for Everyone: Places and Ways to Integrate.* Baltimore, MD: Paul H. Brookes, 1991. 256 pp. $32.00. ISBN 1-55766-155-3.

This practical manual discusses strategies for including people with disabilities in both school-based and community recreational activities, such as school clubs and teams, summer camps, community recreation programs, and sports leagues. It discusses relevant federal legislation and ways to use the law to get people with disabilities included in activities, and also provides examples of successful inclusive programs.

O'Brien, John, and Marsha Forest. *Action for Inclusion: How to Improve Schools by Welcoming Children with Special Needs into Regular Classrooms.* Toronto: Inclusion Press. 55 pp. $15.00.

This is a hands-on guide to the nuts and bolts of including elementary and middle-school students with disabilities. Included are practical tips for developing action plans (MAP) for inclusion, as well as information on building a circle of friends.

Schaffner, C. Beth, and Barbara E. Buswell. *Breaking Ground: Ten Families Building Opportunities Through Integration.* Colorado Springs, CO: PEAK Parent Center, 1989. 75 pp. $10.00.

Parents speak to parents about inclusion in this book. Strategies, advocacy, and how inclusion works in the school and community are the focus. These families create a can-do spirit as they and their children set out to break the bonds of segregation. Inclusion for these children did not "just happen." Their parents moved ahead as advocates, always placing their child as the focus for the advocacy, inclusive friendships, and partnerships.

Schaffner, C. Beth, and Barbara E. Buswell. *Connecting Students: A Guide to Thoughtful Friendship Facilitation for Educators and Families.* Colorado Springs, CO: PEAK Parent Center, 1992. 48 pp. $9.50.

These authors acknowledge that friendships cannot be made to occur, they must develop over time. This book helps to nurture relationships and guide them toward a self-initiated and self-supporting friendship. Scenarios and vignettes are provided and followed by exercises for reflection. This approach establishes an understanding of how and why friendships occur and the implications of this new bond.

Schaffner, C. Beth, and Barbara E. Buswell. *Opening Doors: Strategies for Including All Students in Regular Education.* 4th ed. Colorado Springs, CO: PEAK Parent Center, Inc., 1993. 54 pp. $10.00.

A terrific resource. This publication provides a realistic look at the concerns teachers have when including a student in their classroom. The authors address the new roles the teachers and special education teachers acquire with inclusion. The authors offer a hard look at the supports both professionals and parents need for success. Schaffner and Buswell have a wonderful way of looking at children's strengths. A generous list of references and resources is provided.

Stainback, Susan, and William Stainback, eds. *Inclusion: A Guide for Educators.* Baltimore: Paul H. Brookes, 1996. 416 pp. $32.00. ISBN 1-55766-231-2.

As the title suggests, this guide is intended to show teachers and administrators how to make inclusion work. Parents may be interested in learning about specific approaches to inclusion, curriculum adaptation, classroom behavior management, and using augmentative and alternative communication methods in the inclusive classroom.

Staub, Debbie. ***Delicate Threads: Friendships between Children with and without Special Needs in Inclusive Settings.*** Bethesda, MD: Woodbine House, 1998. 256 pp. $16.95. ISBN 0-933149-90-5.

> For several years, the author of this unique book observed seven pairs of friends in an inclusive elementary school in the Pacific Northwest. In each pair of friends, one child had a significant developmental disability and one did not. The children's stories offer readers a rare insight into the problems and possibilities inherent in such friendships. The author also spends a good deal of time discussing children's friendships in general and how friendships between children with and without special needs resemble and differ from typical friendships. For parents, the information on how adults (parents and teachers) can support or undermine friendships is especially valuable.

Young, Rebecca. ***Mikey Goes to Our School.*** Carbondale, CO: Hometown Press, n.d. 14 pp. $3.95.

> This oversized illustrated booklet explains how one family and school worked together to include Mikey, a second grader with multiple disabilities, in his local school. It includes comments from the special education teacher, classroom teacher, teaching assistants, and classmates about how they adapted their attitudes and teaching methods to help Mike succeed. This may be a useful publication for parents to share with teachers to help them understand that where there's a will, there's a way to include a child.

■ ORGANIZATIONS

Beach Center on Families and Disability
University of Kansas
3111 Haworth Hall
Lawrence, KS 66045
(785) 864-7600 voice & TDD; (785) 864-7605 FAX
E-mail: beach@dole.lsi.ukans.edu
Web site: http://www.lsi.ukans.edu/Beach/Beachhp.htm

> PURPOSE: Conducts research on training and disability issues affecting families, sponsors conferences, publishes and disseminates a wide range of publications on family issues.
> PUBLICATIONS: A series of fact sheets ($.50 each) are available on topics such as *"Identify Special Education Needs," "Due Process Hearings," "Mediation in Special Education,"* and *"Private School Placement of Children with Disabilities." **Going Mobile,*** a video on transition, is offered for $12.00.

Center for Law and Education
1875 Connecticut Ave., NW, Ste. 510
Washington, DC 20009
(202) 462-7688

> PURPOSE: Dedicated to ensuring all children the right to quality public school education.
> PUBLICATIONS: Distributes a *"School Improvement Catalog"* that lists publications for legal and education advocates. A packet for advocates for students with disabilities is available for $25.00, or individual titles can be ordered separately, including: *"When Parents and Educators Do Not Agree: Using Mediation to Resolve Conflicts about Special Education"* ($4.00); *"Promoting Inclusion for All Students with Disabilities"* ($4.00); *"Assistive Technology for Students with Disabilities: Rights under Federal Law"* ($4.00); *"Obtaining Appropriate Educational Services for Three-through Five-Year-Old Children with Disabilities"* ($4.00).

Center on Human Policy

National Resource Center on Community Integration
Syracuse University
805 S. Crouse Ave.
Syracuse, NY 13244-2280
(800) 894-0826; (315) 443-4355 (TTY); (315) 443-4338 FAX
E-mail: thechp@sued.syr.edu
Web site: http://soeweb.syr.edu/thechp/

> PURPOSE: "To promote the full inclusion of people with developmental disabilities in community
> life" through training, technical assistance, consultation, and the dissemination of information.
> PUBLICATIONS: Offers a variety of low-cost information packets on topics such as supported liv-
> ing, housing, personal relationships and social networks, inclusive education, and integrated rec-
> reation. Also many original and reprinted papers, articles, and news bulletins on integrating per-
> sons with disabilities into the community. Request a copy of *"Resources and Reports on Commu-
> nity Integration"* for a complete list.

Consortium on Inclusive Schooling Practices

Child and Family Studies Program
Allegheny-Singer Research Institute
320 E. North Ave.
Pittsburgh, PA 15212
Web site: http://www.asri.edu/CFSP/brochure/abtcons.htm

> PURPOSE: "To build the capacity of state and local education agencies to serve children and youth
> with and without disabilities in school and community settings. The focus of the project is on
> systematic reform rather than changes in special education systems only."
> PUBLICATIONS: Publishes a *"Catalog of Products from Funded Projects"*—a list of manuals, ar-
> ticles, videotapes, brochures, fact sheets, etc. produced by investigators who have received grants
> from the U.S. Dept. of Education, Office of Special Education and Rehabilitative Services. Avail-
> able online, or in print format.

Council for Exceptional Children (CEC)

1920 Association Dr.
Reston, VA 20191
(703) 620-3660; (703) 264-9494 FAX
800-CEC-READ (information on publications only)
Web site: http://www.cec.sped.org

> PURPOSE: "To improve educational outcomes for individuals with exceptionalities."
> SERVICES: A nonprofit membership organization for professionals and students that focuses on 17
> different areas of Special Education. Learning disabilities, mental retardation, early childhood
> education, and communication disorders are just a few of the areas of focus.
> PUBLICATIONS: Publishes a variety of teacher-oriented materials on topics such as Inclusion,
> ADD, At Risk Students, Early Childhood, Social Skills, Professionalism and Ethical Practices,
> and Assessment.

DO-IT

(Disabilities, Opportunities, Internetworking, and Technology)
University of Washington
4545 15th Ave., NE
Seattle, WA 98105
(206) 685-DOIT; (206) 685-4054 FAX
E-mail: doit@u.washington.edu
Web site: http://weber.u.washington.edu/~doit/

> PURPOSE: "To increase the participation of individuals with disabilities in academic programs and careers."
>
> SERVICES: Conducts workshops on adaptive technology, college transition, access to employment, etc.; sponsors a discussion list; lends computers, modems, software, and adaptive technology for use by high school students with disabilities who have an interest in majoring in science, engineering, mathematics, or technology in college.
>
> PUBLICATIONS: Print copies of the following are available free from the address above: *"College: You Can DO IT!"; "Financial Aid for Students with Disabilities"; "Working Together: Faculty and Students with Disabilities";* and others. The articles may also be downloaded from DO-IT's web site.

ERIC Clearinghouse on Disabilities and Gifted Education (ERIC EC)

Council for Exceptional Children
1920 Association Dr.
Reston, VA 20191
(800) 328-0272; (703) 264-9449 TTY
E-mail: ericec@cec.sped.org
Web site: http://www.cec.sped.org/ericec.htm

> PURPOSE: One of 16 federally funded clearinghouses in the ERIC system, ERIC EC focuses on professional literature, information, and resources related to the education and development of individuals who have disabilities or are gifted.
>
> SERVICES: Provides access to the ERIC database with 60,000 citations on disabilities or gifted issues; provides general information on education and referrals to other sources and organizations over the phone; prepares publications on disability issues.
>
> PUBLICATIONS: Digests and research briefs ($1.00 each, or view online) on topics including: *"Integrating Students with Severe Disabilities"* (#468); *"Life Skills Mastery for Students with Special Needs"* (#469); *"Including Students with Disabilities in General Education Classrooms"* (#521); *"Children with Communication Disorders"* (#528); *"Behavioral Disorders: Focus on Change" (#518); "Down Syndrome"* (#457), etc. Also offers minibibliographies that contain annotated readings on a particular topic and fact sheets.

HEATH/American Council on Education

Dept. 36
Washington, DC 20055-0036
(202) 939-9320; (202) 833-4760 FAX
E-mail: heath@ace.nche.edu
Web site: http://www.acenet.edu
gopher://bobcat-ace.nche.edu

> PURPOSE: A national clearinghouse on postsecondary education for individuals with disabilities.
>
> PUBLICATIONS: Offers a variety of resource papers, including *"Head Injury Survivor on Campus"; "Students Who Are Blind or Visually Impaired"; "Students Who Are Deaf or Hard of Hearing";*

"Educational Software for Students with LD"; "Financial Aid for Students with Disabilities." Also newsletter article reprints, including: *"Community Colleges and Students with Disabilities"; "Career Development"; "Get the Most Out of College: Mobility Limitations"; "Students with Disabilities and Law School."* There is a nominal charge for publications in print, computer diskette, or audiocassette format. Publications can also be downloaded free at gopher site above.

Institute on Community Integration

University of Minnesota
109 Pattee hall
150 Pillsbury Dr. SE
Minneapolis, MN 55455
(612) 624-4512; (612) 624-9344 FAX

> PURPOSE: To improve community services and social supports for persons with disabilities and their families.
>
> PUBLICATIONS: Include resource guides on self-advocacy, inclusion, transition, and supported employment; curricula for teachers and for paraprofessionals to help them develop inclusive classrooms; reports on residential services. One copy of the following brochures is free, additional copies are $.50: *"Integration Checklist: A Guide to Full Inclusion for Students with Disabilities"; "Inclusive School Communities: 10 Reasons Why."* Request a publications catalog and a complimentary issue of the newsletter **Impact.**

Institute on Disability/UAP

University of New Hampshire
7 Leavitt Lane, Ste. 101
Durham, NH 03824-3522
(603) 862-4320; (603) 862-0555 FAX
E-mail: institute disability@unh.edu
Web site: http://iod.unh.edu

> PUBLICATIONS: Include *"Petroglyphs: The Writing on the Wall"* (photographic essay about inclusion in high school, $10.00); *"Aqui Se Habla Espanol: Designing and Implementing an Inclusive Foreign Language Program"* ($5.00); **From Special to Regular, From Ordinary to Extraordinary** (a book about the benefits of inclusive education, $7.00); *"Treasures: A Celebration of Inclusion"* (photographic essay, $7.00).

National Challenged Homeschoolers (NATHHAN)

5383 Alpine Rd., SE
Olalla, WA 98359
(253) 857-4257; (253) 857-7764
E-mail: Nathanews@AOL.COM

> PURPOSE: "A Christian, non-profit organization dedicated to providing encouragement to families with special needs children who are homeschooling."
>
> PUBLICATIONS: Publishes a quarterly magazine, **NATHHAN NEWS,** with articles on educational, medical, and religious issues; letters from parents; information on resources. Included in the price of membership ($25). Also offers articles, pamphlets, and **NATHHAN Resource Guide** ($20).

National Information Center for Children and Youth with Disabilities (NICHCY)

P.O. Box 1492
Washington, DC 20013-1492
(800) 695-0285; (202) 884-8441 FAX
E-mail: nichcy@aed.org
Web site: http://www/nichcy.org

> PURPOSE: A clearinghouse that provides information on disabilities and disability-related issues, with an emphasis on children and young people birth to age 22.
>
> SERVICES: Personal responses to questions on disability issues; referrals to other organizations and agencies; database searches; technical assistance to parent and professional groups.
>
> PUBLICATIONS: Examples include: *"Planning for Inclusion"; "Assessing Children for the Presence of a Disability"; "Promising Practices and Future Directions for Special Education"; "Transition Services in the IEP"; "A Student's Guide to the IEP."* There is a small charge for many publications in print format; materials may also be downloaded free of charge on the Internet.

National Parent Network on Disabilities

1200 G St., NW, Ste. 800
Washington, DC 20005
(202) 434-8686 V/TDD
E-mail: npnd@cs.com
Web site: http://www.npnd.org/

> PURPOSE: Established to serve as a national voice for parents of children and adults with disabilities. Aims to empower parents to obtain inclusive educations for their children.
>
> PUBLICATIONS: Include **Inclusion: A Parent's View** ($19.95) and **All Children Belong Trainer Manual** ($25.00).

PACER Center

4826 Chicago Ave. South
Minneapolis, MN 55417-1098
(612) 827-2966 Voice/TTY; (612) 827-3065 FAX
E-mail: mnpacer@edu.gte.net
Web site: http://www.pacer.org

> PURPOSE: The Parent Advocacy Coalition for Educational Rights (PACER) "strives to improve and expand opportunities that enhance the quality of life for children and adults with disabilities and their families." An important focus is on helping parents understand special education laws and obtain appropriate educations for their children.
>
> PUBLICATIONS: **Pacesetter** (a free news magazine); **Begin the Between: Planning for the Transition from High School to Adult Life for Youth with Developmental Disabilities** ($5); **Point of Departure** (a free newsletter for parents of transition-aged students); **FASTWork** (a free newsletter that covers education issues of interest to parents of children with and without disabilities; *"Transition Tips and Tools"* ($9). Many publications are free to Minnesota residents.

PEAK Parent Center, Inc.

6055 Lehman Dr., Ste. 101
Colorado Springs, CO 80918
(719) 531-9400; (719) 531-9452 FAX

> PURPOSE: As Colorado's Parent Training and Information Program, PEAK provides training and information to parents to help them participate effectively with professionals in meeting their child's educational needs.

PUBLICATIONS: Include *Connecting Students: A Guide to Thoughtful Friendship Facilitation for Educators & Families* ($9.50); *Individualizing Learner Outcomes* ($7.00); *"Building Integration with the IEP"* ($5.00); the newsletter *SPEAK OUT* ($9.00); *Discover the Possibilities* ($14.50); and other publications described in "Inclusion" section above.

President's Committee on Mental Retardation
Hubert H. Humphrey Bldg., Rm. 352G
200 Independence Ave., SW
Washington, DC 20201-0001
(202) 619-0634; (202) 205-9519 FAX
Web site: http://www.acf.dhhs.gov/programs/pcmr/

PUBLICATIONS: Offers several book-length reports, free of charge, including: *The Journey to Inclusion* and *Voices and Visions: Building Leadership for the 21st Century.* Request a publication list.

The Roeher Institute
Kinsmen Building
York University
4700 Keele St.
North York, Ontario
Canada M3J 1P3
(416) 661-2023 Voice/TDD; (416) 661-5701 FAX
Web site: http://indie.ca/roeher/intro.html

PURPOSE: "promotes the equality, participation, and self-determination of people with intellectual and other disabilities."

SERVICES: Information services include reference and referral information, customized responses to questions, the development of information packages on specific topics, and operation of an extensive library. Also conducts research and public policy analysis and social development and training.

PUBLICATIONS: *Literacy and Labels: A Look at Literacy Policy and People with Mental Handicaps* ($16.00); *"Inclusion of Individuals with Disabilities in Post-Secondary Education: A Review of the Literature"* ($10.00); *How it Happens: A Look at Inclusive Educational Practice in Canada for Children and Youth with Disabilities* ($10.00).

The Science Linkage in the Community
American Association for the Advancement of Science
1333 H Street, NW
Washington, DC 20005
(202) 326-7067; (800) 351-SLIC

PURPOSE: To promote an "enthusiasm for science, mathematics, and technology," *especially for children with disabilities.*

SERVICES: Offers accommodation program that can meet the need of public and private organizations serving children from preschool age through 12 years old with any type of disability. They offer workshops and conferences.

PUBLICATIONS: A variety of booklets that explain how to organize barrier-free working and learning environments, including *"Barrier Free in Brief: Access to Science Literacy, Access in Word and Deed."*

TASH
29 W. Susquehanna Ave.
Suite 210
Baltimore, MD 21204
(410) 828-6706
Web site: http://www.tash.org

PURPOSE: TASH advocates strongly for inclusion of all individuals in every aspect of life. Their membership is a blend of parents, self advocates, and professionals. Among their goals: "building communities in which no one is segregated and everyone belongs"; "advocating for opportunities and rights"; "promoting inclusive education"; "disseminating knowledge and information."

PUBLICATIONS: Include a quarterly peer-reviewed journal *(JASH)* and a monthly newsletter. Information in the newsletter is pertinent to most parents, addressing current topics regarding inclusive schools, education methods, community living, and politics.

8.

Health Care

■ BOOKS

Ferguson, Tom. *Health Online: How to Find Health Information, Support Groups, and Self-Help Communities in Cyperspace.* Reading, MA: Addison-Wesley Publishing Co., 1996. 308 pp. $17.00. ISBN 0-201-40989-5.

> For readers with little or no experience searching for health or medical information on the Internet, this guide provides a useful starting point. It begins by covering the basics of going online—equipment needed, uses of e-mail, the meaning of common terminology, online do's and don't's. It then discusses the pros and cons of using the major commercial networks to access health information and online support groups. Finally, the book describes some of the existing web sites, newsgroups, and mailing lists on the Internet concerned with health and medical issues. For the most part, this is *not* the place to look for information on locating information dealing with specific disabilities; throughout, the emphasis is more on illnesses.

Kuttner, Leora. *A Child in Pain: How to Help, What to Do.* Point Roberts, WA: Hartley & Marks Publishers, 1996. $14.95. 271 pp. ISBN 0-88179-128-8.

> For any parent who would like to reduce the physical and psychological hurt associated with their child's pain, this is a useful and comprehensive guide. The author discusses such topics as how pain works, its purpose, how parents should and should not respond to their child's pain. She also goes into specifics about methods for assessing and relieving all sorts of pain. Individual chapters are devoted to managing pain on visits to the doctor, to the dentist, and to the emergency room, as well as preparing a child for hospitalization and dealing with pain from medical treatments.

Malloy, JoAnne M. *Benefits Planning for Children and Youth with Disabilities.* Durham, NH: Institute on Disability, 1995. 93 pp. $5.00.

> This manual includes information on health insurance, individual benefits, and programs and services for children and young people ages birth to 21. It was written specifically for young people with disabilities and their families.

Rosenfeld, Lynn R. *Your Child and Health Care: A "Dollars & Sense" Guide for Families with Special Needs.* Baltimore: Paul H. Brookes, 1994. 608 pp. $29.00. ISBN 1-55766-154-5.

> The goal of this guide is to help parents obtain affordable but good quality health care for their children with special needs. It discusses government services and benefits, how to select a health insurance plan and appeal denied claims, how to locate organizations to help with expenses, and paying for out-of-pocket medical expenses.

Sternbach, Richard. *Mastering Pain: A Twelve-Step Program for Coping with Chronic Pain.* New York, NY: Ballantine, 1988. 239 pp. $5.99. ISBN 0-345-35428-1.

> This guide offers excellent information about how pain works, coping strategies for pain management, and suggestions for the family support team.

■ ORGANIZATIONS

Alliance of Genetic Support Groups
35 Wisconsin Circle, Ste. 440
Chevy Chase, MD 20815-7015
E-mail: alliance@capaccess.org
Web site: http://medhelp.org/www/agsg.htm

> PURPOSE: A network of people with genetic conditions, parents, and professionals with an interest in the "consumer" approach toward genetics.
> PUBLICATIONS: *Health Insurance Resource Guide* ($10.00; free to members).

American Chronic Pain Association
P.O. Box 850
Rocklin, CA 95677
(916) 632-0922

> PURPOSE: Mutual support.
> SERVICES: Disseminates guidelines for selecting pain management facilities.
> PUBLICATIONS: Ask for their *Family Manual* and the *ACPA Chronicle,* a quarterly newsletter.

Association for the Care of Children's Health
7910 Woodmont Ave., Ste. 300
Bethesda, MD 20814
800/808-2224; 301/654-6549
E-mail: acch@clark.net
Web site: http://www.acch.org

> PURPOSE: A multidisciplinary membership organization that strives to improve the quality of care for children and their families through education, dissemination of resources, research, and advocacy.
> PUBLICATIONS: *"Pain, Pain, Go Away"* ($1.50) was written to help children express their feelings about being in physical pain. *"Your Child and Home Healthcare"* ($1.50); *"Your Child in the Hospital"* ($1.50); and *"Your Child and Managed Healthcare"* ($1.50) were written for parents and other caregivers. Also has products designed to help children articulate the degree of their pain.

University Hospital School

UI Publications Order Dept. - M105 OH
University of Iowa
Iowa City, IA 52242-5000
(800) 235-2665
Web site: http://www.uiowa/edu/~ddd-uhs/catalog.html

PUBLICATIONS: The Resource Catalog offers print and video materials of general interest to parents and professionals working with children with developmental disabilities. Examples: *"A Guide to Oral Care for Children Who Are Disabled"* (free); *"The Home Health Record"* ($3.75); *"The Iowa Health Care Guidelines Project: Guidelines for Families"* ($3).

9.

Advocacy and Legal Rights

■ BOOKS AND PERIODICALS

Advocacy

The resources in this section cover advocacy in general. For information specific to educational advocacy, see under **"Education"** (p.37).

The Americans with Disabilities Newsletter. P.O. Box 365, Hillsdale, NY 12529-0365. (800) 818-3111.
Aimed at empowering people with disabilities, their families, advocates, and employers, this newsletter covers information on issues such as laws, benefits, housing and access, and employment. Topics recently addressed include: "State Institutions vs. Community Living," "How to Accommodate Mental Disabilities in the Workplace," "Cost-Effective Accommodations," and "Are Pre-Existing Condition Clauses Barred by the ADA?" For subscription rates, call the toll-free number above, or visit their web site at <http://www.wizvax.net/awd/>.

Bishop, Kathleen Kirk, Josie Woll, and Polly Arango. **Family/Professional Collaboration for Children with Special Health Needs and Their Families.** Burlington, VT: University of Vermont, Family/Professional Collaboration Project, 1993. 48 pp. No charge.
This monograph explores seven principles that make for successful family/professional collaboration. The text is enlivened with many quotations and examples from families, professionals, and local and national programs of how these principles have worked. One copy is available free from the National Maternal and Child Health Clearinghouse (stock #G017), at the address listed in the Publishers section at the end of the book.

Des Jardins, Charlotte. *How to Get Services by Being Assertive.* 2nd ed. Chicago: Family Resource Center on Disabilities, 1993. 250 pp. $11.00.

> This is a helpful guide to making decision making for a child less stressful. The author takes great care to explain the difference between assertiveness and aggression, including why one works and the other doesn't. Practical information such as how to access your child's records and how to prepare for a due process meeting is included. The book also summarizes special education rights and lists resources such as Parent Training and Information Centers. Many personal accounts from parents provide guidance and support.

Des Jardins, Charlotte. *How to Organize an Effective Parent/Advocacy Group and MOVE BUREAUCRACIES.* 2nd ed. Chicago: Family Resource Center on Disabilities, 1993. 267 pp. $12.00.

> This manual offers clear, step-by-step instructions for developing a parent/advocacy group. It explains what advocacy is and is not; how to reach out to other parents; how to open the door to new services; and how to keep your parent/advocacy group thriving. The Appendix provides a list of Parent Training and Information Centers, Federal Agencies, and National Resources.

Disability Advocates Bulletin. Pike Institute on Law and Disability, Boston University School of Law, 765 Commonwealth Ave., Boston, MA 02215. (617) 353-2904; (617) 353-2906 FAX.

> This bimonthly newsletter for parent-advocates, self-advocates, and professionals summarizes decisions of state and federal courts on disability-related issues; provides information on new state and federal laws and regulations and on proposed changes to existing laws and regulations; quotes policy letters of federal agencies that clarify and interpret federal laws and regulations. In many cases, the full text of the abstracts summarized in the newsletter can be ordered from the Pike Institute for a nominal fee. Subscriptions are $60 yearly for nonprofessionals; $120 for professionals.

Duffy, Susan et al. *We're All in This Together, So Let's Talk: Effective Communication between Parents of Children with Disabilities and the Professionals Who Work with Them.* Missoula, MT: Montana University Affiliated Rural Institute on Disabilities, Dynamic Communication Process Project, 1994. 159 pp. $10.50 (includes S&H).

> This manual is chock full of helpful, to-the-point advice for achieving just what the subtitle says: effective communication between parents and professionals. Included are tips on becoming a better listener, sending clear messages, interpreting and sending nonverbal cues, and resolving conflicts assertively so that everyone feels like a winner. The chapter on changing from a nonassertive to assertive style should be especially valuable to all but the most seasoned parent-advocate. Using plenty of examples drawn from other parents' experiences, the authors show how parents can ask for what they believe their child needs. This chapter also provides a list of assertive responses to school systems' common excuses for not providing appropriate services. A useful resource list and glossary of terms and acronyms used by early intervention and special education professionals round out the book. (Also available from the Rural Institute on Disabilities is a guide to effective communication written from the professionals' viewpoint: *Effective Communication between Professionals and Parents*—$8.00.)

Dybwad, Rosemary. *Perspectives on A Parent Movement: The Revolt of Parents of Children with Intellectual Limitations.* Cambridge, MA: Brookline, 1990. 182 pp. $17.95. ISBN 0-914797-74-3.

> In a sense, this is a world history book. It is a collection of speeches written over a two-decade period by an early parent advocate who was one of the first to insist that people with disabilities be considered members of their community. These speeches given all over the world are a reminder that children with disabilities are found everywhere and are a universal concern. The author's sensitivity, understanding, courage, and strength are evident in every address. She indeed gives strength to all parents *and* a new energy for the future.

Fishly, Pat. *I AM JOHN.* Washington, DC: National Association of Social Workers Inc., 1992. $3.00. Code: 0360-7283/92.

> This paper was written to establish the need for advocacy for people with mental retardation over time. "John" represents treatment of the mentally retarded since the 1700s, offering a glimpse of what it was like to have mental retardation and how it was treated in 1720, 1850, 1880, 1890, and into the twentieth century. This is sometimes heart-breaking reading, but it also shows how far we have come. This is a great tool to use for inservices for parent advocates and professionals working with parents.

Leff, Patricia Taner, and Elaine H. Walizer. *Building the Healing Partnership.* Cambridge, MA: Brookline, 1992. 307 pp. $34.95. ISBN 0-914797-60-3.

> Page after page of this important book provides parents and professionals with a visit to each other's worlds, an opportunity to respect each other's values. Members of parent/professional teams learn about mutual vulnerability, mutual concerns, and mutual responsibilities. Parents share their experiences and reflect on how past experiences with professionals can create new learning opportunities. Perhaps the most important message in this book is that ideally the most important people in the life of the child with special needs are truly caring individuals with a common bond—the child and his or her needs.

Shapiro, Joseph P. *No Pity: People with Disabilities Forging a New Civil Rights Movement.* New York: Times Books/Random House, 1993. 372 pp. $25.00. ISBN 0-8129-1964-5.

> The title of this splendid book refers to "the new thinking by disabled people that there is no pity or tragedy in disability, and that it is society's myths, fears, and stereotypes that most make being disabled difficult." In exploring the rationale behind this "new thinking," the author presents the riveting personal stories and political maneuverings behind the great gains made in rights to education, employment, community integration, and life. In the end, he makes it crystal clear why society must no longer underestimate the abilities of people with disabilities, prevent them from making their own decisions, and, in general, treat them like second class citizens.

Turnbull, Ann P., and H.R. Turnbull. *Families, Professionals, and Exceptionality: A Special Partnership.* 3rd ed. Upper Saddle River, NJ: Prentice Hall, 1996. 448 pp. $47.00. ISBN 0-13-568551-6.

> This book teaches students how to collaborate with families in a way that promotes equal, meaningful partnerships. Part I explains current thinking about empowerment--how professionals and families can take action to get what they want and need. Part II shows students how they can use the family-systems approach to better understand families. Part III highlights seven key ways to form partnerships with families. Not only does this book combine general and special education approaches, but each of the fifteen chapters ends with a vignette about real families, working with real educators, in real communities across America. These vignettes help students to stand in family members' shoes to better comprehend families' perspectives. (Author's note: Dr. Ann Turnbull provided this review.)

Washington Watch. United Cerebral Palsy, 1660 L St., N.W., Ste. 700, Washington, DC 20036. (800) 872-5827; (202) 785-3508 FAX. Web site: http://www.ucpa.org

> Providing "dependable, timely information for America's disability community" is the mission of this bimonthly newsletter. It is devoted to reporting up-to-the-minute news on legislation and court rulings that will affect people with disabilities. In addition to reporting the facts, the newsletter offers family-friendly information about the possible impact of changes on people with disabilities and their families. The newsletter can be viewed on UCP's web site, or can be received by mail or e-mail for $25.00 a year; by fax, for $50.00.

Self-Advocacy

Abery, Brian, et al. ***Self-Determination for Youth with Disabilities: A Family Education Curriculum.*** Minneapolis, MN: Institute on Community Integration, 1994. 166 pp. $10.00.

> The authors of this practical manual define self-determination as "the intrinsic drive to exercise control over one's thoughts, feelings, and behaviors." The manual is designed to help parents teach their transition-aged children with disabilities the skills and information needed to become self-determined and more in control of their lives. Strategies discussed include using personal future planning sessions to determine the child's abilities, values, and interests; helping the child learn to make his own choices; teaching self-advocacy skills and information about community resources.

Community Advocacy Press. Capabilities Unlimited, 2495 Erie Ave., Cincinnati, OH 45208. (800) 871-2181; (513) 871-5893. E-mail: Countusin@brugold.com.

> This quarterly newsletter is written and edited by persons with disabilities for other self-advocates. Writers share their experiences as self-advocates and in pursuing lives of independence. Subscriptions are free.

DeMerit, K.S., P.L. Halter, G. Jauron, L. Jirovetz, and M. Krueger. ***Charting a Bold Course: A Self-Advocacy Course.*** Green Bay, WI: Brown County ARC, 1988. 45 pp. $14.95.

> This 45-page booklet is a concise guide for looking at and implementing plans for the future. It is designed to assist in the facilitation of a training course or individual sessions with people who have health and/or mental challenges. The individual first looks at his "self," identifies his own values, and finally completes the decision-making procedure. While the approach appears simplistic, the sequence is powerful. The ultimate intent is empowerment and enhanced self-esteem.

Dybwad, Gunnar, and Hank Bersani, Jr., eds. ***New Voices: Self-Advocacy by People with Disabilities.*** Cambridge, MA: Brookline Books, 1996. 269 pp. $29.95. ISBN 1-57129-004-4.

> This collection looks at the self-advocacy movement from an international perspective. Contributors, both with and without developmental disabilities, come from the United States, Canada, Australia, Great Britain, Sweden, and Austria. The writers who do not have disabilities offer accounts—often from first-hand experience--of the origin, impetus, and events leading to the growth of self-advocacy in their countries. The writers with disabilities tell why self-advocacy is needed and what they hope to gain. They speak of the obstacles they encounter in their attempts to be like everyone else—the indignities, loss of privacy, restrictions on freedom, and rigid and petty rules that apply only to them. They talk about their dreams--to have a home with a bathroom and a small kitchen, a job, the opportunity to learn about their disability, a chance to decide what TV show to watch, and the right to get married and have children, no questions asked. The book is an eye-opener for anyone who believes that laws like the ADA have vanquished discrimination against people with disabilities.

Halter, Pamela L. ***Reaching for Independence.*** Green Bay, WI: Brown County ARC, 1985. 44 pp. $8.95.

> This is a handbook that contains a complete curriculum for teaching self-esteem and self-advocacy. The modules are complete with material needs, role play suggestions, and checklists. The sessions allow ample time for discussion and self-awareness. The hoped-for result of this training is that individuals will be aware of socially correct attire, manner, and approach. Plus, they will learn how to assert themselves because they will be more familiar of their value and support systems.

Sands, Deanna J., and Michael L. Wehmeyer, eds. *Self-Determination Across the Life Span: Independence and Choice for People with Disabilities.* Baltimore: Paul H. Brookes, 1996. 384 pp. $35. ISBN 1-55766-238-X.

> The emphasis of this text is on teaching people with disabilities to make their own decisions. The authors provide suggestions for fostering self-determination in both school and community settings. They also include comments from parents about the process of "letting go."

Legal Rights

Boyer, Carol, and Dan Wendling. *NARIC Guide to Resources for the Americans with Disabilities Act (ADA).* 2nd ed. Silver Spring, MD: NARIC, 1996. 67 pp. $5.00.

> This exhaustive directory is a guide to sources of information on the Act's four main titles: employment, public services, public accommodations, and telecommunications. It lists guides, manuals, publications, training programs, and technical assistance programs concerning the ADA, together with ordering or contact information. Also included is information on getting copies of the ADA and ADA regulations.

Citizens Alliance to Uphold Special Education. *Rulings Manual: A Compilation of Selected Rulings.* 3rd ed. Lansing, MI: Citizens Alliance to Uphold Special Education, 1994. Not paginated. $25.00

> This manual includes a great deal of information that parents want and need to know about special education law—literally from A to Z, Access to Zero Reject. The focus is on how court cases have decided different questions, and on the rulings that resulted. This should be a part of every parent resource library and is the perfect companion to CAUSE'S **Section 504**, descibed below. Updates are provided by CAUSE quarterly for a $15.00 fee.

Citizens Alliance to Uphold Special Education. *Section 504 of the Rehabilitation Act of 1973: How to Use the Law to Effectively Service Students.* Lansing, MI: Citizens Alliance to Uphold Special Education, 1995. Not paginated. $15.00.

> Sometimes a child may not "fit" the criteria for special education services under Individuals with Disabilities Education Act (IDEA), yet still need special supports or accomodations to succeed in school. Section 504 provides important support for these students who may otherwise fall through the cracks in the system. This complete guide to 504 explains what the law means and how court cases have been decided regarding access. Referral and eligibility are comprehensibly defined. The handouts are simple and extremely useful "one-pagers" that are easily adaptable to any location in the United States. Sample letters requesting evaluation and re-evaluation and how to determine least restrictive environments are included. This is a fine product for parents, teachers, administrators, and advocates to have on hand.

Goldberg, Daniel, and Marge Goldberg. *The Americans with Disabilities Act: A Guide for People with Disabilities, Their Families and Advocates.* Minneapolis: PACER, 1993. 56 pp. $8.00.

> This useful resource outlines every aspect of the ADA, including how it applies to the areas of employment, public services, public accommodations, and telecommunications. Reasonable accommodation is defined and examples of ways to modify work areas or services are provided.

Malloy, JoAnne M. *Benefits Planning for Children and Youth with Disabilities.* Durham, NH: Institute on Disability, 1995. 93 pp. $5.00.

> This manual includes information on health insurance, individual benefits, and programs and services for children and young people ages birth to 21. It was written specifically for young people with disabilities and their families.

National Center for Law and Deafness. *Legal Rights.* 4th ed. Washington, DC; Gallaudet University Press, 1992. 270 pp. ISBN 1-56368-000-9. $19.95.

> The authors take apart and explain the Americans with Disabilities Act and the Rehabilitation Act of 1973. They discuss how those laws apply to the deaf and hard of hearing. Education, mental health, employment, and a variety of issues regarding this sensitive issue are discussed. Suggestions, strategies, and legal rights are explained.

Ordover, Eileen L., and Kathleen B. Boundy. *Educational Rights of Children with Disabilities: A Primer for Advocates.* Cambridge, MA: Center for Law and Education, 1991. 120 pp. $12.50. ISBN 0-91285-05-4.

> The Center for Law and Education has produced this guide as an overview of the Individuals with Disabilities Act of 1990 (IDEA). The authors provide the reader with good, basic information about every important provision of the law—assessment, eligibility, Individualized Education Program, due process rights. There are useful references at the end of each chapter. Pair this book up with your state's statutes, regulations, and laws and you will have a fine resource for educational advocacy.

Perske, Robert. *Unequal Justice? What Can Happen When Persons with Retardation and Other Developmental Disabilities Encounter the Criminal Justice System.* Nashville, TN: Abingdon Press, 1991. 122 pp. $11.95. ISBN 0-687-42983-8.

> This powerful and disturbing book describes a system of justice that seems to lack any understanding of individuals with developmental disabilities. The author offers a ray of hope or two, but overall, the message is that parents of children in special education and their professional partners have a lot of educating to do in the criminal justice system. Perske does not write in legal-eez, he simply, and masterfully, does what he does best . . . reports what he has observed. A must read for all of us.

Summary of Existing Legislation Affecting People with Disabilities. Washington, DC: U.S. Department of Education, Office of Special Education and Rehabilitative Services, 1992. 235 pp. No charge.

> This book summarizes the provisions of over 60 key federal laws affecting individuals with disabilities. It covers laws relating to education, employment, health, housing, income maintenance (SSI), nutrition, rights, social services, transportation, vocational rehabilitation, and more.

■ ORGANIZATIONS

ADA Disabilities Information Line
U.S. Department of Justice
Civil Rights Division
Disabilities Rights Section
Box 66730
Washington, DC 20035-66738
800-514-0301; 800-514-0383 (TDD)
202-514-6193 (electronic modem)
Web site: http://www.usdoj.gov/crt/ada/

> PURPOSE: The Dept. of Justice is responsible for enforcing Titles II and III (Public Services and Public Accommodations) of the ADA and for disseminating information about the act.

SERVICES: By calling ADA Information Line, callers can listen to an overview of the ADA and complaint process, obtain information on Titles II and III, order materials in print and alternative format on the ADA, and be referred to other agencies for additional assistance.

PUBLICATIONS: Include *"The Americans with Disabilities Act: Questions and Answers"* (32-page booklet written for the general public); fact sheets; *"Regulations for Title II of the ADA"*; and *"Regulations for Title III of the ADA."* All materials are free.

The ARC of Maryland
49 Old Solomon's Island Rd., Suite 205
Annapolis, MD 21401
(410) 571-9320

PUBLICATIONS: The booklet *"Celebrating Lives"* ($6.00) explains the responsibilities of service coordinators/case managers as they advocate with consumers who are developmentally disabled and their parents. The booklet *"Signs of Quality"* ($6.00) includes suggestions from consumers as to what they expect from professionals and service providers in the areas of health and safety, privacy, rights, choices, and opportunities.

The Arc of the United States
500 E. Border St., Ste. 300
Arlington, TX 76010
(817) 261-6003; (817) 277-0553 (TDD)
E-mail: thearc@metronet.com
Web site: http//TheArc.org/welcome.html

PURPOSE: The Arc (formerly the Association for Retarded Citizens) works to improve the lives of all children and adults with mental retardation and their families.

SERVICES: Information and referral about mental retardation, the Arc's programs, and local chapters. Advocates for inclusion of individuals with mental retardation in community life; fosters research and education regarding prevention of mental retardation.

PUBLICATIONS: **Directory of Self-Advocacy Programs** ($5); **Building Self-Advocacy in the Community** ($6); *"A Call to Action: The Roles of People with Mental Retardation in Leadership"* ($3.50); a thrice-yearly newletter for self-advocates, **Advocates' Voice** ($9). Also, *"Using the Plans for Achieving Self-Support to Provide Employment Opportunities for People with Mental Retardation"*; *"Social Security and SSI Benefits for Children with Disabilities"*; *"Appealing a Social Security Disability Benefits Decision"* are free with a self-addressed, stamped envelope. Other publications cover disability laws for business owners, employers, and individuals with mental retardation.

Beach Center on Families and Disability
Bureau of Child Research
University of Kansas
3111 Haworth Hall
Lawrence, KS 66045
(785) 864-7600; (785) 864-4850
E-mail: beach@dole.lsi.ukans.edu
Web site: http://www.lsi.ukans.edu/beach/beachhp.htm

PURPOSE: A university affiliated program providing information for and about families of children with disabilities and national parent resources.

SERVICES: Information and referral.

PUBLICATIONS: Include: *"Use Group Parent Power to Make Things Happen"* ($.50); *"Tell People What You Want"* ($.50); *"Getting Educational Services for Your Child Who Needs Technical Assistance"* ($.50); *"Learn About the Laws That Impact Your Family's Life"* ($.50).

Center for Innovations in Special Education
Parkade Center, Ste. 152
601 Business Loop 70 West
Columbia, MO 65211
Web site: http://tiger.coe.missouri.edu/~mocise
> PURPOSE: "To provide quality continuing education training, information dissemination activities, and resource materials to support educators who strive to help young people with disabilities achieve their potential."
>
> PUBLICATIONS: Has a variety of instructional modules, including *"Accessibility and Accommodation"* ($7.35); *"Self-Advocacy"* ($6.90); *"Rights and Responsibilities of Students with Disabilities in the Postsecondary Setting"* ($1.75); other publications primarily for educators. Note: Publications must be ordered from the Instructional Materials Laboratory at University of Missouri-Columbia. Phone (800) 669-2465; (573) 882-1992 FAX.

Children's Defense Fund
25 E St., NW
Washington, DC 20001
(202) 662-3652
E-mail: cdfinfo@childrensdefense.org
Web site: http://www.childrensdefense.org
> PURPOSE: "A nonprofit research and advocacy organization that exists to provide a strong and effective voice for the children of America."
>
> PUBLICATIONS: Include ***An Advocate's Guide to the Media, An Advocate's Guide to Fund Raising, Your Child's School Records, Stand of Children: A Parent's Guide to Child Advocacy.*** Request a publications catalog.

Disability Rights Education & Defense Fund (DREDF)
2212 6th Street
Berkeley, CA 94710
(510) 644-2555; (510) 644-2629 (TDD); (510) 841-8645 fax
> PURPOSE: DREDF considers itself a guardian of civil rights for people with disabilities.
>
> SERVICES: Advocacy, information, and referral.
>
> PUBLICATIONS: Newsletter and various booklets on the Americans with Disabilities Act.

Disabled Peoples' International
101-7 Evergreen Place
Winnipeg, Manitoba
Canada R3L 2T3
(204) 287-8010; (204) 453-1367 FAX
Web site: http://www.escape.ca/~dpi/
> PURPOSE: "to promote the Human Rights of People with Disabilities through full participation, equalization of opportunity and development. DPI is a grassroots, cross-disability network with member organizations in over 110 countries."
>
> PUBLICATIONS: Examples include: ***Tools for Power*** ($9.00), a resource kit for independent living; ***Non-Government Funding & Networking Contact List*** ($30.00); *"Organizing a Meeting"* ($8.00); *"The Role of Disabled Persons' Organizations"* ($2.00); ***Funny You Should Ask: Living with a Disability*** ($10.00); and proceedings of DPI's World Congresses. ***Disability International Magazine,*** which includes information on products and resources, first person accounts, and news about DPI, can be viewed on the web site.

Equal Employment Opportunity Commission

1801 L St., NW
Washington, DC 20507
(800) 669-EEOC; (800) 800-3302 TDD

PURPOSE: The EEOC is one of the federal agencies responsible for providing information to the public about the ADA.

PUBLICATIONS: Free publications include *"The ADA: Your Employment Rights as an Individual with a Disability"; "Facts about Disability-Related Tax Provisions"; "The ADA: Your Responsibilities as an Employer."*

House Document Room

Ford House Office Building
Room B18
Washington, DC 20515
(202) 225-3456

PUBLICATIONS: Copies of public laws (such as IDEA) can be obtained from this address.

JKL Communications

P.O. Box 40157
Washington, DC 20016
(202) 223-5097

PURPOSE: Provides advocacy resources for parents of children with special needs.

PUBLICATIONS: JKL distributes publications such as *"Documentation and the Law," "ADD and the Law," "Learning Disability and the Law," "Succeeding in the Workplace,"* plus many more. Videos are also available.

Michigan Protection and Advocacy

106 W. Allegany, Suite 210
Lansing MI: 48933-1760
517-487-1755; 800-288-5923 (V/TDD); 517-487-0827

PURPOSE: Provides services for individuals with exceptional needs.

PUBLICATIONS: Quarterly newsletter. Each issue focuses on current topics in advocacy such as inclusion and assistive technology.

National Association of Protection & Advocacy Systems

900 Second St., NE, Suite 211
Washington, DC 20002
202-408-9514; 202-408-9520 FAX; 202-408-9521 TDD
E-mail: NAPAS@earthlink.net
Web site: http://protectionandadvocacy.com/

PURPOSE: National umbrella organization for the "federally mandated system in each state and territory which provides protection of the rights of persons with disabilities through legally based advocacy."

SERVICES: Information and referral and advocacy.

PUBLICATIONS: NAPAS offers a number of publications which include "A Resource for Rights Enforcement" ($2.00); "The Right of Persons with Disabilities to be Free from Discrimination in Housing Pursuant to the Federal Fair Housing Law and other Statutes" ($15.00); and "Frequently Asked Questions about Hiring People Who Have Developmental Disabilities" ($.25).

People First International

P.O. Box 12642

Salem, OR 97309

(503) 362-0336

> PURPOSE: A self-advocacy organization of people with mental retardation or other developmental disabilities who are interested in learning to speak for themselves, become leaders, and take responsibility for improving their lives.
>
> PUBLICATIONS: Include information on People First, setting up local chapters, and officers' handbook.

President's Committee on Employment of People with Disabilities

1331 F St., NW

Washington, DC 20004-1107

(202) 376-6200; (202) 376-6205 (TDD); (202) 376-6219 FAX

Web site: http://www.pcepd.gov

> PUBLICATIONS: Offers a variety of fact sheets, brochures, and longer publications for individuals with disabilities and potential employers. Examples of complimentary fact sheets include: *"Interviewing Tips for the Job Applicant"; "Job Accommodations Come in Groups of One"; "Employment Rights, Who Has Them and Who Enforces Them"; "Supported Employment"; "Job Accommodations—Situations and Solutions"; "Pre-Employment Inquiries."* Most publications available on web site.

The Roeher Institute

Kinsmen Building

York University

4700 Keele St.

North York, Ontario

Canada M3J 1P3

(416) 661-2023 Voice/TDD; (416) 661-5701 FAX

Web site: http://indie.ca/roeher/intro.html

> PURPOSE: "promotes the equality, participation, and self-determination of people with intellectual and other disabilities."
>
> SERVICES: Information services include reference and referral information, customized responses to questions, the development of information packages on specific topics, and operation of an extensive library. Also conducts research and public policy analysis and social development and training.
>
> PUBLICATIONS: ***As If Children Matter: Perspectives on Children, Rights and Disability*** ($24.00); many publications with a Canadian focus such as *"The Right to Fair and Equal Treatment: A Straightforward Guide to the Canadian Human Rights Act"* ($7.00) and *"The Right to Have Enough Money: A Straightforward Guide to the Disability Income System in Canada"* ($7.00).

Washington PAVE (Parents Are Vital in Education)

6316 South 12th

Tacoma, WA 98465

(253) 565-2266 (V/TDD)

> PURPOSE: To provide support and advocacy.
>
> SERVICES: Information and referral, parent-to-parent support, and advocacy.
>
> PUBLICATIONS: Resources list (free); information sheets on different disabilities ($2.00 to $8.00); ***PAVE Newsletter*** (a marvelous resource, full of useful information).

10.

Sign Language and Augmentative and Alternative Communication (AAC)

■ BOOKS AND PERIODICALS

Sign Language

Bornstein, Harry, ed. *Manual Communication: Implications for Education.* Washington, DC: Gallaudet University Press, 1990. 272 pp. $34.95. ISBN 0-930323-57-2.

> A comprehensive look at all of the sign systems currently used to educate deaf students is provided in this book. American Sign Language, Contact Sign (Pidgin Sign), Signed English, Signing Exact English, and Cued Speech are each described in detail by their acknowledged designer, administrator, or scholar. There are also interesting discussions of the history of sign language, conflicts about its use, and factors that affect the choice of manual communication systems.

Klein, Marsha Dunn. *Pre-Sign Language Motor Skills.* Tucson, AZ: Communication Skill Builders, 1992. $23.00. ISBN 0-88450-821-8.

> Written by a registered occupational therapist, this book provides special insight into why understanding motor development is crucial for the child and professional who need to learn and use

sign language. A very clear and important message is shared right at the beginning: there must be a balance "between language and motor instruction." The sections have instructions, paired with illustrations and then a quiz to check the reader's lesson memory. There are pages of sign analysis worksheets to monitor and "score" the signs as the child produces the sign. The illustrations are exceptionally clear.

Schein, Jerome D., and David A. Stewart. *Language in Motion: Exploring the Nature of Sign.* Washington, DC: Gallaudet University Press, 1995. 221 pp. $24.95. ISBN 1-56368-039-4.

A blend of practical information on using sign language and theoretical and historical background of its use, this book is a fascinating introduction to the world of sign. American Sign Language (ASL) is the focus, although information on sign languages used around the world, Pidgin Sign English (contact signing), Cued Speech, and Manual Codes for English (MCE) is also provided. For readers interested in learning ASL, there are chapters on the components of signs and the grammar of ASL; fingerspelling alphabets (including why you should not use the ASL handshape for "t" in some foreign countries); and how to learn to sign. Also included are chapters on the history of sign language, on sign language interpreting, and on the place of ASL in Deaf culture.

AMERICAN SIGN LANGUAGE (ASL)

Costello, Elaine. *Random House American Sign Language Dictionary.* New York, NY: Random House, 1994. 1067 pp. $50.00. ISBN 0-394-58580-1.

With over 5,600 signs, this is billed as the largest, most complete dictionary of ASL. Each entry includes a definition of the word, a line drawing illustrating the sign, and a description of how to make the sign.

Fant, Lou. *The American Sign Language Phrase Book.* 2nd ed. Chicago: Contemporary Books, 1994. 346 pp. $18.95. ISBN 0-8092-3500-5.

This is a guide for people who want to converse in ASL but do not yet understand the grammar. It explains how to say a number of phrases, expressions, sentences, and questions that are helpful in everyday conversation. There is also a brief overview of grammar.

Lane, Leonard G. *Gallaudet Survival Guide to Signing.* 2nd ed. Washington, DC: Gallaudet University Press, 1990. 224 pp. $6.95. ISBN 0-930323-67-X.

A guide to 500 of the most frequently used ASL signs, this book also includes suggestions for successful signing. The vocabulary included is designed to be useful in home, school, work, and social situations.

O'Rourke, Terrence J. *A Basic Vocabulary: American Sign Language for Parents and Children.* Silver Spring, MD: TJ Publishers, 1978. 240 pp. $8.95. ISBN 0-932666-00-0.

In alphabetical order, this book illustrates the ASL signs most commonly used by children.

Riekehof, Lottie L. *The Joy of Signing.* 2nd ed. Springfield, MO: Gospel Publishing House, 1987. 353 pp. $17.95. ISBN 0-88243-520-5.

What makes this well-known dictionary of signs unique is that it explains the origins of the signs illustrated to make learning and remembering them easier. About 1500 ASL signs are illustrated.

Sternberg, Martin L.A. *American Sign Language Dictionary.* New York, NY: HarperCollins, 1995. 737 pp. $10.00. ISBN 0-06-27-32757.

This chunky paperback includes clear illustrations and written descriptions for almost every sign imaginable.

SIGNED ENGLISH

Bornstein, Harry, Karen L. Saulnier, and Lillian B. Hamilton. *The Comprehensive Signed English Dictionary.* Washington, DC: Gallaudet, 1983. 455 pp. $28.95. ISBN 0-913580-81-3.

> Over 3100 signs are illustrated in this book for all ages. The book also shows how to make sign markers, compounds, and contractions. Signs are depicted with two-color line drawings. Also included is an overiview of Signed English as a language.

Bornstein, Harry, and Karen L. Saulnier. *The Signed English Starter: A Beginning Book in the Signed English System.* Washington, DC: Gallaudet University Press, 1984. 208 pp. $13.95. ISBN 0-913580-82-1.

> This book is designed to be used at home or in the classroom as a first course in Signed English. About 900 sign words (vocabulary words) are covered within topical chapters (for example, The Body, Food, Actions, Nature and Animals). The 14 sign markers, which are used to change the form or meaning of a word to match the spoken English word, are also introduced.

Gustason, Gerilee and Esther Zawolkow. *Signing Exact English.* Las Alamitas, CA: Modern Signs Press, 1993. $29.95. ISBN 0-916708-23-3.

> This guide contains over 4400 signs for beginners to advanced signers. The book also includes a thorough discussion of morphological markers and the argument for using them.

FOR CHILDREN

This is just a small sample of the many children's books on sign currently available.

Baker, Pamela. *My First Book of Sign.* Washington, DC: Gallaudet University Press, 1986. 76 pp. $14.95. ISBN 0-930323-20-3.

> Signs for 150 of the words most often used by young children are shown in this brightly illustrated book. Signs for different parts of speech (nouns, verbs, adjectives, etc.) are included, with the number of each based on the findings of early language acquisition research. Sign descriptions are included.

Bourke, Linda. *Handmade ABC.* Reading, MA: Addison Wesley, 1981. Not paginated. $6.95. ISBN 0-201-00015-6.

> For each letter, pictures of items that begin with that letter are illustrated, as well as the hand illustrating the sign. No reading is required, so this book is terrific for preschools.

Charlip, Remy, Mary Beth and George Ancona. *Handtalk: An ABC of Fingerspelling and Sign Language.* New York, NY: Four Winds Press, 1974. ISBN 0-590-07766-X.

> Color photographs are used to illustrate each letter sign, as well as words that begin with the letter represented. Fun words are used as examples. For instance, right in the middle of the book there is a hand with peanut butter slopped on it on the left side of the page. On the right side of the page, there is another hand with jelly plopped in its palm. The top pictures illustrate peanut butter and jelly sandwiches.

Gillen, Patricia Bellan. *My Signing Book of Numbers.* Washington, DC: Gallaudet University Press, 1987. 56 pp. $14.95. ISBN 0-930323-37-8.

> The signs for the numbers 1-20 are illustrated, together with the appropriate number of objects, in this colorful book for young sign language learners. The signs for the numbers 30, 40, 50, 60, 70, 80, 90, and 100 are also included.

Hafer, Jan C., and Robert M. Wilson. ***Come Sign with Us: Sign Language Activities for Children.***
2nd ed. Washington, DC: Gallaudet University Press, 1990. 144 pp. $29.95. ISBN 1-56368-051-3.

> This manual presents twenty short lessons aimed at teaching children the rudiments of sign language. The book is written for adults with no previous knowledge of sign language and focuses on Pidgen Sign English (contact signing)--using ASL signs in English word order. Signs are illustrated with line drawings and defined in both English and Spanish. The annotated bibliography at the end points the way to additional publications useful in learning and teaching about sign.

Hill, Eric. ***Where's Spot? Sign Language Edition.*** New York, NY: Putnam, 1987. 22 pp. $12.95.
ISBN 0-399-20758-9.

> Preschoolers lift the flaps to find where Spot the dog is hiding. This is an excellent book for introducing and teaching positional concepts and yes/no questions. Line drawings added to the original illustrations show American Signed English hand movements.

Sesame Street Sign Language ABC with Linda Bove. New York, NY: Random House, 1985. 32
pp. $3.50. 0-394-87516-8.

> Deaf actress Linda Bove is featured in this friendly introduction to ASL. There are photographs of Bove signing each letter of the alphabet, along with several words beginning with that letter, against a colorful background of Muppet characters.

Slier, Debby. ***Animal Signs: A First Book of Sign Language.*** Washington, DC: Gallaudet University Press, 1995. 16 pp. $6.95. ISBN 1-56368-049-1.

> This board book introduces signs for some of the most common animals to children ages one through four. It is illustrated with color photographs.

Slier, Debby. ***Word Signs: A First Book of Sign Language.*** Washington, DC: Gallaudet University Press, 1995. 16 pp. $6.95. ISBN 1-56368-048-3.

> This board book introduces signs for household objects and other basic words for toddlers and preschoolers. It is illustrated with color photographs.

Wheeler, Cindy. ***Simple Signs.*** New York, NY: Penguin Books, 1995. 32 pp. $12.99. 0-670-86282-7.

> Written by the mother of a child with Down syndrome, this book introduces twenty-eight ASL signs that appeal to preschoolers. Each page features a colorful illustration of a word (cat, dog, milk, happy, friend, sleep) with a line drawing showing how to make the sign.

Alternative and Augmentative Communication (AAC)

The focus of this section is on publications dealing with both low- and high-tech devices used specifically to help children communicate. Additional helpful resources may be found in the next chapter on **"Technology,"** *which lists resources related to multipurpose high-tech devices.*

Donovan, Claire. ***Communicating with Signs, Sounds, and Symbols.*** Self-published by Claire Donovan, 1996. 134 pp. $20.00. ISBN 0-9698308-1-5. (Available from Claire Donovan, 726 Mays Rd., RR#4, Duncan, B.C. V9L 3W8 Canada.)

> This self-published book is a good basic parents' guide to AAC. Using a parent friendly style, it covers common communication difficulties, evaluating and selecting an AAC method, and guidelines for teaching the system to your child. An important emphasis is on developing a communication system that reflects the desires and interests of the user. This is not the book to turn to for information on the types of AAC devices currently available, or for information on funding sources.

Holcomb, Nan. *Sarah's Surprise.* Hollidaysburg, PA: Jason & Nordic, 1990. $13.95.
ISBN 0-944727-0707.

> Sarah can walk, play and socialize, but she cannot talk. Her mom's birthday is in a few days and Sarah wants more then anything to sing "Happy Birthday" to her. She is frustrated and sad until her speech-language pathologist helps her make the switch from a picture board to an augmentative communication device. This children's story emphasizes the importance of identifying the needs of children with communication problems and then creating alternative forms of communication for them to use.

Munson, Joyce H., Carol L. Nordquist, and Susan L. Thuma-Rew. *Communication Systems for Persons with Severe Neuromotor Impairment.* Iowa City, IA: The University of Iowa, University Hospital School, 1987. 253 pp. No charge.

> This monograph summarizes the approach of the University Affiliated Program at the University of Iowa to achieving "maximal communicative potential" in nonspeaking children, primarily those with cerebral palsy. This method emphasizes an interdisciplinary approach to evaluating a child's need for augmentative communication and then implementing a system. As this is an older book, it is not a source for information on the latest technology. It is, however, a good source of information on such general topics as: deciding whether a child would benefit from AAC; the role of positioning in allowing a child to communicate; deciding on an appropriate system; designing a communication board; and setting goals for communication development. A chapter on Integrating Communication Systems into the Classroom offers many practical suggestions for ensuring that the child is truly included in his classroom, not just "parked in the back." Although written for a professional audience, the text is generally clear and jargon-free. Many photos and illustrations of kids and their communication systems are included. One copy of the book is available free from the National Maternal and Child Health Clearinghouse (stock #B272), at the address listed in the Publishers section at the end of the book.

Reichle, Joe, Jennifer York, and Jeff Sigafoos. *Implementing Augmentative and Alternative Communication: Strategies for Learners with Severe Disabilities.* Baltimore: Paul H. Brookes, 1991. 302 pp. $46.00. ISBN 1-55766-044-1.

> The focus of this comprehensive, multi-author volume is on graphic augmentative communication systems (i.e., not gestures) for people with severe communication impairments related to severe or profound mental retardation or autism. The authors begin by explaining in exhaustive detail all the possible forms that augmentative communication can take. Successive chapters explain how to determine who is a candidate for AAC, how to select an appropriate system for a potential user, and how to teach beginning communication skills. Included are several chapters on using AAC systems with individuals who have severe physical disabilities. Although intended primarily for professionals, most of the chapters in the book would not be too heavy going for parents with an interest in the subject.

The Trace Resourcebook: Assistive Technologies for Communication, Control, and Computer Access. Madison, WI: Trace Research & Development Center, 1996. 933 pp. $50.00.

> This directory of software, hardware, and augmentative communication equipment includes descriptions, manufacturer information, and photos for more than 1500 products from 400 manufacturers.

■ ORGANIZATIONS

ISAAC

P.O. Box 1762, Station R

Toronto, Ontario M4G 4A3

Canada

(905) 737-9308; (905) 737-0624

> PURPOSE: A transdisciplinary organization that strives to advance the field of augmentative and alternative communication (AAC); to facilitate information exchange; and to focus attention on work in the field.
>
> PUBLICATIONS: Newsletters include *ISAAC Bulletin; Communication Outlook* (information on state-of-the-art technology in AAC); *Communicating Together* (information on communication systems and everyday experiences of nonspeaking persons). Also publishes a membership directory and professional journal. Reduced subscription rates for members of ISAAC. *Note: Residents of Canada should contact* ISAAC-Canada at this address; residents of the United States should contact USSAAC at the address *below.*

Trace Research & Development Center

University of Wisconsin-Madison

S-151 Waisman Center

1500 Highland Ave.

Madison, WI 53705-2280

(608) 262-6966; (608) 263-5408 TDD; (608) 262-8848 FAX

E-mail: info@trace.wisc.edu

Web site: http://trace.wisc.edu

> PURPOSE: "To advance the ability of people with disabilities to achieve their life objectives through the use of communication, computer and information technologies."
>
> PUBLICATIONS: Offers a variety of publications for users and developers of technology. Examples include: *"Activities Using Headsticks and Optical Pointers"; "Beyond Yes/No in the Early Childhood Classroom"; "Construction Notes of Laptrays, Portable Communication Boards, and Adaptive Pointers";* and *The Trace Resourcebook,* described above.

USSAAC

P.O. Box 5271

Evanston, IL 60204-5271

(847) 869-2122

> PURPOSE: The United States Society for Augmentative and Alternative Communication (USSAAC) is the U.S. chapter of ISAAC (see above). It works on an international, national, and state level to advance the field of augmentative and alternative communication and to help people overcome communication difficulties.
>
> PUBLICATIONS: Newsletters include *USSAAC Bulletin; Communication Outlook* (information on state-of-the-art technology in AAC); *Communicating Together* (information on communication systems and everyday experiences of nonspeaking persons). Reduced subscription rates for members of USSAAC.

11.

Technology

■ BOOKS AND PERIODICALS

Alliance for Technology Access. ***Computer Resources for People with Disabilities: A Guide to Exploring Today's Assistive Technologies.*** 2nd ed. Alameda, CA: Hunter House, 1997. 288 pp. $17.95 (paper) ISBN 0-89793-196-3; $22.95 (spiral) ISBN 0-89793-197-1.

> The authors intend this book as a jumping off point for individuals interested in learning about available assistive technology and its uses. In Part I of the book, the authors discuss how to define your needs, develop a technology plan, and build a supportive team. In Part II, the authors provide examples of assistive technologies to give readers an idea of products that may be useful to them. Part III lists resources, references, and organizations. The information is presented in a logical, step-by-step fashion that should be easily understandable even to readers with no knowledge of technology whatsoever. The book includes many stories about adults and children who use technology in their everyday lives.

Bender, Renet L., and William N. Bender. ***Computer-Assisted Instruction for Students at Risk for ADHD, Mild Disabilities, or Academic Problems.*** Needham Heights, MA: Allyn & Bacon, 1996. 240 pp. $29.95. ISBN 0-205-16062-X.

> This text was written for teachers, but covers some helpful information for parents. It includes information on how computers can help students with particular learning characteristics, as well as how to select appropriate software. Also provided are examples of activities for children of all ability levels.

Children's Software Revue. 44 Main St., Flemington, NJ 08822. (800) 993-9499; (908) 284-0405.

> Although this magazine is targeted at all parents who are looking for guidance in selecting software for children aged 2-15, it would also be useful for parents of children with special needs in

particular. Each software title selected for review is reviewed by one or two test families and/or schools in addition to a staff member. Printed reviews include information on the suggested age range, the concepts that are taught, price, ordering information, a description of the program and features that young users like and do not like, and an overall numerical rating from 1-5. Each issue contains reviews of approximately 120 software titles, for both Mac and Windows. An annual subscription (6 issues) is $24.00; $35.00 in Canada or Mexico. Reviews from back issues of the magazine can be viewed on the magazine's web site: <http://www2.childrenssoftware.com/childrenssoftware/>.

Church, Gregory, and Sharon Glennen. ***The Handbook of Assistive Technology.*** San Diego, CA: Singular Publishing Group, 1991. 394 pp. $39.95. ISBN 1-879105-53-5.

> Although written primarily for educators, the style and content of this text make it useful for parents as well. For novices, the book offers an easy-to-follow overview of computer technology and terminology. Other chapters of interest to parents cover powered mobility aids; augmentative and alternative communication; adaptive toys and environmental control units; and using assistive technology in inclusive settings. Real-life examples of individuals whose lives were enhanced with technology are included throughout the book.

Closing the Gap. P.O. Box 68, Henderson, MN 56044. (612) 248-3294.

> The publishers describe this newsletter as "an internationally recognized source for information on the use of microcomputer related technology by and for exceptional individuals." It may be too advanced for readers who are new to computers or technology. A one-year subscription (6 issues) is $29.00 in the U.S.; $44.00 in Canada and Mexico. **Closing the Gap** also publishes an annual ***Resource Directory*** ($14.95 plus S&H), which lists commercially available hardware and software for use by people with disabilities.

Flippo, Karen F., Katherine J. Inge, and J. Michael Barcus, eds. ***Assistive Technology: A Resource for School, Work, and Community.*** Baltimore: Paul H. Brookes, 1995. 301 pp. $34.00. ISBN 1-55766-189-8.

> The editors intend this book to be "a comprehensive resource guide that can answer users' and professionals' questions about assessment, training, implementation, and funding issues related to assistive technology services and devices." The emphasis of the book is on adult users of technology, but there are several chapters of special interest to parents of children with disabilities. The chapter on Assistive Technology and School System Personnel would be especially useful for parents hoping to get technology included in their child's IEP. There is also a chapter on sports and recreation activities that lists specific adaptations for different activities and explains what the ADA says about allowing individuals with disabilities to participate in inclusive activities. In addition, the chapter on Creative Financing of Assistive Technology would be helpful for anyone looking for public or private sources of funding for technology. Photographs of many of the devices described are included.

Lazzaro, Joseph J. ***Adapting PC's for Disabilities.*** Reading, MA: Addison-Wesley, 1996. 352 pp. $39.95. ISBN 0-201-48354-8.

> The emphasis of this book is on making IBM compatible computers accessible to users with disabilities. Included are tips on adapting keyboards and monitors; on making workstations more convenient and comfortable; and on using PCs for the purpose of augmenting communication abilities. The book is packaged with a CD-ROM, which includes demonstrations of software that can be used to make computers accessible, as well as the full text of the book.

Lazzaro, Joseph J. *Adaptive Technologies for Learning and Work Environments.* Chicago: American Library Association, 1993. 251 pp. $45.00. ISBN 0-8389-0615-X.

The focus of this readable text is on personal computers and adaptive technology that enable information access for people with visual, hearing, motor, and speech disabilities (but *not* cognitive disabilities). The book begins with a thorough introduction to computers designed to give computer novices the vocabulary to understand the rest of the book and some guidance in choosing a personal computer. There are separate chapters on technology for persons with vision impairments, hearing impairments, and motor and/or speech impairments. Here the author discusses not only general types of adaptive technologies useful for specific purposes, but also more than 120 specific adaptive products on the market. There is also a lengthy chapter on funding sources, as well as information on networking computers, using online databases, and CD-ROMs with adaptive technology. Lists of adaptive technology providers, organizations and conferences, and publications for further information round out this useful volume. Note: the author tends to assume that readers are using DOS operating systems rather than Windows, but examples should be readily translatable by readers familiar with both systems.

Male, Mary. *Technology for Inclusion: Meeting the Special Needs of All Students.* 3rd ed. Boston: Allyn and Bacon, 1996. 224 pp. $46.00. ISBN 0-205-19654-3.

Although written with an audience of teachers in mind, this book has much to offer parents of children of all ages. Topics discussed include: guidelines to selecting technology that is age appropriate and permits students to be as included and independent as possible; using technology to support learning of communication, cognitive, and recreation skills; selecting appropriate software; classroom learning strategies/adaptations when several students must share computers; using spreadsheets & databases. An especially useful chapter—on integrating technology with IEPs--covers writing goals and objectives that specify how a student is to use technology to achieve them and how progress can be monitored. The book's emphasis on using technology to enhance learning of academic subjects may make it most useful for children with milder disabilities.

Pacer Center. *Kids Included through Technology Are Enriched: A Guidebook for Teachers of Young Children.* Minneapolis: Pacer Center, 1997. 124 pp. $10.00.

This spiral-bound guide was written for teachers and parents of children with disabilities ages 3-8. It clearly explains the rationale for using technology with young children, as well as how to assess a child's technology needs, what types of technology have been used successfully with young children with disabilities, and how to integrate technology into the classroom and IFSP/IEP. Case histories of children who have been helped through technology are sprinkled throughout the book. Appendices include descriptions of software appropriate for children with disabilities ages 3-8, a list of technology vendors and organizations, information about what federal laws say about assistive technology, and a list of organizations to contact for information and assistance.

Scherer, Marcia. *Living in the State of Stuck: How Technologies Affect the Lives of People with Disabilities.* 2nd ed. Cambridge, MA, Brookline Books, 1993. 189 pp. $17.95. ISBN 1-57129-027-3.

In *Living in the State of Stuck,* the author set out to explore how assistive technology really affects the day-to-day lives of individuals with disabilities. She found that "technology alone is rarely the answer to a person's enhanced qualify of life." Although assistive technology *can* help increase an individual's independence and sense of well-being, it can only do so when it is carefully selected with an eye to the individual's capabilities, personality, and preferences, and when appropriate training and support are provided. To illustrate this message, the author includes the stories of many adults with either lifelong or acquired disabilities who use assistive technologies in their daily activities.

Technology and Inclusion News. Box 92109, Austin, TX 78709. (512) 280-7235.

This newsletter covers information and resources of interest to parents and teachers interested in incorporating technology into the education process. An individual subscription is $25 per year.

The Trace Resourcebook: Assistive Technologies for Communication, Control, and Computer Access. Madison, WI: Trace Research & Development Center, 1996. 933 pp. $50.00.

This directory of software, hardware, and augmentative communication equipment includes descriptions, manufacturer information, and photos for more than 1500 products from 400 manufacturers.

■ ORGANIZATIONS

ABLEDATA

8455 Colesville Rd., Ste. 935

Silver Spring, MD 20910

(800) 227-0216; (301) 608-8912 (TTY); (301) 608-8958 FAX

Web site: http://www.abledata.com

PURPOSE: "A national database of information on assistive technology and rehabilitation equipment available from domestic and international sources." Includes information on commercial products, non-commercial prototypes, and one-of-a-kind and do-it-yourself products.

SERVICES: Consumers can search the database free of charge from the ABLEDATA web site, or can have an information specialist perform a search for a small fee. Information specialists also answer requests for information and provide referrals at no cost.

PUBLICATIONS: Include ***Wheelchair Information Packet*** ($7), ***Sports & Recreation Resource Packet*** ($5), ***Blindness/Low Vision Resource Packet*** ($6), ***Funding Assistive Technology Fact Sheet*** ($1.25 each, minimum order $5); and ***Company Telephone Directory*** ($25)—a listing of all manufacturers and distributors listed in ABLEDATA which is updated quarterly.

Alliance for Technology Access

2175 E. Francisco Blvd., Ste. L

San Rafael, CA 94901

(415) 455-4575; (415) 455-0654 FAX

E-mail: atainfo@ataccess.org

Web site: http://www.ataccess.org/atacess/

PURPOSE: A national network of technology resource centers and technology vendors that seek "to redefine human potential by making technology a regular part of the lives of people with disabilities."

SERVICES: Operates ATA technology resource centers that help people with disabilities and others explore computer software and adaptive devices.

PUBLICATIONS: Publishes ***Computer Resources for People with Disabilities,*** described above. *"Solutions Paks,"* which describe how real people have solved technology access issues, are available to members for $17.50. Also offers an Online Bookmark Update Service, which provides monthly lists of online resources related to assistive technology products, issues, and access.

Apple Computer, Inc.
Worldwide Disability Solutions Group
1 Infinite Loop
Cupertino, CA 95014
(800) 600-7808; (800) 755-0601 (TTY)
Web site: http://www2.apple.com/disability/disability_home.html

> PURPOSE: To ensure that Macintosh computers are fully accessible to individuals with disabilities.
>
> PUBLICATIONS: **Macintosh Access Passport (MAP)** is a database that includes descriptive information about more than 100 Macintosh solutions for individuals with a disability. Consumers can access the database through the web site above, or can request a free printout. *"Resource Sheets,"* one-page summaries of adaptive hardware and software available for the Macintosh, are available on the following topics: Visual Disability, Physical Disability, Learning and Speaking Disability, and Special Education.

DO-IT (Disabilities, Opportunities, Internetworking, and Technology)
University of Washington
4545 15th Ave., NE
Seattle, WA 98105
(206) 685-DOIT; (206) 685-4054 FAX
E-mail: doit@u.washington.edu
Web site: http://weber.u.washington.edu/~doit/

> PURPOSE: "To increase the participation of individuals with disabilities in academic programs and careers."
>
> SERVICES: Conducts workshops on adaptive technology, college transition, access to employment, etc.; sponsors a discussion list; lends computers, modems, software, and adaptive technology for use by high school students with disabilities who have an interest in majoring in science, engineering, mathematics, or technology in college.
>
> PUBLICATIONS: Print copies of the following are available free from the address above: *"Working Together: People with Disabilities and Computer Technology"*; *"Equal Access to Computer Labs"*; *"World Wide Access,"* accessible WWW page design; *"Adaptive Technology Used by DO-IT Scholars."* The articles may also be downloaded from DO-IT's web site.

DREAMMS for Kids, Inc.
273 Ringwood Rd.
Freeville, NY 13068-9618
(607) 539-3027
E-mail: DREAMMS@aol.com
Web site: http://users.aol.com/dreamms/

> PURPOSE: DREAMMS for Kids (Developmental Research for the Effective Advancement of Memory and Motor Skills) is a parent-run nonprofit organization committed to facilitating the use of computers and assistive technology for students and young people with special needs in schools, homes, and the community.
>
> PUBLICATIONS: A newsletter that provides information helpful for parents new to technology. Sample topics include adaptive keyboards, software, adapting toys for motor skills. Also offers *"Tech Paks"* (informative packets on a variety of topics related to assistive technology and augmentative communication).

HEATH/American Council on Education

Dept. 36
Washington, DC 20055-0036
(202) 939-9320; (202) 833-4760 FAX
E-mail: heath@ace.nche.edu
Web site: http://www.acenet.edu
gopher://bobcat-ace.nche.edu

> PURPOSE: A national clearinghouse on postsecondary education for individuals with disabilities.
> PUBLICATIONS: *"Educational Software for Students with Learning Disabilities"; "Computers, Technology, and Disability"* (newsletter article reprint); *"EASI Brochure on Technology."* There is a nominal charge for publications in print, computer diskette, or audiocassette format. Publications can also be downloaded free at gopher site above.

Institute for the Study of Developmental Disabilities

2853 E. 10th St.
Bloomington, IN 47408-2601
(812) 855-6508; (812) 855-9396 TDD
Web site: http://www.isdd.indiana.edu/

> PURPOSE: "To provide leadership that enables communities to include, support, and empower people with disabilities and family members. The Institute accomplishes this by promoting innovative practices and policies that facilitate community membership."
> PUBLICATIONS: *"Early Learning Software Guide"* ($2.00); *"What Is Assistive Technology? A Basic Guide for Consumers and Their Families"* ($10.00).

Macomb Projects

27 Horrabin Hall
Western Illinois University
Macomb, IL 61455
(309) 298-1634; (309) 298-2305 FAX
Web site: http://www.wiu.edu/users/mimacp/wiu
Web site: http://www.mprojects.wiu.edu

> PURPOSE: Macomb Projects is the umbrella title for eight separate projects based at Western Illinois University that deal with young children with disabilities (birth to age 8). Most of the projects involve research related to technology and young children.
> PUBLICATIONS: Macomb Projects has a catalog of tested educational products for early childhood special education (books, software, videotapes, instructional materials). Examples of publications include: ***Good Leads for Software Needs: Suggested Macintosh Software for Young Children*** ($15.00); ***A Switch to Turn Kids On***, a guide to making homemade switches ($12.00); ***ACTTive Technology,*** a quarterly newsletter with technology resources, reviews of software programs, articles on cirriculum adaptations ($16.00).

National Lekotek Center

2100 Ridge Ave.
Evanston, IL 60201
(800) 366-PLAY; (708) 328-5514 FAX
E-mail: lekotek@lekotek.org

> PURPOSE: A resource center on play-centered programs for children with disabilities.
> SERVICES: Operates sites across the country with lending libraries of toys, adaptive equipment, computers, and other resources.
> PUBLICATIONS: Software resource guides, newsletters, training manuals, videos. Call for a product guide.

RESNA

1700 N. Moore St., Ste. 1540

Arlington, VA 22209-1903

(703) 524-6686

> PURPOSE: "Interdisciplinary association for individuals and organizations concerned with the advancement of rehabilitation and assistive technologies for persons with disabilities."
>
> PUBLICATIONS: Include *Assistive Technology Sourcebook* ($30) and *Assistive Technology and the IEP* ($10).

Trace Research & Development Center

University of Wisconsin-Madison

S-151 Waisman Center

1500 Highland Ave.

Madison, WI 53705-2280

(608) 262-6966; (608) 263-5408 TDD; (608) 262-8848 FAX

E-mail: info@trace.wisc.edu

Web site: http://trace.wisc.edu

> PURPOSE: "To advance the ability of people with disabilities to achieve their life objectives through the use of communication, computer and information technologies."
>
> PUBLICATIONS: Offers a variety of publications for users and developers of technology. Examples include: *"Nonvisual Alternative Display Techniques for Output from Graphics-Based Computers"; "Access Issues Related to Virtual Reality of People with Disabilities"; "Technological Approaches to Performance Enhancement";* publications on augmentative communication; and *The Trace Resourcebook,* described above.

12.

Internet Resources

■ BOOKS AND PERIODICALS

Disability-Related Resources on the Internet. Seattle, WA: DO-IT, University of Washington. 20 pp. Free.

> This helpful directory describes hundreds of disability-related discussion lists, electronic newsletters, newsgroup discussion groups, and bulletin board systems accessible via the Internet. Included are resources that deal with general issues such as education, technology, and legal rights, as well as resources concerned with specific disabilities. The most current copy of this publication can be found on the World Wide Web at <http://weber.u.washington.edu/~doit/Brochures/internet_resources.html>. The print version can be ordered from DO-IT, as listed in the Appendix at the back of this book.

Ferguson, Tom. ***Health Online: How to Find Health Information, Support Groups, and Self-Help Communities in Cyperspace.*** Reading, MA: Addison-Wesley Publishing Co., 1996. 308 pp. $17.00. ISBN 0-201-40989-5.

> For readers with little or no experience searching for health or medical information on the Internet, this guide provides a useful starting point. It begins by covering the basics of going online—equipment needed, uses of e-mail, the meaning of common terminology, online do's and don'ts. It then discusses the pros and cons of using the major commercial networks to access health information and online support groups. Finally, the book describes some of the existing web sites, newsgroups, and mailing lists on the Internet concerned with health and medical

issues. For the most part, this is *not* the place to look for information on locating information dealing with specific disabilities; throughout, the emphasis is more on illnesses.

Resources for Families and People Who Work with Families. Lawrence, KS: Beach Center on Families and Disability, updated twice yearly. $3.00.

> Hundreds of resources helpful to families of children with disabilities are listed in this directory. It includes up-to-date listings of useful publications, publishing companies, information and support services, Internet resources, and research and training centers.

■ WEB SITES

As explained in the Introduction, the primary purpose of this book is to list sources of print materials of interest to parents of children with special needs. When an organization's web site is listed in the book, it is generally because that organization also has helpful publications for parents. There are, however, many useful web sites that do not distribute print materials. The very few web sites that are described below were chosen as a representative sample of what is available because they are especially comprehensive, have links to sources of print materials, and/or are good starting points for new Internet users.

Disability Resources on the Internet

Disability Resources, Inc.
4 Glatter Lane
Centereach, NY 11720-1032
(516) 585-0290
Web site: http://www.disabilityresources.org

> PURPOSE: To provide links to the "best disability resources on the web," including "national and international sites, documents, databases, and other informational materials."
>
> FEATURES: Users can browse the main index for the site's "WebWatcher" service, which lists thousands of topics, or can zero in on a specific area of interest by choosing the shortcut index. There are links to information on many disability diagnoses, as well as to topics of general interest, such as inclusion, types of therapy, technology, and legal issues. The site is updated every few days with new resources.

ERIC Clearinghouse on Disabilities and Gifted Education (ERIC EC)

The Council for Exceptional Children
1920 Association Dr.
Reston, VA 20191
(800) 328-0272; (703) 264-9449
E-mail: ericec@cec.sped.org
Web site: http://www.cec.sped.org/ericec.htm

> PURPOSE: ERIC EC is one of 16 clearinghouses sponsored by the U.S. Dept. of Education, National Library of Education. It collects and disseminates professional literature, information, and resources related to the education and development of people who have disabilities or are gifted.
>
> FEATURES: This web site is notable for the access it provides to the ERIC (Educational Resources Information Center) database, the information database of the U.S. Department of Education. For no cost, anyone can search the database, which lists publication data and abstracts for over 60,000 journal articles, conference proceedings, papers, speeches, research reports, teaching guides, and books. Users can then order copies of publications that satisfy their search criteria. The site also offers access to the "AskERIC Question-Answering Service," which allows parents and profession-

als to ask ERIC staff questions about special education. In addition, the ERIC EC web site has links to many related information sources and listservs. See the Education section of this book for information about the types of print material that can be ordered from ERIC EC.

Family Village
1500 Highland Ave.
Madison, WI 53705
(608) 263-5973; (608) 263-0802 TDD; (608) 263-0529 FAX
Web site: http://www.familyvillage.wisc.edu/

> PURPOSE: The Family Village is "a global community that integrates information, resources, and communication opportunities" for people with disabilities, their families, and professionals.
>
> FEATURES: The organization and design of this web site are very user friendly. Icons on the home page are labeled with the names of places found in any real community, for example "Library," "Coffee Shop," "Hospital," "School," "Bookstore," etc. Clicking on the icons brings you to the cyberspace equivalent of those places. For instance, clicking on "Post Office" brings up a "Parent-to-Parent Web Board" on which users can post and read messages about their child's diagnosis, about a specific medical procedure, about an undiagnosed condition, to others who live in the same geographical area, etc. Clicking on "Bookstore" brings up reviews of recommended books; links to publishers and other sources of books on special needs; links to on-line periodicals; and more. The web site also offers a helpful "Guide to Using the Internet for Parents of Children with Disabilities or Chronic Health Conditions," with helpful tips for communicating with others and finding information via the Internet.

Our-Kids
Web site: http://rdz.stjohns.edu/library/support/our-kids

> PURPOSE: Our-Kids is an online support group (listserv) for parents and others worldwide who care about children with disabilities or delays. It was founded by parents for parents, and the material that can be accessed from the web site was contributed by parents.
>
> FEATURES: Our-Kids is a forum for parents of children with widely varying diagnoses to ask questions, seek support, and share information. Instructions for joining the list are on the home page; messages that have been posted by members of the Our-Kids list can be accessed through the archives by members or nonmembers of the list. Home pages and pictures of participants on the list can also be accessed from the Our-Kids web site. In addition, there are reviews of books for parents and children written by members of the list, links to online magazines, and links to publishers and bookstores. Links to other web sites of interest to parents of children with specific diagnoses or disabilities in general can be found under "Internet Resources."

PediaNet
2348 Ralph Ave.
Brooklyn, NY 11234
(718) 444-0440; (718) 241-3477 FAX
E-mail: info@pedianet.com
Web site: http://www.pedianet.com

> PURPOSE: To provide developmental and medical information to the public and professionals that will enhance and safeguard children's lives.
>
> FEATURES: PediaNet is designed to provide health-related information about children in general, but also includes several features of special interest to parents of children with special needs. First, under "Resources," it provides an easy link to Medline, which permits the general public to search the National Library of Medicine's database for free. Second, under "News and Informa-

tion," PediaNet maintains a "Disease Database," which parents can search for information on hundreds of pediatric disorders, including many rare disabilities. The site also provides information about new products for children, as well as products that have been recalled.

Special Education Resources on the Internet (SERI)
Web site: http://www.hood.edu/seri/serihome.htm

PURPOSE: To provide links to online information resources related to special education.

FEATURES: This web site provides an exhaustive list of links to special education resources, including informational sites operated by universities, organizations, government agencies, publishers, professionals, and others; databases; listservs; sources for products; and more. Categories of information covered include special information resources related to specific disabilities; Disability Products and Commercial Sites; Legal and Law Resources; Special Education Discussion Groups; Inclusion Resources; Special Needs and Technology; Transition Resources; Parents & Educator's Resources. An excellent first stop for those seeking information on any aspect of special education or early intervention.

13.

Community Integration and Friendship

The resources listed here focus on the benefits and how-to's of inclusion in general. Resources on specific types of inclusion can be found under **"Education"** (p. 37) and **"Recreation"** (p. 87).

■ BOOKS AND PERIODICALS

Amado, Angela Novak, ed. *Friendships and Community Connections between People with and without Developmental Disabilities.* Baltimore, MD: Paul H. Brookes, 1993. 416 pp. $30.00. ISBN 1-55766-121-9.

> Many of the foremost proponents of inclusion contributed to this splendid volume about the how's and why's of fully integrating people with developmental disabilities into their communities. There are chapters on relationships on the job and recreational activities; on community programs specifically designed to foster friendships; on using religion to build relationships; and on historical changes in the way relationships between people with and without disabilities have been viewed. The emphasis is on using naturally occurring situations as a springboard to social integration. Numerous real-life stories of relationships between people with and without disabilities are included.

Condeluci, Al. *Interdependence: The Route to Community.* 2nd ed. Winter Park, FL: G.R. Press, Inc., 1995. 232 pp. $34.95. ISBN 1-878205-11-0.

> This text is a good resource for parents and professionals who promote inclusion and empowerment. This author provides what some may consider a controversial look at our present system of services for children. He provides a realistic look at the "old paradigm" of "the client has the problem, people are homogeneously congregated, segregated, controlled by experts, and [need] to be fixed." Then he offers the hope of "interdependence," a guide for changing the system, where the focus is "not on people who are [or have] problems, but on the [limiting] viewpoints of others."

Heyne, Linda A., Stuart J. Schleien, and Leo H. McAvoy. *Making Friends: Using Recreation Activities to Promote Friendship between Children with and without Disabilities.* Minneapolis: University of Minnesota, School of Kinesiology and Leisure Studies, 1993. 74 pp. $10.00. (Available from Institute on Community Integration.)

> This practical handbook for parents and educators describes how structured and informal recreation activities can be used to encourage friendships between children in grades K-6, with and without disabilities. Topics covered include typical barriers to friendship, steps for using recreational activities to promote friendships, and using focus groups to solve problems related to friendship development.

Inclusion News. Inclusion Press International, 24 Thome Crescent, Toronto, ONT Canada M6H 2S5. (416) 658-5363; (416) 658-5067 FAX. Web site: http://www.inclusion.com

> The focus of this free newsletter is inclusion in all aspects of life. It is published "occasionally" by a privately funded source. Articles are inspiring and offer suggestions to make inclusion work. Anecdotes, personal messages, poetry, and resources are sprinkled throughout this publication.

Mannix, Darlene. *Life Skills Activities for Special Children.* West Nyack, NY: Center for Applied Research in Education, 1992. $27.95. ISBN 0-87628-547-7.

> Included in this collection of lesson plans are dozens of activities designed to help teach "life skills" to children with disabilities. The skills are organized into four sections: 1) Basic Survival Skills (personal information about oneself, telephone skills, using money, time concepts, etc.); 2) Personal Independence (dressing, grooming, food and eating, etc.); 3) Community Independence (community places such as restaurants and movie theaters, getting around, reading a map or schedule, etc.); 4) Getting Along with Others (recognizing diversity, cooperating with others, understanding others, good manners). The activities are designed primarily to be used by teachers with students in upper elementary grades, but might also be useful at home.

Mannix, Darlene. *Social Skills Activities for Special Children.* West Nyack, NY: Center for Applied Research in Education, 1993. $27.95. ISBN 0-87628-868-9.

> Primarily a practical manual for teachers, this book includes ready-to-use lesson plans for teaching a variety of social skills to children with special needs in upper elementary grades and beyond. Topics covered include: Accepting Rules and Authority at School; Relating to Peers; and Developing Positive Social Skills. Skills are taught within the context of real-life activities and sections are clearly organized and full of reproducibles. Many of the lessons in this book could be applied to home and recreational planning for children with and without special needs.

Nowicki, Stephen, Jr., and Marshall P. Duke. *Helping the Child Who Doesn't Fit In.* Atlanta, GA: Peachtree Publishers, 1992. 178 pp. $14.95. ISBN 1-56145-025-1.

> The authors of this practical guide coined the term *dyssemia* to describe unusual difficulty in using and understanding nonverbal signs or signals. According to the authors, this difficulty is at the root of many children's problems in forming relationships and fitting in. Children can have

problems with many types of nonverbal communication, or with just one specific type--for example, with use of touch and personal space, facial expressions, tone of voice, or gestures and postures. For each possible type of dyssemia, the authors provide specific strategies for parents to use to help their child overcome problems in this area. There is also an overview chapter that explains how to develop a plan to help a child overcome problems with dyssemia in general. Most of the treatment strategies seem to have been developed with children who do not have other disabilities in mind, but some may be useful to parents of children with Down syndrome, mental retardation, autism, or other disabilities that affect social skills acquisition.

O'Brien, John, and Connie Lyle O'Brien. ***Members of Each Other: Building Community in Company with People with Developmental Disabilities.*** Toronto: Inclusion Press, 1996. 140 pp. $15.00.

This collection of essays and reflections focuses on the reasons and means for including people with developmental disabilities in their communities. Topics covered include building circles of support, helping individuals with disabilities connect one-on-one with those without, and connecting people to community associations.

Pearpoint, Jack. ***From Behind the Piano: The Building of Judith Snow's Unique Circle of Friends.*** Toronto, Ontario: Inclusion Press, 1990. 132 pp. $10.00. ISBN 1-895418-00-3.

Plan to sit an evening with this book because you will simply be unable to put it down. As you read how Judith Snow, a woman with severe disabilities, was enabled to become a member of her community, you will understand the true meaning of "circle of friends." You will understand how friendship can and has moved bureaucratic mountains. You will also understand the inadequate understanding that exists in the world regarding persons who are disabled. This book will give you strength to go on. As often said by the author, "If Judith can do it, anyone can. . . ."

Perske, Robert. ***Circles of Friends: People with Disabilities and Their Friends Enrich the Lives of One Another.*** Nashville, TN: Abingdon Press, 1988. 94 pp. $12.95. ISBN 0-687-08390-7.

This is a collection of short essays about real-life friendships between people with and without disabilities. Perske writes about the classmate who helped her friend with multiple disabilities learn to walk; the girl with profound mental retardation who learned all sorts of skills and behaviors once she was included in a typical classroom; the friendship between a young woman with severe brain damage and her roommates in a co-op housing arrangement; and the staff person who befriended a young blind boy diagnosed with mental retardation and taught him to play the accordian, paving the way for his participation in the musical life of his community. Interspersed with these vignettes are Perske's musings about subjects such as the need for friendship and what is wrong with using the word "special" to describe people. The book is beautifully illustrated with sketches by Martha Perske.

■ ORGANIZATIONS

Beach Center on Families and Disability
University of Kansas
3111 Haworth Hall
Lawrence, KS 66045
(785) 864-7600 voice & TDD; (785) 864-7605 FAX
E-mail: beach@dole.lsi.ukans.edu
Web site: http://www.lsi.ukans.edu/beach/beachhp.htm

PURPOSE: Conducts research on training and disability issues affecting families, sponsors conferences, publishes and disseminates a wide range of publications on family issues.

PUBLICATIONS: *Amistad,* a collection of stories of Hispanic children with disabilities and their friendships, is available in English or Spanish for $6.00. Also available: *"What Research Says: Friendship and Children with Disability* ($2.00) and the fact sheet *"Encourage Friendships between Children with and without Disabilities"* ($.50).

Canadian Association for Community Living

Kinsmen Building, York University
4700 Keele St.
North York, Ontario M3J 1P3
Canada
(416) 661-9611; (416) 661-5701 (fax)
Web site: http://indie/ca/cacl/index.htm/

PURPOSE: The CACL focuses on developing a welcoming, supportive community for all Canadians by working to ensure that people with mental handicaps become active members of their communities.

SERVICES: The CACL publishes a newsletter and other publications; advocates for people with mental handicaps and their families; and has a network of local chapters across Canada.

Center on Human Policy

National Resource Center on Community Integration
Syracuse University
805 S. Crouse Ave.
Syracuse, NY 13244-2280
(800) 894-0826; (315) 443-4355 (TTY); (315) 443-4338 FAX
E-mail: thechp@sued.syr.edu
Web site: http://soeweb.syr.edu/thechp/

PURPOSE: "To promote the full inclusion of people with developmental disabilities in community life" through training, technical assistance, consultation, and the dissemination of information.

PUBLICATIONS: Offers a variety of low-cost information packets on topics such as supported living, housing, personal relationships and social networks, inclusive education, and integrated recreation. Also many original and reprinted papers, articles, and news bulletins on integrating persons with disabilities into the community. Request a copy of *"Resources and Reports on Community Integration"* for a complete list.

Institute on Community Integration

University of Minnesota
109 Pattee Hall
150 Pillsbury Dr. SE
Minneapolis, MN 55455
(612) 624-4512; (612) 624-9344 FAX

PURPOSE: To improve community services and social supports for persons with disabilities and their families.

PUBLICATIONS: Include resource guides on self-advocacy, inclusion, transition, and supported employment; curricula for teachers and for paraprofessionals to help them develop inclusive classrooms; reports on residential services. Request a publications catalog and a complimentary issue of the newsletter *Impact.*

Religion and Disability Program
910 16th St., NW, Suite 600
Washington, DC 20006
(202) 293-5960; (202) 293-5968 TDD

> PURPOSE: This program of the National Organization on Disability helps religious groups break down barriers against people with disabilites, both within the congregation and on the outside.
>
> PUBLICATIONS: *That All May Worship,* an interfaith handbook to assist congregations in welcoming people with disabilities; *Loving Justice,* which describes and clarifies the Americans with Disabilities Act (ADA) and other relevant laws as they relate to the religious community; *From Barriers to Bridges,* a guide to help get a dialogue going between people with disabilities, their families, and the religious community. It provides step-by-step planning for a conference called *That All May Worship,* and promotes other community-building activities.

The Roeher Institute
Kinsmen Building
York University
4700 Keele St.
North York, Ontario
Canada M3J 1P3
(416) 661-2023 Voice/TDD; (416) 661-5701 FAX
Web site: http://indie.ca/roeher/intro.html

> PURPOSE: "Promotes the equality, participation, and self-determination of people with intellectual and other disabilities."
>
> SERVICES: Information services include reference and referral information, customized responses to questions, the development of information packages on specific topics, and operation of an extensive library. Also conducts research and public policy analysis and social development and training.
>
> PUBLICATIONS: Examples include: *Making Friends: Developing Relationships between People with a Disability and Other Members of the Community* ($16.00); *Hugs All Around! How Nicholas McCullough Came Home* ($10.00); *"Planning for Change"* ($5.00); *"Closing Institutions, Opening Communities"* ($10.00); *"The Contradiction of Kindness; The Clarity of Justice: An Occasional Paper"* ($7.00). *Entourage,* the Institute's quarterly magazine, promotes community living for people with intellectual or other disabilities ($20.00 in the U.S.; $19.26 in Canada).

TASH
29 W. Susquehanna Ave., Ste. 210
Baltimore, MD 21204
(410) 828-6706
Web site: http://www.tash.org

> PURPOSE: TASH advocates strongly for inclusion of all individuals in every aspect of life. Their membership is a blend of parents, self-advocates, and professionals. Among their goals: "building communities in which no one is segregated and everyone belongs"; "advocating for opportunities and rights"; "promoting inclusive education"; "disseminating knowledge and information."
>
> PUBLICATIONS: Include a quarterly peer-reviewed journal *(JASH)* and a monthly newsletter. Information in the newsletter is pertinent to most parents, addressing current topics regarding inclusive schools, education methods, community living, and politics.

14.

Recreation

■ BOOKS

Bailey, Sally Dorothy. *Wings to Fly: Bringing Theatre Arts to Students with Special Needs.* Bethesda, MD: Woodbine House, 1993. 409 pp. $17.95. ISBN 0-933149-58-1.

> *Wings to Fly* explains how parents and professionals can use drama activities to enable children with special needs to visit places they have never been, be what they never thought they could be, and, in the end, grow socially by leaps and bounds. The book describes practical strategies for including students with disabilities in drama programs and theatre programs, as well as how to use drama to teach life skills or academic skills. There is also a great deal of information on teaching to students' individual learning styles.

Block, Martin E. *A Teacher's Guide to Including Students with Disabilities in Regular Physical Education.* Baltimore, MD: Paul H. Brookes, 1994. 276 pp. $38.00. ISBN 1-55766-156-1.

> This book was designed to provide physical education teachers, special educators, and parents with practical strategies for including children with disabilities in regular physical education programs. An especially important section provides actual accommodations for many sports activities, including team sports, archery, and dancing. Also included are examples of goals and objectives, as well as an excellent checklist for determining needed instructional modifications.

Froese, Mary Frances. *Heroes of a Special Kind.* Ventura, CA: Evergreen, 1990. 220 pp. $12.95. ISBN 0-926284-15-0.

> This book chronicles the stories of some very special Olympians, as well as the coaches and volunteers of Special Olympics who helped them triumph. Along the way, there are many uplifting examples of people helping other people to reach their dreams.

Greenstein, Doreen. *Backyards and Butterflies: Ways to Include Children with Disabilities in Outdoor Activities.* Cambridge, MA: Brookline, 1995. 72 pp. $14.95. ISBN 1-57129-001-7.

> This book makes gardening a possibility for everyone (green thumbs *not* included). First the author helps you decide where the garden needs to be—raised, on a table, in a bucket, in a bag. Adaptations are described for all stages of gardening, from planting seeds to harvesting. The author also describes adaptations for many other outdoor activities, including feeding birds, picking berries, catching insects, getting involved in 4-H, riding a tricycle, swinging and sliding, and picnicking. Nearly all the gadgets and creative ideas can be created with "stuff" you have in the garage. A terrific book.

Heyne, Linda A., Stuart J. Schleien, and Leo H. McAvoy. *Making Friends: Using Recreation Activities to Promote Friendship between Children with and without Disabilities.* Minneapolis: University of Minnesota, School of Kinesiology and Leisure Studies, 1993. 74 pp. $10.00. (Available from Institute on Community Integration.)

> This practical handbook for parents and educators describes how structured and informal recreation activities can be used to encourage friendships between children in grades K-6, with and without disabilities. Topics covered include typical barriers to friendship, steps for using recreational activities to promote friendships, and using focus groups to solve problems related to friendship development.

Learning Disabilities Association of Canada. *Winners, No Losers: A Handbook for Recreational Providers of Cooperative Activities for Everyone.* Ottawa: LDAC, 1993. 48 pp. $3.50. ISBN 0-919053-43-2.

> This booklet is a terrific resource for parents, teachers, and recreational professionals. Each page is filled with information about the identification of learning disabilities, what can be done about it, and the benefits of following the suggestions or strategies that are indicated. It explains such problems as language processing problems, low self-esteem, distractibility, hyperactivity and impulsiveness, inappropriate social behavior, frustration, anxiety, and procrastination. An extensive resource list is provided.

Maddox, Sam, ed. *Spinal Network: Total Wheelchair Resource Book.* 2nd ed. Malibu, CA: Spinal Network, 1994. 568 pp. ISBN 0-943489-03-2.

> A major focus of this book is sports for people with physical disabilities. Everything from air guns to bungee-cord jumping to sea kayaking are discussed. There are personal reports from individuals who share information about how they participate in their favorite sport. Although the book is mainly targeted at the adult reader who has a physical disability, the book can also give parents and children a glimpse of the possibilities that lie ahead.

Moon, M. Sherril, ed. *Making School and Community Recreation Fun for Everyone: Places and Ways to Integrate.* Baltimore, MD: Paul H. Brookes, 1991. 256 pp. $32.00. ISBN 1-55766-155-3.

> This practical manual discusses strategies for including people with disabilities in both school-based and community recreational activities, such as school clubs and teams, summer camps, community recreation programs, and sports leagues. It discusses relevant federal legislation and ways to use the laws to get people with disabilities included in activities, and also provides examples of successful inclusive programs.

Morris, Lisa Rappaport, and Linda Schulz. ***Creative Play Activities for Children with Disabilities: A Resource Book for Teachers and Parents.*** 2nd ed. Champaign, IL: Human Kinetics, 1989. 217 pp. $16.95 ISBN 0-87322-933-9.

> The projects and activities presented here are designed to meet the simplest to most complex needs of children with a variety of disabilities and their families. The focus is on the family and how playing together can pull everyone together and strengthen their coping skills as well as the child's developmental skills. Play indoors, outdoors, arts and crafts, and attention to all the senses are addressed. Activities are designed for infants to 8-year-olds. Adaptations are included and games are designed to be cost effective. Often household items are the main ingredients of the game or activity.

Nordoff, Paul, and Clive Roberts. ***Music Therapy in Special Education.*** 2nd. ed. St Louis, MMB Music, 1983. 272 pp. $17.50. ISBN 0-918812-22-4.

> This text defines the importance of music in the lives of children with exceptional needs, emphasizing that music "gets through" to children with special needs. It explains how music therapists and educators can use music as a socialization and therapy tool.

Roth, Wendy, and Michael Tompane. ***Easy Access to National Parks: The Sierra Club Guide for People with Disabilities.*** San Francisco: Sierra Books, 1992. 404 pp. ISBN 0-87156-620-6. $16.00.

> This is a useful manual for planning vacations that everyone can enjoy. The "Best Visits and Accessibility" chapter will help you plan where you want to go. Then, each Region is addressed and little maps are provided to show how to get there. All kinds of information is provided, from daily temperatures, to the amount of slope on trails, to bathroom accessibility...and more. Authors' notes provide a personal touch as they explain what the area is really like.

Rynders, John E., and Stuart J. Schleien. ***Together Successfully: Creating Recreational and Educational Programs That Integrate People with and without Disabilities.*** Arlington, TX: The Arc, 1991. 113 pp. $12.50.

> This is a practical manual for structuring recreational, social, and educational activities in the community so that participants with and without disabilities can experience positive social interactions, learn, and grow. Many of the suggestions are provided in easy-to-use checklist format, and cover topics such as Guidelines for Positive Interactions, Guidelines for Adapting Activities, and Traits of Quality Integrated Programs. Included are specific instructions for thirty inclusive recreational activities suitable for preschoolers through adults.

Schleien, Stuart J., M. Tipton Ray, and Frederick P. Green. 2nd ed. ***Community Recreation and People with Disabilities: Strategies for Inclusion.*** Baltimore, MD: Paul H. Brookes, 1997. 368 pp. $39.00. ISBN 1-55766-259-2.

> This is a guide to inclusion in community recreation programs for professionals and advocates. Many practical techniques for including people with disabilities are described, as well as the authors' system for observing programs and devising ways to overcome obstacles to participation. An important emphasis is on fostering social relationships through inclusion in recreational activities.

Schwartz, Sue, and Joan E. Heller Miller. ***The New Language of Toys: Teaching Communication Skills to Children with Special Needs.*** 2nd ed. Bethesda, MD: Woodbine House, 1996. 279 pp. $16.95 ISBN 0-933149-08.

> The focus of this friendly guide is on using toys and games to promote language acquisition in an entertaining way. The authors provide numerous examples of specific play strategies, games, and

toys that are helpful for children at different developmental ages, from birth through age six. Adaptations for children with specific types of disabilities are included, as appropriate. Home-made alternatives to store-bought toys are suggested at each age level, since not all parents can afford to purchase a load of toys. The authors also describe many books that are useful for teaching speech and language concepts to children of different ages.

Sports & Recreation Resource Packet. Silver Spring, MD: ABLEDATA. $5.00.

This information packet contains the following fact sheets written for individuals with disabilities and their families: "Cycling"; "Winter Sports and Recreation Equipment"; "Aquatic Sports and Recreation Equipment"; "Funding Assistive Technology."

Winston, Lynn. ***Ideas for Kids on the Go.*** Bloomington, IL: Cheever, 1984. 69 pp. $6.95. ISBN 0-915708-17-5.

This is a dual purpose book. First there are suggestions for parents as they manage the challenges of raising a child with a disability. Then, kids talk about having a disability, developing coping skills, and increasing self-esteem. This little book provides a support system, an awareness program, and a resource for recreation, all in one.

Zulewski, Richard. ***The Parents Guide to Coaching Physically Challenged Children.*** Cincinnati, OH: Betterway Books, 1994. 133 pp. $12.95. ISBN 1-55870-347-0.

In this manual written for anyone involved in coaching children with special needs, the author begins by introducing a variety of disabilities. With this overview completed, the exercises begin. Instructions are provided to acquaint the coach with warm-ups, isometrics, isotonic, and cool-down exercises. Games of every sort are described. Information about adaptations and safety is included. The author also offers straight talk about including children with disabilities in typical athletic events. A long list of references and resources is provided.

■ ORGANIZATIONS

California Deaf-Blind Services
650 Howe Ave., Ste. 300
Sacramento, CA 95824
(916) 641-5855

PUBLICATIONS: *"Relaxation Strategies"* and *"Ideas for Recreational and Leisure Activities"* are part of a series of fact sheets. No charge.

National Library Service for the Blind and Physically Handicapped
Library of Congress
1291 Taylor St., NW
Washington, DC 20542
(800) 424-8567
E-mail: nls@loc.gov
Web site: http://www.loc.gov/nls

PURPOSE: Distributes reading materials in alternate formats (braille, audiotape) to U.S. citizens who are blind or have a physical impairment that prevents them from using ordinary printed materials.

PUBLICATION: *"Sports, Outdoor Recreation and Games for Visually and Physically Impaired Individuals"* is a free, 30-page flyer with information about national organizations that sponsor athletic events, literature on sports, and adapted equipment and games.

North American Riding for the Handicapped Association (NHRHA)

P.O. Box 33150
Denver, CO 80233
(303) 452-1212; (800) 369-7433

PURPOSE: To support and promote therapeutic riding for individuals with special needs.
SERVICES: Member Operating Center, a riding facility for members of NHRHA.
PUBLICATIONS: Request their newsletter and list of NHRHA locations nearest to you.

Very Special Arts

1300 Connecticut Ave., NW
Washington, DC 20036
(202) 628-2800; (202) 737-0645 TDD; (202) 737-0725 FAX

PURPOSE: "An international organization that provides programs in creative writing, dance, drama, music and the visual arts for individuals with physical and mental disabilities" and "promotes worldwide awareness of the educational benefits of the arts for all people."
PUBLICATIONS: *Start with the Arts Teacher's Guide* (282 pp., $32) and *Learning Log* ($10.50) are two parts of an instructional program for young children aimed at helping educators and parents create "meaningful learning experiences" using all of the arts. The Teacher's Guide details hands-on activities using commonly available materials and books on the themes of: All about Me, the weather, transportation, My Outdoor World, and Good Food for Good Health. The optional Learning Log contains suggested follow-up activities for parents to do with their children at home. The activities are appropriate for use in daycare, schools, and homes.

15.

Sexuality and Relationships

■ BOOKS

Enright, Rick. *Caution: Do Not Open Until Puberty!* London, Ontario: Thame's Valley Children's Centre, 1995. (Distributed by Devinjer House.) 37 pp. $9.95. ISBN 0-9680415-0-7.

> This paperback book offers a down-to-earth, easy-to-understand introduction to the topic of sexuality for adolescents with physical disabilities. Roughly half of the manual covers physical and emotional issues related to "normal" sexual functioning; the other half covers differences that can occur in people with physical disabilities.

Fegan, Lydia, Anne Rauch, and Wendy McCarthy. *Sexuality and People with Intellectual Disability.* Baltimore: Paul H. Brookes, 1993. 131 pp. $32.00. ISBN 1-55766-140-5.

> This slim volume provides an overview of the major issues related to sexuality confronting parents and residential staff. For the most part, the authors concentrate on describing *what* it is important for young people with disabilities to learn, rather than on *how* to teach it. For instance, there is little advice given about preventing sexual abuse, or on how to help a child understand the concept of privacy. There is also no information specific to the needs of individuals with Down syndrome, Fragile X syndrome, or other genetic conditions that result in mental retardation. The book is probably most valuable for its explanations of the rights and needs of individuals with mental retardation to sexual expression and fulfillment.

Haseltine, Florence B., Sandra S. Cole, and David B. Gray. *Reproductive Issues for Persons with Physical Disabilities.* Baltimore: Paul H. Brookes, 1993. 400 pp. $34.00. ISBN 1-55766-111-1.

> Although primarily a book for professionals, this book is useful for the specific information it provides about fertility, pregnancy, delivery, and other reproductive issues in people with different physical disabilities. Included are personal experiences of adults with physical disabilities.

Heaton, Caryl. *Let's Talk about Health: What Every Woman Should Know.* North Brunswick, NY: The Arc of New Jersey, 1995. 170 pp. $20.00.

> This clear, straightforward workbook was written to help women with developmental disabilities understand the following subjects: Healthy Habits; People's Bodies; Being a Grown Woman; Premenstrual Syndrome; We're All Sexual; What a Trip to the Doctor Is Like; Preventing Sexual Abuse; Contraception and Family Planning; Diseases You Can Get from Having Sex; Growing Older; and Cancer and Other Dangerous Diseases. Audiotapes that provide a word-for-word recording of the book are available.

Hingsburger, David. *I Openers: Parents Ask Questions about Sexuality and Their Children with Developmental Disabilities.* Vancouver, British Columbia: Family Support Institute Press, 1993. 88 pp. $15.00 (plus $2.50 S&H). ISBN 0-9696944-0-7.

> With respect and humor, the author answers dozens of questions submitted by parents of children and adults with mental disabilities from Canada and the United States. His answers stress the importance of teaching children about privacy and safety so that they can make the most responsible decisions possible for themselves. The book does not soft pedal the many reasons parents worry about encouraging their children's sexual expression, but emphasizes that it is better to confront these worries by educating your child than to do nothing. The book does not discuss issues related to specific causes of disability, but would be a good general introduction to the issues for parents of children and adolescents with mental disabilities.

Madaras, Linda, and Area Madaras. *My Feelings, My Self: A Growing-up Guide for Girls.* New York, NY: Newmarket Press, 1993. 152 pp. $11.95. ISBN 155704-157-1.

> The authors speak directly to middle school and high school girls (without disabilities) about relationships with parents and friends, self-awareness, and other concerns. They use text, quizzes, exercises and letters as the format to present information to girls in a non-threatening style that encourages interaction. The authors also give pointers on getting extra help if this book is not enough.

Maksym, Diane. *Shared Feelings: A Parent Guide to Sexuality Education for Children, Adolescents and Adults Who Have a Mental Handicap.* North York, Ontario: The Roeher Inst., 1990. 104 pp. $16.00. ISBN 0-920121-91-8.

> With input from many parent and professional reviewers, the author wrote this non-threatening guide to help parents teach their children with mental retardation about relationships and sexuality. The early chapters lay the groundwork for later teaching about sexuality by helping parents to focus on their feelings about their child, to put their child's sexuality into perspective, and to learn basic principles of listening and talking to their child. Later chapters address "Talking to Children about Bodies and Feelings"; "Decisions" related to marriage, parenthood, and birth control; "Facts about STDs"; and "Sexual Abuse."

Schwier, Karin Melberg. *Couples with Intellectual Disabilities Talk about Living and Loving.* Bethesda, MD: Woodbine House, 1994. 212 pp. $15.95. ISBN 0-933149-65-4.

> In their own words, fifteen couples with intellectual disabilities talk about their experiences in searching for a meaningful and fulfilling relationship. Although some of the couples are now hap-

pily married and a few have children, most of them have faced or are still facing obstacles thrown in their way by society. The men and women interviewed range in age from their late teens to over seventy, and come from the United States, Canada, Australia, and New Zealand.

■ ORGANIZATIONS

The Arc of the United States
500 E. Border St., Ste. 300
Arlington, TX 76010
(817) 261-6003; (817) 277-0553 (TDD)
E-mail: thearc@metronet.com
Web site: http//TheArc.org/welcome.html
> PUBLICATIONS: *"Let's Talk about Health: What Every Woman Should Know: The Gyn Exam,"* a booklet for women with developmental disabilities that explains what happens during a breast exam, pap smear, and mammogram ($3.50); *"HIV & AIDS Prevention Guide for Parents"* ($3.50); *"Learn to Be Safe,"* an HIV prevention training kit for teens and adults with mental retardation ($8).

National Association of Protection & Advocacy Systems
900 2nd St., NE, Ste. 211
Washington, DC 20002
(202) 408-9514; (202) 408-9521 TDD; (202) 408-9520 FAX
E-mail: NAPAS@earthlink.net
Web site: http://protectionandadvocacy.com/
> PURPOSE: A membership organization for disability rights agencies, protection & advocacy systems, and client assistance programs.
> PUBLICATIONS: *"HIV Education for People with Mental Disabilities"* ($7.00); *"HIV and Mental Health Institutions"* ($7.00); ***Abuse/Neglect Investigations Manual*** ($25.00).

National Committee to Prevent Child Abuse
332 S. Michigan Ave., Ste. 1600
Chicago, IL 60604-4357
(312) 663-3520
> PUBLICATIONS: Offers many low-cost educational publications geared to parents and children on the topics of sexual, physical, and emotional abuse. Although not specifically written with children with disabilities in mind, publications include comic books, coloring books, and other easy-reading materials.

Planned Parenthood: Shasta Diablo
Resource Center
2185 Pacheco St.
Concord, CA 94520
(510) 676-0505, ext. 215
> PUBLICATIONS: ***The Family Education Program Manual,*** a curriculum for teaching sexuality, self-esteem, and abuse prevention to middle and high school students with developmental and learning disabilities, is available for $30.00. Information packet on *"Current Issues in Sexuality and Disability"* ($2); brochures.

The Roeher Institute
Kinsmen Building
York University
4700 Keele St.
North York, Ontario
Canada M3J 1P3
(416) 661-2023 Voice/TDD; (416) 661-5701 FAX
Web site: http://indie.ca/roeher/intro.html

> PURPOSE: "Promotes the equality, participation, and self-determination of people with intellectual and other disabilities."
>
> SERVICES: Information services include reference and referral information, customized responses to questions, the development of information packages on specific topics, and operation of an extensive library. Also conducts research and public policy analysis and social development and training.
>
> PUBLICATIONS: ***No More Victims: Addressing the Sexual Abuse of People with a Mental Handicap—Families' and Friends' Manual*** ($18.00); ***Vulnerable: Sexual Abuse and People with an Intellectual Handicap*** ($20.00); and, for self-advocates: *"The Right to Control What Happens to Your Body: A Straightforward Guide to Issues of Sexuality and Sexual Abuse"* ($7.00).

SIECUS
130 W. 42nd St., Ste. 350
New York, NY 10036-7802
(212) 819-9770; (212) 819-9776 FAX

> PURPOSE: The Sexuality Information and Education Council of the United States (SIECUS) "develops, collects and disseminates information, promotes comprehensive education about sexuality, and advocates the right of individuals to make responsible sexual choices."
>
> PUBLICATIONS: The April/May 1995 edition of ***SIECUS Report*** (vol. 23, no. 4) is on the topic of *"Meeting the Needs of People with Developmental Disabilities"* and includes articles on: "Comprehensive Sexuality Education for Children and Youth with Disabilities"; "Special Education Meets Sexuality Education"; "Sexuality and Sexual Expression in Persons with Mental Retardation," and "Why Do People with Mental Retardation Need Sexuality Education?" Cost is $9.20. The bibliography *"Sexuality and Disability"* is $2. Also available are free fact sheets on subjects of general interest.

16.

Planning for the Future

Resources in this section provide information on planning for the physical, emotional, and financial well-being of individuals with disabilities after their parents' deaths. Topics covered include adult services and benefits, estate planning, and planning for a life of maximum independence. Additional resources on independent living can be found under **"Community Integration and Friendship"** (p. 81).

■ BOOKS AND PERIODICALS

Abery, Brian, et al. ***Self-Determination for Youth with Disabilities: A Family Education Curriculum.*** Minneapolis, MN: Institute on Community Integration, 1994. 166 pp. $10.00.

> The authors of this practical manual define self-determination as "the intrinsic drive to exercise control over one's thoughts, feelings, and behaviors." The manual is designed to help parents teach their transition-aged children with disabilities the skills and information needed to become self-determined and more in control of their lives. Strategies discussed include using personal futures planning sessions to determine the child's abilities, values, and interests; helping the child learn to make his own choices; teaching self-advocacy skills and information about community resources.

Berkobien, Richard. ***A Family Handbook on Future Planning.*** Arlington, TX: The Arc of the United States, 1991. 133 pp. $15.00. Order #10-2.

> This practical workbook is designed to help parents of children with developmental disabilities plan for their child's future personal, financial, and legal well-being. It includes information

about wills, trusts, guardianship, educational and employment rights, residential options, government benefits, and resources. Especially helpful are the many charts and checklists intended to help parents figure out their child's needs and how they can be met. The book comes with several pages of updated information which make the book current.

The Life Planning Newsletter. CMS Publications, 44 W. 17th St., #5, New York, NY 10011. Web site: http://sonic.net/nilp/news.html

Current information on issues such as government benefits, wills, trusts, housing, employment, advocacy, and transitions from school to community is provided in this newsletter. An annual subscription is $24.95.

Pearpoint, Jack, John O'Brien, and Marsha Forest. ***PATH: Planning Possible Positive Futures.*** 2nd ed. Toronto: Inclusion Press. 60 pp. $15.00.

This practical workbook outlines an eight-step problem solving approach to planning for future opportunities in learning, living, and working. Using PATH, families, schools, and others begin by choosing a desired outcome for the future and then working backwards to develop steps that can be undertaken in the present.

Russell, L. Mark, Arnold E. Grant, Suzanne M. Joseph, and Richard W. Fee. ***Planning for the Future: Providing a Meaningful Life for a Child with a Disability after Your Death.*** Evanston, IL: American Publishing Co., 1993. 417 pp. $24.95. ISBN 0-9635780-0-6.

The emphasis of this practical and readable guide is on developing a comprehensive estate plan that will assure your child's continued care and well-being. The authors discuss how to make sure that your hopes and dreams for your child's future, as well as his own, are carefully considered and recorded in a Letter of Intent. Other important issues addressed include deciding whether to appoint a guardian or advocate; deciding how to bequeath and manage your financial resources through wills, trusts, and safe-guarding of government benefits; and understanding income taxes, estate taxes, and probate.

Stengle, Linda J. ***Laying Community Foundations for Your Child with a Disability: How to Establish Relationships That Will Support Your Child after You're Gone.*** Bethesda, MD: Woodbine House, 1996. 217 pp. $15.95. ISBN 0-933149-67-0

The human side of estate planning is the subject of this empathetic and practical guide. The author first encourages parents to develop a vision of the best possible life for their children in their absence—in terms of living arrangements, employment, activities, and friendships. She then systematically guides readers through steps that will help families make this vision a reality. According to the author, the key is to ensure that the child develops a network of caring friends who will be interested in being involved in his life over the long term. The book includes many useful checklists and tables intended to help parents plan for various aspects of their child's future.

Wehman, Paul. ***Life Beyond the Classroom: Transition Strategies for Young People with Disabilities.*** 2nd ed. Baltimore: Paul H. Brookes, 1996. 533 pp. $55.00. ISBN 1-55766-248-7.

This text focuses on ways to help young adults with disabilities "adjust to the challenges of adulthood"—and, in particular, the workplace." The emphasis is on carefully planning and then implementing individualized life-skills training at school by the age of 14 or 16. Because it is written for professionals, the book talks about parents, rather than to them, and is not an easy read. Parents of older children may find it worthwhile, however, to read the overview chapter on developing an Individualized Transition Plan (ITP), with its many examples of goals for employment, vocational education/training, financial/income needs, independent living, transportation/mobility, social relationships, recreation/leisure, health/safety, and self-advocacy. There are also separate chapters on developing ITPs for students with mild mental retardation, severe disabilities, sensory impairments, learning disabilities, behavior disorders, orthopedic and other health impairments, and traumatic brain injury. Parents whose children have already left high school may be interested in the chapters on finding jobs, vocational placements, and independent living.

■ ORGANIZATIONS

The Arc of the United States
500 E. Border St., Ste. 300
Arlington, TX 76010
(817) 261-6003; (817) 277-0553 (TDD)
E-mail: thearc@metronet.com
Web site: http//TheArc.org/welcome.html

> PURPOSE: The Arc (formerly the Association for Retarded Citizens) works to improve the lives of all children and adults with mental retardation and their families.
>
> SERVICES: Provides information and referral about mental retardation, the Arc's programs, and local chapters. Advocates for inclusion of individuals with mental retardation in community life; fosters research and education regarding prevention of mental retardation.
>
> PUBLICATIONS: The following fact sheets are free with a self-addressed, stamped envelope: *"Residential Options for People with Mental Retardation"* (#101-3); *"Facts on Transition from School to Work and Community Life"* (#101-4); *"Individual Service Coordination for Individuals with Mental Retardation"* (#101-22); *"The Education of Students with Mental Retardation: Preparation for Life in the Community"* (#101-28); *"Managed Care and Long-Term Services for People with Mental Retardation"* (#101-46). The Arc also operates a future planning web site: <http://TheArc.org/misc/futplan.html>.

Beach Center on Families and Disability
University of Kansas
3111 Haworth Hall
Lawrence, KS 66045
(785) 864-7600 voice & TDD; (785) 864-7605 FAX
E-mail: beach@dole.lsi.ukans.edu
Web site: http://www.lsi.ukans.edu/beach/beachhp.htm

> PURPOSE: Conducts research on training and disability issues affecting families, sponsors conferences, publishes and disseminates a wide range of publications on family issues.
>
> PUBLICATIONS: *"Group Action Planning as a Strategy for Getting a Life"* ($4.50); *"How to Make Positive Changes in Your Family Member's Life with Group Action Planning"* ($4.00); *"What You Should Know about Person-Centered Planning"* ($.50).

Institute for the Study of Developmental Disabilities
2853 E. 10th St.
Bloomington, IN 47408-2601
(812) 855-6508; (812) 855-9396 TDD
Web site: http://www.isdd.indiana.edu/

> PURPOSE: "To provide leadership that enables communities to include, support, and empower people with disabilities and family members. The Institute accomplishes this by promoting innovative practices and policies that facilitate community membership."

PUBLICATIONS: *"A Family Guide to Transition Planning"* ($2.75); *"Student and Consumer Profiles: Functional Vocational Assessment"* ($2.50); *"Transition Services: Systems Components Checklist"* ($1.00); **Community Job Training for High School Students with Severe Disabilities: Developing Jobs and Teaching Job Skills** ($11.50).

National Information Center for Children and Youth with Disabilities (NICHCY)

P.O. Box 1492
Washington, DC 20013-1492
(800) 695-0285; (202) 884-8441 FAX
E-mail: nichcy@aed.org
Web site: http://www.nichcy.org

> PURPOSE: A clearinghouse that provides information on disabilities and disability-related issues, with an emphasis on children and young people birth to age 22.
> SERVICES: Personal responses to questions on disability issues; referrals to other organizations and agencies; database searches; technical assistance to parent and professional groups.
> PUBLICATION: The NICHCY news digest on Estate Planning is $2.

PACER Center

4826 Chicago Ave. South
Minneapolis, MN 55417-1098
(612) 827-2966 Voice/TTY; (612) 827-3065 FAX
E-mail: mnpacer@edu.gte.net
Web site: http://www.pacer.org

> PURPOSE: The Parent Advocacy Coalition for Educational Rights (PACER) "strives to improve and expand opportunities that enhance the quality of life for children and adults with disabilities and their families."
> PUBLICATIONS: **Supported Employment and Transition Resources** ($10.00); **Transition Tips and Tools** ($9.00); **The Road to Work: An Introduction to Vocational Rehabilitation.**

Rehabilitation Research and Training Center (RRTC) on Aging with Mental Retardation

Institute on Disability and Human Development
University of Illinois
1640 W. Roosevelt Rd.
Chicago, IL 60608
(800) 996-8845; (312) 996-6942 FAX
Web site: http://www.uic.edu/orgs/rrtcamr/index.html

> PURPOSE: "To promote the independence, productivity, community inclusion, and full citizenship of older adults with mental retardation through a coordinated program of research, training, technical assistance and dissemination activities."
> SERVICES: Operates the Clearinghouse on Aging and Developmental Disabilities, a computerized database of publications.
> PUBLICATIONS: Subscriptions to *A/DDVANTAGE* newsletter, published two times a year, are free. Also available: *Information Directory on Aging and Developmental Disabilities* ($10.00); Research Briefs on topics including age-related physical changes, funding for community living options, adjusting to changes in housing, and health and social supports among families.

The Roeher Institute
Kinsmen Building
York University
4700 Keele St.
North York, Ontario
Canada M3J 1P3
(416) 661-2023 Voice/TDD; (416) 661-5701 FAX
Web site: http://indie.ca/roeher/intro.html

> PURPOSE: "promotes the equality, participation, and self-determination of people with intellectual and other disabilities."
>
> SERVICES: Information services include reference and referral information, customized responses to questions, the development of information packages on specific topics, and operation of an extensive library. Also conducts research and public policy analysis and social development and training.
>
> PUBLICATIONS: ***Planning ...To Have a Life*** ($30.00); ***The Power to Choose: An Examination of Service Brokerage and Individualized Funding as Implemented by the Community Living Society*** ($20.00); *"Service Brokerage: Individual Empowerment and Social Service Accountability"* ($16.00).

17.

Death and Dying

■ BOOKS

For Adults

Finkbeiner, Ann K. *After the Death of a Child: Living with Loss through the Years.* New York, NY: Free Press, 1996. 273 pp. $23.00. ISBN 0-684-82965-7.

> The author of this thoughtful book set out to explore the long-term, large-scale effects of the death of a child on a family. To find out, she interviewed dozens of parents about how their lives had been changed five or more years following the loss of a child. Families that she interviewed detailed changes in their marriages, their child's brothers and sisters, their relationships with others, their religious beliefs, their feelings about the nature of life, their priorities, and more. Interwoven with the stories of interviewees is research about how parents typically react to a child's death. In the end, the author concludes that it is impossible to "let go" of a child completely, and that parents all work out different ways of preserving the bond with their child. This is not for newly bereaved readers who hope the pain will go away soon, but may be comforting to parents who have settled in to their grief for a while.

Grollman, Earl. *Talking about Death: A Dialogue between Parent and Child.* 3rd ed. Boston: Beacon Press, 1990. 128 pp. $14.00. ISBN 0-8070-2501-1.

> This book is really three books in one. First it is a children's book designed to create an atmosphere in which the child feels comfortable sharing her feelings about death, dying, and the loved one lost. The illustrations created by Susan Avishai are beautifully clear and promote discussion

about feelings. Next, it is a book to help prepare adults to talk to children about death and dying. Finally, it is a resource book which includes 15 pages of resources and an additional 20 pages of helpful books and tapes. The author has created an exceptional tool for families and individuals to use as they cope with and talk about the grieving process.

Kushner, Harold S. ***When Bad Things Happen To Good People.*** New York: Avon Books, 1983. 149 pp. $4.99. ISBN 0-380-60392-6.

This book was written by a Rabbi after his 14-year-old son died from a condition know as progeria (rapid aging). He sought to create "some blessing out of Aaron's pain and tears" by helping others to continue to believe that God is good and fair in spite of the tragedies they have seen—tragedies that happen to "good people." This is a book you will keep on a near shelf to read again and again.

Rosof, Barbara D. ***The Worst Loss: How Families Heal from the Death of a Child.*** New York, NY: Henry Holt, 1994. 290 pp. $25.00. ISBN 0-8050-3240-1.

A psychotherapist wrote this very readable book to help families who have lost a child "know what they were facing, understand what they were feeling, and appreciate their own needs and time-tables." This is a good general guide to coping over both the short and long terms. The author describes how death affects mothers and fathers differently, as well as how it affects siblings of different ages. She explains the tasks that parents need to accomplish in their grieving, as well as what they may be feeling and why. Although the author does not specifically address the issue of a child with disabilities dying, there are separate chapters on dealing with infant deaths, sudden deaths, and deaths that result from terminal illness. The concluding chapter offers many paths for choosing what to do with the rest of your life. Heartfelt quotations from family members who have lost a child illustrate the author's points.

Schaefer, Dan, and Christine Lyons. ***How Do We Tell the Children? A Step-by-Step Guide for Helping Children Two to Teen Cope When Someone Dies.*** New York: Newmarket Press, 1993. 172 pp. $10.95. ISBN 1-55704-181-4.

This book is designed to help parents and significant others talk about death and dying to children. The authors provide a variety of options and scenarios for those very difficult and often avoided discussions about the death of a loved one. The book includes sections on explaining the death of an infant or sibling, as well as a *crisis section,* which provides a quick reference for the book. A reader's resource guide is included.

Schiff, Harriett Sarnoff. ***The Bereaved Parent.*** New York, NY: Penguin Books, 1978. 146 pp. $11.95. ISBN: 0-14-005043-4.

This is not written specifically for the family of a child with disabilities, but would be helpful for any parent who is grieving. The author lost a ten-year-old son and offers supportive and compassionate thoughts to help other families through the pain of their sorrow.

Jewette, Claudia. ***Helping Children Cope with Separation and Loss.*** Boston, MA: Harvard Common Press, 1982. 146 pp. $8.95. ISBN 0-916782-53-0.

This is a valuable tool for helping children cope with a variety of losses—a friend who moves away, the loss of a favorite toy, a family move, the death of a loved one. The author offers guidance in helping children reflect and cope and move on. An excellent bibliography is included.

For Children

Grollman, Earl. *Straight Talk about Death for Teenagers: How to Cope with Losing Someone You Love.* Boston: Beacon Press, 1993. 146 pp. $8.95. ISBN 0-8070-2501-1.
>   This book gives teens something that often eludes them when someone they love dies. That is support. The author touches on the soul of the teen with poetry; on their grieving with frank discussion; and on their fears with answers and strategies as they survive their loss. Each page provides space for the reader to note feelings and concerns or just explain their loss in their own words. At the end of the book, there are questions for teens to ask themselves to help them identify where they are emotionally.

Mills, Joyce C. *Gentle Willow: A Story for Children about Dying.* New York, NY: Magination Press, 1993. Not paginated. $11.95. ISBN 0-945354-54-1.
>   In a few pages illustrated with soft watercolors, children learn about death, dying, letting go, and keeping precious memories of special friends and loved ones. The book is appropriate for children aged 4 to 8.

Simon, Norma. *The Saddest Time.* Morton Grove, IL: Albert Whitman, 1986. 38 pp. $4.95. ISBN 0-8075-7204-7.
>   This illustrated book for children aged 6-10 offers three different scenarios to use as starting points for discussing the death of a loved one. It includes stories about an uncle, a classmate, and a grandmother dying.

Stein, Sara Bonnett. *About Dying: An Open Family Book for Parents and Children Together.* New York, NY: Walker & Company, 1974. 47 pp. $8.95. ISBN 0-8027-6172-0. Out of print.
>   This is an interactive book, written for preschoolers and kindergartners. The beginning focus is on the death of a pet, then the story eases into the death of a family member—grandpa. Each page is designed to be a catalyst for discussion, sharing, and coping.

■ ORGANIZATIONS

The Compassionate Friends
P.O. Box 3696
Oak Brook, IL 60522-3696
(708) 990-0010; (708) 990-0246
>   PURPOSE: "A mutual assistance self-help organization offering friendship and understanding to bereaved parents and siblings." Helps bereaved people resolve their grief and provides information and education about bereaved parents and siblings.
>   PUBLICATIONS: Has a resource catalog with extensive listings of books and booklets from a variety of publishers in the categories of Parental Bereavement; Miscarriage, Stillbirth, and Infant Death; Suicide; General Bereavement; Parents & Sibling Grief; For Children; For Teens; For Family and Friends. Publishes two quarterly newsletters: *STAGES* (for bereaved siblings) and *We Need Not Walk Alone* (for bereaved parents). The first issue of each is free to bereaved siblings or parents; subscriptions are $10 and $20, respectively ($13 and $23 for Canadian subscriptions).

National Maternal and Child Health Clearinghouse

2070 Chain Bridge Rd., Ste. 450

Vienna, VA 22182-2536

(703) 356-1964; (703) 821-2098 FAX

E-mail: nmchc@circsol.com

Web site: http://www.circsol.com/mch

PURPOSE: "Disseminates state-of-the-art information about maternal and child health." Most of the publications distributed were developed through programs funded by grants from the Maternal and Child Health Bureau.

PUBLICATIONS: *"Peter's Story"* is an illustrated booklet written by the mother of a baby boy who died at three months of a variety of complications associated with a rare chromosome disorder. The author discusses her feelings before and after her son's death and mentions some coping techniques that helped. One copy is available free (pub. #J088).

Part 2

Specific Disabilities

18.

Attention Deficit Disorders

A word about terminology: The term ADD is commonly used when talking about attention deficit disorders. However, more correct is the term Attention-Deficit/Hyperactivity Disorder (AD/HD), as defined in the **Diagnostic and Statistical Manual, Fourth Edition (DSM IV),** published by the American Psychiatric Association in 1994. The new definition recognizes three subtypes of AD/HD:

- ADHD, Predominantly Inattentive Type
- ADHD, Predominantly Hyperactive-Impulsive Type
- ADHD, Combined Type

What this means for readers: Most books are about all subtypes and their characteristics. However, authors vary widely as to what terms they use, which can be confusing to their audience. Readers are advised to first look at a book's preface or introduction to find out how the author defines his or her terminology and the book's focus.

■ BOOKS AND PERIODICALS

Basic Information

Bain, Lisa J. *A Parent's Guide to Attention Deficit Disorders.* New York, NY: Dell, 1991. 211 pp. $12.95. ISBN 0-440-50639-5.

This easy-to-read and understand book offers a good introduction to attention deficit disorders. The book's "Core Symptoms" checklist can help readers determine whether their child may have

ADD. An especially helpful section discusses behaviors and strategies for management. Traditional and non-traditional treatments are explained. An excellent book for parents and teachers to read together.

Barkley, Russell A. ***Taking Charge of ADHD: The Complete Authoritative Guide for Parents***. New York, NY: The Guilford Press, 1995. 294 pp. $16.95. ISBN 0-89862-099-6.

> An uplifting and useful book that empowers parents to make balanced and informed decisions for their child and family. The book offers a new perspective on ADHD, which is that the hallmark symptoms--inattention, impulsivity, and hyperactivity--all boil down to a problem of inhibiting behavior. This viewpoint, that ADHD is a disorder of self-control, helps parents develop greater respect for their children as they come to understand and accept their child's daily struggle. Included are a comprehensive overview of ADHD, current research, behavior management strategies for home and school, medications and other interventions, and advice for how parents should nurture themselves.

Coleman, Wendy S. ***Attention Deficit Disorders, Hyperactivity & Associated Disorders: A Handbook for Parents & Professionals.*** 6th ed. Madison, WI: Calliope, 1993. 104 pp. $12.95. ISBN 0-9620187-2-4.

> The best part of this book is that it is so practical. For parents just getting the diagnosis, there is a thorough discussion of the evaluation process, with special considerations to bear in mind. The chapters on medication and treatment are packed with information about pros and cons of different treatments, medication side effects, and even what to do if a dose is missed. There are many question-and-answer sections and an extensive list of resources is provided.

Dendy, Chris A. Zeigler. ***Teenagers with ADD: A Parents' Guide.*** Bethesda, MD: Woodbine House, 1995. 370 pp. $16.95. ISBN 0-933149-69-7.

> This comprehensive guide to ADD in the teen years addresses the concerns of parents who merely suspect that their child has ADD, as well as of parents who have known their child's diagnosis for years. The book thoroughly covers the differences among the different types of ADD and explores what is known about causes. It then addresses common problems at home, at school, and in the community, offering dozens of practical, parent-tested solutions. It takes an indepth look at medications, behavior management, classroom adaptations, parent-teacher collaboration, homework struggles, post-secondary education, risky behaviors, and other health and medical problems frequently associated with ADD. Particularly useful is the chapter that details how the Individuals with Disabilities Education Act (IDEA) and Section 504 can be used to obtain educational adaptations for students with ADD. Many helpful tables designed to help parents individualize adaptations and interventions for their teenager are included. Throughout the book, quotations from families and teens themselves colorfully illustrate points made in the text.

Fowler, Mary. ***Maybe You Know My Kid: A Parents' Guide to Identifying, Understanding and Helping Your Child with Attention-Deficit Hyperactivity Disorder***. New York, NY: Birch Lane Press, 1993. 239 pp. $12.95. ISBN 1-55972-209-6.

> This guide, written by a parent and advocate, is a classic. While providing solid information, it also offers a realistic portrayal of one family's struggle with their child's ADHD. A good read for families who suspect their young child has ADHD or whose child has recently been diagnosed. This is not the place to go for the latest on research.

Garber, Stephen W., Garber, Marianne Daniels, and Spizman, Robyn Freedman. *Is Your Child Hyperactive? Inattentive? Impulsive? Distractible?: Helping the ADD/Hyperactive Child*. New York, NY: Villard Books, 1995. $12.95. ISBN 0-679-75945-X.

> With a focus on managing symptoms of ADHD--with or without medication--the authors describe for parents how to encourage and nurture positive behaviors while extinguishing negative ones. A variety of strategies are discussed for helping the child acquire skills to deal with ADHD. Starting with the very young child, these include games that teach the child how to control his activity level, such as "the statue game," and for the older child, training to respond to situations in a more controlled, reasoned fashion, such as "calmness training" and "impulse control training." Very practical.

Gordon, Michael. *ADHD/Hyperactivity: A Consumer's Guide for Parents and Teachers*. DeWitt, NY: GSI, 1991. 174 pp. $14.95. ISBN 0-9627701-0-8.

> If you have limited time for reading, try to read at least one book written by Dr. Gordon. This book, like his others, is packed with useful information and written in a parent-friendly style. It concentrates exclusively on children with the hyperactive type of ADD. Several chapters are devoted to helping teachers and students survive each other. Issues such as homework, ways to present instructional materials, and ways to structure the classroom are discussed. Also included are many practical pointers to help parents obtain an accurate evaluation of their child, develop a good educational plan, and cope with raising and teaching a child with ADHD. This book offers the kind of assistance that can mean success for the student.

Hallowell, Edward M., and John J. Ratey. *Driven to Distraction: Recognizing and Coping with Attention Deficit Disorder from Childhood through Adulthood*. New York, NY: Touchstone, 1995. 319 pp. $12.00. ISBN 0-684-80128-0.

> This national bestseller is a comprehensive guide to attention deficit disorders. The chapters on diagnosing ADD and managing ADD within the family should be especially useful for parents of children newly diagnosed with ADD. There is also a great deal of advice on behavior management. The authors use many stories about the experiences of their patients to help illustrate the different forms that ADD can take. Many useful resources are included.

Hallowell, Edward M., and John J. Ratey. *Answers to Distraction*. New York, NY: Bantam Books, 1996. 334 pp. $12.00. ISBN 0-553-37821-X.

> This follow-up to **Driven by Distraction** is a compilation of answers to frequently asked questions about ADD in children, adolescents, and adults. Chapters cover a wide variety of issues including typical concerns such as causes and treatment, as well as lesser known topics such as creativity and ADD. Appendices of tips for managing ADD, resources, and a reading list are included. A good reference to pull off the shelf again and again.

Hallowell, Edward. *When You Worry about the Child You Love*. New York: Simon & Schuster, 1996. 281 pp. $23.00. ISBN 0-684-80090-X.

> For parents who suspect, or have just learned, that their child has an emotional or learning problem, this book provides an excellent overview of disorders that may make children mad, sad, afraid, or confused. The book explains when parents should worry about their children's behavior and seek professional help; discusses steps parents can take to help children manage their emotions and learn, no matter what the disorder; and discusses treatment options, including medication. Information on a number of disorders with a biologic or genetic basis is included; among them, ADD, obsessive-compulsive disorder, conduct disorder, oppositional defiant disorder, and learning disability. The author's conversational style and numerous anecdotes make this an easy read.

Ingersoll, Barbara D. *Daredevils and Daydreamers: New Perspectives on Attention-Deficit/Hyperactivity Disorder*. New York, NY: Main Street Books/Doubleday, 1998. 239 pp. $10.95. ISBN 0-385-48757-6.

> Comprehensive and clear, this book describes advances in ADHD research and understanding during the last decade and what they mean for raising, treating, and educating children and adolescents. Chapters begin with a summary of what was known ten years ago compared to today, then move on to in-depth coverage of basic issues such as evaluations, causes, and medications. The author devotes extensive coverage to comorbidity (co-existing related disorders and problems such as mood disorders, learning disabilities, conduct disorder, sleep apnea, wetting and soiling, etc.), social problems, and the effects upon family dynamics. Highly recommended.

Kajander, Rebecca. *Living with ADHD.* Minneapolis, MN: Park Nicollet Medical Foundation, 1995. 67 pp. $9.95. ISBN 1-884153-08-9.

> Just the right amount of information to start with is provided in this slim paperback. It includes straightforward "criteria for diagnosing ADHD" and wonderful coping instructions. A chart is provided for easy medication reference. The "Tips for Teens" section offers quick strategies for teens to use as they learn to live with ADHD. There is an example of a letter for parents to send their child's teachers, which would be a handy way to begin parent/teacher collaborations. Several pages of resources are also included.

Koplewicz, Harold S. *It's Nobody's Fault: New Hope and Help for Difficult Children and Their Parents.* New York, NY: Times Books/Random House, 1996. 305 pp. $25.00. ISBN 0-8129-2473-8.

> This book focuses on what the author calls "no fault brain disorders"--emotional and behavioral disorders that are known or presumed to be caused by brain chemical abnormalities, rather than environmental causes such as poor parenting. Conditions covered include attention deficit hyperacivity disorder, obsessive compulsive disorder, separation anxiety disorder, social phobia, generalized anxiety disorder, conduct disorder, and others. For each disorder, the author discusses symptoms, diagnosis, brain chemistry, treatment (with an emphasis on medications that can improve brain chemical functioning), and issues involved in parenting a child with the disorder. The book is very readable and filled with examples of children treated by the author.

McEwan, Elaine K. *Attention Deficit Disorder.* Wheaton, IL: Harold Shaw, 1995. 311 pp. $11.99. ISBN 0-87788-056-5.

> This introductory book includes chapters on diagnosing ADD, survival skills, and keeping the family functioning smoothly. Chapter 9, "Why Me, Lord," may be helpful for parents who need to reflect upon where they are personally in coping with attention deficit disorder. The classroom intervention list is terrific, and the case study flow chart is a great resource for student study teams. The stories of 23 families touched by ADD are interwoven throughout the book.

Moss, Robert A., and Helen Huff Dunlap. *Why Johnny Can't Concentrate: Coping with Attention Deficit Problems.* Rev. ed. New York, NY: Bantam, 1996. 240 pp. $12.95. ISBN 0-553-37541-5.

> The authors write about coping with ADD over a lifetime. They provide many examples of strategies for success that can be used by the classroom teacher and parent. Medicine as an option is a special focus and discussed in depth. There are also chapters devoted to behavior management and to locating support and resources.

Paltin, David M. *The Parents' Hyperactivity Book.* New York, NY: Plenum, 1993. 291 pp. $27.50. ISBN 0-306-44465-8.

> This well-researched book is a valuable resource for both parents and professionals. The author begins by describing, defining, and explaining relevant and current research about ADHD. He

writes in a clear manner, carefully explaining each point. Emphasis is placed on how parents can work with their child and respond to his needs for direction and monitoring, all the while maintaining an appreciation of the child's strengths. Parents tell their stories in a chapter devoted to real-life coping with the frustration of ADHD. The book includes resources and references.

Parker, Harvey C. *The ADD Hyperactivity Workbook for Parents, Teachers, and Kids*. Plantation, FL: Specialty Press, Inc., 1994. 142 pp. $16.00. ISBN 0-9621629-6-5.

> A good, beginning book for understanding ADD with an emphasis on how to effectively manage its symptoms. Charts for teachers and parents help monitor behavior and academic progress, plus medication and its effects. Token cards and sticker charts (stickers included!) motivate and reward children for desired behaviors.

Causes

Hartmann, Thom. *Beyond ADD: Hunting for Reasons in the Past and Present*. Grass Valley, CA: Underwood Books, 1996. 216 pp. $12.95. ISBN 0-385-48757-6.

> For readers wondering about the origin of ADD, this author puts forth a number of interesting theories as to why it exists. His own pet theory is that ADD is a vestigal psychological and physiological advantage of our ancestral hunter/gatherers that enabled them to stay alive and thrive. Among other theories he offers, but does not necessarily support, is that ADD, characterized by a short attention span, is a trained response to modern advertising. Stimulating reading.

Family Issues

Kilcarr, Patrick J., and Quinn, Patricia O. *Voices From Fatherhood: Fathers, Sons and ADHD*. New York, NY: Brunner/Mazel, 1997. 184 pp. $19.95. ISBN 0-87630-858-2.

> As fathers become more involved in their children's care, they need support and information about the special challenges of raising a son with ADHD. Through a blend of basic information and fathers' personal accounts, readers gain insight into what works best and what doesn't, and how to foster a mutually satisfying relationship full of personal growth for both father and son.

Education

Bramer, Jennifer S. *Succeeding in College with Attention Deficit Disorders: Issues and Strategies for Students, Counselors and Educators.* Plantation, FL: Specialty Press, Inc., 1996. 189 pp. $18.00. ISBN 1-886941-06-8.

> Although intended as a primer for both college students with ADD and college professionals, this book is geared more to the professional audience of college administrators, instructors, and counselors. The first half focuses on ADD, its symptoms, causes, diagnosis, and treatment. Based on extensive interviews, the author provides a look at what it's like to be a college student with ADD. The second half takes a closer look at these interview findings with regard to making college for the student with ADD a successful experience. For the student, there are practical discussions about special services, accomodations, study tips, and note-taking strategies. Also covered are the attitudes, policies, programs, and accommodations that colleges should have in place for helping students succeed. Appendices summarize and reinforce suggestions for students and college professionals.

Latham, Patricia and Peter S. Latham. *Higher Educational Services for Students with Learning Disabilities and Attention Deficit Disorder: A Legal Guide.* Cabin John, MD: National Center for Law and Learning Disabilities, 1994. 32 pp. $18.00.

> Prepared by attorneys, this guide provides an overview of disability services and then a general discussion of the Americans with Disabilities Act (ADA). There is an exceptionally good explanation of Applicable Case Law that includes information about obligatory aids and remedial services.

Nadeau, Kathleen G. *Survival Guide for College Students with ADD or LD*. New York, NY: Magination Press, 1994. 64 pp. $9.95. ISBN 0-945354-63-0

> This slim, yet comprehensive guide is written expressly for students. Choosing a college can be a complex process, but in the case of students with ADD or LD, there are special considerations. Does the college have LD and ADD programs; is early registration an option; can certain required courses be waived, or changed to meet the student's needs? These and other important questions are covered here. Once on campus, there are a number of steps students should take to get the academic accommodations and services they need. Discussions include how to work with the Office of Disabled Student Services to get assistance such as extended-time examinations and note-takers, and the best ways to alert professors to difficulties and enlist their help. Other supports— medical consultations to monitor medications and counseling services—are recommended. In addition, students are advised on ways to help themselves succeed, including time management techniques, study tips, and maintaining a positive attitude.

Parker, Harvey C. *The ADD Hyperactivity Handbook for Schools: Effective Strategies for Identifying and Teaching Students with Attention Deficit Disorders in Elementary and Secondary Schools.* Plantation, FL: Specialty Press, 1992. 330 pp. $27.00. ISBN 0-9621629-2-2.

> This handbook can help both teachers *and* parents develop a plan to help the child with ADD succeed in school. Assessment, treatment, and problem solving in the classroom are covered in a comprehensive manner. Many practical suggestions are offered to help parents and teachers deal with the specific problems they are confronting. The author provides a list of references especially for children. In addition, fact sheets, guides, helpful checklists, and other resources are included.

Richards, Karen Kirk. *Turning the Tide: How to Be an Advocate for the ADD/ADHD Child.* Kansas City, MO: Midgard Press, 1992. 76 pp. $8.95. ISBN 0-939644-88-6.

> This guide looks at parents as "classroom consultants." It provides information on how best to work with professionals on parent-centered, child-centered, and professional-centered interventions. Medication is also discussed as a type of intervention to consider. A useful glossary and resource list are included.

Rief, Sandra F. *The ADD/ADHD Checklist: An Easy Reference for Parents & Teachers*. Paramus, NJ: Prentice Hall, 1997. 256 pp. $11.95. ISBN 0-13-762395-X.

> This is a well-organized book full of information in concise list format. Five sections cover information for teachers and parents, including the basics about ADD/ADHD, strategies to improve academic and behavioral functioning, and an extensive listing of resources. A detailed table of contents, index, and section summaries help readers quickly locate the specific information needed.

Rief, Sandra F. *How to Reach and Teach ADD/ADHD Children: Practical Techniques, Strategies, and Interventions for Helping Children with Attention Problems and Hyperactivity*. West Nyack, NY: The Center for Applied Research in Education, 1993. 240 pp. $27.95. ISBN 0-87628-413-6.

> Chapters address specific challenges and offer methods to help students with ADD succeed in this guide for teachers, resource specialists, and other educators working with elementary school stu-

dents. From instructional strategies to managing behavior to teaching organization and study skills, this book delivers.

Medical Treatment

Garber, Stephen W., Marianne Daniels Garber, and Robyn Freedman Spizman. *Beyond Ritalin: Facts about Medication and Other Strategies for Helping Children, Adolescents, and Adults with Attention Deficit Disorders.* New York, NY: Harper Perennial, 1997. 255 pp. $13.00. ISBN 0-06-097725-6.

> This book is about the effectiveness of medication as a treatment for ADHD. The authors repeatedly state that medication, when warranted, should be used in conjunction with other treatments for optimal results. They sort through the facts and fallacies concerning Ritalin and other medications and how they influence self-control, learning, attention, social skills, and organization.

First Person Perspectives

Hartmann, Thom. *ADD Success Stories: A Guide to Fulfillment for Families with Attention Deficit Disorder.* Grass Valley, CA: Underwood Books, 1995. 238 pp. $11.95. ISBN 1-887424-03-2.

> The author interviewed thousands of children and adults with ADD to come up with the real-life stories that fill this book. He describes how individuals with ADD have found fulfilling lives at school, at work, and within their relationships, and suggests strategies to help others achieve similar successes.

Kelly, Kate, and Peggy Ramundo. *You Mean I'm Not Lazy, Stupid Or Crazy?!* New York, NY: Simon & Schuster, 1996. 444 pp. $14.00. ISBN 1-864-81531-1.

> Written from the point of view of two adults with ADD, this book is billed as "a self-help book for adults with attention deficit disorder." The authors provide up-to-date information about research related to ADD in adulthood, and especially about managing ADD as an adult. If your child has ADD, the authors' strategies for daily living may help you help him. A resource list and reading list are included.

For Children

FICTION

Caffrey, Jaye Andras. *First Star I See.* Fairport, NY: Verbal Images Press, 1997. 150 pp. $9.95. ISBN 1-884281-17-6.

> Paige Bradley is a bright, creative girl whose active imagination gets the better of her when she has trouble focusing on the task at hand. To win an interview with her favorite actress from *Star Warriors*, she tries her best to write an award-winning essay on stars (the celestial kind) for the school contest. Despite her best intentions, her plans go awry when her imagination takes her every place except where she's supposed to be. But with the help of a sympathetic assistant principal, Paige is determined to master the challenge of "focusing her own telescope" to overcome her difficulties with ADD. This novel will appeal to children in middle school, especially girls with ADD.

Corman, Clifford L., and Esther Trevino. *Eukee: The Jumpy Jumpy Elephant.* Plantation, FL: Specialty Press, 1995. 24 pp. $15.00. ISBN 0-921629-8-1.

> Eukee is a smart little elephant who likes to chase butterflies, blow bubbles, and do cartwheels. He always feels jumpy inside, however, and can never finish the Elephant March at school. Unhappy that he does not have any friends, he consents to a visit to the doctor, where he learns he

has ADD. With the help of a behavior chart and medicine, Eukee learns to behave more like the other animals, and soon is proudly leading the Elephant March.

Galvin, Matthew. ***Otto Learns about His Medicine.*** New York, NY: Magination Press, 1995. 28 pp. $11.95. ISBN 0-945354-71-1.

> Otto the car likes school, but has trouble settling down to learn. Otto's motor runs too fast and everyone is losing patience with him. After his parents take him to a specialist for help, they learn how medicine can help Otto. This fanciful story sets the stage for children to talk about their concerns. This illustrated story is appropriate for children from about 5-10.

Gehret, Jeanne. ***The Don't-Give-Up Kid.*** Fairport, NY: Verbal Images, 1990. 40 pp. $9.95. ISBN 0-9625136-2-8.

> Alex has dyslexia and attention deficit disorder. School is such a challenge that he feels like crawling under his seat sometimes. Eventually, a special teacher helps him get just what he needs to be successful: a smaller class size and one-to-one assistance. This is an excellent awareness tool for parents and elementary-school children.

Gehret, Jeanne. ***Eagle Eyes: A Child's Guide to Paying Attention.*** Fairport, NY: Verbal Images, 1991. 40 pp. $9.95. ISBN 0-9625136-4-4.

> Ben describes what it is like to have ADD. He explains not only what he does but how he feels when he cannot focus on tasks, when he forgets, and when he makes his sister angry. Clues to helping a child with this disorder are included in the story. After the story, a selective resource list is provided. This is a fine awareness tool and story for siblings in elementary school.

Gordon, Michael. ***Jumping Johnny Get Back to Work! A Child's Guide to ADHD/Hyperactivity.*** DeWitt, NY: GSI, 1995. 24 pp. $10.00. ISBN 0-9627701-1-6.

> Johnny can't sit still, pay attention, or keep his hands from pulling, tearing, tapping, or swinging. After some tests, a psychologist is finally able to explain why Johnny is so active and to suggest some strategies to help him manage his behavior and focus his attention. For elementary school children, this book provides an interesting and amusing explanation of the evaluation and treatment of ADHD.

Hip-Hop, The Hyperactive Hippo. Peapack, NJ: Tim Peters and Co., 1996. 20 pp. $15.95.

> Hip-Hop just cannot keep still. He disturbs all the other animals during quiet time, stomping his feet and splashing through the water. After a visit to the doctor, he learns that he has attention deficit hyperactivity disorder, and that his behavior is not his fault. The doctor mentions teaching Hip-Hop activities to change his behavior, but does not mention medication. The oversized pages and illustrations of friendly African animals should appeal to young children.

Janover, Caroline. ***Zipper, the Kid with ADHD.*** Bethesda, MD: Woodbine House, 1997. 108 pp. $11.95. ISBN 0-933149-95-6.

> Zach Winson (a.k.a. Zipper) is a bright fifth-grader who excels at baseball, enjoys Scouting, and dreams of becoming a drummer. He has no close friends, however, and is constantly landing in hot water because of his impulsiveness and disorganization. With the help of some caring adults, Zach learns to become more focused, but not before he has a run-in with the law and lets down his teammates. Facts about ADHD and strategies for coping with it are subtly woven into this fast-paced, illustrated novel for children in grades 3-6.

Moss, Deborah M. *Shelley, the Hyperactive Turtle.* Bethesda, MD: Woodbine House, 1988. 24 pp. $14.95. ISBN 0-933149-31-X.

> Shelley the turtle simply is not like any other turtle in school. He just *can't* sit still and, as a result, is constantly in trouble. After a trip to the doctor, he learns that it is not his fault that he feels so "wiggly" and he begins to feel better about himself. With medication and understanding, Shelley begins to calm down and make friends. Rich, full-colored illustrations make this an appealing book for children 4-8 years of age.

NONFICTION

Brakes: The Interactive Newsletter for Kids with ADD. Available through ADD WareHouse, 300 NW 70th Ave., Ste. 102, Plantation, FL 33317. 800-233-9273; 954-792-8545

> This newsletter is for kids with ADD ages 7-14. Included are feature stories, interviews, mazes, cartoons, games, and other activities designed to help young people cope with ADD. An annual subscription (6 issues) is $24; $30 in Canada.

Gordon, Michael. *I Would If I Could: A Teenager's Guide to ADHD/Hyperactivity.* DeWitt, NY: GSI, 1993. 34 pp. $12.50. ISBN 0-9627701-3-2.

> In this thin paperback, the author takes a humorous, straightforward approach to educating teens about ADD. He focuses on what ADD is, what can be done about it, and how ADD can affect relationships and self-esteem.

Quinn, Patricia O. *Adolescents and ADD: Gaining the Advantage.* New York: Magination Press, 1995. 81 pp. $12.95. ISBN 0-945354-70-3.

> Written in a very reader-friendly style, this book tackles topics such as strategies for getting organized at home and in school; self-advocacy; and kid-to-kid support. A long list of resources is included.

Quinn, Patricia O., and Judith M. Stern. *Putting On the Brakes: Young People's Guide to Understanding Attention Deficit Hyperactivity Disorder.* New York, NY: Magination Press, 1991. 64 pp. $9.95. ISBN 0-945354-32-0.

> This is an excellent first book on ADHD, aimed primarily at ages 8-13. The authors write informally, as if they are speaking with their readers. For example, after listing good and bad feelings that children with ADHD frequently experience (confused, overloaded, angry, energetic, athletic, creative) the authors ask "What are your feelings?" The book explains what ADHD is and how a child can work with it in this interactive fashion. The book is liberally illustrated.

Quinn, Patricia O., and Judith M. Stern. *The "Putting On the Brakes" Activity Book for Young People with ADHD.* New York, NY: Magination Press, 1993. 88 pp. $14.95. ISBN 0-945354-57-6.

> Like *Putting On the Brakes,* this is an interactive book. It includes stories, worksheets ("Me and My ADHD"), mazes, and exercises designed to help children aged 8-12 learn skills such as sequencing, task completion, and setting priorities. There is a fine final section on succeeding at school.

FOR SIBLINGS

Gehret, Jeanne. *I'm Somebody Too.* Westport, NY: Verbal Images Press, 1992. 159 pp. $13.00. ISBN 1-884281-12-5.

> Emily feels left out because her brother gets all the attention. She doesn't understand her brother's disability and tries to compensate by being a perfect little girl. This story, for children aged 9 and up, explains how families and siblings can benefit from counseling, support, and anger management.

Gordon, Michael. *My Brother's a World-Class Pain: Sibling's Guide to ADHD/Hyperactivity.* Dewitt, NY: GSI, 1992. 34 pp. $11.00.ISBN 0-9627701-2-4.

> This short book takes a realistic and humorous look at what it is like to have a brother or sister with ADHD. The author explains the nature of ADHD and helps young readers acknowledge and understand their feelings about having a sibling with ADHD. He also suggests ways that siblings can help make family life a little smoother.

■ ORGANIZATIONS

CH.A.D.D. (Children and Adults with Attention Deficit Disorder)
499 Northwest 70th. Ave., Suite 109
Plantation, FL 33317
(305) 587-3700; (305) 587-4599 FAX
Web site: http//www.chadd.org/

> PURPOSE: "A nonprofit parent-based organization formed to better the lives of individuals with attention deficit disorders and those who care for them."
> SERVICES: CH.A.D.D. provides parent-to-parent education, support, advocacy; encourages scientific research; and sponsors a legislative awareness office in Washington, DC.
> PUBLICATIONS: *ATTENTION!* magazine is full of relevant articles, resources, personal accounts, and strategies for anyone raising and teaching children with attention deficit disorder. Also available: *ADD and Adolescence: Strategies for Success from CH.A.D.D.* ($17.75), fact sheets, and audiotapes from conferences.

Council for Exceptional Children (CEC)
1920 Association Dr.
Reston, VA 20191
(703) 620-3660; (703) 264-9494 FAX
800-CEC-READ (information on publications only)
Web site: http//www.cec.sped.org

> PURPOSE: "To improve educational outcomes for individuals with exceptionalities."
> SERVICES: A nonprofit membership organization for professionals and students that focuses on 17 different areas of Special Education.
> PUBLICATIONS: Publishes and distributes a variety of teacher-oriented materials, including the booklet *"Education of Children with Attention Deficit Disorder"* ($4.50) and other publications about ADD.

Learning Disabilities Association of America
4156 Library Road
Pittsburgh, PA 15234
(412) 341-1515; (412) 344-0224 FAX
E-mail: ldanatl@usaor.net
Web site: http//www.ldanatl.org

> PURPOSE: A nonprofit national organization "devoted to defining and finding solutions for the broad spectrum of learning problems."
> SERVICES: Advocacy, public awareness, research, and dissemination of information on learning disabilities.
> PUBLICATIONS: Distributes many booklets and books for parents, children, and teachers published by a variety of publishers on the topics of learning disabilities and ADD. Request a publications catalog.

Learning Disabilities Association of Canada
323 Chapel St., Ste. 200
Ottawa, Ontario K1N 7Z2
Canada
(613) 238-5721; (613) 235-5391
E-mail: ldactaac@fox.nstn.ca
> PUBLICATIONS: Offers *"A Guide for Parents on Hyperactivity in Children."*

National Center for Law and Learning Disabilities (NCLLD)
P.O. Box 368
Cabin John, MD 20818
(301) 469-8308; (301) 469-9466 FAX
> PUBLICATIONS: Examples include *"ADD in School"; "ADD in College"; "ADD in the Workplace"; "Confidentiality Under the Law"; "Documentation, Disclosure & the Law"; "The Armed Forces (and ADD/LD)."* Most publications are $2.00.

■ CATALOG

A.D.D. WareHouse
300 NW 70th Ave., Ste. 102
Plantation, FL 33317
(800) 233-9273; (954) 792-8944; (954) 792-8545
Web site: http://www.addwarehouse.com
> PURPOSE: A comprehensive resource for the understanding and treatment of attention deficit disorders and related problems for teachers, parents, health-care professionals, adults, and kids. Has a free catalog full of ADD-related books, videos, training programs, games, professional texts, and assessment products produced by a variety of publishers.

19.

Autism and Pervasive Developmental Disorders (PDD)

▪ BOOKS AND PERIODICALS

Basic Information

Frith, Uta. *Autism: Explaining the Enigma.* Malden, MA: Blackwell Publishers, 1992. 204 pp. $23.95. ISBN 0-631-16824-9.

Uta Frith's premise is that people with autism experience life as a series of fragmented events and that it is very difficult, if not impossible, for them to make sense of these events and view them as a coherent whole. She devotes several chapters to exploring how the mental abilities and perceptions of children with autism typically differ from other children's, focusing in particular on how their beliefs, emotions, and thoughts differ. She also takes an in depth look at how and why communication and social skills are a problem. The book was originally published in Great Britain, so some of the terminology (classification of levels of mental retardation) and word usages (referring to a child as "it," speaking of "suffering" from autism) may be jarring to American readers.

Hallowell, Edward. ***When You Worry about the Child You Love.*** New York, NY: Simon & Schuster, 1996. 281 pp. $23.00. ISBN 0-684-80090-X.

For parents who suspect, or have just learned, that their child has an emotional or learning problem, this book provides an excellent overview of disorders that may make children mad, sad, afraid, or confused. The book explains when parents should worry about their children's behavior and seek professional help; discusses steps parents can take to help children manage their emotions and learn, no matter what the disorder; and discusses treatment options, including medication. Information on a number of disorders with a biologic or genetic basis is offered, including pervasive developmental disorders (PDD) and Asperger syndrome. The author's conversational style and numerous anecdotes make this an easy read.

Pollak, Richard. ***The Creation of Dr. B: A Biography of Bruno Bettelheim.***

In 1967, Bruno Bettelheim published *The Empty Fortress,* a highly praised book in which he expounded upon his theory that autism was the result of emotional abandonment by parents who wished that their children had not been born. For many years, this book negatively colored how parents of children with autism felt about themselves and how they were treated by professionals. Pollak's biography reveals how little Bettelheim understood about children with autism, or indeed, anything that he was supposedly an expert in. Bettelheim is unmasked as an Austrian lumber dealer who used faked academic credentials after emigrating to the U.S. to begin practicing as a psychotherapist. As the director of a school for emotionally disturbed children in Chicago, he invented data to support his theories and wrote authoritatively about children he had never met or treated. The book also offers revealing looks at other aspects of Bettelheim's renown that were unmerited.

Powers, Michael D., ed. ***Children with Autism: A Parents' Guide.*** Bethesda, MD: Woodbine House, 1989. 368 pp. $14.95. ISBN 0-922149-16-6.

This comprehensive introduction to autism provides straightforward and accurate information for parents of children from birth to about age six. Chapters were contributed by both professionals and parents, and cover the following topics: What Is Autism?; Adjusting to Your Child's Diagnosis; Medical Problems, Treatments, and Professionals; Daily Life; Family Life; Your Child's Development; Finding the Right Educational Program; Legal Rights and Hurdles; Becoming an Advocate; and The Years Ahead. Parents share personal experiences at the end of each chapter, and the book includes a glossary and suggested reading list.

Siegel, Bryna. ***The World of the Autistic Child.*** New York, NY: Oxford University Press, 1996. 351 pp. $25.00. ISBN 0-19-507667-2.

Here is a book that parents can use throughout the lifetime of their child with autism or PDD. Ms. Siegel has written a guide that will help parents of young children make those early decisions that seem so overwhelming, and later, those decisions that involve education, training, and socialization. The book begins with a very thorough discussion of the spectrum of autistic disorders—PDD, autism, late onset autism, and Asperger syndrome. The author then offers common sense information about coping, parent supports, education, and treatments, including alternative therapies such as facilitated communication, dietary regimens, and auditory training. Examples of programs are provided and a whole chapter is devoted to medications. The tone of the book is objective throughout, even when unorthodox treatments for autism are being discussed.

Education

Holmes, David L. *Autism through the Lifespan: The Eden Model.* Bethesda, MD: Woodbine House, 1998. 400 pp. $21.95. ISBN 0-933149-28-X.

> This informative book explains how the Eden Family of Services, based in Princeton, NJ, provides services to people with autism, starting from diagnosis and continuing, if necessary, for the rest of their lives. Written by the founder of the program, the book goes into detail about how Eden provides early intervention services, special education, work experiences, and services to prepare children or adults to transition into inclusive settings. Although written primarily for professionals, parents interested in a detailed glimpse into how a successful program is run will value this book.

Koegel, Robert L., and Lynn Kern Koegel. *Teaching Children with Autism: Strategies for Initiating Positive Interactions and Improving Learning Opportunities.* Baltimore: Paul H. Brookes, 1995. 256 pp. $32.00. ISBN 1-55766-180-4.

> After discussing typical learning and behavior characteristics in children with autism, this book provides practical guidelines for handling specific challenges in the classroom. It includes information on creating a supportive environment, dealing with disruptive behavior, and teaching social and language skills. Helpful reading for both parents and educators.

Lovaas, Ivar O. *Teaching Developmentally Disabled Children: The Me Book.* Austin, TX: PRO-ED, 1981. 244 pp. $34.00. ISBN 0-936104-78-3.

> The author presents a behavior management technique that has been successfully used to teach young children with autism and PDD developmental skills and to decrease undesirable behaviors. In the method here described by Lovaas, parents and volunteers work intensely with the child to teach him components of individual skills, using rewards to reinforce every small step forward. One family's experiences with the method are described in Catherine Maurice's *Let Me Hear Your Voice,* listed below under First Person Perspectives.

Maurice, Catherine, Gina Green, and Stephen Luce, eds. *Behavioral Intervention for Young Children with Autism: A Manual for Parents and Professionals.* Austin, TX: Pro-Ed, 1996. 400 pp. $34.00. ISBN 0-89079-683-1.

> This technical manual offers detailed information about the use of applied behavior analysis in the treatment of autism. It also includes a chapter about the laws involved in obtaining funding for a behavioral intervention program, as well as information about the research supporting behavioral intervention and points to consider in evaluating research studies in general.

Penning, Marge. *A Language/Communication Curriculum for Students with Autism and Other Language Impairments.* Lansing, MI: CAUSE, 1992. $90.00. No ISBN.

> This impressive work, originally written for children with autism, has been updated and expanded to provide a structured, ecological approach to language intervention for all children. This is a *complete curriculum,* with information provided in developmental sequence. Assessments and guidelines for inclusion of augmentative communication are included. It is a massive work, but worth the effort to read, digest, and use. While the author strongly recommends the consultation of a speech and language pathologist, the material is easily adaptable for use by teachers, aides, and childcare workers.

Schopler, Eric, and Gary B. Mesibov. *Learning and Cognition in Autism.* New York, NY: Plenum, 1995. 346 pp. $49.50. ISBN 0-306-44871-8.

> This semi-technical text sums up what researchers have learned about learning and cognition in individuals with autism. The book also decribes strategies, ideas, and state-of-the art procedures that have been geared to meet the unique learning needs of children with autism. For example, the book focuses on Project TEACCH at the University of North Carolina-Chapel Hill, explaining the program's structured process of teaching with many examples. The authors also examine the educational approaches used by other programs for children with autism.

Simons, Jeanne, and Sabine Oishi. *The Hidden Child: The Linwood Method for Reaching the Autistic Child.* Bethesda, MD: Woodbine House, 1987. $17.95. ISBN 0-933149-06-9.

> The focus of this book is a teaching method developed at the Linwood School in Ellicott City, Maryland. The authors underscore that this method is one method among many. While they do not suggest that the Linwood method can perform miracles, they do share throughout the book successes that they have had. Laced with the success is description after description of the challenges staff and students face as therapy goes on. The structure that Linwood uses focuses on these "basic tenets": 1) The child is accepted in his environment; 2) The focus of treatment is on the health of the child; 3) All education is therapy, all therapy is education; 4) Therapy is flexible.

Behavioral Issues

Kozloff, Martin A. *Reaching the Autistic Child.* 2nd ed. Cambridge, MA: Brookline, 1998. 245 pp. $15.95. ISBN 1-57129-056-7.

> This is a parent training program designed to help parents understand and develop strategies for dealing with the behaviors of their child with autism. It is based on the *social exchange theory* principle, which revolves around socialization within the family, especially between parent and child. Each section discusses a different child, his or her behaviors, and the training program for limiting those behaviors. Summaries of procedures and technical information are provided.

Schopler, Eric, and Gary B. Mesibov. *Behavioral Issues in Autism.* New York, NY: Plenum, 1994. 295 pp. $49.50. ISBN 0-306-44600-6.

> This semi-technical book provides an indepth look at behavior management of individuals with autism. The authors provide a complete analysis of behaviors and interventions, and discuss both aversive and nonaversive interventions. Since assessment today in many areas of the country focuses on a functional analysis, parents may find the chapter devoted to that topic extremely helpful.

Schopler, Eric, ed. *Parent Survival Manual: A Guide to Crisis Resolution in Autism and Related Developmental Disorders.* New York, NY: Plenum, 1995. 224 pp. $29.95. ISBN 0-306-44977-3.

> To compile this eminently practical manual, the editor collected anecdotes from parents of children with autism and other developmental disabilities about day-to-day challenges they have confronted and how they solved them. The parent stories were then analyzed by professional behavior therapists. Problematic behaviors covered include aggression, toilet training difficulties, communication problems, eating and sleeping problems, and perseveration. Besides offering ready-made solutions to common problems, the book also provides information about working out solutions to unique problems.

Siblings

Harris, Sandra. *Siblings of Children with Autism: A Guide for Parents.* Bethesda, MD: Woodbine House, 1994. 127 pp. $12.95. ISBN 0-933149-71-9.

> Parents speak out, brothers and sisters share, and Dr. Harris explains potential problems and feelings associated with having a sibling with autism. This book offers practical suggestions for sibling support that can be easily incorporated into the daily routine. Advice for playtime, communication strategies, and tips for explaining what autism is are all included.

Siegel, Bryna, and Stuart Silverstein. *What about Me? Growing Up with a Developmentally Disabled Sibling.* New York, NY: Plenum, 1994. 316 pp. $24.95. ISBN 0-306-44650-2. Out of print.

> This book was written, in part, by a sibling for siblings. It is for adult siblings, parents, and professionals who counsel families. In the first chapter, Stu Silverstein describes growing up with a brother who has autism. Later chapters look at families from a clinical point of view. Feelings, adjustments, and coping strategies are reviewed, discussed, and analyzed, and ideas for support are offered. There are a number of questionnaires that can provide the catalyst for expression during support group meetings and counseling sessions.

Advanced Reading

Gillberg, Christopher, and Mary Coleman. *The Biology of the Autistic Syndromes.* 2nd ed. New York, NY: Cambridge University Press, 1992. 317 pp. $69.95. ISBN 0-521-432286.

> This book is an exceptionally well-referenced research text about autism and syndromes associated with it. Beginning with the work of Leo Kanner, the authors explain important research into genetic, biochemical, immunological, and epidemiological issues in autism. The authors emphasize that their philosophy is to maintain a "cautious attitude when discussing autism with parents." They explain that all children are different; just as the future for all children is different. It is the responsibility of the professional to diagnose, but not to assume the future for the child. With that said, there is a lot of information in this book *about* autism. Chapter 20 focuses on other syndromes with a secondary diagnosis of autism such as Cornelia de Lange syndrome, fetal alcohol syndrome, Mobius syndrome, neurofibromatosis, Rett syndrome, Tourette syndrome, tuberous sclerosis, and Williams syndrome. A glossary of genetic terminology is included.

Schopler, Eric, and Gary B. Mesibov. *High Functioning Individuals with Autism.* New York, NY: Plenum, 1992. 316 pp. ISBN 0-306-44064-4.

> A variety of professionals contributed chapters devoted to diagnostic, social, and educational issues related to high functioning individuals with autism. While the text written by professionals is fairly technical, parent's perspectives have been included that not only provide real-life information, but validate the importance of the parent as a team member in treatment. Also highly accessible is the chapter by Temple Grandin, in which she writes about her continuing struggles with autism and uses her experiences to define what works and does not work with individuals with autism.

Schreibman, Laura. *Autism.* Newbury Park, CA: SAGE, 1988. 160 pp. $18.95. ISBN 0-8039-2810-6.

> This is a technical guide written for professionals. It is important for parents, however, because it is a good research book. It is fairly easy to read and loaded with references for additional research. The book provides a history of the research about autism, while focusing on parent participation as the essential component in the treatment of an individual with autism.

Sigman, Marian, and Lisa Capps. *Children with Autism: A Developmental Perspective.* Cambridge, MA: Harvard University Press, 1997. 270 pp. $14.00. ISBN 0-674-05314-1.

> Although not a primer for the new parent, this book should interest parents who would like to understand how we know what we know about children with autism. The authors look at autism "through the lens of developmental psychopathology"—that is, by comparing the atypical development in children with autism with typical development. The book examines how development of children with and without autism differs in the areas of early pysiological regulation, perception, and cognition; social and emotional understanding; and language acquisition and use. The book also discusses the range of development in children with autism and attempts to single out factors in early development that may help determine how well an individual with autism eventually functions in the world. Extensive references make this a useful jumping off point for parents interested in what research has found.

Alternative & Controversial Treatments

Crossley, Rosemary. *Facilitated Communication Training.* New York, NY: Teachers College Press, 1994. 150 pp. ISBN 0-8077-3327-X. $15.95.

> The author describes the highly controversial technique of facilitated communication from the philosophy that everyone should be provided an opportunity to learn to communicate, no matter what their apparent functioning level is. There are cautions about the use of this technique, especially where legal issues such as assigning rights, agreeing to medical treatment, and other self-advocacy decisions are involved. Several case studies are provided. Photographs showing techniques for holding and support are included.

Gerlach, Elizabeth K. *Autism Treatment Guide.* Eugene, OR: Four Leaf Press, 1994. 130 pp. $7.99. ISBN 0-9637578-0-6.

> The purpose of this little book is to give parents an overview of the major treatment methods currently espoused for children with autism. A variety of treatment options—both mainstream and controversial—are discussed: including educational treatment, holding therapy, facilitated communication, and vitamin supplements. In addition, resources are provided at the end of each section.

Shane, Howard. **Facilitated Communication: The Clinical and Social Phenomenon.** San Diego, CA: Singular, 1994. 323 pp. $45.00. ISBN 1-56593-341-9.

> This is a very close, critical look at facilitated communication. The book focuses on the known history and facts that relate to facilitated communication and describes empirical studies of this phenomenon. This is not easy reading, and some parents may find it a rather negative book, but it is a valuable resource for deciding whether or not to accept facilitated communication as a valid communication tool.

Stehli, Annabel. *Dancing in the Rain.* Westport, CT: The Georgiana Organization, 1995. 303 pp. $14.95. ISBN 0-9644838-0-7.

> This collection includes twenty-two stories written by parents of children with a variety of disabilities, including attention deficit disorder, dyslexia, hyperlexia, central auditory processing disorder, pervasive developmental delay, and autism. The families used a variety of traditional and controversial methods to reach their children, including auditory integration training, vitamin therapy, the Lovaas method, the TEACCH program, sensory integration therapy, and the Option Institute.

First Person Perspectives

Barron, Judy, and Sean Barron. ***There's a Boy in Here.*** New York, NY: Simon & Schuster, 1992. 264 pp. $20.00. ISBN 0-671-76111-0.

> This is a fascinating story written by a mother and son about the son's emergence from autism. This is not a book about a cure, but about the struggle to shed the safe restraints and rules of autism. The Barrons talk candidly about their struggles, feelings, and ultimate successes. The reader leaves this book with hope for the future and a profound admiration for Sean, whose challenges continue to this day, and his family, who worked endlessly with Sean.

Christopher, William and Barbara. ***Mixed Blessings.*** New York, NY: Avon, 1989. 224 pp. $4.95. ISBN 0-380-70999-6.

> For years, the Christophers' adopted son, Ned, was a puzzle to everyone. At two and a half, he could write all the letters of the alphabet, identify most of the flags of the world, and give the name of any flower in the garden, but his social and language skills seemed a bit odd. Although he was diagnosed as "atypical with autistic features" at three and a half, other professionals and the Christophers continued to doubt this diagnosis for several years. With the passage of time, the gap between Ned and typical children widened, and he became more self-stimulatory and aggressive. The Christophers tried a succession of treatments, including sensory integration therapy, megavitamins, anticonvulsants, Ritalin, and the patterning program of the Institutes for the Achievement of Human Potential. Despite the authors' celebrity (William Christopher starred as Father Mulcahy on M*A*S*H), their story reads like the story of every family desperate to find some answers and to do what is right for their child.

Gorman, Jacqueline. ***The Seeing Glass: A Memoir.*** New York, NY: Putnam, 1997. 288 pp. $22.95. ISBN 1-57322-061-2.

> For ten weeks, the author of this engrossing memoir temporarily lost her sight to optic neuritis. While unable to relate to the outside world as she was accustomed to, she turned her thoughts inwards and began to vividly recall memories of her older brother, Robin, who had autism. When he was institutionalized at 12, Robin had become a non-member of the family; years later he was killed in an accident. In this account, the author eloquently reveals the long-suppressed emotions she felt toward her brother which were reawakened by her bout with blindness.

Grandin, Temple, and Margaret M. Scariano. ***Emergence: Labeled Autistic.*** Novato, CA: Academic Therapy Publications, 1993. 184 pp. $12.99. ISBN 0-446-67182-7.

> In this autobiography of her early years, Temple Grandin opens up her life, challenges, and successes as an individual with autism for all to experience. She describes what and how she feels, and tries to analyze why autistic characteristics are important to her and perhaps to others. She also explores how her mother and other significant persons in her life had an impact on her abilities to function in the outside world. Some of the therapy suggestions the author makes may be considered controversial, but many parents and professionals have found her insights into the world of autism invaluable.

Grandin, Temple. ***Thinking in Pictures and Other Reports from My Life with Autism.*** New York, NY: Doubleday, 1995. 222 pp. $22.95. ISBN 0-385-47792-9.

> The title of this astounding book refers to the author's ability to translate "both spoken and written words into full-color movies, complete with sound, which run like a VCR tape in [her] head." Grandin, who has autism, believes most people with autism share her relative talent in visual spatial skills, and her relative weakness in verbal skills. In the series of essays that make up

this book, she shares many additional fascinating insights into the differences between people with and without autism. Among the topics she discusses are: why people with autism have trouble with abstract thought; her difficulties understanding how to act in different types of relationships; how she prepares herself for transitions; her interpretation of why some people with autism are "low functioning" and some "high functioning"; why people with autism often have unusual reactions to sensory stimuli; how she experiences emotions; how to help children with autism build on their strengths and interests in school; and her views on religion and the meaning of life. This gracefully written book includes photographs of the author at different ages, as well as of some of the lifestock handling devices and facilities she has developed in her career. ***Thinking in Pictures*** is essential reading for anyone who would like greater insight into the way individuals with autism experience life.

Greenfeld, Josh. ***A Child Called Noah.*** New York, NY: Henry Holt, 1972. 224 pp. $7.95. ISBN 0-03-091384-5.

> Through journal entries, the author recounts important events in the first six years of his son, Noah, who has autism. The entries reflect the family's puzzlement and pain as they struggle to understand Noah's difficulties connecting with the world, his unusual behaviors, his sleep problems, and his developmental delays.

Greenfeld, Josh. ***A Place for Noah.*** New York, NY: Henry Holt, 1978. 295 pp. $10.00. ISBN 0-03-089896-X.

> Taking off where ***A Child Called Noah*** left off, this book reflects the family's increasing anger and loss of hope—in the education system, in the medical establishment, and in their son's future. After extensive efforts at modifying Noah's behavior, the author concludes that the correct label for his son is not the "glamorous" term *autistic,* but rather, *brain-damaged.*

Greenfeld, Josh. ***A Client Called Noah: A Family Journey Continued.*** Orlando, FL: Harcourt Brace Jovanovich, 1989. $8.00. ISBN 0-15-6181-68-1.

> The third book in the "Noah" series, this book consists of day-to-day journal entries by the author concerning himself, his wife, their nondisabled son, and Noah, their son with autism. This is a work about struggle and burnout. After eighteen years, the Greenfeld family finally decides to separate from Noah and places him in a residential setting.

Hart, Charles. ***Without Reason: A Family Copes with Two Generations of Autism.*** Arlington, TX: Future Horizons, 1989. 292 pp. $19.95. ISBN 0-06-016143-4.

> The author writes of his experiences both as the younger brother of an individual with autism and as the father of his own child with autism. The story gives a heartening glimpse of how far society, as well as the author, have come in understanding and accepting people with autism. There are vast differences between the way the author's brother, born in the 1920s, was considered the source of all the family's problems, and the way that his son, born in the 1970s, has been given the support and understanding to become an integral and accepted part of his family and community.

Johnson, Carol, and Julia Crowder. ***Autism: From Tragedy to Triumph.*** Boston, MA: Branden, 1994. 185 pp. $12.95. ISBN 0-8282-1965-0.

> This is the story of a mother's relentless journey to find a diagnosis and treatment for her child with autism. The treatment focus is that of Dr. Ivar Lovaas; however, the author does not provide a detailed description of the sessions or techniques used. The reader catches glimpses of success but the loudest voice heard is that of the mother, her stress, and her anxiety.

Martin, Russell. ***Out of Silence: A Journey into Language.*** New York, NY: Henry Holt, 1994. 300 pp. $22.50. ISBN 0-8050-1998-7.

In this provocative biography, the uncle of a little boy with autism set out to chronicle his nephew's struggle to learn to communicate. Along the way, he discovered a great deal about the development of language, the brain's role in understanding and producing speech and language, and how differences in brain structure might contribute to speech problems in people with autism. These discoveries, and his speculations about how they might apply to his nephew, Ian, are skillfully interspersed with vignettes about Ian's progress in acquiring language and fitting into the larger world. Although Ian's parents eventually began to use facilitated communication with him with some success, facilitated communication is not represented as a miracle cure for autism, and indeed, seems to make some of Ian's behaviors worse. The book should be of great interest to anyone who would like to understand more about the nature and causes of language delay, not just to parents of children with autism.

Maurice, Catherine. ***Let Me Hear Your Voice: A Family's Triumph Over Autism.*** New York, NY: Fawcett, 1993. 371 pp. $12.00. ISBN 0-449-90664-7.

The beginning of Catherine Maurice's story will be familiar to anyone who has a child with autism or has read other parents' accounts of the early years of their child with autism. There are the mounting questions and concerns, the dismissals of these concerns by well-meaning friends and professionals, and then the tidal wave of unbearable emotions once a diagnosis is reached. The Maurices (a pseudonymn) received not just one, but five diagnoses of autism or PDD in their daughter from a variety of respected specialists. In a twist on the usual story, however, the family refused to cope with autism; they wanted to "blast it out of existence." After trying holding therapy, the family relied primarily on the Lovaas method of intensive behavioral therapy combined with frequent private speech therapy sessions. (In the Lovaas method, each task is broken into small units and the child is systematically rewarded for every step toward mastering the units.) In the end, the Maurices used these techniques to help both their daughter and their younger son overcome autistic tendencies. The book includes a foreword by Bernard Rimland, who states that he met the children and detected no residual signs of autism in them. There is also an afterword by Ivar Lovaas, who explains the basis of his method and clarifies that it is not a sure-fire "cure" for all children with autism, although he believes it can help most children to varying degrees. Helpful appendices contain information on resources and elements of the Maurices' behavioral program for parents interested in exploring this method.

Park, Clara Claiborne. ***The Seige: The First Eight Years of an Autistic Child, With an Epilogue, Fifteen Years After.*** Boston: Little, Brown and Co., 1982. 328 pp. $14.95. 0-316-69069-4.

When "Elly" Park was born in 1958, the word *autism* had only recently come into use. Parents were still often blamed for causing autism, and it was widely considered a psychosis. Although a psychiatrist strongly recommended psychotherapy as treatment for Elly, her mother thought the advice she was given at diagnosis was much more helpful: "Take her home. . . . Do what you've been doing . . . give her plenty of affection." The commonsense approach she developed on her own to teach Elly needed skills was later greatly admired by psychiatrists on staff at Anna Freud's clinic in England. The Epilogue, written when Elly (real name, Jessy) was in her mid-twenties, underscores the importance of a loving, involved family in helping children with autism achieve their potential: in her early twenties, Elly had graduated from high school with a regular degree, had single-handedly typed the Spanish translation of *The Siege,* was employed in a college mailroom, and was an accomplished cook and artist. Photographs are included.

Schulze, Craig. *When Snow Turns to Rain: One Family's Struggle to Solve the Riddle of Autism.* Bethesda, MD: Woodbine House, 1993. $14.95. ISBN 0-933149-63-8.

> This is the story of a family that looked relentlessly for a cure, a fix, *something,* that would help their son, Jordan, who seemed brighter than average until he was two. Special schools, medications, therapies, and parental devotion simply did not help him regain his "normalcy." He went from speaking in full sentences to speaking only in grunts and whines; from a happy, sociable toddler, to a child prone to sudden bouts of aggression who seemed disconnected from others. Through diary entries and narration, Dr. Schulze shares his frustration and his grief. Finally, the family came to accept Jordan as he is and to feel some inner peace. This is an extraordinary book. If you have a child who is autistic or "autistic like," you may very well feel an alliance with this family.

Sperry, Virginia Walker. *Fragile Success: Nine Autistic Children, Childhood to Adulthood.* North Haven, CT: Archon Books, 1995. 234 pp. $27.50. ISBN 0-208-02413-1.

> This unique book profiles seven boys and two girls with autism or PDD from their preschool years to early adulthood. The common denominator among the children is that they all attended the Elizabeth Ives School for Special Children in New Haven, Connecticut--a pioneer in preschool education for children with autism. Their stories are told through case studies written by a former teacher at the school, incorporating reports from teachers, medical professionals, and social workers. In most cases, the mother has also contributed an account of her family's experiences with the child. The work provides a fascinating overview of the wide range of abilities and disabilities in children with autism and how those characteristics do or do not change over the years.

Stehli, Annabel. *The Sound of a Miracle.* Westport, CT: The Georgiana Organization, 1996. 226 pp. $20.95. ISBN 0-9644838-1-5.

> This is a story of perseverance against all odds. The author shares her struggles, her anger, and her anguish while pursuing a "cure" for her child with autism. For her family, the solution eventually proves to be auditory integration training. The author's courage in the face of incomprehensible hostility and her determination to stick with an arduous course of therapy are inspiring.

Williams, Donna. *Nobody, Nowhere: The Extraordinary Autobiography of an Autistic.* New York, NY: Doubleday, 1992. 224 pp. $14.95. ISBN 0-385-25425-3.

> This is a remarkable book worth the time and close attention of any reader, with or without an interest in autism. Donna Williams is an exceptionally gifted writer who just happens to have autism. She calls this book "a story of two battles, a battle to keep out 'the world' and a battle to join it." What kept her from joining the world for twenty-five years was her utter confusion about why she was as she was. Her hostile mother at first suspected she was deaf, and later, "a retard" and "mad." Ms. Williams had very logical reasons for acting as she did, however--tolerating some people and not others, having tantrums, using echolalic speech, other typically "autistic" behaviors--and explains these reasons with great clarity. Be prepared for some shocks and some laughs, as Ms. Williams does not mince words.

Williams, Donna. *Somebody, Somewhere: Breaking Free From the World of Autism.* New York: Times Books, 1994. 238 pp. $23.00. ISBN 0-8129-2287-5.

> Continuing where *Nobody, Nowhere* left off, this book covers the four years since the author's diagnosis with autism. The narration alternates between scenes from the past and scenes from the present, and includes the author's insights and experiences trying out different jobs, including a stint as a special education aide, pursuing a college degree in education, and handling the onerous task of publicizing her first book.

FOR CHILDREN

Armenta, Charles A. *Russell Is Extra Special: A Book about Autism for Children.* New York, NY: Magination Press, 1992. 17 pp. $11.95. ISBN 0-945354-43-6.

> In this picture book written for children 4-8 years old, Russell's dad introduces the reader to his son and explains autism in the process. This picture album makes it clear how the family copes with Russell's autistic behaviors and how much they love him. An excellent awareness book.

Katz, Illana, and Edward Ritvo. *Joey and Sam.* Northridge, CA: Real Life Story Books, 1993. 38 pp. $16.95. ISBN 1-882388-00-3.

> Sam is a five-year-old with autism, and Joey is his six-year-old brother. The story follows the two brothers through an ordinary day at home and at school, showing some of the ways the two boys are different and alike. Although Joey wrestles with his feelings about having a brother with autism, he does not hesitate to express his love for Sam and his pride in his accomplishments, which include reading and knowing facts about the planets. The book is illustrated with black and white drawings.

Martin, Ann M. *Kristy and the Secret of Susan.* New York, NY: Scholastic, 1990. 148 pp. $3.99. ISBN 0-590-42496-3.

> Kristy Thomas, 13, is intrigued when she lands the job of babysitting 8-year-old Susan Feldman for a month. Although Susan has autism and is basically nonverbal, she is a musical savant with perfect pitch and can also immediately tell the day of the week of any date in history. Kristy decides it is her mission to help Susan make friends and to act more "normally" so that she can stay home and go to the neighborhood school. Some adult readers may feel that Kristy fails more because of her parents' disinterest in inclusion than because of her autism, but others may value this book as a means to explain why some children with autism live in residential settings. The book is #32 in "The Baby-Sitters Club" series.

Martin, Ann M. *Inside Out.* New York, NY: Scholastic, 1984. 152 pp. $3.99. ISBN 0-590-43621-X.

> At the beginning of this engrossing and multi-dimensional novel, Jonathan's family is struggling with a horrible dilemma. They must either succeed in changing his little brother's autistic behaviors, or put him in an institution. At four, James is nonverbal, sometimes screams all night, hits himself in the face, and is prone to tantrumming and taking off his clothes in public. Although Jonathan is convinced that a new school will help his little brother become "normal" again, progress is very slow. In coming to terms with James's needs and his own feelings about those needs, Jonathan learns many valuable lessons about himself and society. Interesting subplots involve a succession of money-making schemes dreamed up by Jonathan and his friends and dealing with a classmate who has special needs of his own.

Thompson, Mary. *Andy and His Yellow Frisbee.* Bethesda, MD: Woodbine House, 1996. 20 pp. $14.95. ISBN 0-933149-83-2.

> Sarah, the new girl at school, is fascinated by Andy and his yellow frisbee. All recess long, Andy keeps to himself, spinning his frisbee around and around. When Sarah devises a plan to get to know Andy, Rosie, Andy's older sister, gets involved. Through Rosie's eyes, the reader learns what it is like to live with a brother like Andy, in all his complexity. The story, appropriate for children in grades K-5, ends on a hopeful, if realistic, note.

Watson, Esther. *Talking to Angels.* San Diego: Harcourt Brace Co., 1996. 26 pp. $16.00. ISBN 0-15-201077-7.

> Colorful drawings tell us about autism and the love and understanding sisters have for each other.

■ ORGANIZATIONS

Autism Network International (ANI)
P.O.Box 448
Syracuse, NY 13210-0448
E-mail: bordner@uiuc.edu.
Web site: http//www.students.uiuc.edu/~bordner/nai.html

> PURPOSE: An advocacy and self-help organization for individuals with autism.
>
> SERVICES: An avenue for peer counseling and support for all ages. Pen-Pal directory, chat room, speaker referral services, and reference library are available.
>
> PUBLICATIONS: *Our Voice,* published quarterly.

Autism Research Review International (formerly *Institute for Child Behavior Research*)
4182 Adams Ave.
San Diego, CA 92116
(619) 281-7165; (619) 563-6840 FAX

> PURPOSE: A nonprofit organization dedicated to research into autism and related disorders.
>
> PUBLICATIONS: The quarterly newsletter, *Autism Research Review International,* summarizes research findings in layperson's language and reports on investigations into conventional and unconventional treatments ($16.00 in the USA; $18.00 international subscriptions). Request a list of publications, which include information packs, books, and video tapes.

Autism Services Center (ASC)
Pritchard Building
605 9th Street
P.O. Box 507
Huntington, WV 25710-0507
(304) 525-8026; (304) 525-8026 FAX

> PURPOSE: Provides "professional training, consulting and advocacy information to people working with autistic individuals."
>
> SERVICES: Maintains a listing of therapists and educators and other professionals who focus on working with individuals with autism. Offers workshops, seminars, and research.
>
> PUBLICATION: Publishes a newsletter, *Behind the Lines.*

Autism Society of America (ASA)
7910 Woodmont Ave., Suite 650
Bethesda, MD 20814
(800) 328-8476; (301) 657-0869 FAX
(800) 329-0899 FAX ON DEMAND SERVICE
Web site: http//www.autism-society.org/

> PURPOSE: The ASA is dedicated to increasing public and professional awareness about autism and to advocating for the rights and needs of individuals with autism and their families.
>
> SERVICES: Information and referral services include parent to parent assistance, and a fax on demand service. The ASA also provides educational and habilitation services and is involved in goverment advocacy and public awareness. Sponsors over 225 local chapters.
>
> PUBLICATIONS: *The Advocate* newsletter for members of ASA ($20.00 yearly) is published bimonthly, and includes information on research, legislation, and family issues. Information packets (free to members) are available on a wide range of topics.

Autism Society of Michigan

809 Center St., Ste. 8A
Lansing, MI 48906-5257
(517) 487-9260; (517) 487-2377 FAX

> PUBLICATIONS: This chapter of the ASA operates a mail-order bookstore specializing in titles on autism. The catalog includes publications on the topics of behavioral management, communication, current approaches, education, employment, families, personal experiences, related disabilities, and siblings.

Autism Society of North Carolina

505 Oberlin Rd., Ste. 230
Raleigh, NC 27605-1345
(919) 743-0204; (919) 743-0208 FAX

> PUBLICATIONS: This chapter of the ASA considers itself the largest bookstore specializing in titles on autism. The bookstore catalog lists over 150 titles. This organization also publishes *The Spectrum,* a quarterly newsletter, and *"Autism Primer: Twenty Questions and Answers,"* a booklet with basic information about autism. Members of the Autism Society of North Carolina receive discounts on books; access to the lending library and resource center; and the quarterly newsletter.

Autism Support Center

64 Holten St.
Danvers, MA 01923
(508) 777-9135
and
66 Canal Street, 6th Floor
Boston, MA 02114
(617) 723-6738

> PURPOSE: Information and referral for individuals with autism, their families, and professionals. Membership is free, but donations gladly accepted.
> SERVICES: Support groups and information dissemination.
> PUBLICATION: *Autism Support Center Newsletter,* quarterly.

Future Horizons

422 E. Lamar, Suite 106
Arlington, TX 76011
(800) 489-0727

> PUBLICATIONS: This publishing company publishes and distributes books, videos, and tapes only on autism-related topics. Publications cover subjects such as communication, medical treatments, educational advancements, behavior management, improving social skills, and recreation ideas. The company also publishes parent-to-parent conference papers in an annual compilation.

The Georgiana Organization

P.O. Box 2607
Westport, CT 06880
(203) 454-1221; (203) 454-3788 FAX

> PURPOSE: A center that collects teaching materials for Auditory Integration Training (AIT) and encourages the practice of AIT.
> SERVICES: Data repository service, information, and education.
> PUBLICATIONS: Newsletter ($12.00); other publications.

Institute for the Study of Developmental Disabilities
Indiana University
2853 E. 10th St.
Bloomington, IN 47408-2601
(812) 855-6508; (812) 855-9396 TTY
Web site: http//www.isdd.indiana.edu/

PURPOSE: "To provide leadership that enables communities to include, support, and empower people with disabilities and family members. The Institute accomplishes this by promoting innovative practices and policies that facilitate community membership."

PUBLICATIONS: **Autism Training Sourcebook,** a compilation of training papers on Assessment, Autism, Behavior Management, Communication, and Functional Programming, is $10.00. Other publications include: *"Helpful Responses to Some of the Behaviors of Individuals with Autism"* ($4.00); *"Helping People with Autism Manage Their Behavior"* ($5.00); *"Identifying High Functioning Children with Autism"* ($2.00).

International Rett Syndrome Association
9121 Piscataway Rd.
Clinton, MD 20735
(300) 856-3334; (800) 818-RETT

PURPOSE: "To support and encourage medical research to determine the cause and find a cure for Rett synrome, to increase the public awareness of Rett syndrome, and to provide informational and emotional support to families of children with Rett syndrome."

SERVICES: Information and referral, advocacy, regional support groups.

PUBLICATIONS: Newsletter, educational materials, fact sheets. NOTE: This association is listed in this section because Rett syndrome, a neurological disorder affecting only girls and causing impairments in language, hand function, and intellectual development, is frequently misdiagnosed as autism.

TEACCH Division
Administration & Research
CB #7180, Medical School Wing E
University of North Carolina at Chapel Hill
Chapel Hill, NC 27599-7180
(919) 966-2174; (919) 966-4127 FAX

PURPOSE: To improve the understanding and services available for all children and adults with autism and related communication difficulties.

SERVICES: Offers a wide range of services, such as: diagnosis and assessment; individualized treatment training for professionals and parents; consultations to classrooms, also demo. classrooms used for training and observation; social skills groups; crisis intervention; job coaching with competitive and supported employment, and model program development.

PUBLICATIONS: Request a list of publications.

Trace Research & Development Center
University of Wisconsin-Madison
S-151 Waisman Center
1500 Highland Ave.
Madison, WI 53705-2280
(608) 262-6966; (608) 262-8848 FAX; (608) 263-5408 TTY

E-mail: info@trace.wisc.edu

Web site: http//trace.wisc.edu

> PURPOSE: "To advance the ability of people with disabilities to achieve their life objectives through the use of communication, computer and information technologies."
>
> PUBLICATIONS: Offers several papers on facilitated communication, including *"Final Report 1: Literature Review"* ($2.00) and *"Final Report 2: Description of Case Studies on Facilitated Communication"* ($1.00).

U.S. Dept. of Health and Human Services

Public Health Service

National Inst. of Neurological and Communicative Disorders and Stroke,
   Office of Scientific Health Reports

9000 Rockville Pike, Bldg. 31

Bethesda, MD 20892

(800) 352-9424

> PUBLICATIONS: Request the free publications: *"Autism: Hope Through Research"; and "AUTISM: Fact Sheet."*

20.

Cerebral Palsy

■ BOOKS

Basic Information

Finnie, Nancie R. *Handling the Young Cerebral Palsied Child at Home.* 3rd ed. Newton, MA: Butterworth-Heinemann, 1995. 306 pp. $40.00. ISBN 0-7506-0579-0.

> This is the classic guide to daily care of infants and children with cerebral palsy. The author clearly explains abnormal movements and postures and how to minimize them in handling and positioning a child with cerebral palsy. She also provides in-depth information about handling daily care routines such as sleeping, toilet training, dressing, feeding, and bathing. In addition, there is useful information on how cognitive, speech, and other skills develop in children with cerebral palsy, with practical information about how parents can help. Numerous line drawings illustrate the text.

Geralis, Elaine, ed. *Children with Cerebral Palsy: A Parents' Guide.* 2nd ed. Bethesda, MD: Woodbine House, 1998. 434 pp. $16.95. ISBN 0-933149-82-4.

> From the beginning definition of cerebral palsy to the final extensive list of resources and reading suggestions, the reader will collect information that will support, challenge, and comfort. Chapters provide current information and ideas about: the nature and causes of cerebral palsy; coping with the diagnosis; medical concerns and treatment; daily care; family life; development; therapies; early intervention and special education; legal rights and benefits; and advocacy. Each chapter ends with parent statements; thoughts from other parents that let you know that you are not alone. The book is liberally illustrated with photographs of children and equipment, as well as drawings showing positioning and handling techniques.

Miller, Freeman, and Steven J. Bachrach. *Cerebral Palsy: A Complete Guide for Caregiving.* Baltimore, MD: Johns Hopkins University Press, 1995. 465 pp. $35.95. ISBN 0-8018-5091-6.

> This encyclopedic work covers many of the concerns of parents with children with cerebral palsy from birth through early adulthood. Strong points of the book include its detailed coverage of medical concerns and treatments, as well as of daily care issues (including home modifications, car seats, wheelchairs, positioning and mobility equipment, shoes, feeding, toilet training, using enemas or suppositories, and more). There are also individual chapters on diplegia, hemiplegia, and quadriplegia with helpful information specific to developmental and medical concerns that commonly arise from birth through age eighteen. The "Cerebral Palsy Encyclopedia" (glossary) at the end is especially comprehensive. The book is less helpful and even outdated in some cases where emotional, educational, and legal issues are concerned. Although the book would be a very useful resource for many parents, its descriptions of everything possible that could go wrong may be too overwhelming for some new parents.

First Person Perspectives

Bratt, Berneen. *No Time for Jello: One Family's Experiences with the Doman-Delacato Patterning Program.* Cambridge, MA: Brookline Books, 1989. 201 pp. $17.95. ISBN 0-914797-56-5.

> The "Jello" in the title of this book is the family goldfish. Nobody has time to change its water, or to do anything else, once the family enrolls in the Philadelphia-based Institutes for the Achievement of Human Potential, hoping to cure six-year-old Jamie of his cerebral palsy. For close to a year, Jamie, his parents, and scores of volunteers spend twelve hours a day "patterning" Jamie--forcing him to crawl, creep, swing from an overhead ladder, walk, run, and rebreathe his own carbon dioxide. (This "treatment" is supposed to work by increasing sensory input to his unused brain cells, according to the theories of Glenn Doman, the Institutes' founder.) There is often not enough time for Jamie to eat a sit-down meal; instead, his mother feeds him bits of egg or fruit while he is endlessly crawling or creeping around the house. The Institute requires that his parents keep him home from school so they can devote all their time to the program. After spending thousands of dollars and hours on the program, the family finally concludes that the negligible improvements they have seen in Jamie's physical abilities are not worth the effort and sacrifice. An excellent book for any parent who is contemplating trying an alternative therapy with their child.

Grimm, Eric. *Walk with Me.* Washington, DC: UCPA, 1992. 50 pp. $6.00. Available through United Cerebral Palsy Associations (UCPA).

> The author, a young man with cerebral palsy, wrote this account of his life to help readers understand what it is like to have CP, and to help others understand that people with CP are just like everyone else.

Kramer, Laura Shapiro. *Uncommon Voyage: Parenting a Special Needs Child in the World of Alternative Medicine.* Winchester, MA: Faber & Faber, 1996. 205 pp. $24.95. ISBN 0-571-19887-2.

> Ever since the author's son, Seth, was diagnosed with cerebral palsy, she has devoted herself to researching any and all methods and treatments that might help him. In this book, she recounts how and why she decided to pursue both mainstream and alternative treatments, including physical therapy, occupational therapy, cranial-sacral therapy, the Feldenkrais method, a privately-devised physical strengthening program, homeopathy, and "breathing lessons" from a Yoga instructor. Along the way, the author also discusses how having a sibling with cerebral palsy has affected her daughter, her family's struggles to find the best school for Seth, and her ultimately successful suit against the obstetrician who delivered Seth. The author's primary message is that it is the parents' responsibility to research all possible avenues of treatment and to make decisions about what is right for their child.

Nolan, Christopher. *Under the Eye of the Clock: The Life Story of Christopher Nolan.* New York, NY: Dell, 1987. 176 pp. $7.95. ISBN 0-385-29713-0. Out of print.

> Christopher Nolan is a young Irish poet who has severe cerebral palsy. Unable to speak, he communicates through body language and by poking out letters with a typing stick attached to his head. In this book, he writes about his childhood and adolescence in the third person, referring to himself as Joseph Meehan. Nolan has a prodigious vocabulary, a fondness for coining new words, and a style that sometimes borders on stream-of-consciousness, so this is difficult reading. It is also tremendously rewarding, however. There are many insights into how it feels to have a brilliant mind trapped inside a "zoo-caged" body. He writes, for example, of how it feels to seem "a fool in other people's eyes," and how it feels to be "castrated by crippling disease, molested by scathing mockery, silenced by paralysed vocal muscles yet ironically blessed with a sense of physical well-being."

Papazian, Sandy. *Growing Up with Joey: A Mother's Story of Her Son's Disability and Her Family's Triumph.* Santa Barbara, CA: Fithian Press, 1997. 272 pp. $24.00. ISBN 1-56474-184-2.

> Sandy Papazian has four children, including a son with cerebral palsy. This book gives a slice of an often overwhelming life, in which everything that needed to be done for her children each day literally added up to more than twenty-four hours.

For Children

Aaseng, Nathan. *Cerebral Palsy.* New York, NY: Franklin Watts, 1991. 96 pp. $22.00. ISBN 0-531-12529-7.

> "Cerebral Palsy affects only the muscles, not the heart or soul," says Mary who is now a guidance counselor, and has had cerebral palsy since birth. This is also the author's attitude about cerebral palsy. With the help of clear, understandable pictures, this book outlines the basics—from characteristics and causes, to effects on childhood development and beyond. This is an excellent, brief picture, for older children and teens of what CP is and how people live with it.

Bergman, Thomas. *Going Places: Children Living with Cerebral Palsy.* Milwaukee, WI: Gareth Stevens Publishing, 1991. 48 pp. $18.60. ISBN 0-8368-0199-7.

> This book introduces us to Mathias, a six-year-old who has cerebral palsy and is deaf. Black and white photographs depict the day-to-day effort Mathias and each family member must expend to help him live life to the fullest. Treatments and classes are explained, but mostly this book reveals Mathias's personality and his strength.

Emmert, Michelle, and Gail Owens. *I'm the Big Sister Now.* Niles, IL: Albert Whitman & Co., 1989. 32 pp. $14.95. ISBN 0-8075-3458-7.

> Michelle, 9, describes what it is like to live with her older sister, Amy, who has cerebral palsy. This well-written and beautifully illustrated book does a good job of explaining CP in understandable terms. Although written for children aged 7-11, the book should be shared with adults as well.

Fassler, Joan. *Howie Helps Himself.* Morton Grove, IL: Albert Whitman & Co., 1975. 32 pp. $14.95. ISBN 0-8075-3422-6.

> Howie has cerebral palsy. He gets around in a wheelchair, or rather, *other people* get him around in his wheelchair. More than anything, Howie wants to move that chair himself. This is the story of how he works at accomplishing his goal. This children's story for preschoolers and early elementary grades provides information about cerebral palsy, children who live with it, and some insight about coping with it.

Moran, George. *Imagine Me on a Sit-Ski*. Morton Grove, IL: Albert Whitman and Co., 1995. 32 pp. $14.95. ISBN 0-80753-618-0.

> Billy is so excited. He's going skiing with his friends. He's a little scared, too, because this is his first experience skiing. Billy happens to have cerebral palsy and ordinarily uses a wheelchair to get around. With adaptations, however, Billy and his friends enjoy the slopes.

Perske, Robert. *Don't Stop the Music.* Nashville: Abingdon Press, 1986. 140 pp. $9.95. ISBN 0-687-11060-2.

> This young adult novel has all the thrills, romance, and adventure you could ever want in a good book. It also has another ingredient: a teenaged hero and heroine who have cerebral palsy. The plot centers around the characters' efforts to crack an auto-theft and gives Robert Perske a forum for promoting independence, inclusion, and awareness of disabilities. He uses the characters to help the reader identify their feelings about persons with disabilities. Through them, we are able to sort out our own prejudices, concerns, and even fears. All this and a fine "who-done-it" too.

Slepian, Jan. *The Alfred Summer.* New York, NY: Simon & Schuster, 1980. 132 pp. ISBN 0-02-782920-0. Out of print.

> When this story opens in the summer of 1937, Lester feels that he is an object of pity and derision. Although he can walk awkwardly and talk well enough to be understood when he takes his time, his cerebral palsy seems to scare every possible friend away. Then he meets Alfred, a happy-go-lucky boy with mental retardation and a limp. The two fall in with two other children who feel like misfits and spend the summer building a rowboat that they plan to use to get away from it all. Along the way, Lester learns that he is stronger both physically and emotionally than he ever knew and that some people, at least, are worth getting close to.

Wanous, Suzanne. *Sara's Secret.* Minneapolis: Carolrhoda Books, 1995. 40 pp. $18.95. ISBN 0-87614-856-9.

> Five-year-old Justin has cerebral palsy and mental retardation. He "can't walk or talk or feed himself, or even sit up," but still, he makes his sister Sara happy. Sara is not happy, however, when the teacher at her new school plans a unit on disabilities. Sara does not want to let her friends know about her brother, for fear that they will tease her about him. When her secret gets out, however, she finds that her classmates are curious, not mean, and she even feels brave enough to explain why her brother is sometimes "slobbery." This liberally illustrated book has a fair amount of text and is suitable for children from about grades 3-6.

Yates, Sarah. *Can't You Be Still?* Winnipeg, Manitoba: Gemma B. Publishing, 1992. 28 pp. $8.95. ISBN 0-9696477-0-0.

> It's the first day of school and four-year-old Ann, who has CP, lets us join her. Ann loves to swim and shows everyone in her class what fun it is. Children will enjoy the illustrations and learning about turning the challenges of cerebral palsy into strengths.

Yates, Sarah. *Nobody Knows!* Winnipeg, Manitoba: Gemma B. Publishing, 1994. 24 pp. $8.00. ISBN 0-9696477-1-9.

> Explore Ann's world with her and her friend Jay as they go for an adventure out of the yard. Although Ann can't talk yet, she sure can think and problem solve, as this story clearly demonstrates.

■ ORGANIZATIONS

March of Dimes
Resource Center
1275 Mamaroneck Ave.
White Plains, NY 10605
(888) MODIMES; (914) 997-4764 TTY; (914) 997-4763 FAX
Web site: http://www.modimes.org

> PURPOSE: The Resource Center of the March of Dimes provides information to the public about birth defects, pregnancy, and children's health issues.
>
> PUBLICATIONS: Has free fact sheets on disabilities such as achondroplasia, cleft lip and palate, Down syndrome, neurofibromatosis, PKU, and spina bifida, as well as on genetic testing.

NIH Neurology Institute
National Institute of Neurological Disorders and Stroke
P.O. Box 5801
Bethesda, MD 20824
(800) 352-9424; (301) 402-2186 FAX
Web site: http://www.ninds.nih.gov

> PURPOSE: Supports research into brain and nervous system disorders.
>
> PUBLICATIONS: Free publications include: ***Neurological Disorders: Voluntary Health Agencies and Other Patient Resources*** (a directory); *"Know Your Brain"* (fact sheet on anatomy and function); *"Hope Through Research"* brochures on cerebral palsy and head injury.

United Cerebral Palsy (UCP)
1660 L St., N.W., Ste. 700
Washington, DC 20036
(800) 872-5827; (202) 776-0414 FAX; (202) 973-7197 TTY
Web site: http//www.ucpa.org

> PURPOSE: "To advance the independence, productivity and full citizenship of people with cerebral palsy and other disabilities, through our commitment to the principles of independence, inclusion, and self-determination."
>
> SERVICES: Information and referral; legislative advocacy; research. Local affiliates provide direct services to people with disabilities and their families, including therapy, assistive technology training, advocacy, and employment assistance.
>
> PUBLICATIONS: ***Washington Watch,*** a bimonthly newsletter, is described in the Advocacy section of this book. Offers fact sheets on topics such as, *"Cerebral Palsy - Facts and Figures"; "Multiple Births and Developmental Brain Damage"; "Aging and Cerebral Palsy"; "Alternative and Complementary Medicine"; "Surgical Treatment of Drooling"; and "Gait Analysis."* Also has a catalog of publications of interest to parents and advocates published by a variety of companies and organizations. Many publications can be downloaded from the web site.

21.

Cleft Palate and Facial Differences

■ BOOKS AND PERIODICALS

Basic Information

Charkins, Hope. *Children with Facial Differences: A Parent's Guide.* Bethesda, MD: Woodbine House, 1996. 361 pp. $16.95. ISBN 0-933149-61-1.

> This compassionate and readable guide was written for parents of children with congenital craniofacial anomalies—differences in the structure of the head or face present at birth. Specific conditions covered include: cleft lip and palate, hemifacial microsomia, microtia and atresia, craniosynostoses syndromes (e.g., Apert and Crouzon syndromes), Treacher Collins syndrome, Nager syndrome, and Pierre Robin sequence. The book thoroughly explains the nature and causes of various types of facial difference, and then provides the support and information parents need to cope with the many challenges—medical, emotional, social, educational, legal, and financial—that facial differences can pose. The book includes many candid photographs of children with their families and offers extensive listings of helpful publications and organizations.

Jung, Jack H. *Genetic Syndromes in Communication Disorders.* Austin, TX: PRO-ED, 1989. 285 pp. $38.00. ISBN 0-89079-280-1.

> Written primarily for speech, language, and hearing professionals and students, this semi-technical text covers genetic syndromes that involve communication disorders. The first chapter pro-

vides a clear overview of medical genetics, explaining terminology, how chromosomal and single gene disorders occur, how family pedigrees are taken, and determining recurrence risks. The book then examines individual disorders with a genetic component, discussing causes, effects on hearing and speech, treatment of communication difficulties, and prognosis for people with the disorder. Conditions of facial difference covered include: Apert syndrome, branchio-oto-renal syndrome, Crouzon syndrome, cleft lip and palate, ectrodactyly-ectodermal dysplasia-clefting syndrome, hemifacial microsomia, Moebius syndrome, Pierre-Robin sequence, Stickler syndrome, Treacher Collins syndrome, oro-facial-digital syndrome. Chapters on specific syndromes are 4-10 pages long and include references.

Miller, Nancy B. *Nobody's Perfect: Living & Growing with Children Who Have Special Needs.* Baltimore: Paul H. Brookes, 1994. 307 pp. $21.00. ISBN 1-55766-143-X.

Parents of children with facial difference may want to take special note of this book. The author wrote it in close consultation with four mothers of children with special needs, including the mother of a child with Pierre Robin sequence. Many quotations from the parents about their experiences and feelings are used to illustrate the author's ideas about helping parents cope with the special challenges of raising a child with special needs.

Moller, Karlind, Clark D. Starr, and Sylvia A. Johnson. *A Parent's Guide to Cleft Lip and Palate.* Minneapolis: University of Minnesota, 1990. 130 pp. $16.95. ISBN 0-8166-1491-1.

This is a practical guide for parents and professionals. The authors carefully explain just what clefts are and describe the different types of clefts. From the very beginning, they stress that technology has advanced to the point where clefts can be treated with great success. Chapters cover concerns such as surgery, feeding, speech development, and ear problems. There are many clear diagrams and photographs of children with repaired and unrepaired clefts.

Resources for People with Facial Difference. Bellingham, WA: Let's Face It, published annually. One copy available free with a 9" x 12" self-addressed envelope, with $3 postage and a note telling about yourself.

This is an annotated listing of organizations, books, booklets, periodicals, and videos dealing with issues of interest to persons with facial difference and their families. Included are listings of general interest, as well as resources on specific conditions—both congenital and acquired, common (cleft palate) and uncommon (Mobius syndrome, Freeman-Sheldon syndrome, Treacher Collins syndrome, and Sturge-Weber syndrome). Ordering information for most publications is provided.

Thoene, Jesse G., ed. *Physician's Guide to Rare Diseases.* 2nd ed. Montvale, NJ: Dowden Publishing Co., 1995. 1200 pp. $129.99. ISBN 0-9628716-1-3.

This text provides information on approximately 900 rare disorders. The following information is given for each disorder: description, synonyms, signs and symptoms, etiology (cause), epidemiology (prevalence), standard and investigational treatments, and resources for more information. Many rarer conditions of facial difference are described in the book. Although written primarily as a diagnostic tool for medical professionals, the book would be understandable to an interested lay person.

For Children

Brink, Benjamin. *David's Story: A Book about Surgery.* Minneapolis: Lerner Publications, 1996. 32 pp. $19.95. ISBN 0-8225-2577-1.

Seven-year-old David was born with a number of facial differences, including a missing nostril and widely spaced eyes. With clear color photos and matter-of-fact text, this book shows what happened before, during, and after the operation to create a new nostril and straighten David's eyes.

The author acknowledges, but does not dwell on, the emotions that David and his family feel at various stages. A slight amount of blood is visible in one photograph, so parents should use care in reading the book to a child who might be frightened. The suggested reading level is grades 3-5.

Krementz, Jill. ***How It Feels to Live with a Physical Disability.*** New York, NY: Simon & Schuster, 1992. 136 pp. $18.00. ISBN 0-671-72371-5.

In their own words, twelve children with a variety of physical disabilities tell what it is like to look and feel different from other children. Francis Smith, age 16, has Treacher Collins syndrome. He tells of meeting other children and adults with facial differences, and about his hopes, fears, and dreams. This young adult book includes black-and-white photographs of the children, their families, and friends.

■ ORGANIZATIONS

AboutFace—Canada

99 Crowns Lane, 4th Floor
Toronto, Ontario M5R 3P4
Canada
(800) 665-3223

PURPOSE: To provide support and information to people with facial differences and their families.
PUBLICATIONS: *"My Newborn Has a Facial Difference"; "Apert, Crouzon, and Other Craniosynostosis"; "A School Program to Introduce Facial Differences";* others.

AboutFace—USA

P.O. Box 93
Limekiln, PA 19535
(800) 225-3223

PURPOSE: To provide support and information to people with facial differences and their families.
PUBLICATIONS: See under AboutFace—Canada.

Children's Craniofacial Association

9441 LBJ Freeway, Ste. 115-LB46
Dallas, TX 75243
(800) 535-3643

PURPOSE: To provide support, information, and financial assistance to children with craniofacial anomalies and their families.
PUBLICATIONS: Publishes booklets for parents about the following disorders: Apert syndrome, craniosynostosis, hemifacial microsomia, microtia, and Treacher Collins syndrome.

Cleft Palate Foundation

1218 Grandview Ave.
Pittsburgh, PA 15211
(412) 481-1376; (412) 481-0487; (800) 24-CLEFT (v/TTY)

PURPOSE: This Foundation is the "public service arm" of the American Cleft Palate-Craniofacial Association.
SERVICES: 24-hour hotline for information.
PUBLICATIONS: Examples include: *"The Genetics of Cleft Lip and Palate: Information for Families"; "Feeding an Infant with a Cleft"; "Cleft Lip and Palate—The First Four Years"; "Information about Dental Care of a Child with Cleft Lip and Palate"; "Cleft Lip and Palate—The Child from Three to*

Twelve Years"; "Information about Crouzon Syndrome"; "Information about Pierre Robin Sequence"; "Information about Treacher Collins Syndrome"; "Information about Submucous Cleft Palate." There is a small charge for most publications. Some publications available in Spanish.

FACES
National Association for the Craniofacially Handicapped
P.O. Box 11082
Chattanooga, TN 37401
(423) 266-1632: (800) 332-2373; (423) 267-3124 FAX

> PURPOSE: Serves children and adults with any type of facial or head disorder.
> SERVICES: Provides financial assistance to individuals with severe facial deformities resulting from congenital defects or accidents. Provides a resource file of available treatment centers.
> PUBLICATION: Quarterly newsletter, **Faces** (no charge).

La Leche League International
P.O. Box 4079
Schaumburg, IL 60168-4079
(847) 519-7730; (847) 519-0035 FAX
E-mail (orders only): OrderDepartment@llli.org
Web site: http//www.lalecheleague.org/

> PURPOSE: To provide education, information, support, and encouragement to women interested in breastfeeding.
> PUBLICATIONS: Has a variety of books, booklets, and fact sheets on breastfeeding in general, as well as on "Special Situations" such as breastfeeding a baby who is premature, chronically ill, or has a cleft lip or palate. Request a publications catalog.

Let's Face It
P.O. Box 29972
Bellingham, WA 98228-1972

> PURPOSE: To help people world-wide understand and solve the problems of living with a facial difference.
> SERVICES: Information, referral, and support.
> PUBLICATIONS: **Resources for People with Facial Difference,** described above ($3.00 S&H). Also reprints of articles on reconstructive surgery, self-esteem, and other issues.

March of Dimes
1275 Mamaroneck Ave.
White Plains, NY 10605
(914) 428-7100

> PURPOSE: To prevent birth defects and infant mortality through advocacy, research, and education.
> PUBLICATIONS: *"Cleft Lip and Palate Public Health Information Sheet"; "Birth Defects"; "Genetic Counseling."*

National Easter Seal Society
230 W. Monroe St., Ste. 1800
Chicago, IL 60606
(800) 221-6827; (312) 726-1494 FAX; (312) 726-4258 TTY

> PURPOSE: To help individuals with disabilities become as independent as possible.
> SERVICES: Operates a 24-hour hotline to answer questions and provide referrals (800 number above).
> PUBLICATION: *"Bright Promise: For Your Child with Cleft Lip and Cleft Palate."*

22.

Deafness and Hearing Loss

■ **BOOKS AND PERIODICALS**

Basic Information

Directory: Resources for Human Communication Disorders. Bethesda, MD: NIDCD Information Clearinghouse, 1996. 102 pp. Free.

> This is a directory of 129 associations and organizations in the United States that have an interest in deafness and other communication disorders. Most of the organizations listed are national in scope and focus on health issues relating to hearing, balance, smell, taste, voice, speech, and language. Descriptions include contact information, including e-mail and Internet addresses, descriptions of the organizations, and information about publications and meetings.

Freeman, Roger D., Clifton F. Carbin, and Robert J. Boese. ***Can't Your Child Hear? A Guide for Those Who Care about Deaf Children.*** Austin, TX: Pro-Ed, 1981. 368 pp. $26.00. ISBN 0-936104-40-6.

> This older book was written for parents of children with a severe to profound hearing loss that occurred before the development of speech. It offers answers to the most common questions about raising a deaf child, with an emphasis on information about communication approaches. The authors' preference is for the total communication approach.

Luterman, David M., with Mark Ross. ***When Your Child Is Deaf.*** Parkton, MD: York Press, 1991. 182 pp. $22.95. ISBN 0-912752-27-0.

> This would be an excellent first choice for hearing parents looking for an overview of issues related to parenting a child who is deaf or hard of hearing. Using a conversational style and many anecdotes about deaf children he has known, the author quickly reassures parents about typical emotions and concerns they may have as their child grows from infancy to young adulthood. There are chapters on dealing with initial emotions; parenting traps to avoid; fostering healthy, supportive relationships within the family; the measurement and types of hearing loss; and hearing aids and systems. In discussing educational options, the author admits to a bias against using ASL or the aural (auditory-verbal) method with young children, although information about all methods is given. The book does not include photographs or an index.

Marschark, Marc. ***Raising and Educating a Deaf Child: A Comprehensive Guide to the Choices, Controversies, and Decisions Faced by Parents and Educators.*** New York, NY: Oxford University Press, 1997. 256 pp. $25.00. ISBN 0-19-509467-0.

> This guide aims to give parents of deaf children the information they need to make decisions about a variety of educational and practical issues. The goal is to empower parents to help their child succeed in both academic and social circles, but to do so by making the choices that are right for their family and their child. Issues addressed include: types of schools and classroom placements; communication options; technological aids; social opportunities; and Deaf culture.

Medwid, Daria, and Denise Chapman Weston. **Kid-Friendly Parenting with Deaf and Hard of Hearing Children: A Treasury of Fun Activities toward Better Behavior**. Washington, DC: Gallaudet Press, 1995. 373 pages. $24.95. ISBN 1-56368-031-9.

> Written for parents of children aged 3 to 12, this book highlights play activities for teaching communication, social, and problem-solving skills. Also described are parenting techniques to aid in setting limits and changing behavior. Topics covered include setting limits and avoiding power struggles; fears and anxieties; and moodiness. A useful bonus is the "201 Rewards Children Love to Work For." A great resource for parents and teachers.

Ogden, Paul W. ***The Silent Garden: Raising Your Deaf Child.*** 2nd ed. Washington, DC: Gallaudet University Press, 1996. 304 pages. $29.95. ISBN 1-56368-058-0.

> For parents new to the world of deafness, this is a good source of information and support. The main focus is on making informed choices--about communication approaches, educational issues, technology—that will enable a deaf child to reach his or her potential. It also covers the basics about the types of hearing loss and emotions related to receiving the diagnosis of deafness in a child. Comments from parents of deaf children help reassure parents that it can be done.

Silent News. 133 Gaither Dr., Ste. E., Mount Laurel, NJ 08054-1710.

> A newspaper for deaf and hard of hearing people covering news, opinion, sports, and entertainment. Free sample available. A one-year subscription is $20.00 ($30.00 outside of the U.S.).

Education

Flexor, Carol, Denise Wray, Ron Leavitt, and Robert Flexor, eds. ***How the Student with Hearing Loss Can Succeed in College: A Handbook for Students, Families, and Professionals.*** 2nd ed. Washington, DC: Alexander Graham Bell, 1996. 304 pp. $24.95.

> In this useful book, college students who are deaf and hard of hearing are urged to become knowledgeable self-advocates in order to succeed in college. The book provides background information

about hearing loss, federal laws, and program accessibility, as well as guidelines on using support services and resources in college. Also included is helpful information on career and college planning (options for post secondary education, thinking about a career, selecting and financing an educational program).

Grant, June. *The Hearing Impaired: Birth to Six.* Boston: College-Hill Press, 1987. 182 pp. $29.95. ISBN 0-316-32402-7.

> The purpose of this older book is to help teachers "advance the quest for language facility" for young children with mild to profound hearing losses. A fair amount of the content is targeted directly at classroom teachers, but parents may find interesting the information on the nature of language; stages of language development and how they differ for children with hearing losses; elements of good preschool programs; and using creativity (the arts) to spark language learning.

Oberkotter, Mildred, ed. *The Possible Dream: Mainstream Experiences of Hearing-Impaired Students.* Washington, DC: Alexander Graham Bell, 1990. 66 pp. $7.95.

> This is a collection of essays written by student winners of AG Bell scholarships and their parents. The students, who use the oral method to communicate, write about the challenges and successes they have experienced living in the hearing world.

Smith, Maureen A., and Patrick Schloss. *Teaching Social Skills to Hearing-Impaired Students.* Washington, DC: Alexander Graham Bell, 1990. 203 pp. $21.95. ISBN 0-88200-169-8

> Written for parents and teachers of elementary to high school students with hearing loss, this guide offers suggestions for developing social competence. The book explains how to set goals and objectives, how to plan activities for teaching social skills, and how parents and teachers can work together to maximize learning.

Tucker, Bonnie Poitras. *IDEA Advocacy for Children Who Are Deaf or Hard-of-Hearing: A Question and Answer Book for Parents and Professionals.* San Diego: Singular Publishing, 1997. 134 pp. $14.95. ISBN 1-56593-896-8.

> This guide explains how the 1997 Amendments to the Individuals with Disabilities Education Act apply to deaf and hard-of-hearing students. In question-and-answer format, it also discusses issues that parents need to understand to be the most effective advocates for their child. Topics covered include developing the IEP, least restrictive environment, related services, private schools, discipline, dispute resolution, and infants and toddlers.

Communication Approaches

Included in this section are books that describe the methodology and rationale of one or more of the approaches currently used by deaf individuals to communicate. For practical manuals on signing, see "Sign Language and Alternative and Augmentative Communication" in Part I (p. 63).

Bornstein, Harry, ed. *Manual Communication: Implications for Education.* Washington, DC: Gallaudet University Press, 1990. 272 pp. $34.95. ISBN 0-930323-57-2.

> A comprehensive look at all of the sign systems currently used to educate deaf students is provided in this book. American Sign Language, Contact Sign (Pidgin Sign), Signed English, Signing Exact English, and Cued Speech are each described in detail by their acknowledged designer, administrator, or scholar. There are also interesting discussions of the history of sign language, conflicts about its use, and factors that affect the choice of manual communication systems.

Cornett, R. Orin, and Mary Elsie Daisey. ***Cued Speech Resource Guide for Parents of Deaf Children.*** Raleigh, NC: National Cued Speech Association, 1992. 832 pp. $27.50. ISBN 0-9633164-0-0.

> This comprehensive manual explores using cued speech--a method of augmenting speech reading with hand and mouth shapes or cues--as a communication option for children with hearing losses. The book covers the basics of cued speech, encouraging communication, speech reading, auditory training, educational issues, and family and peer relationships. Included are case histories of families who chose this method of communication.

Estabrooks, Warren. ***Auditory-Verbal Therapy for Parents and Professionals.*** Washington, DC: Alexander Graham Bell, 1994. 300 pp. $36.95.

> This is the basic text for parents and professionals interested in learning about auditory-verbal therapy--a method that emphasizes optimizing a child's listening skills so that he can listen, understand spoken language, and speak. Actual therapy sessions with infants and children of different ages are described, as well as sample activities. The book also explains AVT's aggressive methods of audiological management, considers the family-professional partnership, and discusses cochlear implants.

Lynas, Wendy. ***Communication Options in the Education of Deaf Children.*** San Diego: Singular Publishing, 1994. 117 pp. $32.50. ISBN 1-56593-373-7.

> The intent of this slim volume is to objectively examine three broad categories of communication approaches: Auditory-Oral, Total Communication, and Bilingual. For each approach, the author discusses how the approach works, the arguments in favor of it, the evidence supporting claims, and problems with the approach. Woven throughout the book are the author's thoughts on whether all deaf children *can* be taught to use speech as well as whether they *should*. Most of the references are to British Sign Language rather than to American Sign Language and the writing has a scholarly tone, but the book should still be of interest to North American parents who are evaluating communication options for their child.

Schein, Jerome D., and David A. Stewart. ***Language in Motion: Exploring the Nature of Sign.*** Washington, DC: Gallaudet University Press, 1995. 221 pp. $24.95. ISBN 1-56368-039-4.

> A blend of practical information on using sign language and theoretical and historical background of its use, this book is a fascinating introduction to the world of sign. American Sign Language (ASL) is the focus, although information on sign languages used around the world, Pidgin Sign English (contact signing), Cued Speech, and Manual Codes for English (MCE) is also provided. For readers interested in learning ASL, there are chapters on the components of signs and the grammar of ASL; fingerspelling alphabets (including why you should not use the ASL handshape for "t" in some foreign countries); and how to learn to sign. Also included are chapters on the history of sign language, on sign language interpreting, and on the place of ASL in Deaf culture.

Schwartz, Sue, ed. ***Choices in Deafness: A Parents' Guide to Communication Options.*** 2nd ed. Bethesda, MD: Woodbine House, 1996. 304 pp. $16.95. ISBN 0-933149-85-9.

> For families trying to decide which communication method to use with their child, this readable, unbiased guide is invaluable. At the heart of the book are chapters contributed by experts on the five communication approaches most commonly used by children who are deaf or hard of hearing: auditory verbal, bilingual-bicultural (ASL), cued speech, oral, and total communication. Following the descriptions of each communication approach are accounts written by families, and, in some cases, children, who have chosen to use that particular approach. Also included are helpful chapters on the nature and causes of hearing loss; audiological assessments; and cochlear implants. Useful appendices list publications and resources for further information.

Simmons-Martin, Audrey Ann, and Karen Glover Rossi. *Parents and Teachers: Partners in Language Development.* Washington, DC: Alexander Graham Bell, 1990. 386 pp. $27.95. ISBN 0-88200-167-1.

> The authors intend this guide to be "a comprehensive in-depth tutorial for parent-teacher partnership in fostering language development" in young children with hearing losses. By "language development," the authors are referring to the development of speech and listening skills through the oral approach. Topics covered include: stages of language development and objectives for parents to work on at each stage; adapting your parenting style to maximize language learning; helping your child develop listening skills; and ways of motivating young children to use and expand their language skills. Anecdotes about parents who successfully taught their children using the oral approach are woven throughout the book.

Tye-Murray, Nancy. *Cochlear Implants and Children: A Handbook for Parents, Teachers, and Speech and Hearing Professionals.* Washington, DC: Alexander Graham Bell, 1993. 189 pp. $26.95. ISBN 0-88200-173-6.

> This illustrated guide was written for families and professionals working with a child using the Nucleus 22-Channel cochlear implant. It explains what the implant is and how it works; potential benefits; helping the child adjust to it; and communication and academic goals for children in the classroom.

Winefield, Richard. *Never the Twain Shall Meet: Bell, Gallaudet, and the Communications Debate.* Washington, DC: Gallaudet University Press, 1987. 152 pp. $19.95. 1-56368-056-4.

> This book traces the controversy about which communication approach to use in educating the deaf to the nineteenth century, when Alexander Graham Bell and other oralists locked horns with Edward Miner Gallaudet and other sign language champions. The author also examines how this controversy still colors deaf education today.

Deaf Culture

DeafNation. P.O. Box 3521, Grand Rapids, MI 49501-3521. (616) 774-8162; (616) 774-8106 FAX.

> A monthly, full-color newspaper for the Deaf community. A one-year subscription is $19.95 ($45.00 outside of the U.S.).

Gannon, Jack R. *The Week the World Heard Gallaudet.* Washington, DC: Gallaudet University Press, 1989. 176 pp. $19.95. ISBN 0-930323-50-5.

> Liberally illustrated with black and white photographs, this book recounts the events that led to the appointment of Gallaudet University's first deaf president in 1988.

Moore, Matthew S., and Linda Levitan. 2nd ed. *For Hearing People Only.* Rochester, NY: MSM Productions, 1993. 336 pp. $19.95. 0-9634016-1-0.

> In Q&A format, this book sets out to answer "some of the most commonly asked questions about the Deaf community, its culture, and the 'Deaf Reality.'" A good introduction to Deaf culture issues and terminology.

Schein, Jerome D. *At Home Among Strangers.* Washington, DC: Gallaudet University Press, 1989. 254 pp. $24.95. ISBN 0-930323-51-3.

> This book by a long-time professor at Gallaudet University takes a close look at the Deaf community in the United States. Among the questions it sets out to answer are: "What is the Deaf community? Where is it? Who are its members? How did they come together? Why have they created the society

in the way they have? How do they conduct their affairs? In what direction is the Deaf community moving?" Along the way, the author examines the evolution of ASL; the nature and purpose of organizations for the Deaf; the role of the school in Deaf culture; and how the Deaf are treated on the job, and by the medical and legal establishment.

First Person Perspectives

Altman, Ellyn. *Talk with Me! Giving the Gift of Language and Emotional Health to the Hearing Impaired Child.* Washington, DC: Alexander Graham Bell, 1988. 222 pp. $19.95. ISBN 0-88200-163-9.

> In this book, the author writes as one parent to another about the important issues that she believes affect a child's social, language, and emotional development. Topics covered include: coping with emotions, language development and how parents can enhance it, teaching deaf children to speak and listen to the best of their abilities, self-esteem, and family life issues.

Bradford, Tom. *"Say That Again, Please!"* Dallas, TX: Bradford Publications, 1991. 370 pp. $16.95. ISBN 0-9630738-5-0.

> After beginning with a lighthearted look at his experiences living with a hearing loss, the author becomes an interviewer. He poses a series of questions about issues in deafness to a group of teachers, parents, and deaf persons and reports their responses in topical chapters. Some of the many topics discussed include: communication methods, hearing aids, academic skills, socialization, irritations with hearing people, irritations with deaf people, siblings, and dating and marriage.

Cohen, Leah Hager. *Train Go Sorry: Inside a Deaf World.* New York, NY: Vintage Books, 1994. 296 pp. $10.95. ISBN 0-679-76165-9.

> On the surface, this book is a fascinating inside look at a year in the life of students and staff at the Lexington School for the Deaf in Queens, New York. The book focuses on two deaf seniors—a Russian immigrant and a native New Yorker—exploring their struggles with themselves, their families, and society to maintain their own identities in a hearing world and to choose the direction *they* want their lives to take. Along the way, the author also weighs the pros and cons of controversial questions such as: Should all deaf schools be closed and all deaf children be mainstreamed in public schools, or will this sever "deaf children from a culture that offers them strength"? Is the cochlear implant of real benefit to anyone? Are deaf administrators and teachers always preferable to hearing staff in educating deaf children and young adults? The author spent her early years living in the Lexington School, as her father was an administrator; both of her paternal grandparents were deaf.

Fletcher, Lorraine. *Ben's Story: A Deaf Child's Right to Sign.* Washington, DC: Gallaudet University Press, 1988. 267 pp. $7.95. ISBN 0-930323-47-5.

> When Ben Fletcher was born profoundly deaf, the thinking in the local British schools was that signing would make a deaf child lazy and prevent him from learning to speak. As a result, Ben's parents were pressured into fitting him with hearing aids and an auditory trainer, and to working endlessly to teach him to listen and speak. Eventually, his parents went out on a limb and insisted that Ben be taught using first Total Communication and then British Sign Language (BSL). This story of how one family's dogged advocacy efforts and self-education finally led to a breakthrough in communication skills should be interesting to other parents who are unsure about the communication approach to use with their own children.

Forecki, Marcia Calhoun. *Speak to Me.* Washington, DC: Gallaudet University Press, 1985. 154 pp. $12.95. ISBN 0-930323-68-8.

> After her son, Charlie, was diagnosed as profoundly deaf at eighteen months, Marcia Forecki felt inadequate in many ways. She felt guilty that it had taken her so long to realize that Charlie could not hear; scornful of her early clumsy attempts at signing; ashamed that she had not thought to develop a name sign for him; overwhelmed because she was a single mother who had to work and eke out quality time with her son. Gradually, however, as Charlie was enrolled first in a hearing-impaired preschool classroom and then in a state school for the deaf, she began to regain her confidence in her abilities as a mother. That the author never lost her sense of humor is apparent in the self-deprecating but witty way she describes her difficulties in learning to parent a young deaf son.

Gray, Daphne, with Gregg Lewis. *Yes, You Can, Heather! The Story of Heather Whitestone, Miss America 1995.* Washington, DC: Alexander Graham Bell, 1995. 236 pp. $18.95.

> The mother of the first deaf Miss America here recounts her daughter's life story. Diagnosed with a profound hearing loss at 18 months, Heather Whitestone was encouraged to develop speech, dance, and otherwise excel in the hearing world. Not surprisingly, her achievements did not come without struggles and sacrifices from everyone in her family.

Kisor, Henry. *What's That Pig Outdoors: A Memoir of Deafness.* New York, NY: Viking Penguin, 1990. 270 pp. $10.95. ISBN 0-14-014899-X.

> When he was three, Henry Kisor lost his hearing to a bout of meningitis. He regained his communication skills through an unusual method named after its inventor, Miss Doris Mirrielees of Alabama. Using this method, Kisor's mother first taught him to read English words and sentences; then moved on to teach him speechreading and speaking. Kisor was well suited to the Mirrielees method, and was successfully mainstreamed from elementary school through graduate school with no special supports except preferential seating and note taking. Eventually he rose to become the book editor at the Chicago Sun-Times. Kisor writes of his successes in a modest yet witty manner. His story is a testament to his own persistence and motivation, as well as to his family's boundless support. His mother, for instance, refused to accept "that a deaf child should not be too ambitious, because the world will not allow him to achieve his goals." Kisor acknowledges feeling a stranger to Deaf Culture, and is unabashedly proud of fitting in and doing so well in the hearing world.

Sacks, Oliver. *Seeing Voices: A Journey into the World of the Deaf.* New York, NY: HarperCollins, 1989. 224 pp. $11.00. ISBN 0-06-097347-1.

> In the course of three long essays, Oliver Sacks explores a variety of issues related to deafness that fascinate him as a physician and a human being. Among the topics he discusses are: the relation of language to thought; the differences between how deaf and hearing children learn language; the controversy between manualists and oralists, both historically and currently; the mother's role in helping her child learn to communicate and think; different forms of sign; and the "Deaf President Now" campaign at Gallaudet University. The text is generously sprinkled with anecdotes about historical figures and people Dr. Sacks has personally known.

Schrader, Steven L. *Silent Alarm: On the Edge with a Deaf EMT.* Washington, DC: Gallaudet University Press, 1995. 140 pp. $17.95. ISBN 1-56368-044-4.

> This is the story of Steven Schrader's fifteen years as an emergency medical technician and firefighter. Although Schrader's severe hearing loss occasionally made it more difficult to do his job, it was mostly irrelevant and not a major obstacle to success in his chosen career.

Thomsett, Kay, and Eve Nickerson. ***Missing Words: The Family Handbook on Adult Hearing Loss.*** Washington, DC: Gallaudet University Press, 1993. 256 pp. $24.95. ISBN 1-56368-023-8.

> This is the personal account of an adult who slowly becomes deaf and the changes she faces in her life. Do's and don't's for dealing with a loved one's hearing loss—all learned from experience—are shared. There is also information on cochlear implants and on adaptations to the environment such as lighting, furniture placement, and acoustics. The coping suggestions from someone who has "been there" are a strongpoint of the book.

Zazone, Philip. ***When the Phone Rings, My Bed Shakes.*** Washington, DC: Gallaudet University Press, 1993. 295 pp. $22.95. ISBN: 1-56368-024-6.

> These are the memoirs of a sensitive and caring family doctor and professor of medicine who just happens to be deaf. The book focuses on Zazone's experiences as a student, a doctor, and a family man, and includes a great deal of detail about how Dr. Zazone interacts with his patients. A great read.

For Children

FICTION

Hodges, Candri. ***When I Grow Up.*** Hollidaysburg, PA: Jason & Nordic Publishers, 1995. 30 pp. $14.95. ISBN 0-944727-26-3.

> It is career day and Jimmy sees people of all ages who are either deaf or hard of hearing working at lots of different jobs. The message is that if you are deaf you can be anything you want to be. The story incorporates 24 signs.

Lakin, Patricia. ***Dad and Me in the Morning.*** Morton Grove, IL: Albert Whitman, 1994. 32 pp. $14.95. ISBN 0-8075-1419-5.

> Jacob and his father get up early one morning and walk to the beach to see the sun rise. Jacob is deaf, but he and his father have many special ways of communicating (beyond signing and speech reading) and the closeness between them is evident. The illustrations and the words used to describe what the two experience are very colorful. For preschoolers and early elementary grades.

Levi, Dorothy Hoffman. ***A Very Special Sister.*** Washington, DC: Gallaudet University Press, 1992. 36 pp. $9.95. ISBN 0-930323-96-3.

> Laura, who is deaf, is very excited when she learns she will soon be a big sister (she appears to be about six). But when her friends suggest that her mother might love the baby more if she is hearing, Laura becomes very depressed. When Laura discusses her concerns with her mother, her mother has the perfect answer for any child worried about being displaced by a younger brother or sister.

Litchfield, Ada B. ***A Button in Her Ear.*** Chicago, IL: Albert Whitman & Company, 1976. 32 pp. $14.95. ISBN 0-8075-0987-6.

> Angela is not hearing well, which leads to many misunderstandings with playmates and others. After a trip to the doctor and the audiologist, she is fitted with a hearing aid. By the end of the story, she is happily showing it off to her friends. Suitable for children in grades 2-4.

Martin, Ann M. ***Jessi's Secret Language.*** New York, NY: Scholastic, Inc., 1988. 148 pp. ISBN 0-590-41586-7. $3.99.

> In agreeing to babysit for the Braddock family several afternoons a week, Jessica Ramsey also commits herself to learning a new language. Matthew Braddock, age seven, is profoundly deaf and communicates with American Sign Language. His older sister, Haley, is sometimes embarrassed to be seen with a brother who talks with his hands and rides a special bus, but finds she can

discuss her feelings with Jessica, who is black and sometimes feels like an outsider too. Subplots about Jessi's lead in the community ballet, and a fellow ballet dancer who cannot communicate with her deaf sister, add interesting layers to the story. The book is number 16 in "The Baby-Sitters Club" series.

Peterson, Jeanne Whitehouse. *I Have a Sister, My Sister Is Deaf.* New York, NY: HarperCollins, 1977. 32 pp. $5.95. ISBN 0-06-443059-6.

> An older sister describes what it is like to have a little sister who is deaf, making it clear that her sister is more like other children than unlike them. The book is appropriate for children in early elementary school grades.

Riskind, Mary. *Apple Is My Sign.* Boston: Houghton Mifflin, 1981. 160 pp. $5.95. ISBN 0-395-65747-4.

> Ten-year-old Harry has spent all of his life on his family's apple farm in turn-of-the-century Pennsylvania. Everyone in the family is deaf and somewhat mistrustful of the hearing world. Harry's horizons are expanded when he is sent to the Bertie School for the Deaf in Philadelphia. Not only does he see his first motorcar, but he also learns that there is nothing odd or shameful about being deaf, and he starts to dream of becoming a teacher. When a hearing friend uses sign language to cheat during a spelling bee, he feels he has been taken advantage of, but eventually gains important insights into the ways that deaf and hearing people are alike. Throughout the book, conversations of deaf characters are given in sign order; useful for readers interested in understanding how English and ASL differ.

Scott, Virginia M. *Belonging.* Washington, DC: Gallaudet University Press, 1986. 176 pp. $2.95. ISBN 0-930323-33-5.

> Like all teenagers, fifteen-year-old Gustie puts a premium on "belonging" to the right crowd. When she contracts meningitis and loses her hearing, however, her world is turned upside down. Her parents and some of her teachers seem so hard to get along with, and her best friend rejects her. Eventually, with the help of a new boyfriend who has a deaf brother, Gustie begins to feel as if she fits in again.

NONFICTION

Abbott, Deborah, and Kisor, Henry. *One TV Blasting and a Pig Outdoors: A Concept Book.* Morton Grove, IL: Albert Whitman, 1994. 40 pp. $14.95. ISBN 0-8075-6075-8.

> The narrator of this illustrated book tells what it is like to live with a deaf father. He touches on sign language, speech reading, and TTY's, as well as on some of the humorous misunderstandings that can occur when there are both deaf and hearing family members. Appropriate for older elementary grades.

Okimoto, Jean Davies. *A Place for Grace.* Seattle, WA: Sasquatch Books, 1996. 32 pp. $7.95. ISBN 1-57061-069-X.

> This is the tale of Grace, a dog who is training to become a hearing dog. She is doing well, until she comes to the wake-up portion of the test and decides she would rather sleep. In the end, Grace graduates and goes home to alert her owner to ringing doorbells, phones, and other noises. Appropriate for children in preschool and early elementary grades.

Showers, Paul. *Ears Are for Hearing.* New York, NY: Thomas Y. Crowell, 1990. Not paginated. $12.95. ISBN 0-690-04718-5.

> A colorful and easy-to-read children's book that explains how we hear and what can happen to damage hearing. Great for kindergarten to fifth grade.

■ ORGANIZATIONS

Alexander Graham Bell Association for the Deaf
3417 Volta Place, N.W.
Washington, DC 20007-2778
(202) 337-5220 V/TTY; (202) 337-8270 FAX
E-mail: agbell2@aol.com
Web site: http//www.agbell.org

>PURPOSE: "To promote universal rights and optimal opportunities for people who are hearing impaired to communicate verbally through speaking, using residual hearing, speechreading, and processing both spoken and written communication.
>
>SERVICES: Responds to requests for information, promotes public awareness about hearing loss, offers financial aid and scholarships to individuals with hearing loss and their families, provides support and networking through local affiliates.
>
>PUBLICATIONS: Has an extensive catalog of their own and others' publications. Selections include: *Advocacy Handbook* ($15.00), *Auditory Training* ($21.95), *"Cochlear Implants for Children"* (free), *The Possible Dream: Mainstream Experiences of Hearing-Impaired Students* ($7.95), *25 Ways to Promote Spoken Language in Your Child with a Hearing Loss* ($6.00), *"Communication, Consistency, Caring: A Parent's Guide to Raising a Hearing-Impaired Child"* ($1.25), *"Oral Interpreting: Facts for Consumers"* ($1.00), *Families and Their Hearing-Impaired Children* ($9.95). Members receive *The Volta Review,* a research journal, and the magazine *Volta Voices* and a discount on book purchases.

American Deafness and Rehabilitation Association
P.O. Box 251554
Little Rock, AR 72225
(501) 868-8850 (V/TTY); (501) 868-8812 FAX

>PURPOSE: A professional organization dedicated to enhancing the quality of life with people who are deaf or hard of hearing.
>
>SERVICES: Information and referral about careers, university programs, job opportunities, deafness; advocacy; professional meetings and workshops.
>
>PUBLICATIONS: Publishes a quarterly journal, *JADARA,* and a quarterly newsletter; monographs.

American Society for Deaf Children
1820 Tribute Rd., Ste. A
Sacramento, CA 95815
(800) 942-2732 V/TTY
E-mail: asdc1@aol.com
Web site: http//www.educ.kent.edu/deafed/asdchome.html

>PURPOSE: A membership organization that acts as a clearinghouse for the exchange of information between parents and professionals and supports the use of sign language.
>
>SERVICES: Information and referral; local affiliates.
>
>PUBLICATIONS: A quarterly newsletter, *Endeavor,* covers educational and legislative issues.

Auditory/Verbal International
2121 Eisenhower Ave., Ste. 402
Alexandria, VA 22314
(703) 739-1049; (703) 739-0874

>PURPOSE: To promote the use of the auditory verbal approach to communication.

SERVICES: Information and referral about hearing loss and auditory verbal therapy.

PUBLICATIONS: Quarterly magazine.

Beginnings for Parents of Hearing Impaired Children

3900 Barrett Dr., Suite 100
Raleigh, NC 27609
(800) 541-4327; (919) 571-4846 FAX

PURPOSE: To provide unbiased counseling and provide resources for families who have children with hearing impairments.

SERVICES: Information and referral, advocacy, parent-to-parent connections.

PUBLICATIONS: *Beginnings,* a free quarterly newsletter.

Captioned Films & Videos Program

5000 Park St., North
St. Petersburg, FL 33709
(800) 237-6213; (800) 237-6819 TTY; (800) 538-5636 FAX
E-mail: nadcfv@aol.com

SERVICES: Provides captioned 16mm films and videos for free. S&H may be charged. Request their catalog and send for the films/videos on a 5-7 day loan basis.

Deafpride

1350 Potomac Ave., SE
Washington, DC 20005
(202) 675-6700

PURPOSE: An advocacy organization that works to educate deaf and hearing people about the rights of deaf people.

SERVICES: Holds educational programs, activities, workshops; offers interpreting services and speakers and panelists from the Deaf community.

PUBLICATIONS: Quarterly newsletter; position papers; booklet on access to medical services.

Hereditary Hearing Impairment Resource Registry

Boystown National Research Hospital
555 N. 30th St.
Omaha, NE 68131
(800) 320-1171

PUBLICATIONS: Has fact sheets on a number of hereditary causes of hearing loss, including Alport syndrome, branchio-oto-renal syndrome, neurofibromatosis, osteogenesis imperfecta, Stickler syndrome, Usher syndrome, and Waardenburg syndrome.

John Tracy Clinic

806 W. Adams Blvd.
Los Angeles, CA 90007
(800) 522-4582 (V/TTY); (213) 749-1651 FAX

PURPOSE: Supports and trains parents of children who are deaf or deaf-blind.

PUBLICATIONS: Offers two correspondence courses for parents of children with hearing losses (for ages birth to 18 months, and 18 months through 5 years); and one correspondence course for parents of children who are deaf-blind. The courses focus on communication needs, child development, and family relationships. Courses are offered in English and Spanish. Parents receive the correspondence courses free of charge; professionals pay a small fee. The Clinic also publishes a bulletin and other educational publications.

Meniere's Network

The Ear Foundation
1817 Patterson St.
Nashville, TN 37203
(800) 545-4327; 615-329-7807; 615-329-7935

PURPOSE: Promotes integration of individuals with hearing loss into the mainstream.

SERVICES: Information and referral, Support groups, hearing preservation, continuing education credits.

PUBLICATIONS: Publishes *Otoscope,* a free quarterly publication.

National Association of the Deaf

814 Thayer Ave.
Silver Spring, MD 20910
(301) 587-1788; (301) 587-1789 TDD; (301) 587-1791 FAX
E-mail: NADHQ@juno.com
Web site: http//www.nad.org

PURPOSE: A consumer organization that focuses primarily on grassroots advocacy and empowerment, captioned media, certification of American Sign Language and Deaf Studies professionals; information dissemination, legal assistance and youth leadership development.

SERVICES: information and referral services through its Public Information Center; handles legal issues related to deaf and hard of hearing individuals through its Law Center; disseminates information on legislative activities through its Government Affairs Unit; operates a Youth Program to support and guide deaf students.

PUBLICATIONS: *The NAD Broadcaster* (newspaper distributed to members), fact sheets, deaf awareness materials. The Deaf American Monograph series includes book-length publications on topics such as *Communication Issues Among Deaf People, Viewpoints on Deafness,* and *Deafness: Life & Culture*.

National Cued Speech Association

Nazareth College
4245 East Ave.
Rochester, NY 14618
(800) 459-3529

PURPOSE: To advocate for and support the use of cued speech.

SERVICES: Education about cued speech; information and referral.

PUBLICATIONS: Journal published annually. Membership: $25.00 a year.

National Information Center on Deafness

Gallaudet University
800 Florida Ave., NE
Washington, DC 20002-3695
(202) 651-5051; (202) 651-5052 TTY; (202) 651-5054 FAX
E-mail: nicd@gallux.gallaudet.edu
Web site: http//www.gallaudet.edu/~nicd

PURPOSE: "A centralized source of information about hearing loss and deafness. NCD collects, develops, and disseminates up-to-date information on deafness, hearing loss, organizations, and services for deaf and hard of hearing people."

SERVICES: Information and referral.

PUBLICATIONS: Offers many free and low-cost publications on the topics of Assistive Devices and Hearing Aids, Careers and Employment, Communication and Sign Language, Education, Gallaudet University, Health and Mental Health, Legal Issues, Parenting, and more. Request a publications catalog.

National Institute on Deafness and Other Communication Disorders (NIDCD)

Information Clearinghouse
1 Communication Ave.
Bethesda, MD 20892-3456
(800) 241-1044; (800) 241-1055 TTY; (301) 907-8830 FAX
E-mail: nidcd@aerie.com
Web site: http//www.nih.gov/nidcd/

PURPOSE: "Collects, produces, and disseminates information on normal and disordered processes of human communication."

SERVICES: Provides information and resource materials on hearing, balance, smell, taste, voice, speech, and language. Operates a database with materials on these subjects. Information specialists respond to professional and public inquiries by phone.

PUBLICATIONS: Include the **Directory** described above; *"Cochlear Implants Information Packet"*; *"Hearing and Hearing Loss Information Packet"*; *"Recent Research on Hereditary Deafness"*; *"Update on Developmental Speech and Language Disorders."* Publications are free.

Phonic Ear, Inc.

3880 Cypress Dr.
Petaluma, CA 94954-7600
(707) 769-1110; (707) 769-9624 FAX

PUBLICATIONS: Free publications include *"All about FM"*; *"Facts, Figures & FM: What Every Parent, Teacher, and Child Should Know about Listening and Learning"*; and *"Communication, Caring, Consistency: A Parent's Guide to Raising a Hearing Impaired Child."*

SHHH—Self Help for Hard of Hearing People, Inc.

7910 Woodmont Ave., Suite 1200
Bethesda, MD 20814
(301) 657-2248; (301) 657-2249 TTY

PURPOSE: A consumer-education organization that strives to develop acceptance of people with hearing loss and to promote education about hearing loss detection, management, and prevention of further loss.

SERVICES: Information and referral, local chapters.

PUBLICATIONS: Bimonthly journal; brochures on topics such as hearing aids, psychological effects of hearing loss, assertiveness for individuals with hearing loss. There is a charge for most publications.

TRIPOD

2901 N. Keystone St.
Burbank, CA 91504-1620
(818) 972-2080 V/TTY; (818) 972-2090

PURPOSE: To provide assistance to families raising children who are deaf or hard of hearing.

SERVICES: Information and referral.

PUBLICATIONS: Quarterly newsletter with information on child development, speech, and sign language; videos; information packets.

◼ CATALOG

Harris Communications
15159 Technology Dr.
Eden Prairie, MN 55344-7714
(800) 825-6758; (800) 825-9187 TTY; (612) 906-1099 FAX

> This company has an extensive catalog of publications and videos about deafness and hearing loss produced by a variety of publishers. Topics covered include: Children's Materials, Coping with Hearing Loss, Education, Deaf Culture, Parent's Resources, Sign Language, and more. Also sells assistive devices.

23.

Down Syndrome

■ BOOKS AND PERIODICALS

Basic Information

Cunningham, Cliff. ***Understanding Down Syndrome: An Introduction for Parents.*** Revised ed. Cambridge, MA: Brookline, 1996. 243 pp. $14.95. ISBN 0-57129-009-5.

> This fine guide presents an overview of some of the major issues facing families of young children with Down syndrome. Topics covered include: coping with emotions; family issues; causes; characteristics; personality and temperament; and development. Among the strong points of the book are the detailed explanations of the range of development in children with Down syndrome, possible cognitive limitations and strengths, and interpretating tests of mental ability. Weaker points for American readers may be the British slant and the lack of information about daily care concerns and special education. Much of the information in the book was drawn from studies of 200 young children with Down syndrome conducted by the author over the course of twenty years. Quotations from the families of the children involved in these studies are sprinkled throughout the book, and several pages of photographs are included.

Disability Solutions. 9220 S. W. Barbur Blvd., #119-179, Portland, OR 97219-5428. E-mail: dsolns@teleport.com

> This parent-friendly bimonthly newsletter is subtitled "A resource for families and others interested in Down syndrome and related disabilities." Issues are usually organized around a central theme such as sibling issues, writing better IEPs, curricular adaptations, or adaptive and alternative communication. Feature articles examine the issue in some depth, and may be written by parents or professionals. Each issue also includes useful resources related to the subject theme, as well as book reviews. Subscriptions are free. The current newsletter and back issues can also be downloaded from the web site: <http://www.teleport.com/~dsolns>.

Nadel, Lynn, and Donna Rosenthal, eds. ***Down Syndrome: Living and Learning in the Community.*** New York, NY: Wiley-Liss, 1995. 297 pp. $17.95. ISBN 0-471-02201-2.

> Compiled from papers and presentations from the Fifth International Down Syndrome Congress sponsored by the National Down Syndrome Society, this book covers a wide variety of subjects. Broad subject areas include: 1) personal observations; 2) behavior; 3) family issues; 4) development; 5) education; 6) medical care; and 7) community participation. Although some of the papers are technical, most are quite readable and informative. Several of the essays on inclusion will be of interest to parents of school-age children.

Pueschel, Siegfried M. ***A Parent's Guide to Down Syndrome: Toward a Brighter Future.*** Baltimore: Paul H. Brookes Publishing Co., 1990. 315 pp. $20.00 ISBN 1-55766-060-3.

> This guide is a general introduction to Down syndrome written and compiled by a prominent doctor in the field. The book covers issues from birth to adulthood, including causes, genetics, development, education, recreation, and future planning. This is a useful and informative resource. Photographs are included. (The book is also available in Spanish for $25.00; ISBN 84-345-2429-5.)

Rynders, John E., and J. Margaret Horrobin, ***Down Syndrome: Birth to Adulthood. Giving Families an EDGE.*** Denver: Love Publishing Co., 1995. 344 pp. $29.95. ISBN 0-89108-236-0.

> This useful, comprehensive guide provides practical and in-depth information about a wide range of issues facing parents and families of children and adults with Down syndrome. The authors bring together much research information, but do so in readable terms. A particular strength of the book is the amount of information provided about making the right educational decisions for your child. Quotes from parents whose children have been followed by the authors from infancy to young adulthood and lots of pictures make this book a good, general infancy-to-adulthood guide.

Selikowitz, Mark. ***Down Syndrome: The Facts.*** New York, NY: Oxford Press, 1997. 2nd ed. 176 pp. $17.95. ISBN 0-19-262662-0.

> Authored by an Australian developmental pediatrician, this guide provides a positive introduction to the topic of parenting a child with Down syndrome. Included are chapters on coping; what Down syndrome is and what causes it; development; health; the heart; behavior; early intervention and preschool; choosing a school; adolescence; adulthood; controversial treatments. Because the author is Australian, the chapters on educational options, and, in particular, inclusion may not be as useful to American readers as some of the other books reviewed in this section.

Stray-Gundersen, Karen, ed. ***Babies with Down Syndrome: A New Parents' Guide.*** 2nd ed. Bethesda, MD: Woodbine House, 1995. $15.95. 340 pp. ISBN 0-933149-64-6.

> Written by a team of parents and professionals, this compassionate book is intended as a first guide for parents of young children with Down syndrome, ages birth through five. While acknowledging the very real challenges that often confront parents of children with Down syndrome, the book emphasizes the many reasons for optimism that families of today have. Topics covered include: characteristics and causes; coping emotionally; medical concerns and treatments; daily care; family life; development; early intervention; and legal rights and benefits. Each chapter concludes with parent statements—quotations from parents about their experiences and emotions raising a child with Down syndrome. Many candid photographs of children are included. A glossary, reading list, and listings of state, national, and iternational resources make up the appendices. (The book is also available from the same publisher in Spanish; ISBN 0-933149-91-3.)

Education

Hanson, Marci. *Teaching the Infant with Down Syndrome: A Guide for Parents and Professionals.* 2nd ed. Austin, TX: PRO-ED, 1987. 268 pp. $29.00. ISBN 0-89079-103-1.

> First published in 1977 and updated in 1987, this helpful manual explains many different ways for parents (and professionals) to work with or "teach" babies with Down syndrome up to about the age of three. The book focuses on what is now commonly called "early intervention," and provides many parent-infant activities aimed at fostering good development. Included is information on teaching children with Down syndrome in general, as well as strategies for teaching specific gross motor, cognitive and fine motor, communication, and social and self-help skills. Many photos are included, but they appear somewhat dated.

Oelwein, Patricia Logan. *Teaching Reading to Children with Down Syndrome: A Guide for Parents and Teachers.* Bethesda, MD: Woodbine House, 1995. 370 pp. $16.95. ISBN 0-933149-55-7.

> The author shares her twenty-plus years of experience teaching students with Down syndrome to read in this clearly written and practical manual. She begins by describing learning characteristics of children with Down syndrome, and discussing in a general way teaching techniques that are helpful. She then discusses how to teach children (or adults) with Down syndrome how to read using a sight-word-based individualized approach. The method makes use of many homemade games, as well as flashcards which are provided in the appendix. Many photographs of and anecdotes about children the author has worked with are included.

Teaching Strategies for Children with Down Syndrome: A Resource Guide (K-3). Calgary, Alberta: Ups and Downs and The PREP Program, 1996. 60 pp. $20.00.

> This friendly little guide was designed to introduce teachers to Down syndrome and to some strategies that often work when teaching young children with Down syndrome. The book covers typical strengths and needs in many areas, including Communication Skills, Basic Concepts, Self-Help Skills, Social Interaction, and Computers, and gives a few examples of accomodations to try. The section on accomodations for Graphic Skills (printing and using scissors) offers perhaps the most specific help. This is a great overview for parents and teachers new to the world of Down syndrome.

Motor Skills

Burns, Yvonne, and Pat Gunn. *Down Syndrome: Moving Through Life.* Co-published: London: Chapman & Hall; San Diego: Singular Publishing Group, Inc., 1993. 223 pp. $44.75. ISBN 0-412-46180-3.

> Although expensive for a paperback, this book provides useful information about the gross and fine motor skills of children with Down syndrome from birth to adulthood. Written and compiled by an Australian therapist and special educator, the book explains the causes of motor problems and offers advice and activities. Most of the activities provided are for young children; for older children and young adults, the authors mainly describe characteristic problems with gross and fine motor skills. There is some technical language, but parents with some background or exposure to physical therapy should be able to use this book.

Share, Jack, and Ron French. *Motor Development of Children with Down Syndrome: Birth to Six Years.* Kearney, NE: Educational Systems Assoc., 1993. 140 pp. $35.00. ISBN 1-878276-46-8.

> This workbook presents activities for parents and professionals to use with young children with Down syndrome to encourage their motor development. Exercises are presented with the goal, the expected age to acquire the skill, and the suggested activities and exercises. The resource information at the back of the book is quite outdated.

Winders, Patricia C. *Gross Motor Skills in Children with Down Syndrome: A Guide for Parents and Professionals.* Bethesda, MD: Woodbine House, 1997. 236 pp. $16.95. ISBN 0-933149-81-6.

> For parents of children with Down syndrome aged birth through age six, this is a goldmine of information about enhancing motor development. The author explains the physical and medical problems that may interfere with motor development, then provides step-by-step instructions for working with a child to acquire motor skills appropriate to his developmental stage. Skills run the gamut from head control, rolling, sitting, and crawling, to walking, kicking a ball, using stairs, jumping, and riding a tricycle. Many clear photographs accompany the activities described. An appendix lists the age range at which children with Down syndrome normally acquire each motor skill.

Communication Skills

Communicating Together. P.O. Box 6395, Columbia, MD 21045-6395. (410) 995-0722; (410) 997-8735 FAX.

> This bimonthly newsletter edited by Dr. Libby Kumin is devoted to speech and language issues for parents of children with Down syndrome. The newsletter is $20 per year in the U.S.; $25/year U.S. funds (outside USA).

Kumin, Libby. *Communication Skills in Children with Down Syndrome: A Guide for Parents.* Bethesda, MD: Woodbine House, 1994. 241 pp. $14.95. ISBN 0-933149-53-0.

> Providing the foundation for good, strategic planning for speech and language intervention is the goal of this handy guide. The author first describes typical communication problems in children with Down syndrome, and then offers suggestions for optimizing communication development at different developmental stages, from birth through the elementary school years. Many home activities for working on specific speech and language goals are included for each age range. The author also discusses how speech-language pathologists assess and treat communication difficulties, and offers tips for developing strong parent-professional partnerships. A Spanish translation of the book is available from the publisher for $20.00.

Medical Concerns

Marino, Bruno, and Siegfried M. Pueschel. *Heart Disease in Persons with Down Syndrome.* Baltimore, MD: Paul H. Brookes Publishing Co., 1996. 240 pp. $59.00. ISBN 1-55766-224-X.

> This is a collection of papers from the May 1992 International Congress on Heart Disease in Down Syndrome, held in Rome, Italy. Written primarily for pediatric cardiologists, pediatricians, and other health professionals, the text covers congenital heart malformations and anomalies and surgical interventions.

Neill, Catherine A., Edward B. Clark, and Carleen Clark. *The Heart of a Child: What Families Need to Know about Heart Disorders in Children.* Baltimore: Johns Hopkins University Press, 1992. 331 pp. $24.95. ISBN 0-8018-4234-4.

> Two physicians and a nurse teamed together to write this comprehensive and readable guide to heart disorders in children. Chapters cover background information on how the heart works and how heart defects are diagnosed, as well as detailed information on all of the major types of heart defects in children and their treatment. A chapter on Children with Multiple Handicaps lists the syndromes commonly associated with heart defects and discusses special considerations in planning treatment and long-term care. Many helpful illustrations and case stories are included.

Pueschel, Siegfried M., and Jeanette K. Pueschel, eds. *Biomedical Concerns in Persons with Down Syndrome.* Baltimore: Paul H. Brookes Publishing Co., 1992. 320 pp. $48.00. ISBN 1-55766-089-1.

> This compilation of articles about medical issues in people with Down syndrome is useful reading for parents who have a medical background or who have done extensive reading on the subject. It is not useful as a basic source of information for lay parents, but may be of interest to those who want indepth information on seizures, orthopedic concerns, heart problems, or other medical issues. This book could be recommended by parents to their pediatricians to help them learn more about the medical treatment of patients with Down syndrome.

Van Dyke, D.C., Phillip Mattheis, Susan Eberly, and Janet Williams, eds. *Medical & Surgical Care for Children with Down Syndrome: A Guide for Parents.* Bethesda, MD: Woodbine House, 1995. 395 pp. $14.95. ISBN 0-933149-54-9.

> Written specifically for parents, this is a one-stop source of information about the most common medical and healthcare problems in individuals with Down syndrome. Numerous professionals contributed to this book, each with their special working knowledge; each with their special talent to share about medical issues. The book covers the full range of medical issues: heart, skin, eye, ear, nose, throat, orthopedic, thyroid, and neurological problems are just a few of the conditions discussed. There are also chapters on alternative therapies, anesthesia and surgical concerns, and nutrition. A great list of resources is provided.

Adolescent and Adult Issues

Lawrence, Patricia, Roy I. Brown, Josephine Mills, and Irene Estay. *Adults with Down Syndrome: Together, We Can Do It.* North York, Ontario, Canada: Captus Press, Inc., 1993. 130 pp. $10.00 (plus $5.00 for U.S. shipping). ISBN 1-895712-28-9.

> Written for families with adult-age members with Down syndrome, this short book draws on the expertise of the authors as well as interviews with families that include an individual with Down syndrome. Topics discussed include home living, wellness, work, residential options, leisure and social activities, and friendship and relationships. The book is intended to promote discussion of the often-difficult issues of the adult with Down syndrome.

Pueschel, Siegfried, and Maria Sustrova. *Adolescents with Down Syndrome: Toward a More Fulfilling Life.* Baltimore: Paul H. Brookes Publishing Co., 1997. 396 pp. $35.95. ISBN 1-55766-281-9.

> Through twenty-five separately authored articles, this book explores numerous issues surrounding adolescence and Down syndrome. Divided into five sections—Health and Physical Development; Behavioral, Psychologic, and Psychiatric Issues; Education; Life in the Workplace; and Life in the Community—the book is written mostly from the perspective of professionals, but parents with a good knowledge background will find useful information here.

Research

Down Syndrome Quarterly. Samuel J. Thios, Ph.D., Editor, Denison University, Granville, OH 43023. (614-587-6338); (614-587-6338). E-mail: THIOS@DENISON.EDU

> This quarterly journal is "devoted to advancing the state of knowledge on Down syndrome and will cover all areas of medical, behavioral, and social scientific research." It contains original reports of research, as well as articles summarizing previous research. Frequently, reviews of current books on Down syndrome are included, as well as abstracts or references to recently published research on Down syndrome. Portions of the journal may be tough going for parents without a strong background in the subject area, but parents who are interested in keeping up to date on the latest research will want to subscribe or find a copy in the library. A one-year subscription for individuals is $24.00 in the U.S. and $30.00 in Canada and Mexico.

First Person Perspectives

Berube, Michael. *Life As We Know It: A Father, a Family, and an Exceptional Child.*
New York, NY: Pantheon Books/Random House, 1996. 284 pp. $24.00. ISBN 0-679-44223-5.

> On one level, this is the story of the first four years in the life of Jamie Berube, a little boy with
> Down syndrome. There are vignettes about his birth, medical problems, language development,
> and interactions with his older brother. On another level, the book is an indepth analysis of how
> having a son with Down syndrome has changed the author's thinking. The author uses his son's
> story as a jumping off point to expound upon human differences, prenatal testing, special educa-
> tion, society's views of disability, and other issues. Some readers may find the philosophizing
> overly cerebral; others may find it thought-provoking.

Josephson, Gretchen. *Bus Girl.* Cambridge, MA: Brookline Books, 1997. 107 pp. $14.95.
ISBN 1-57129-041-9.

> The poems in this fascinating collection were written over the course of 25 years, between the author's
> teens and early 40s. Gretchen Josephson, who happens to have Down syndrome, addresses universal
> themes with her spare, unrhymed poetry. She writes of love, both requited and frustrated, of peace, of
> the beauty of nature, of death. There are poems that are frankly autobiographical—about working as
> a bus girl in a tea room, her travels, her relationship with her parents—and others that raise philo-
> sophical or spiritual questions. The book, which was edited by Lula Lubchenco and Allen Crocker,
> succeeds both as a window into the thoughts and feelings of a young woman with Down syndrome, and
> also as a collection of thoughtful and moving poems to be enjoyed in their own right.

Kingsley, Jason, and Mitchell Levitz. *Count Us In: Growing Up with Down Syndrome.*
San Diego: Harcourt, Brace & Company, 1994. 183 pp. $9.95. ISBN 0-15-622660-X.

> In this unique book, Jason Kingsley and Mitchell Levitz, two highly accomplished men with Down
> syndrome, share their life stories and their dreams for the future. Kingsley and Levitz discuss a
> wide variety of issues that affect their lives, including society's perception of people with Down
> syndrome, politics, independence, and relationships.

Rogers, Dale Evans. *Angel Unaware.* Grand Rapids, MI: Fleming H. Revell, 1984. 94 pp. $8.99.
ISBN: 0-8007-5434-4.

> Originally published in 1953, this slim volume is a biography of sorts of the author's daughter,
> Robin, who was born with Down syndrome. After Robin died of an inoperable heart defect at age
> two, Dale Evans (of the Roy Rogers-Dale Evans western show) wrote this book from her daughter's
> perspective. Robin "explains" why God sent her to earth and narrates her return to heaven. Chris-
> tians may find this book's message uplifting.

Stallings, Gene, with Sally Cook. *Another Season: A Coach's Story of Raising an Exceptional
Son.* Boston: Little, Brown, 1997. 216 pp. $22.95. ISBN 0-316-81196-3.

> Gene Stallings, football coach at the University of Alabama, dreamed of having a son who would
> be an athletic superstar. In 1962, when his only son, John Mark, was born with Down syndrome,
> he and his wife were crushed. On top of everything, John Mark was diagnosed with a serious
> inoperable heart defect, and was not expected to live past one. As he relates his family's life with
> "Johnny" over the past 35 years, Stallings is very open about his own and others' ambivalent
> feelings about having a child with Down syndrome in an era when there was little public accep-
> tance of differences. He comes across as a loving family man who was just as proud of his four
> daughters for teaching John Mark to walk, tie his shoes, and ride a bike as he was of John Mark
> for learning these skills. The book provides a sobering reminder of how far society has come from
> the days when institutionalization was recommended for babies with "mongolism" and early in-

tervention was a foreign concept. Interwoven with John Mark's story are highlights from Stallings's coaching careers at Texas A&M and Alabama and with the Houston Oilers.

Trainer, Marilyn. ***Differences in Common: Straight Talk on Mental Retardation, Down Syndrome, and Life.*** Bethesda, MD: Woodbine House, 1991. 231 pp. $14.95. ISBN 0-933149-40-9.

> The essays in this collection were written over the course of 25 years by a mother with an inimitable way of looking at the rewards and challenges of raising a child with Down syndrome. Essays about her son's infancy and childhood tackle subjects such as grappling with your emotions; early school experiences; the sometimes unintentional humor in inappropriate behavior; the "up" side of having a child with Down syndrome; and society's perceptions of individuals with disabilities. Essays about her son's adolescence and early adulthood look at issues such as sibling involvement; the risks that go with independence; friendships; abuse; weight problems; and the transition from school to work. Some essays are humorous; others more somber or philosophical. All are interesting and insightful.

For Children

FICTION

Becker, Shirley. ***Buddy's Shadow.*** Exton, PA: Jason & Nordic Publishers, 1991. 30 pp. $7.95. ISBN 0-944727-08-5.

> Buddy, a young child with Down syndrome, feels lonely and wants to have a best friend of his own. He decides to save up to buy a puppy for a companion. Although the story has some troubling elements, it does show Buddy saving money and being responsible for his new pet. This illustrated book is appropriate for preschoolers and slightly older children.

Booth, Zilpha. **Finding a Friend.** Mount Desert, ME: Windswept House Publishers, 1996. 36 pp. $8.95. ISBN 1-883650-32-1.

> Through text and illustrations, this book for children in early elementary grades tells an interesting story of friendship. Eight-year-old Andy lives on a large orchard and eagerly awaits the arrival of a new family with a boy his age, only to learn that his new playmate, Mike, has Down syndrome. This small book does a good job of tracing the developing relationship of these two boys and explores how Mike's Down syndrome affects their friendship.

Buchanan, Dawna Lisa. ***The Falcon's Wing.*** New York, NY: Orchard Books, 1992. 131 pp. $13.95. ISBN 0-531-05986-3.

> After her mother's death, Bryn, 12, and her father move from Ohio to Ontario to stay with Aunt Pearl. Bryn is surprised to learn that her aunt has a fourteen-year-old daughter, Winnie, who happens to have Down syndrome. At first, Bryn has a difficult time adjusting to living in Canada and to her cousin's differences. By the end of the novel, she has gained new understanding about many things—including mental retardation, love, and human nature. The characters in this novel are extremely well fleshed out and believable, and the evolution of the relationship between Bryn and her cousin with Down syndrome seems very genuine. For ages 9 through 14.

Christopher, Matt. ***Fighting Tackle.*** Boston: Little, Brown & Co., 1995. 147 pp. $3.95. ISBN 0-316-13794-4.

> One of the long series of Matt Christopher sport stories, ***Fighting Tackle*** stars Terry and his brother Nicky, who has Down syndrome. Terry learns lessons about adjusting to change on his football team and in his life with help from his brother. Although a little contrived, this young adult book does weave a main character—an athletic child with Down syndrome—into a story football-minded children will like.

Dodds, Bill. *My Sister Annie.* Honesdale, PA: Boyds Mills Press, 1993. 94 pp. $14.95.
ISBN 1-56397-114-3.

> Charlie is an eleven-year-old with lots on his mind: the championship baseball game, a girl he has
> a big crush on, a club he really wants to join, and his big sister, Annie, who has Down syndrome.
> Through this story, Charlie expresses many emotions siblings of children with Down syndrome
> may feel and comes to new insights about his sister and his priorities. The book is recommended
> for ages 9 through 14.

Fitzgerald, John, and Lyn Fitzgerald. *Barnaby's Birthday.* New York, NY: Macmillan/McGraw Hill
(SRA), 1994. 16 pp. $11.30. ISBN 0-383-03618-6.

> In rhyming verse, this colorfully illustrated book for the very young describes children arriving at
> Barnaby's party, Barnaby opening presents, and blowing out his birthday cake candles. Although
> it is difficult to tell from the illustrations that Barnaby has Down syndrome (the book's cataloging
> information states that he has Down syndrome), the book does a good job conveying just how
> typical Barnaby really is.

Fleming, Virginia. *Be Good to Eddie Lee.* New York, NY: Putnam, 1993. $15.95. 32 pp.
ISBN 0-399-21993-5.

> Christy's mom tells her to be good to Eddie Lee, a neighbor boy with Down syndrome, but Christy
> secretly suspects that he's one of God's "mistakes." One summer day when Eddie Lee joins her in
> a walk through the woods, however, Christy realizes that Eddie Lee is far more perceptive than
> she ever imagined. This charming story of friendship illustrated in full color is appropriate for
> children in lower elementary school grades.

Haines, Sandra. *Becca and Sue Make Two.* Boise, ID: Writer's Press, 1995. 32 pp. $6.99.
ISBN 1-885101-15-5.

> This colorfully illustrated children's book looks at the friendship between Becca and her best friend, Sue,
> who has Down syndrome. Through a shared school music project, Becca and Sue learn about differences.
> The book has a positive tone, but is not very believable in how it explains Sue's Down syndrome.

Harris, Margaret L. **Adventures in Wonderland.** Minneapolis, MN: Parent Advocacy Coalition for
Educational Rights Center Inc., (PACER). 36 pp. Call for price.

> This is a delightful little book with charming illustrations written by a girl called Maggie, who has
> Down syndrome. It is a take-off on *Alice in Wonderland,* with some of the same characters, but
> the story is definitely Maggie's—a fun read.

Hatch, Ann, and Randy Hatch. *Tommyelf in the City of Love.* Salt Lake City: Buffalo River Press,
1995. 32 pp. $16.95. ISBN 1-887727-00-0.

> In this fantasy book for all ages, Tommy and his friends are whisked away from a drab institu-
> tion by a mysterious elfwoman. The children are magically transported to the North Pole. Here
> Tommy lives with Santa and the elves, and finds family, love, and a vocation. Photographs of
> children with Down syndrome are incorporated into the colorful illustratrations. Although the
> story involves much fantasy, it is uplifting.

Klein, Lee. *Are There Stripes in Heaven?* Mahwah, NJ: Paulist Press, 1994. 32 pp. $4.95.
ISBN 0-8109-6618-6.

> Patrick's sister Colleen, who has Down syndrome, has a knack for saying quirky or "special"
> things. At church, Colleen teaches a lesson of understanding to two girls who are uncomfortable
> with and rude to Colleen. Although Patrick resists going to church because he would rather be at
> the video arcade, he too learns to appreciate his sister's gift of expression.

Kneeland, Linda. *Cookie.* Exton, PA: Jason & Nordic Publishers, 1989. 30 pp. $7.95.
ISBN 0-944727-05-0.

> Although the central character in this illustrated children's book is not identified as having
> Down syndrome, the communication problems presented are common to children with Down
> syndrome. Molly has limited speech and gets frustrated expressing her wants and needs. But
> with her speech therapist, she learns signing, and things change for the better. This book for
> preschoolers and slightly older children is useful in showing the process of learning signs and
> working with a speech therapist.

Litchfield, Ada B. *Making Room for Uncle Joe.* Morton Grove, IL: Albert Whitman & Co., 1984.
28 pp. $12.95. ISBN 0-8075-4925-5.

> Although it contains some dated material, this book shows the dynamics of a family's adjustment
> to the arrival of Uncle Joe, an adult with Down syndrome who comes to live with his sister (and
> her family with three children) when the institution he lives in is closed. After a rocky start, each
> child learns there is much to like about their uncle. For ages 7-10.

Lott, Brett. *Jewel.* New York, NY: Pocket Books, 1991. 358 pp. $9.00. ISBN 0-671-74039-3.

> Teenagers may enjoy this engrossing adult novel. The book follows Brenda Kay from her birth in
> 1943 in a rural Southern town where little is known about Down syndrome, through a family
> move to California and a chance at real education and a real future. Almost everything positive
> that happens in the novel is sparked by the determination and love of Jewel, Brenda Kay's mother.
> The book is a memorable journey through history, through acceptance, and through the evolution
> of a strong-willed family, and not to be missed by parents and teens who like a good read.

Lowell, Melissa. *The Winning Spirit.* New York, NY: Skylark Books/Bantam Books, 1995. 121 pp.
$3.50. ISBN 0-553-48321-8.

> Nikki Simon has never met someone with mental retardation until her skating club decides to
> train for a competition with some Special Olympians. When Nikki is paired with Carrie, a thir-
> teen-year-old with Down syndrome, she feels uncomfortable until she begins to see that Carrie is
> a dedicated and graceful skater. As the two girls practice together and become more of a team,
> Nikki learns about the perils of having expectations that are too low or too high, and also that
> winning is not always the most important thing. This book does not provide a clear understanding
> of how Down syndrome typically affects physical and cognitive skills, but it emphasizes attitudes
> that many parents of children with disabilities wish their children's friends and classmates to
> have. Part of the "Silver Blades" series, the book is recommended for ages 9-12.

Martin, Ann M. *Dawn and Whitney, Friends Forever.* New York, NY: Scholastic, Inc., 1994.
144 pp. $3.99. ISBN 0-590-48221-1.

> Dawn Schafer is hired as an afternoon companion for twelve-year-old Whitney Cater, who has
> Down syndrome. Whitney is under the impression that Dawn is her friend, pure and simple,
> which predicatably leads to hurt feelings when she discovers the truth. Despite the stares and
> rude remarks directed their way when they go out in public, Dawn comes to view Whitney as a real
> friend who is fun to be around. The description of Whitney's disability is tastefully handled, with
> references to her "careful" way of speaking and to Dawn's impression that the grown-up part of
> Whitney's mind could only grow up so much. The book is #77 in "The Baby-Sitters Club" series.

Rabe, Berniece. *Where's Chimpy?* Morton Grove, IL: Albert Whitman & Co., 1988. 28 pp. $5.95.
ISBN 0-8075-8928-4.

> In this endearing book, Misty, a young girl with Down syndrome recalls her day as she tries to
> remember where she lost her stuffed pet monkey, Chimpy. Filled with wonderful photographs, the

book subtly presents a child with Down syndrome as the central character without drawing undue attention to it. The book is appropriate for preschoolers and children in early elementary grades.

Rheingrover, Jean Sasso. ***Veronica's First Year.*** Morton Grove, IL: Albert Whitman & Co., 1996. 24 pp. $12.95. ISBN 0-8075-8474-6.

> This illustrated children's book traces the birth of Veronica, a baby with Down syndrome, through her first birthday. Her family's reactions to her birth and her brother's relationship with her are portrayed in words and pictures. Suitable for ages 5-10.

Schwier, Karin Melberg. ***Idea Man.*** Eastman, Quebec: Diverse City Press, 1997. 43 pp. $10.00. ISBN 1-896230-09-1.

> Erin is angry when her parents leave her overnight with family friends. The family's older son, Jim, is in the "dummy class" at school and better known as the Dork. Erin's worst fears are realized when two girls from her seventh grade class witness Jim giving her a hug. After Jim helps Erin with a creative writing homework assignment, however, she begins to see her mistake in judging Jim based on what others say. A good book to get middle schoolers thinking about the importance of being sensitive to others' feelings and looking beneath surface differences.

Shaw, Lou. ***Honor Thy Son.*** Nashville, TN: Abingdon Press, 1994. 180 pp. $12.95. ISBN 0-687099-82-X.

> Teenaged mystery lovers may enjoy this tale of false accusations and family ties. The son in the title is a young man with Down syndrome who is constantly showing his Dad his smarts in searching for a solution to a murder mystery. The author, who has a daughter with Down syndrome, portrays the son and his relationship with his father very realistically.

Testa, Maria. ***Thumbs Up, Rico!*** Morton Grove, IL: Albert Whitman and Co., 1994. 39 pp. ISBN 0-8075-7906-8.

> Three short stories are told from the viewpoint of Rico, a young teen with Down syndrome who enjoys basketball and doing things with his many friends. Although the book may serve as an interesting starting point for discussion about inclusion, readers may wonder why Rico talks more fluently and articulately than teens with Down syndrome they are likely to know, and may be turned off by the unflattering color illustrations of Rico. For upper elementary grades.

NONFICTION

Cairo, Shelley, Jasmine Cairo, and Tara Cairo. ***Our Brother Has Down's Syndrome: An Introduction for Children.*** Willowdale, Ontario, Canada: Annick Press, 1990. $14.95 (Hardcover). ISBN 0-920303-30-7. $4.95 (Paperback). ISBN 0-920303-31-5.

> This is a beautiful book, and is still one of the best books for introducing Down syndrome to siblings, friends, and schoolmates. It is written for children aged about 4-8, but there is not an adult in the world who will not enjoy the photographs of Jai, a little boy with Down Syndrome. The authors, Jai's sisters, begin the book with a simple and clear explanation of Down syndrome. Then they describe Jai, his strengths and needs, and how they help him. Jai's sisters talk about their feelings, too.

Carter, Alden R. ***Big Brother Dustin.*** 30 pp. $14.95. Morton Grove, IL: Albert Whitman & Co., 1997. ISBN 0-8075-0715-6.

> This book, illustrated with photographs, focuses on Dustin, a young boy with Down syndrome whose disability is not mentioned in the story. The book tracks Dustin's efforts to choose a name for his yet-to-be-born sister. There is also a seven-page "album" in the back of the book containing photographs of Dustin and his new sister, MaryAnn. For preschoolers and younger elementary ages.

■ ORGANIZATIONS

The Arc of the United States
500 E. Border St., Ste. 300
Arlington, TX 76010
(817) 261-6003; (817) 277-0553 (TTY)
E-mail: thearc@metronet.com
Web site: http//TheArc.org/welcome.html

> PURPOSE: The Arc (formerly the Association for Retarded Citizens) works to improve the lives of all children and adults with mental retardation and their families.
>
> SERVICES: Information and referral about mental retardation, the Arc's programs, and local chapters. Advocates for inclusions of individuals with mental retardation in community life; fosters research and education regarding prevention of mental retardation.
>
> PUBLICATIONS: Has an extensive publications catalog, which includes many fact sheets (free with a self-addressed, stamped envelope) about specific topics related to mental retardation. *"An Overview of Down Syndrome,"* by Siegfried Pueschel, M.D., is $3.50.

Association for Children with Down Syndrome
2616 Martin Ave.
Bellmore, NY 11710
(516) 221-4700; (516) 221-4311 FAX
E-mail: info@acds.org
Web site: http//www.acds.org

> PUBLICATIONS: Offers a variety of books, manuals, and videos, including a paper on ADD and Down syndrome, a movement and dance curriculum, a children's book about preschoolers with Down syndrome, publications on developmental issues, and a newsletter. Request a publications list.

Canadian Down Syndrome Society
811 Fourteenth St., NW
Calgary, Alberta T2N 2A4
Canada
(403) 270-8500; (403) 270-8291 FAX

> PURPOSE: To enhance the quality of life for people with Down syndrome, to increase public awareness of Down syndrome, to provide information and resources about Down syndrome, and to build a communication network among all people with interests relevant to Down syndrome.
>
> SERVICES: Annual conference, support network and chapters across Canada, newsletters, and information clearing house.
>
> PUBLICATIONS: CDSS publishes several useful booklets, including *"Your Baby: Information about Down Syndrome"; "Preventative Medical Guidelines for Children with Down Syndrome"; "Annotated Bibliography of Journal Articles on Down Syndrome";* and *"Sexuality, Relationships, and Adolescents with Down Syndrome."* Call to request their Resource Catalog.

National Association for Down Syndrome (NADS)
P.O. Box 4542
Oak Brook, IL 60522-4542
708/325-9112
Web site: http//www.nads.org/

> PURPOSE: To promote the growth and development of individuals with Down syndrome and encourage research into Down syndrome. This membership organization focuses its parent work mostly in the Chicago area.

PUBLICATIONS: *"A Baby First"* is a pamphlet used by parent support volunteers for new parents. It is filled with color pictures of kids with Down syndrome and emphasizes how babies with Down syndrome are babies first. Available in English or Spanish for $1.50. Also a newsletter and videos.

National Down Syndrome Congress (NDSC)
1605 Chantilly Dr., Suite 250
Atlanta, GA 30324
800-232-NDSC
E-mail: NDSCcenter@aol.com
Web site: http//www.carol.net/~ndsc
> PURPOSE: To enhance all aspects of life for persons with Down syndrome.
> SERVICES: Information and referral; advocacy; annual convention.
> PUBLICATIONS: Has a newsletter for members published 10 times a year and pamphlets for new parents available in English and Spanish.

National Down Syndrome Society (NDSS)
666 Broadway
New York, NY 10012-2317
212-460-9330
800-221-4602 Information and Referral
212-979-2872 FAX
Web site: http://www.ndss.org/
> PURPOSE: "Creating and carrying out programs that enable people with Down syndrome to achieve their fullest potential and to make possible the scientific research that will improve the health of people today and find the answers to Down syndrome tomorrow."
> SERVICES: Supports research, sponsors symposiums and conferences. Provides free information and referral services. Sponsors local support groups.
> PUBLICATIONS: Fact sheets and booklets on topics such as Speech and Language Skills, Inclusion, Sexuality, The Heart, Endocrine Conditions, and Life Planning; reading lists on selected topics such as Behavior and Speech and Language; booklets for new parents; proceedings of NDSS scientific symposia; ***Home Based Computer Program for Children with Down Syndrome*** (4 manual set); ***Down Syndrome: Advances in Medical Care;*** videos. Request a publications list.

University of Portsmouth
Sarah Duffen Centre
c/o Anne Sewall, Distributor
RR1, Box 100 H
East Corinth, VT 05040
Web site: http//www.downsnet.org/
(Sarah Duffen Centre's DownsNet Home Page, UK)
> PURPOSE: The Sarah Duffen Centre at the University of Portsmouth, England, was founded to study the development of children with Down syndrome and to investigate effective methods of remedial help and educational programs.
> PUBLICATIONS: The following books are available in the U.S. at the address listed above: ***Meeting the Educational Needs of Children with Down Syndrome: A Handbook for Teachers*** ($32.00); ***The Development of Language and Reading Skills in Children with Down Syndrome*** ($15.00); ***The Adolescent with Down Syndrome: Life for the Teenager and Family*** ($10.00). Request a current price list and information on shipping and handling charges.

24.

Epilepsy

■ BOOKS

Basic Information

Freeman, John M., Eileen P.G. Vining, and Diana J. Pillas. *Seizures and Epilepsy in Childhood: A Guide for Parents.* Baltimore, MD: Johns Hopkins University Press, 1990. 287 pp. $16.95. ISBN 0-8018-4649-8.

>   The emphasis of this topnotch, optimistic guide is on helping families put epilepsy into perspective. Throughout, the authors focus on what children with epilepsy can do, rather than what they cannot do, and how they are usually more like other children than unlike them. The five major parts cover: 1) Why Do Seizures and Epilepsy Occur? 2) Diagnosing and Treating Seizures; 3) Treating Seizures and Epilepsy; 4) Coping with Epilepsy; and 5) Living with Epilepsy. The authors are careful to present both sides of issues, to empower parents to make educated decisions about such matters as whether to put their child on medication, whether to stop medication, whether to get counseling for their child, and whether to allow their child to participate in specific activities. One chapter is devoted to the special problems of children with cerebral palsy, mental retardation, or other conditions where epilepsy is a secondary disability.

Gumnit, Robert J. *Living Well with Epilepsy.* New York, NY: Demos, 1990. 166 pp. $12.95. ISBN 0-939957-21-3.

>   This book is written primarily for the adult reader who has epilepsy, but several chapters are addressed to parents of children with epilepsy. There are brief chapters on Seizures in Newborns and Infants, Treating Childhood Seizures, Helping a Child Live Well with Epilepsy, and Transition to Independence: The Teen Years. New parents can also learn from the chapters on general issues such as the causes of epilepsy, treatment, and first aid for seizures.

Hopkins, Anthony, and Richard Appleton. *Epilepsy: The Facts.* 2nd ed. New York, NY: Oxford University Press, 1996. 176 pp. $16.95. ISBN 0-19-262548-9.

> For readers looking for a good general overview of medical aspects of epilepsy, this would be a useful place to start. Types of seizures, causes, testing, diagnosis of epilepsy, treatment, and prognosis are covered succinctly and readably. Little information is provided about educational concerns, however, and the limited information about legal issues, driving, and adult concerns is specific to the United Kingdom.

Kaplan, Peter W., Pierre Loiseau, Robert S. Fisher, and Pierre Jallon. *Epilepsy A to Z: A Glossary of Epilepsy Terminology.* New York, NY: Demos Vermande, 1995. 322 pp. $29.95. ISBN 0-939957-75-2.

> Although written for health care professionals, this book should also be useful for others looking for brief answers to questions about epilespy. Definitions are given for over 300 terms and phrases related to epilepsy, with references for further information.

Moshé, Solomon L., John M. Pellock, and Matthew C. Salon. *The Parke-Davis Manual on Epilepsy.* New York, NY: KSF, 1993. 72 pp. $9.95. ISBN 0-9634953-1-3.

> This easy-to-use little book offers a good overview of epilepsy, the types of seizures, and suggestions about how to treat this disorder. A strong point is its coverage of safety-related topics, such as the use of safety bed pillows, thoughts on driving, and memory tricks that can boost safety. An "Encyclodex" at the back explains the seizure terminology used in the book.

Minnesota Department of Health, Services for Children with Handicaps. *Seizure Disorder.* Minneapolis, MN: Minnesota Dept. of Health, 1991. 60 pp. Free.

> This booklet was created for anyone who is the primary caretaker for a child, adolescent, or adult with a seizure disorder. It provides a good, basic overview of the different types of seizures and the first aid, medical treatment, and support services available. A list of the most common medications, including their potential side effects, is provided. The booklet also touches on social needs, health needs, educational needs, and family support needs.

Wilmer, Andrew. *Epilepsy: 199 Answers—A Doctor Responds to His Patients' Questions.* New York, NY: Demos Vermande, 1996. 128 pp. $24.95. ISBN 1-888799-09-9.

> As the title suggests, this slim volume provides answers to commonly asked questions about epilepsy. Questions are arranged by topic, and cover subjects such as treatment, epilepsy in children, surgery, and research. A helpful resources section lists epilepsy organizations, medical centers, summer camps, and Internet resources.

Seizure Control

Freeman, John M., Millicent T. Kelly, and Jennifer B. Freeman. *The Epilepsy Diet Treatment: An Introduction to the Ketogenic Diet.* 2nd ed. New York, NY: Demos, 1996. 181 pp. $24.95. ISBN 0-939957-86-8.

> The ketogenic diet is usually regarded as a last resort for children with epilepsy whose seizures cannot be controlled with anticonvulsants. Children on the diet receive most of their calories through fat and very few through protein and carbohydrates. This book explains the theory and practice of the diet and information on day-to-day meal planning. The ketogenic must *always* be administered under the guidance of a physician, so the book should not be regarded as a complete how-to guide.

Richard, Adrienne, and Joel Reiter. *Epilepsy: A New Approach.* 2nd ed. New York, NY: Walker & Co., 1995. 238 pp. Out of print.

> The focus of this book is on controlling seizures without medication. It discusses ways to recognize that a seizure is approaching, as well as techniques that may help reduce the incidence of seizures. The authors emphasize the importance of a healthy lifestyle, and include guidelines on good nutrition, appropriate exercise, relaxation, journal keeping, and specific stress reduction techniques.

First-Person Perspectives

Schachter, Steven C., ed. *Brainstorms: Epilepsy in Our Words: Personal Accounts of Living with Epilepsy.* Philadelphia: Lippincott-Raven Press, 1993. 128 pp. $22.00. ISBN 0-88167-997-6.

> In this fascinating collection, nearly seventy people of all ages describe what it is like to have a seizure. Additional narrative explains how epilepsy affects each of their lives. Also available from the same author is *The Brainstorms Companion* (ISBN 0-7817-0230-5), a collection of descriptions by family members and friends about what it is like to witness a seizure, and *The Brainstorms Family* (ISBN 0-397-51839-0), stories by children about living with epilepsy.

For Children

Bergman, Thomas. *Moments That Disappear: Living with Epilepsy.* Milwaukee, WI: Gareth Stevens Publishing, 1992. 48 pp. ISBN 0-8368-0739-1. Out of print.

> Joakim is a good-looking twelve-year-old. He is an athlete, musician, and all-around kid--with one difference; he has epilepsy. The book focuses on the changes that Joakim has experienced since he had his first seizure six months ago. Photographs show Joakim having an absence seizure, an EEG, and day-to-day life with epilepsy. We see the concerns in Joakim's eyes, we learn about the changes he has had to make in his life, and begin to ask the same questions he does about the future.

Dottie the Dalmation Has Epilepsy. Peapack, NJ: Tim Peters and Co., 1996. 20 pp. $15.95.

> Dottie, a Dalmation puppy, dreams of being the firehouse mascot. Then, one day, she has a seizure in the yard behind the firehouse. Although the doctor prescribes a medication to control her seizures, Dottie is initially embarrassed by her diagnosis. Her self-esteem returns when she helps Fireman Bob rescue a baby from a burning building. Younger children will be attracted to this book's large pages and dramatic illustrations of the fire.

Karolides, Nicholas. *Focus on Physical Impairments: A Reference Handbook.* Santa Barbara, CA: ABC-CLIO, 1990. 332 pp. $39.50. ISBN 0-87436-428-0.

> This book was designed to provide young readers with information and resources about nine physical conditions, including epilepsy. In the 25-page chapter on epilepsy, the author provides a definition and statistics about the incidence, then discusses types of epilepsy, developmental factors, social factors (including effects on IQ and stigmatization), treatment, education, employment, recent developments, and tips on interacting with someone with epilepsy. The chapter concludes with descriptions of both fiction and nonfiction books suitable for junior high or high school readers and other resources. Although the book is part of the Teenage Perspective series, it would be equally useful to parents and teachers looking for a nontechnical overview of the major issues related to epilepsy. The descriptions provided are quite meaty and include interesting but not commonly known facts such as the names of states that, until the 1980s, had laws prohibiting adults with epilepsy to marry or bear children.

Krementz, Jill. ***How It Feels to Fight for Your Life.*** Boston: Little, Brown and Co., 1989. 132 pp. ISBN 0-316-50364-9. Out of print.

> Fourteen children and teenagers with chronic illnesses or disabilities describe their daily lives and struggle for independence. One of the children profiled is a sixteen-year-old girl with epilepsy who plays varsity sports and is looking forward to getting her driver's license. (Note: some outdated terminology such as "petit mal" and "grand mal" is used.) The book is illustrated with excellent black-and-white photos of the children.

Moss, Deborah M. ***Lee, The Rabbit with Epilepsy.*** Bethesda, MD: Woodbine House, 1989. 24 pp. $12.95. ISBN 0-933149-32-8.

> While fishing with her grandpa, Lee loses her fish because she appears to be just staring into space. This is the beginning of a story that explains, in very simple terms, what epilepsy is and how it is diagnosed. The most important message in this book is that having a seizure disorder does not mean you can't do the things you want to do. Recommended for children 4-8.

Swanson, Susanne M. ***My Friend Emily: A Story about Epilepsy and Friendship.*** Boise, ID: Writer's Press Service, 1994. 36 pp. $5.99. ISBN 1-885101-04-X.

> Emily makes a point of educating her friend, Katy, about her epilepsy. She explains what happens during a seizure, what causes seizures, and what to do if you see someone having a seizure. Katy remembers what to do one day when Emily has a seizure at recess. There is minimal plot in this illustrated story, but the author explains epilepsy well for an elementary school-aged audience.

■ ORGANIZATIONS

American Epilepsy Society

638 Prospect Ave.
Hartford, CT 06105-4250
(203) 586-7505
E-mail: aesmain@aol.com

> PURPOSE: Professional organization devoted to the study and treatment of epilepsy.
> PUBLICATIONS: Members receive the monthly journal ***Epilepsia.***

Epilepsy Canada

1470 Peel St., Ste. 745
Montreal, Quebec H3A 1T1
Canada
(514) 845-7855; (514) 845-7866

> PURPOSE: Canada's "only national, nonprofit organization dedicated to improving the quality of life for people with epilepsy and their families."
> PUBLICATIONS: ***Lumina,*** a twice yearly newsletter (in English and French) contains articles on medications, medical issues, parenting, and Canadian programs, and is included in the price of membership ($20 Canadian). Also informational brochures such as *"Your Medication for Epilepsy," "Epilepsy: Answers to Your Questions,"* and *"Children and Epilepsy: What Parents Need to Know."*

Epilepsy Foundation of America

4351 Garden City Dr.
Landover, MD 20785-2267
(800) EFA-1000; (800) 332-2070 TTY; (301) 577-2684 FAX
E-mail: postmaster@efa.org
Web site: http//www.efa.org/

PURPOSE: The Epilepsy Foundation of America is the national, charitable, non-profit, voluntary agency in the United States dedicated to the welfare of people with epilepsy. Its goals are the prevention and cure of seizure disorders, the alleviation of their effects, and the promotion of independence and optimal quality of life for people who have these disorders.

SERVICES: Information and referral; advocacy; family and public education; parent and family networks; camping and recreational activities; employment services; residential services.

PUBLICATIONS: Has an extensive catalog of books, pamphlets, and videos from the EFA and other publishers. Books available include: ***Epilepsy Parent and Family Networks Resource Manual*** ($19.95); ***Brothers & Sisters: A Guide for Families of Children with Epilepsy*** ($10.95); ***School Planning: A Guide for Parents of Children with Seizure Disorders*** ($12.95); and the four-book ***Issues and Answers*** series for parents of children from birth to young adulthood ($12.95 each). Examples of low-cost pamphlets available include: *"Epilepsy Medicines and Dental Care"; "Surgery for Epilepsy"; "All about Partial Seizures"; "Safety and Seizures"; "Epilepsy: Legal Rights, Legal Issues."* Some publications are available in Spanish. EFA members receive discounts on publications and a subscription to the newspaper ***Epilepsy Today***.

25.

Fetal Alcohol Syndrome and Prenatal Substance Exposure

■ BOOKS

Basic Information

Davis, Diane. *Reaching Out to Children with FAS/FAE: A Handbook for Teachers, Counselors and Parents Who Work with Children Affected by Fetal Alcohol Syndrome & Fetal Alcohol Effects.* West Nyack, NY: The Center for Applied Research and Education, 1994. (Distributed by National Professional Resources.) 192 pp. $27.95. ISBN 0-87628-857-3.

> This eminently readable and practical guide was written to offer support and hope to families and others who care about a child or young adult with FAS or FAE. Opening chapters cover diagnosis and prognosis, cause, family life issues, and strategies for success at school. Next follows a lengthy section detailing specific techniques for helping children and adults with FAS/FAE with specific difficulties—for example, dealing with anger, releasing energy, building self-esteem, and learning basic living skills and social skills. A final resource section includes essays written by parents of children with FAS and lists of books and organizations.

Hallowell, Edward. ***When You Worry about the Child You Love.*** New York, NY: Simon & Schuster, 1996. 281 pp. $23.00. ISBN 0-684-80090-X.

> For parents who suspect, or have just learned, that their child has an emotional or learning problem, this book provides an excellent overview of disorders that may make children mad, sad, afraid, or confused. The book explains when parents should worry about their children's behavior and seek professional help; discusses steps parents can take to help children manage their emotions and learn, no matter what the disorder; and discusses treatment options, including medication. Information on a number of disorders with a biologic or genetic basis, including FAS/FAE, is included. The author's conversational style and numerous anecdotes make this an easy read.

Kleinfeld, Judith, and Siobhan Westcott, eds. ***Fantastic Antone Succeeds! Experiences in Educating Children with Fetal Alcohol Syndrome.*** Fairbanks, AK: University of Alaska Press, 1993. 368 pp. $20.00. 0-912006-65-X.

> This practical and empathetic guide has a hopeful message for families. The authors take the stance that most children with FAS/FAE have the potential to lead happy and satisfying lives, with the right kinds of intervention and education at home and at school. Three broad sections cover how FAS affects the brain and the ability to learn and behave; the role of the family in helping children learn and control behavior; and strategies for helping students with FAS/FAE succeed at school. Contributors include adoptive parents, birth mothers, educators, counselors, and physicians.

Morse, Barbara A., and Lyn Weiner. ***FAS: Parent and Child.*** Brookline, MA: Fetal Alcohol Educational Program, 1993. 32 pp. $7.50.

> For new parents, this booklet offers an excellent overview of issues related to raising a child with FAS. Among the topics addressed are sleeping, developmental milestones, behavioral issues, family relations, and adolescence. Resources are included.

Schoenbrodt, Lisa, and Romayne A. Smith. ***Communication Disorders and Interventions in Low Incidence Pediatric Populations.*** San Diego: Singular Publishing Group, 1995. 250 pp. $39.95. ISBN 1-56593-220-X.

> This text includes a very thorough chapter on children who were exposed prenatally to drugs or alcohol. The forty-page chapter covers incidence, the impact of substance exposure on the fetus, characteristics of children of prenatal substance abuse, and treatment, with special attention to speech, language, and feeding effects. Although intended primarily for speech-language pathologists, the information should also be valuable for parents.

Villareal, Sylvia Fernandez, Lora-Ellen McKinney, and Marcia Quakenbush. ***Handle with Care: Helping Children Prenatally Exposed to Drugs and Alcohol.*** Santa Cruz, CA: ETR Associates, 1992. 200 pp. $17.95. ISBN 1-56071-077-2.

> Although written primarily for service providers, this clearly written guide also contains useful information for caregivers. Included is information on developmental problems in children prenatally exposed to substances; descriptions of the kinds of preschool experiences that can help; suggestions for the daily care of a baby; and ideas for teaching children who are at risk of school failure by respecting different learning styles. The book also contains a good deal of discussion about how a child can be helped by treating a parent's drug or alcohol dependency and by focusing on family problems related to drug abuse. Case stories give an idea of the wide range of effects that prenatal drug and alcohol exposure can have on a child.

First Person Perspective

Dorris, Michael. *The Broken Cord.* New York, NY: HarperCollins, 1990. 300 pp. $12.00. ISBN 0-06-091682-6.

> As a young, single, college instructor, Michael Dorris decided he wanted to adopt a Native American child. "Adam," the three-year-old boy he was offered, was diagnosed as mildly mentally retarded, but Dorris initially believed that was a diagnosis the child would grow out of. Gradually, however, Dorris realized that Adam was not catching up with other children—he had significant speech delays; was not toilet trained; could not grasp colors, numbers, or letters; engaged in self-stimulatory behavior; and developed recurrent seizures. After learning that Adam's birth mother had died of acute alcohol poisoning, Dorris finally began to suspect the true cause of Adam's problems. Interwoven with Dorris's account of raising Adam and two other adoptive children are long blocks of narrative recounting what researchers have learned about the nature and consequences of FAS, particularly in the Native American population. Some readers may find these passages slow going, but overall, the book gives a masterful view of what it is like to raise a child with fetal alcohol syndrome.

For Children

Westridge Young Writers Workshop. *Kids Explore the Gifts of Children with Special Needs.* Santa Fe, NM: John Muir Publications, 1994. 115 pp. $9.95. ISBN 1-56261-156-9.

> Part of the "Kids Explore" series, this slim paperback is meant to help readers learn to respect all people. The authors are students in the third through sixth grades who got to know ten fellow students with disabilities and then wrote short biographical essays about them. One of the students profiled has fetal alcohol syndrome. The essays answer questions commonly asked about each disability, and also offer glimpses into how the students get along at school, in their families, and in the community. Many black and white photographs are included.

■ ORGANIZATIONS

The Arc of the United States
500 E. Border St., Ste. 300
Arlington, TX 76010
(817) 261-6003; (817) 277-0553 (TTY)
E-mail: thearc@metronet.com
http//TheArc.org/welcome.html

> PUBLICATIONS: Offers a variety of publications for young people, pregnant women, and teachers on prevention of FAS and other alcohol-related birth defects. Request a publications catalog.

Fetal Alcohol Syndrome/Family Resource Institute
P.O. Box 2525
Lynnwood, WA 98036
(425) 778-4048

> PURPOSE: Provides families and professionals with information and support.
> SERVICES: Information and referral, legislative updates, workshops.
> PUBLICATIONS: The newsletter *FAS Times* is $15.00 yearly. Parent information packet also available.

The National Organization on Fetal Alcohol Syndrome (NOFAS)
1815 H St., NW, Ste. 1000
Washington, DC 20006
(800) 66-NOFAS; (202) 466-6456 FAX

> PURPOSE: A national nonprofit organization that strives to eliminate FAS and FAE to improve the quality of life for individuals with FAS/FAE.
>
> PUBLICATIONS: Publishes and distributes several books, videos, and brochures on FAS/FAE, including a Resource Guide that lists treatment centers, prevention programs, and support groups nationwide. The newsletter ***Notes from NOFAS*** is free to members.

26.

Fragile X Syndrome

■ BOOKS AND PERIODICALS

Basic Information

National Fragile X Advocate. P.O. Box 17023, Chapel Hill, NC 27516-1702. (800) 434-0322.

> This quarterly newsletter covers research, educational issues, family life and other topics of interest to parents and professionals with an interest in fragile X syndrome. An annual subscription is $36.00.

Schoenbrodt, Lisa, and Romayne A. Smith. ***Communication Disorders and Interventions in Low Incidence Pediatric Populations.*** San Diego: Singular Publishing Group, 1995. 250 pp. $39.95. ISBN 1-56593-220-X.

> One meaty chapter of this readable manual focuses on children with fragile X syndrome. The information is intended to give speech-language pathologists the background they need to work with children with fragile X syndrome, and covers such information as genetics, physical characteristics, sensory integration, cognitive and learning characteristics, assessment, and treatment. There is a great deal of information on speech and language characteristics of children with fragile X syndrome at different ages.

Schopmeyer, Betty B., and Fonda Lowe. ***The Fragile X Child.*** San Diego: Singular Publishing, 1992. ISBN 1-879105-83-7. $39.95

> Because this guide was written by therapists for therapists, some of the language is rather technical. It does, however, provide a thorough discussion of causes, medical concerns, and developmental strengths and needs of children with fragile X syndrome. Several chapters discuss in detail how speech and language therapy and occupational therapy can be used to help children with fragile X learn and handle behavioral challenges. The book includes many references. Overall, the information is accurate and provides the support that only knowledge can bring.

Tranfaglia, Michael R. *A Medication Guide for Fragile X Syndrome.* 2nd ed. West Newbury, MA: FRAXA, 1996. 118 pp. $25.00. No ISBN.

> Dr. Tranfaglia writes about his book: "This guide is not a medical textbook. It is intended to serve as a background to help parents communicate with their physicians regarding medications." Topics covered include: Who should be tested? Who should treat, who should be treated? There is an extensive medication reference section. This book may be purchased from FRAXA, listed under "Organizations," below.

Wilson, Philip, Tracy Stackhouse, Rebecca O'Connor, Sarah Scharfenaker, and Randi Hagerman. *Issues and Strategies for Educating Children with Fragile X Syndrome.* Denver, CO: National Fragile X Foundation, 1994. 98 pp. Please call/write for current cost.

> This monograph provides an overview and discussion of genetic implications of fragile X syndrome, as well as of the medical, behavioral, occupational, and speech therapy techniques that can help address concerns. Excellent strategies for day-to-day life at home and at school are included. The many fine photographs of children with fragile X syndrome are a highlight of the book.

For Children

O'Connor, Rebecca. **Boys with Fragile X Syndrome.** Denver, CO: National Fragile X Foundation. $10.00 ISBN 0-9647355-0-4.

> This story about children with fragile X syndrome provides an overview of the behaviors, some physical characteristics, and strategies for behavioral intervention. Illustrations are colorful and help present the information in a sensitive manner.

■ ORGANIZATIONS

Duke University Medical Center
Box 90660
Durham, NC 27708-0660
(919) 687-3600

> PUBLICATION: Offers a 20-page booklet that includes suggestions for curriculum development and behavior management, as well as suggestions about handling sensory integration problems in the classroom: *"Fragile X: Educating Boys with Fragile X Syndrome"* ($10.00).

The Fragile X Association of Southern California
1528 N. Pepper St.
Burbank, CA 91505
(818) 845-5877

> PURPOSE: To provide vital support and information to fragile X families, and promote awareness of fragile X syndrome.
> SERVICES: Information and referral and parent-to-parent support, for all parents wherever their location.
> PUBLICATIONS: Brochure—an excellent at-a-glance explanation of fragile X syndrome.

FRAXA Research Foundation

P.O. Box 935
West Newbury, MA 01985-0935
(508) 462-1990; (508) 463-9985 FAX
E-mail fraxa@seacoast.com
Web site: http//www.worx.net/fraxa

> PURPOSE: A national non-profit organization whose purpose is to further scientific research to find effective treatment for this disorder.
>
> SERVICES: Directly funds promising research projects aimed at treatment. Funds FRAXA post-doctoral fellowships. Information and referral for parents and professionals interested in fragile X syndrome.
>
> PUBLICATIONS: FRAXA Research Foundation newsletter is published quarterly and included in annual membership fee of $25.00. A variety of informational booklets are also available.

National Fragile X Foundation

1441 York St., Suite 215
Denver, CO 80206
(303) 333-6155; (800) 688-8765; (303) 333-4369 FAX

> PURPOSE: To promote education, diagnosis, treatement and research related to fragile X syndrome and other types of X-linked mental retardation.
>
> SERVICES: Information and referral.
>
> PUBLICATIONS: Publishes a newsletter, conference proceedings, parent and professional packets. *"Fragile X Syndrome: A Handbook for Families and Professionals"* is a 24-page booklet with basic information about fragile X syndrome, the genetic implications, diagnosis, and personal insight for parents. Request a price list.

National Institute of Child Health and Human Development (NICHD)

Public Information and Communications Branch
P.O. Box 29111
Washington, DC 20040
(301) 496-5133
Web site: http//www.nih.gov/nichd/

> PURPOSE: NICHD "seeks to assure that every individual is born healthy, is born wanted, and has the opportunity to fulfill his or her potential for a healthy and productive life unhampered by disease or disability."
>
> PUBLICATIONS: *"Facts about Fragile X Syndrome"* (#2026) is free.

27.

Hydrocephalus

■ BOOKS AND PERIODICALS

Basic Information

Drake, James, and Christian Sainte-Rose. ***The Shunt Book.*** Malden, MA: Blackwell Science, 1994. $26.95. ISBN 0-86542-220-6.

> The authors of this text hope that increased understanding of shunts and their functions will help professionals minimize the effects of hydrocephalus through shunting and maintain the best long-term function of shunt systems. Chapters cover the history of cerebrospinal fluid (CSF) shunts; how shunts work; how they are made; the components of shunts; potential complications of using shunts; and neurosurgical decisions in choosing and inserting a shunt. Although technical, some of the information may be useful to families concerned with optimizing shunt function.

Hydrocephalus News & Notes. National Hydrocephalus Foundation, 1670 Green Oak Circle, Lawrenceville, GA 30243. (770) 995-8982 FAX.

> This quarterly, 20-page newsletter is the official publication of the National Hydrocephalus Foundation. It includes information for individuals with hydrocephalus of all ages, including first-person accounts, medical issues, emotional and family concerns, and resources. Subscription included in NHF dues of $30.00.

Hydrocephalus Newsletter. Hydrocephalus Association, 870 Market St., Ste. 955, San Francisco, CA 94102. (415) 732-7040.

> This quarterly is the official newsletter of the Hydrocephalus Association. It covers medical and educational issues, association news, book reviews, and resources. A subscription is included in the association dues of $20.00.

■ ORGANIZATIONS

Hydrocephalus Association
870 Market St., Ste. 955
San Francisco, CA 94102
(415) 732-7040; (415) 732-7044
Web site: http//neurosurgery.mgh.harvard.edu/ha/

> PURPOSE: Provides support, education, and advocacy for families of people with hydrocephalus and professionals.

> SERVICES: Has an OutReach Program, which provides one-to-one support for families and individuals; holds regional educational meetings and a bi-annual national conference; networks with other support groups.

> PUBLICATIONS: The following publications are free to members; others should phone for costs: *"About Hydrocephalus: A Book for Parents,"* a 36-page booklet available in English or Spanish; *"About Normal Pressure Hydrocephalus: A Book for Adults and Their Families"; "The Resource Guide,"* a list of 350 articles on hydrocephalus available from the Association; and the ***Hydrocephalus Newsletter,*** described above. Fact sheets on 12 topics, including *"Learning Disabilities in Children with Hydrocephalus"* and *"Social Skills Development in Children with Hydrocephalus,"* are also available.

28.

Learning Disabilities

■ BOOKS

Basic Information

Cordoni, Barbara. *Living with a Learning Disability.* 2nd ed. Carbondale, IL: Southern Illinois University Press, 1990. 174 pp. $19.95. ISBN 0-8093-1668-4.

> This important book looks at learning disabilities in an environment other than the school environment. Every effort is made to help the reader understand just what it *means* to have different types of learning disabilities. Using a variety of perspectives, the author offers strategies for success and lessons learned by parents, children, and young adults. Ms. Cordoni uses humor to make her points, always remarking on the lessons learned. A major emphasis is the effect of learning disabilities on young adults and how their problems in school and at home carry over later in life to college and vocational life. Resources include college and adult programs, employment, and vocational opportunities.

Fisher, Gary, and Rhoda Cummings. *When Your Child Has LD (Learning Differences): A Survival Guide for Parents.* Minneapolis: Free Spirit, 1995. 168 pp. $12.95. ISBN 0-915793-87-3.

> This is a basic parents' guide to learning disabilities by the authors of the popular *School Survival Guide for Kids with LD.* Topics covered include: types of LD, causes of LD, signs that your child might have LD, legal rights for your child and family, working with the school, coping with family problems, and advocating for your child.

Hallowell, Edward. *When You Worry about the Child You Love.* New York, NY: Simon & Schuster, 1996. 281 pp. $23.00. ISBN 0-684-80090-X.

> For parents who suspect, or have just learned, that their child has an emotional or learning problem, this book provides an excellent overview of disorders that may make children mad, sad, afraid, or confused. The book explains when parents should worry about their children's behavior and seek professional help; discusses steps parents can take to help children manage their emotions and learn, no matter what the disorder; and discusses treatment options, including medication. Information on a number of disorders with a biologic or genetic basis is included: among them, learning disability, ADD, conduct disorder, oppositional defiant disorder, overanxious disorder, and panic attacks. The author's conversational style and numerous anecdotes make this an easy read.

Mackenzie, Leslie, and Amy Lignor, eds. *The Complete Learning Disabilities Directory: Comprehensive Guide to LD Resources.* Lakeville, CT: Greyhouse Publishing, 1994. 678 pp. $99.00. ISBN 0-939300-58-3.

> This comprehensive directory for parents and professionals lists national and state associations and organizations; state and federal government organizations; legal information sources; books and periodicals; classroom information; computer adaptations and software; and programs related to learning disabilities. While it will not fit neatly into your purse, it *will* fit beautifully on the shelf of a family resource center library.

Selikowitz, Mark. *Dyslexia and Other Learning Disabilities: The Facts.* New York, NY: Oxford University Press, 1995. 144 pp. $18.95. ISBN 0-19-262300-1.

> In easy-to-read language, the author provides exceptionally clear, concise definitions and descriptions of learning disabilities, including problems with reading, writing, and socialization. There is a thorough discussion of treatment options, including controversial techniques such as sensory integration therapy and the Doman-Delacato Method. Positive suggestions for parents are included within each section. The resource list includes addresses for organizations that help families of children with learning disabilities.

Silver, Larry. *The Misunderstood Child.* 2nd ed. Bradenton, FL: Human Services Institute, 1992. 322 pp. $9.95. ISBN 0-8306-2837-1.

> This is a great publication which sets the stage for early advocacy for your child with learning disabilities. It includes causes and symptoms of different types of learning disabilities, as well as thorough information on evaluation and assessment, complete with descriptions of the tests. A major focus is on suggestions and approaches that parents can use at home as well as in dealing with the school. Legal issues are covered and an index of resources is included.

Smith, Corinne, and Lisa Strick. *Learning Disabilities: A to Z. A Parent's Complete Guide to Learning Disabilities from Preschool to Adulthood.* New York, NY: The Free Press/Simon & Schuster, 1997. 407 pp. $25.00. ISBN 0-684-82738-7.

> For parents looking for a one-stop source of information, this comprehensive parents' guide would be a good choice. The book covers information that parents in the early stage of getting a diagnosis need to know, including the earliest possible signs of a learning disability and what to expect during an evaluation. For parents whose child has already been diagnosed, there is information on becoming an expert on, and advocating for your child; planning an effective IEP; and strategies for classroom success. The book also includes several chapters about issues outside the classroom, including effects of LD on social and emotional growth; nourishing self-esteem and healthy relationships; and making the transition from high school to work or post secondary education. The book is enlivened with many case stories about children and young adults with LD, sometimes written in their own words.

Smith, Sally L. *No Easy Answers.* New York, NY: Bantam, 1995. 400 pp. $9.95. ISBN 0-553-35450-7.

> Every chapter of this excellent book is full of information about learning disabilities. Learning disabilities are explained so clearly, the reader can see just what it is like to have LD and understand exactly how the behaviors associated with it get in the way of living. The author includes one of the finest and most comprehensive explanations of educational law available. A good selection of books, videos, resources, and organizations is included. Parents will use this book over and over again as a reference, a guide, a manual, and a source for strategic planning.

Smith, Sally L. *Succeeding Against the Odds: How the Learning Disabled Can Realize Their Promise.* New York, NY: Putnam, 1991. 320 pp. $12.95. ISBN 0-87477-731-3.

> Sally Smith, the parent of a child with a learning disability, wrote this book to provide support, education, and acknowledgement for persons with a learning disability (LD) and their families. Individuals with LD speak about their experiences at the beginning of each chapter, adding a personal statement. There is also a chapter in which parents share their experiences, talking about what has and has not worked. The final chapter is devoted to helping individuals with LD develop strategies for coping and success *themselves.* A long list of resources is included.

Stevens, Suzanne H. *The Learning Disabled Child: Ways Parents Can Help.* 2nd ed. Winston-Salem, NC: John F. Blair, 1993. 196 pp. $8.95. ISBN 0-89587-014-2.

> This exceptional book was written for parents who want to learn about learning disabilities and help their child in the process. It provides a clear, basic explanation of learning disabilities with no frills, false promises, or magic cures. Ms. Stevens writes in an easy-to-read, conversational style, offering excellent examples, straight talk, and suggestions regarding what to do and what not to do. This book contains a very clear explanation of tests, what they mean, and how to use the information from the tests to help your child. Realistic expectations about therapy are discussed. The author also provides numerous suggestions regarding working with the school system. Some emphasis is placed on private schools and segregated settings; however, every possible strategy is addressed fairly and openly. A selected bibliography is provided at the end.

Dyslexia

Davis, Ronald D., with Eldon M. Braun. *The Gift of Dyslexia: Why Some of the Smartest People Can't Read and How They Can Learn.* Burlingame, CA: Ability Workshop Press, 1994. 214 pp. $14.95. ISBN 0-929551-23-0.

> The author of this guide looks at the dyslexic learning style as a talent. He believes that dyslexia springs from a tendency to think in pictures rather than words and that this makes it difficult to form mental pictures of written words. He explains how and why he thinks dyslexia develops beginning at infancy and describes his method of focusing attention on the written word and using a multisensory approach to improve memory for written words.

Doyle, James. *Dyslexia: An Introductory Guide.* San Diego: Singular Publishing, 1995. 226 pp. $39.95. ISBN 1-56593-604-3.

> Although intended as an introductory text for educators, this nontechnical book would also be useful to parents. Topics covered include the nature of dyslexia, diagnosis, and strategies for helping students overcome reading difficulties.

Levinson, Harold N. *Smart But Feeling Dumb.* Rev. ed. New York, NY: Warner Books, 1993. 320 pp. $12.99. ISBN 0-446-39545-5.

> Dr. Levinson, the parent of two girls with dyslexia, writes about his research on inner ear dysfunction and his theories that this medical problem can cause dyslexia as well as speech disorders,

changes in temperament, and concentration problems. Vignettes about children who were succesfully treated are included.

Levinson, Harold N. *The Upside-Down Kids: Helping Dyslexic Kids Understand Themselves and Their Disorder.* New York, NY: M. Evans, 1991. 150 pp. $17.95. ISBN 0-87131-625-0.

> This book is valuable for children and adults. Hyper-Harry, Anna the motor-mouth, and six other children identify the world that they live in; the world of the dyslexic. In the simplest of terms, Dr. Levinson explains the why of dyslexia and the how of managing it. Resources for children and parents are included.

Levinson, Harold N., and Addie Sanders. *Turning Around the Upside-Down Kids: Helping Your Dyslexic Kids Overcome Their Disorder.* New York, NY: M. Evans, 1992. 156 pp. $17.95. ISBN 0-87131-700-1.

> This companion to *The Upside-Down Kids* offers a look at techniques for helping children with dyslexia. Views on emotional, personal, social, and academic issues are addressed by the eight Upside-Down Kids and their teacher.

Spafford, Carol S., and George S. Grosser. *Dyslexia: Research and Resource Guide.* Needham Heights, MA: Allyn & Bacon, 1995. 352 pp. $36.96. ISBN 0-205-15907-9.

> This text is intended to be a comprehensive resource for educators and parents of children with reading problems. It describes dozens of approaches to treating dyslexia, as well as the advantages and disadvantages of different classroom placements. Information on the special learning problems of children with attention deficit disorder and dyslexia, and on gifted children with dyslexia, is also included.

Education

Bireley, Marlene. *Crossover Children: A Sourcebook for Helping Children Who Are Gifted and Learning Disabled.* 2nd ed. Reston, VA: Council for Exceptional Children, 1995. 94 pp. $28.00. ISBN 0-86586-264-8.

> The emphasis of this book is on what and how to teach students who are struggling academically in school despite above average intelligence. It covers selecting and adapting teaching methods and materials and dealing with social and behavioral difficulties, while challenging the gifted student with LD to meet his or her potential.

Latham, Patricia, and Peter S. Latham. *Higher Educational Services for Students with Learning Disabilities and Attention Deficit Disorder: A Legal Guide.* Cabin John, MD: National Center for Law and Learning Disabilities, 1994. 32 pp. $18.00.

> Prepared by attorneys, this guide provides an overview of disability services and then a general discussion of the Americans with Disabilities Act (ADA). There is an exceptionally good explanation of Applicable Case Law that includes information about obligatory aids and remedial services.

Levine, Mel. *Educational Care: A System for Understanding and Helping Children with Learning Problems at Home and in School.* Cambridge, MA: Educators Publishing Service, 1994. 325 pp. $28.00. ISBN 0-8388-1987-7.

> Although primarily a textbook, this is a terrific research tool. It offers a step-by-step approach for teachers and parents as they identify those actions and reactions that get in the way of a child learning. Every page is full of valuable information about assessing the child from a functional point of view. Academic and social learning are discussed—not peripherally, but in depth, with

examples and suggestions for interventions. Many worksheets are included in the appendices for help with assessment of learning difficulties.

Nadeau, Kathleen G. ***Survival Guide for College Students with ADD or LD***. New York, NY: Magination Press, 1994. 64 pp. $9.95. ISBN 0-945354-63-0.

> This slim, yet comprehensive guide is written expressly for students. Choosing a college can be a complex process, but in the case of students with ADD or LD, there are special considerations. Does the college have LD and ADD programs; is early registration an option; can certain required courses be waived, or changed to meet the student's needs? These and other important questions are covered here. Once on campus, there are a number of steps students should take to get the academic accommodations and services they need. Discussions include how to work with the Office of Disabled Student Services to get assistance such as extended-time examinations and note-takers, and the best ways to alert professors to difficulties and enlist their help. Other supports--medical consultations to monitor medications and counseling services--are recommended. In addition, students are advised on ways to help themselves succeed, including time management techniques, study tips, and maintaining a positive attitude.

Rosner, Jerome. ***Helping Children Overcome Learning Difficulties.*** 3rd ed. New York, NY: Walker & Co., 1993. 286 pp. $18.95. ISBN 0-8027-7396-6.

> This is an extensive how-to guide for parents and professionals as they work with children who have learning disabilities. The book focuses on developing an "action plan" identifying, understanding, and helping the child with LD. Chapters explain in depth how to achieve each portion of the plan, and include guidelines and activities. This comprehensive book is a *must* for parents and professionals.

Stevens, Suzanne H. ***Classroom Success for the LD and ADHD Child.*** 2nd ed. Winston-Salem, NC: John F. Blair, 1996. $13.95. ISBN 0-89587-159-9.

> This useful book should be in the hands of every parent who has a child with a learning disability and every teacher who is responsible for that child's education. Practical information is provided regarding everything from first identification of a child with LD to adjusting the environment so the child can be successful. Although the focus is on the classroom, the techniques can be carried over to the home. The author uses touching stories about real children and adults to emphasize important points. She also points out what society needs to do to help people with learning disabilities. A selected bibliography completes this fine book.

Tuttle, Cheryl Gerson, and Penny Paquette. ***Parenting Children with Learning Disabilities.*** New York, NY: Doubleday, 1995. 208 pp. $11.00. ISBN 0-385-47582-9.

> The authors, both parents, offer a practical guide for helping a child with LD by creating a strong parent/professional partnership. Definitions, discussion about emotions and self-esteem, complete explanations of the types of learning disabilities, and a resource guide are all provided. This book is packed with information that will provide a lifetime of support for the parent/professional team.

College Directories

Some of the many college guides for students with learning disabilities are listed below. Check your bookstore or **Books in Print** for the most recent edition, as many of these directories are updated regularly.

Lipkin, Midge. ***The Schoolsearch Guide to Colleges with Programs or Services for Students with Learning Disabilities.*** Belmont, MA: Schoolsearch, 1993. 928 pp. $34.95. ISBN 0-9620326-5-4.

Mangrum, Charles, and Stephen Strichart. ***Peterson's Colleges with Programs for Students with Learning Disabilities 1998.*** Princeton, NJ: Peterson's, 1997. 688 pp. $32.95. ISBN 1-56079-853-X.

Princeton Review Publishing Staff. ***K & W Guide to Colleges for the Learning Disabled.*** 4th ed. New York, NY: Random House, 1997. $25.00. ISBN 0-375-75043-6.

Sclafani, Annette, and Michael Lynch. ***College Guide for Students with Learning Disabilities.*** 12th ed. New York, NY: Laurel Publications, 1996. 328 pp. $25.95. ISBN 0-933243-09-X.

Social Skills

Nowicki, Stephen, Jr., and Marshall P. Duke. ***Helping the Child Who Doesn't Fit In.*** Atlanta, GA: Peachtree Publishers, 1992. 178 pp. $14.95. ISBN 1-56145-025-1.

> The authors of this practical guide coined the term *dyssemia* to describe unusual difficulty in using and understanding nonverbal signs or signals. According to the authors, this difficulty is at the root of many children's problems in forming relationships and fitting in. Children can have problems with many types of nonverbal communication, or with just one specific type—for example, with use of touch and personal space, facial expressions, tone of voice, or gestures and postures. For each possible type of dyssemia, the authors provide specific strategies for parents to use to help their child overcome problems in this area. There is also an overview chapter that explains how to develop a plan to help a child overcome problems with dyssemia in general.

First Person Perspectives

Brown, Dale. ***I Know I Can Climb the Mountain.*** Columbus, OH: Mountain Books, 1995. 93 pp. $8.95. ISBN 1-881650-04-9.

> The poems in this short book were written between the ages of 8 and 22 by a woman who was diagnosed at age 19 with learning disabilities, dyslexia, and ADD. Powerfully and succinctly, the poems offer a glimpse of what it feels like to live with learning disabilities. There are poems about struggling in school, feeling like a misfit, imagining a gloomy future, and resolving to "harness" her brain so she can learn, as well as poems about teenage experiences such as dieting, falling in love, and volunteering in the slums of Washington, DC.

Dunn, Kathryn Boesel, and Allison Boesel Dunn. ***Trouble with School: A Family Story about Learning Disabilities.*** Bethesda, MD: Woodbine House, 1993. 32 pp. $9.95. ISBN 0-933149-57-3.

> In this unique illustrated book for parents and children, a mother and daughter take turns telling about the trials and tribulations of living with a learning disability. Allison, a second-grader, describes what it is like to be different and teased by her classmates. Allison's mother recounts her frustrations with Allison and her behavior and the strategies they created to survive. Along the way, the book provides suggestions that may help other families live with a learning disability.

Lelewer, Nancy. ***Something's Not Right: One Family's Struggle with Learning Disabilities.*** Acton, MA: VanderWyk & Burnham, 1994. 184 pp. $21.95. ISBN 0-9641089-0-9.

> This is the autobiography of a mother who has dyslexia and her ups and downs raising four children, three of whom have learning disabilities. When the schools seemed unable to help, the author used her own experiences with dyslexia to devise a plan of instruction that worked for her children.

Osmond, John. *The Reality of Dyslexia.* Rev. ed. Cambridge, MA: Brookline Books, 1995. 150 pp. $14.95. ISBN 1-57129-017-6.

> Designed to offer a window into the world of dyslexia, this collection includes accounts from both children and adults diagnosed with dyslexia. The contributors speak of the common emotions they have felt before and after diagnosis, as well as of the educational and other accommodations that have helped them.

Riddick, Barbara, Marion Farmer, and Christopher Sterling. *Students and Dyslexia: Growing Up with a Specific Learning Disability.* San Diego: Singular Publishing, 1997. 180 pp. $39.95. ISBN 1-56593-886-0.

> This interesting collection presents transcripts of interviews with university students about their experiences growing up with dyslexia.

For Children

Fiction

Borntrager, Mary Christner. *Andy.* Scottdale, PA: Herald Press, 1993. 144 pp. $8.95. ISBN 0-8361-3633-0.

> This is a fictional account of a teenage boy who is "different" from his peers. Andy has a developmental delay and makes poor choices. The story is about Andy's adventure as he runs away from home, later to return to the family and friends he needs for support and, ultimately, success.

Dwyer, Kathleen M. *What Do You Mean I Have a Learning Disability?* New York, NY: Walker and Co., 1991. 48 pp. $14.95. ISBN 0-8027-8102-0.

> Ten-year-old Jimmy has a secret. He just knows that he is stupid. He is sure he is because he always forgets things, gets F's at school, and even though he tries really hard, cannot write or do math the way the other kids do. This story explains why Jimmy is the way he is and describes how his parents find help for him. It also explains that children with learning disabilities can benefit from being taught in a "different way." In the end, Jimmy sees the results of his hard work after he receives help from teachers especially trained to work with children who have learning disabilities.

Herold, Ann Bixby. *The Hard Life of Seymore E. Newton.* Scottdale, PA: Herald Press, 1990. 96 pp. $5.95. ISBN 0-8361-3532-6.

> This is a children's book about a smart third-grader who just cannot think straight under pressure. When he writes, things jumble up, and math is a nightmare. Kids at school make fun of him and overall he hates his life. Everything changes, though, when he learns about a class that will help him with his learning disabilities. As the story unfolds, young readers will be impressed with the friendships that are made, the barriers that are broken, and the family that both supports and frustrates this young man. A wonderful book for a child with LD, an awareness program, or general reading.

Janover, Caroline. *Josh, A Boy with Dyslexia.* Burlington, VT: Waterfront Books, 1988. 100 pp. $7.95. ISBN 0-914525-10-7.

> Josh, a fifth grader, is the new kid on the block. Josh has trouble with writing his letters (they turn every-which-way), remembering what he is supposed to be doing (forgetting what was just said), being able to stay on a task (watching ants build a home instead of going straight to school), and remembering directions (thank goodness he has a wart on his left hand!). These problems are all frustrations for him, and so are the reactions of other kids to his problems. Gradually, however, Josh learns strategies for dealing with his classroom problems and learns to generalize them to the real world. Along the way, he proves to have the makings of a hero and a good friend. A first-class adventure story with information about learning disabilities subtly woven in.

Janover, Caroline. *The Worst Speller in Jr. High.* Minneapolis: Free Spirit Publishing, 1995. 200 pp. $4.95. ISBN 0-915793-76-8.

> Like most seventh graders, Katie Kelso longs to be a P.K. (Popular Kid). She does not have as much time as she would like, however, to work on her image. Because of her dyslexia, she must spend extra time on her homework and working with a tutor, and she frequently has to babysit for her brothers, especially after her mother learns she has breast cancer. Eventually, a new boy helps Katie discover some hidden talents, and she realizes that it is more important to be herself than to be popular. With its fast pace, realistic dialog, and undercurrents of romance, this novel should appeal to readers with and without dyslexia.

Lasker, Joe. *He's My Brother.* Morton Grove, IL: Albert Whitman and Company, 1974. 44 pp. $14.95. ISBN 0-8075-3218-5.

> Jamie is a little boy who is developing just slowly enough that he doesn't fit into school. His older brother writes lovingly about Jamie's differences. A great awareness tool for children ages 3-8 and for sibling groups.

Levy, Myrna Neuringer. *The Summer Kid.* Toronto: Second Story Press, 1991. $5.95. ISBN 0-929005-20-1.

> In this heartwarming and sensitive novel, a ten-year-old girl befriends another "summer kid" during a vacation. Karen notices something strange about Tommy right away, but can't put her finger on it. No matter how many questions she asks her grandma, or anyone . . . they all put her off. Karen learns about Tommy's special talents as she gets to know him and works together with him in a castle building contest. This is a wonderful story that highlights the strengths that children with learning disabilities have and the time it may take to identify those strengths.

NONFICTION

Clayton, Lawrence, and Jaydene Morrison. *Coping with a Learning Disability.* Rev. ed. New York, NY: Rosen Publishing Group, 1995. 115 pp. $15.95. ISBN 0-8239-2212-X.

> Written for middle school and high school students with learning disabilities, this book "speaks" to them with concern, humor, and sincerity. The authors offer suggestions for coping and practical advice for working with teachers, choosing friends, and understanding the family's response to a learning disability. Regard this book as a resource, a reference guide, and a support system.

Cummings, Rhoda, and Gary Fisher. *The School Survival Guide for Kids with LD (Learning Differences): Ways to Make Learning Easier and More Fun.* Minneapolis: Free Spirit, 1991. 176 pp. $10.95. 0-915793-32-6.

> This upbeat book offers students eight years and up specific strategies for dealing with school problems associated with LD. It includes tips on organizing time, setting goals, handling conflicts, requesting help, and taking tests. This book provides strategies that lead to success and increased self-esteem.

Cummings, Rhoda, and Gary Fisher. *The Survival Guide for Teenagers with LD (Learning Differences).* Minneapolis: Free Spirit, 1993. 200 pp. $11.95. ISBN 0-915793-51-2.

> Written for students with LD ages thirteen and up, this supportive guide covers many issues near to a teenager's heart: friends, dating, working, and being independent. It also explains what LD is, what types of educational assistance are available, and what rights students with LD have under the law.

Hayes, Marnell. ***The Tuned-In, Turned-On Book about Learning Problems.*** Revised ed. Novato, CA: Academic Therapy Publications, 1994. 132 pp. $8.00. ISBN 1-57128-090-1.

This book for children and teens who have learning disabilities is written in a way that will make the young reader feel that it was written especially for him. The chapters take the reader through a natural progression of learning. The questions posed *sound* like kids talking; for example, "If I'm so smart, why do I have trouble learning?" Since the author has learning problems too, she is able to express what it is like to live with them. She has even included letters from kids that express real concerns in real language. Strategies that may be successful are provided. No cures are offered, but good, solid, simple advice is provided. There is a glossary and resource list at the end of the book.

Landau, Elaine. ***Dyslexia.*** New York, NY: Franklin Watts, 1991. 62 pp. $21.00. ISBN 0-531-20030-2.

In short chapters, this book covers the basics of dyslexia for upper elementary to middle school readers. It explains what dyslexia is, possible causes, and what can be done to help students overcome dyslexia. Children and adults contributed many anecdotes about what it is like to have dyslexia. The book includes numerous color photographs.

Levine, Mel. ***All Kinds of Minds: A Young Student's Book about Learning Abilities and Learning Disabilities.*** Cambridge, MA: Educators Publishing Service, 1993. 283 pp. $22.00. ISBN 0-8388-2090-5.

This beautifully written book is designed to help children understand learning disabilities and develop strategies that will help them cope with this disability. Each chapter introduces a child with a specific learning disability, then goes on to examine the learning differences of that child. How the child feels about himself, what he can do to help himself, and ideas for others to help him are included. In the last section, the author describes a variety of learning disabilities, including attention deficits, reading disorders, memory problems, language disorders, social skills disorders, and motor problems. This children's book is also extremely valuable for parents and professionals. It is available on audiotape.

Roby, Cynthia. ***When Learning Is Tough: Kids Talk about Their Learning Disabilities.*** Morton Grove, IL: Albert Whitman & Co., 1994. 56 pp. $13.95. ISBN 0-8075-8892-X.

Eight children between the ages of nine and thirteen were interviewed and photographed for this book. The kids talk about their feelings about having a learning disability; strategies they use for coping with school work; teasing and how they handle it; the support they get from teachers and family members; and their dreams for the future. All of the kids come across as typical, well-rounded kids who just happen to have trouble in school.

Stein, Judith, and Uzi, Ben-Ami. ***Many Ways to Learn: Young People's Guide to Learning Disabilities.*** New York, NY: Magination Press, 1996. 82 pp. $12.95. ISBN 0-945354-74-6.

Learning disabilities are hard to live and learn with--unless you understand what's going on. ***Many Ways to Learn*** is written to address first the feelings and concerns of the child, then to provide strategies that will help children with LD cope, succeed, and feel good about being in control of an out-of-control situation. Teachers and students may wish to team up and collaborate, using this manual as a guide. Many resources are included.

■ ORGANIZATIONS

American Hyperlexia Association
479 Spring Rd.
Elmhurst, IL 60126
(708) 530-8551; (708) 530-5909 FAX
> PURPOSE: To promote and facilitate effective teaching techniques at both home and school for individuals with hyperlexia.
> SERVICES: Family assistance with information and referral sources.
> PUBLICATIONS: Quarterly newsletter, directory of services, and informational mailings.

CONNECT Information Service
150 S. Progress Ave.
Harrisburg, PA 17109
(717) 657-5840
> PUBLICATION: One copy of *"Steps to Independence for People with Learning Disabilities,"* a self-remediation handbook by Dale S. Brown for people with LD, is available free. The guide covers living on your own, finding and keeping a job, social skills, and coping skills.

Council for Learning Disabled
Box 40303
Overland, KS 66204
(913) 492-3840
> PUBLICATIONS: *Learning Disability Forum* and the *Learning Disabilities Quarterly Journal.*

Learning Disabilities Association of America
4156 Library Road
Pittsburgh, PA 15234
(412) 341-1515; (412) 341-8077; (412) 344-0224 FAX
E-mail: ldanatl@usaor.net
Web site: http://www.ldanatl.org
> PURPOSE: A membership organization devoted to "defining and finding solutions for the broad spectrum of learning problems."
> SERVICES: Information and referral; legislative advocacy; school program development; sponsorship of local chapters and conferences.
> PUBLICATIONS: Has an extensive catalog of publications on LD, ADD, mental health, and related topics; request a publications list. Publishes a newsletter, *LDA Newsbriefs,* published 6 times a year, which covers legislative, educational, and other developments relevant to LD ($13.50 annually).

Learning Disabilities Association of Canada
200-323 Chapel St.
Ottawa, Ontario K1N 7Z2
CANADA
(613) 238-5721; (613) 245-5391 FAX
E-mail: Idactaac@fox.nstn.ca
> PURPOSE: Non-profit organization similar to organization in USA.
> SERVICES: Information & referral.
> PUBLICATIONS: *"Parents as Advocates"* (information packet); *"The Three R's for Parents"*; *"Winners, No Losers: A Handbook for Recreational Providers of Cooperative Activities for Everyone."*

National Center for Law and Learning Disabilities (NCLLD)

P.O. Box 368

Cabin John, MD 20818

(301) 469-8308; (301) 469-9466 FAX

PUBLICATIONS: Examples include: *"Confidentiality Under the Law"; "Alternative Disputes, Resolutions & The ADA"; "The Criminal Justice System (ADD/LD)"; "How to Pick a Lawyer"; "LD in the Workplace - For Employers & Employees."*

National Center for Learning Disabilities (NCLD)

381 Park Ave. South, Ste. 1240

New York, NY 10016

(212) 545-7510; (212) 545-9665 FAX

PURPOSE: A nonprofit organization dedicated to helping individuals with learning disabilities live independent, fulfilling, and productive lives.

SERVICES: Information and referral; legislative advocacy; funding programs for persons with LD; public education.

PUBLICATIONS: Has quarterly newsletters, annual magazine, fact sheets, videos.

National Institute of Child Health and Human Development (NICHD)

Public Information and Communications Branch

P.O. Box 29111

Washington, DC 20040

(301) 496-5133

Web site: http//www.nih.gov/nichd/

PURPOSE: NICHD "seeks to assure that every individual is born healthy, is born wanted, and has the opportunity to fulfill his or her potential for a healthy and productive life unhampered by disease or disability."

PUBLICATIONS: Up to 50 copies of each of the following publications may be ordered free of charge: *"Learning Disabilities, Advocacy, Science and the Future of the Field"* (#2010); *"Research in Learning Disabilities at the NICHD"* (#2021); *"Facts about Dyslexia"* (#9).

National Library Service for the Blind and Physically Handicapped

Library of Congress

1291 Taylor St., NW

Washington, DC 20542

(800) 424-8567

E-mail: nls@loc.gov

Web site: http//lcweb.loc.gov/nls

PURPOSE: Provides a free library service to people who are blind or have a physical impairment or learning disability that prevents them from using standard printed materials.

SERVICES: Lends books and magazines in braille or talking book format free of charge to eligible readers via postage-paid mail. Also lends cassette players for talking books.

PUBLICATIONS: Request the free *"Reference Circular No. 90-1, March 1990,"* which lists many information and advocacy organizations and publications relating to learning disabilities.

The Orton Dyslexia Society
Chester Building, Ste. 382
8600 LaSalle Rd.
Baltimore, MD 21286-2044
(800) ABCD123; (410) 321-2044 FAX
E-mail: info@ods.org
Web site: http//ods.org

> PURPOSE: "An international non-profit, scientific, and educational organization which supports and encourages interdisciplinary study and research, facilitates the exploration of the causes and early identification of dyslexia, and is committed to the wide dissemination of research-based knowledge."
>
> SERVICES: Forty-five branches provide information, sponsor conferences, and offer referral services.
>
> PUBLICATIONS: Include *Language and the Developing Child* ($15); *Understanding Learning Disabilities: A Parent Guide and Workbook* ($20); *Readings for Educators* ($13); *Many Faces of Dyslexia* ($18.50); *Bridges to Reading* ($21); monograph series. Request a publications list. Free with membership: *Annals of Dyslexia Journal,* an annual publication, and *Perspectives,* a quarterly newsletter (membership ranges from $25.00 students, to $55.00 individual, and $90.00 for a family).

Recording for the Blind & Dyslexic
20 Roszel Rd.
Princeton, NJ 08540
(800) 221-4792; (609) 520-7990 FAX

> SERVICES: For a one-time membership fee, people who are blind or cannot use printed materials due to physical or perceptual disabilities can borrow educational books on cassette tape. Taped books include textbooks, computer manuals, and research materials, as well as fiction, drama, and poetry. A print catalog of materials on tape is available for a small fee, or borrowers can call the toll-free number to ask about specific titles.

Sensory Integration International
1602 Cabrillo Ave.
Torrance, CA 90501
(310) 320-9986; (310) 320-9934 FAX

> PURPOSE: "To develop awareness, knowledge, skills and services in Sensory Integration."
>
> SERVICES: Educational training programs, information and educational materials, evaluation and treatment services, research affiliated programs.
>
> PUBLICATIONS: Quarterly newsletter, *Sensory Integration.* Has a wide variety of publications such as: *"A Parents Guide to Understanding Sensory Integration"; "Movement Is Fun"; "Sensory Motor Handbook";* and reviews of research in Sensory Integration.

29.

Mental Illness and Emotional and Behavioral Disorders

■ BOOKS

Basic Information

Aman, Michael G. *Working Bibliography on Behavioral and Emotional Disorders and Assessment Instruments in Mental Retardation.* Rockville, MD: U.S. Dept. of Health and Human Services, 1991. (Available from National Institute of Mental Health.) 40 pp. Free.

> This is an alphabetical listing of books and articles that deal with the topic of mental retardation in conjunction with a behavioral, psychiatric, or emotional disorder. It covers publications released between the early 1970s and 1991.

Hales, Dianne, and Robert E. Hales. *Caring for the Mind: The Comprehensive Guide to Mental Health.* New York, NY: Bantam, 1995. 896 pp. $39.95. ISBN 0-553-09146-8.

> This is a readable and encyclopedic guide to mental health care today. With the help of case histories, it defines and explains numerous mental health disorders, based on DSM-IV criteria. Different treatments, such as medications, family therapy, talk therapy, and hypnosis, are also thoroughly discussed. Other topics covered include suicide, self-help, violence, sex, and alcohol. Chapters are organized with useful headings and sidebars that make it easy to track down needed information.

Hallowell, Edward. ***When You Worry about the Child You Love.*** New York, NY: Simon & Schuster, 1996. 281 pp. $23.00. ISBN 0-684-80090-X.

> For parents who suspect, or have just learned, that their child has an emotional or learning problem, this book provides an excellent overview of disorders that may make children mad, sad, afraid, or confused. The book explains when parents should worry about their children's behavior and seek professional help; discusses steps parents can take to help children manage their emotions and learn, no matter what the disorder; and discusses treatment options, including medication. Information on a number of disorders with a biologic or genetic basis is included: depression, ADD, obsessive-compulsive disorder, conduct disorder, oppositional defiant disorder, overanxious disorder, panic attacks, PTSD, learning disability, bipolar disorder, frontal lobe syndrome, borderline personality disorder, FAS/FAE, PDD and Asperger syndrome, Tourette syndrome, and trichotillomania. The author's conversational style and numerous anecdotes make this an easy read.

Jordan, Dixie. ***A Guidebook for Parents of Children with Emotional or Behavioral Disorders.*** Minneapolis, MN: PACER Center, 1996. 133 pp. $12.00.

> This handbook has a Minnesota slant, but much of the information would be useful to parents regardless of where they live. The book gives a broad overview of many issues, from when to seek professional assessment and treatment, to finding a mental health provider who will empower the family, not blame it; from rights to educational services, to methods of financing mental health services for a child. The author recommends seeking, if at all possible, "wraparound services"— family focused, community-based, individualized health and support services that follow the child wherever he or she needs them.

Koplewicz, Harold S. ***It's Nobody's Fault: New Hope and Help for Difficult Children and Their Parents.*** New York, NY: Times Books/Random House, 1996. 305 pp. $25.00. ISBN 0-8129-2473-8.

> This book focuses on what the author calls "no fault brain disorders"—emotional and behavioral disorders that are known or presumed to be caused by brain chemical abnormalities, rather than environmental causes such as poor parenting. Conditions covered include attention deficit hyperactivity disorder, obsessive compulsive disorder, separation anxiety disorder, social phobia, generalized anxiety disorder, enuresis, Tourette syndrome, major depressive disorder, bipolar disorder, schizophrenia, eating disorders, conduct disorder, and PDD and autism. For each disorder, the author discusses symptoms, diagnosis, brain chemistry, treatment (with an emphasis on medications that can improve brain chemical functioning), and issues involved in parenting a child with the disorder. The book is very readable and filled with examples of children treated by the author.

Nowicki, Stephen, Jr., and Marshall P. Duke. ***Helping the Child Who Doesn't Fit In.*** Atlanta, GA: Peachtree Publishers, 1992. 178 pp. $14.95. ISBN 1-56145-025-1.

> The authors of this practical guide coined the term *dyssemia* to describe unusual difficulty in using and understanding nonverbal signs or signals. According to the authors, this difficulty is at the root of many children's problems in forming relationships and fitting in. Children can have problems with many types of nonverbal communication, or with just one specific type—for example, with use of touch and personal space, facial expressions, tone of voice, or gestures and postures. For each possible type of dyssemia, the authors provide specific strategies for parents to use to help their child overcome problems in this area. There is also an overview chapter that explains how to develop a plan to help a child overcome problems with dyssemia in general.

Specific Diagnoses

ANXIETY DISORDER

Shaw, Mary Ann. *Your Anxious Child: Raising a Healthy Child in a Frightening World.*
Secaucus, NJ: Birch Lane Press, 1995. 174 pp. $14.95. ISBN 1-55972-318-1.

> For parents who are wondering whether their child's anxiety is something to be concerned about, this is the book to read. The author helps parents distinguish between a variety of types of anxiety, devoting a chapter each to performance anxiety, separation anxiety, trauma-induced anxiety, anxiety related to the divorce of parents, and true anxiety disorders (phobias, panic disorders, and obsessive-compulsive disorder). In addition, there are chapters on physical problems related to anxiety, on ways to adapt parenting skills to better support an anxious child, and on special considerations when a child has another disability in addition to an anxiety disorder.

DEPRESSION

Ingersoll, Barbara D., and Sam Goldstein. *Lonely, Sad and Angry: A Parent's Guide to Depression in Children and Adolescents.* New York, NY: Doubleday, 1995. 225 pp. $16.95. ISBN 0-385-47642-6.

> For parents who know or suspect that their child is depressed, this book offers an in-depth discussion of the basics. It clearly explains the DSM IV criteria for the diagnosis of depression, and differentiates among the different types of depression: major depression, dysthymia, bipolar disorder. As the authors believe that childhood depression frequently accompanies other psychological disorders, the book thoroughly explores the relationship between depression and anxiety disorders, ADD, learning disabilities, conduct disorder, and oppositional defiant disorder. Also covered are pyschological and medical treatments, how to handle a crisis, and what families and teachers can do to help.

Oster, Gerald D., and Sarah S. Montgomery. *Helping Your Depressed Teenager: A Guide for Parents and Caregivers.* New York, NY: John Wiley & Sons, 1995. 184 pp. $16.95. ISBN 0-471-62184-6.

> The purpose of this very reader-friendly guide is to help parents "understand the difference between 'normal' ups and downs of adolescence and signs and symptoms of clinical depression." It explores the many possible reasons for depression in teens—including societal and peer pressures, developmental issues, and family problems. It also describes the behavioral changes commonly associated with depression and provides pointers for parents on dealing with specific signs of depression. Several chapters also examine suicide warning signs and discuss what parents should and should not do if their child may be at risk of attempting suicide. Completing the book are several chapters on the evaluation and treatment process, with discussions of the pros and cons of individual and family counseling, medication, and hospitalization.

Shapiro, Patricia Gottlieb. *A Parent's Guide to Childhood and Adolescent Depression.*
New York, NY: Dell Publishing, 1994. 172 pp. ISBN 0-440-50633-6. Out of print.

> This short guide aims to help parents understand their role in raising a child or adolescent with depression. It explains how parents can recognize the first signs of depression, as well as situations that can make a child vulnerable to depression. There is also information on choosing a therapist and preparing a child to see the therapist; on finding the appropriate treatment approach for a child; and on how parents can adapt communication styles, stress managment, and other interactions to make living with a depressed child easier. Additionally, there is a chapter on causes and prevention of suicide in young people.

Slaby, Andrew, and Lili Frank Garfinkel. *No One Saw My Pain: Why Teens Kill Themselves.*
New York, NY: W.W. Norton & Co., 1996. 208 pp. $12.00. ISBN 0-393-31392-1.

> In researching this book, the author, a psychiatrist, met with the families of eight teens who committed suicide. In a conversational and sensitive style, he recounts the events leading up to

each suicide, and delves into the effects on parents and siblings. In his judgement, adolescent depression was at the root of each of the suicides. The author emphasizes how subtle the signs of teenage depression can be, and the importance of understanding the true reasons for suicide before families can move on. The author also shares the five global themes that he has noticed in analyzing young people's suicide notes, in hopes that other suicides may be prevented. In addition, there is information for parents about how to get help if their teenaged child may be at risk of commiting suicide.

EATING DISORDERS

Abraham, Suzanne, and Llewellyn-Jones, Derek. *Eating Disorders: The Facts.* 4th ed. New York, NY: Oxford University Press, 1997. 256 pp. $17.95. ISBN 0-19-262759-7.

> This is a concise guide to the nature, causes, diagnosis, and treatment of anorexia nervosa, bulimia nervosa, and obesity. The focus is on helping young people with eating disorders learn to help themselves through healthful eating and exercise practices.

Bode, Janet. *Food Fight: A Guide to Eating Disorders for Pre-Teens and Their Parents.* New York, NY: Simon & Schuster, 1997. 153 pp. $16.00. ISBN 0-688-980272-2.

> True to its title, this compassionate book includes information directed at both a middle school audience and at parents. Symptoms, possible causes, and treatments for anorexia, bulimia, and compulsive overeating are explored in detail. There is also solid information on nutrition, and suggestions to help young people regain more healthy eating habits. Throughout the book, young people recount their experiences with eating disorders in their own words.

Claude-Pierre, Peggy. *The Secret Language of Eating Disorders: The Revolutionary New Approach to Curing Anorexia and Bulimia.* New York, NY: Times Books, 1997. 288 pp. $25.00. ISBN 0-812-92842-3.

> The author runs a clinic that treats only people with anorexia or bulimia who have not been helped by other treatments and who are near death. Here she describes how her program works and shares the stories of former patients she has helped. The author also goes into detail about her belief that feelings of worthlessness underlie most people's eating disorders, and explains how she works to help her patients regain their self-esteem.

Jablow, Martha M. *A Parent's Guide to Eating Disorders and Obesity.* New York, NY: Dell, 1992. 164 pp. $10.00. ISBN 0-385-30030-1.

> Written in an easy-to-read, conversational style, this guide illuminates parental concerns related to anorexia, bulimia, and compulsive overeating. The author discusses the history, causes, warning signs, diagnosis, and medical complications related to each eating disorder. The emphasis is on a family approach to treatment. Four composite characters, representing teens with different eating disorders, are followed from diagnosis through treatment.

OBSESSIVE-COMPULSIVE DISORDER

Levenkron, Steven. *Obsessive-Compulsive Disorders: Treating and Understanding Crippling Habits.* New York, NY: Warner Books, 1991. 192 pp. $14.99. ISBN 0-446-39348-7.

> The author of this thought-provoking book regards obsessive-compulsive behavior primarily as an attempt to reduce anxiety, stemming perhaps from "underparenting" or a genetic predisposition toward anxiety. He explains why he thinks today's society is contributing to an uprise of OCD, and how and why OCD behaviors develop in any given individual. Treatment—counseling, medication, hospitalization—is discussed in great detail, using many examples of children and adults with OCD the author has worked with for illustration.

Rapoport, Judith L. *The Boy Who Couldn't Stop Washing: The Experience of Obsessive-Compulsive Disorder.* New York, NY: NAL-Dutton, 1991. 304 pp. $5.99. ISBN 0-451-17202-7.

> The bulk of this fascinating book consists of the stories of many children and adults with Obsessive-Compulsive Disorder—their symptoms, what a typical day is like, their feelings about having OCD, the problems they encounter getting a correct diagnosis, and what has and has not helped them cope with their disorder. Rounding out the book are brief sections on the diagnosis of OCD and what to do if you think you or a loved one has OCD.

SCHIZOPHRENIA

Backlar, Patricia. *The Family Face of Schizophrenia: Practical Counsel from America's Leading Experts.* New York, NY: G.P. Putnam's Sons, 1994. 283 pp. $22.95. ISBN 0-87477-748-8.

> The chapters in this unique book consist of oral histories of families whose "lives have been altered by mental illness" followed by a commentary from a professional working in a specific helping discipline. The family members who tell their stories include a father, a single mother, and several husband and wife couples. The commentators have expertise in law, nursing, police work, psychiatry, psychology, and social work. Although the individuals with schizophrenia are now all adults, many of their stories begin in adolescence. The subject areas discussed—including "Slipping through the Cracks: Failure of the Mental Health System"; "Whereabouts Unknown: Searching for a Missing Family Member"; "At Risk: Suicide and Schizophrenia"—should be of interest to families of children with schizophrenia, regardless of age.

Mueser, Kim T., and Susan Gingerich. *Coping with Schizophrenia: A Guide for Families.* Oakland, CA: New Harbinger Publications, 1994. 355 pp. $13.95. ISBN 1-879237-78-4.

> The authors of this comprehensive book believe that family members should be on the "frontline" of treatment for a relative with schizophrenia, since they are aware of changes in behavior before anyone else is. The book offers many specific suggestions for managing the disorder and for coping with family problems, with chapters grouped under the broad categories of Preventing Relapses, Creating a Supportive Environment, Specific Problems, and Looking Ahead. To help family members take an active role in their relative's treatment, the book includes numerous checklists and worksheets for making observations, evaluating behaviors, watching for signs of a relapse, and dealing with stresses on the family.

Torrey, E. Fuller. *Surviving Schizophrenia: For Families, Consumers, and Providers.* 3rd ed. New York, NY: HarperCollins, 1995. 409 pp. $14.00. ISBN 0-06-095076-5.

> This freshly updated classic explains the science of schizophrenia (causes, symptoms, treatment) in very readable terms, while giving families guidance in helping them cope with schizophrenia. It includes in-depth information on how schizophrenia is diagnosed and other disorders that must be ruled out. Another important focus is on the treatments that can be used to successfully control schizophrenia—specific drugs, their benefits and side effects, drug interactions, and what to do in the case of drug refusal. Numerous case histories and quotations from people with schizophrenia about their experiences are provided. Helpful resources include lists of organizations and recommended further reading. The author, a clinical and research psychiatrist, is considered one of the foremost authorities on schiozophrenia and has a sister with schizophrenia.

FAMILY LIFE

Marsh, Diane T., and Rex M. Dickens. *Troubled Journey: Coming to Terms with the Mental Illness of a Sibling or Parent.* New York, NY: Putnam, 1997. 288 pp. $24.95. ISBN 0-87477-875-1.

> The authors conducted a survey to determine the effects on the family when one or more members has a mental illness. This book describes their findings about short- and long-term effects on a family's functioning.

Secunda, Victoria. *When Madness Comes Home: Help & Hope for the Children, Siblings, & Partners of the Mentally Ill.* New York, NY: Hyperion, 1997. 384 pp. $23.95. ISBN 0-7868-6171-1.

The focus of this empathetic guide is on helping readers who have a spouse, child, sibling, or parent with a mental illness develop better coping skills. The author, who grew up with a sister with mental illness, weaves many of her own experiences into the narrative, as well as stories obtained from interviewing many individuals who have family members with mental illness or substance abuse problems.

Education

Foxx, Richard M., and Ron G. Bittle. *Thinking It Through: Teaching A Problem Solving Strategy for Community Living. Curriculum for Adolescents with Emotional Problems.* Champaign, IL: Research Press, 1989. Not paginated. $14.95. ISBN 0-87822-301-0.

This curriculum provides a structures approach for teens to learn how to react and act appropriately when faced with authority figures, drugs, and alcohol. Community pressures and peer issues are also discussed. This is a professional publication and requires a professional approach to facilitate the program.

Jordan, Dixie. *Honorable Intentions: A Parent's Guide to Educational Planning for Children with Emotional or Behavioral Disorders.* Minneapolis, MN: PACER Center, 1995. 157 pp. $15.00.

The author of this manual advocates that parents "consider the 'honorable intentions' that bring both parents and teachers to the school planning relationship"—to remember that even though conflicts may arise about instruction, services, or discipline, that does not mean that school personnel do not care about a child's success in school. To help parents and teachers ensure that a child's needs in the classroom are being taken into account and met as well as possible, the book includes many helpful checklists of questions to consider—for example, questions to consider in deciding whether a change in placement would be advisable, or whether suspension is warranted. Also helpful is the chapter listing specific adaptations and modifications that can help students with emotional or behavioral problems. The book discusses educational rights and benefits under both IDEA and Section 504.

Psychotherapy

Doft, Norma, with Barbara Aria. *When Your Child Needs Help: A Parent's Guide to Therapy for Children.* New York: Harmony Books/Crown Publishers, 1994. 224 pp. $12.00. ISBN 0-517-88169-1.

This is a useful guide for parents who are considering psychotherapy for a child under the age of twelve. Topics discussed include deciding whether your child needs help, finding a good therapist, what happens during play therapy, and the parents' role in meeting therapy goals. The author also clearly explains when it is important for parents to seek counseling or training to help them learn how to defuse power struggles or minimize parent-child mismatches that can fuel emotional problems. The book is enlivened by many anecdotes about real-life children who were helped through therapy with the author, a child psychologist.

Fishman, Katharine Davis. *Behind the One-Way Mirror: Psychotherapy and Children.* New York: Bantam Books, 1995. 558 pp. $27.50. ISBN 0-553-07886-0.

The author, a journalist, spent three years observing and talking with psychotherapists, psychopharmacologists, their students, their parents, and their patients' families. The resulting book is her attempt to show what children with emotional or behavioral problems such as ADD, anxiety disorder, anorexia, depression, OCD, and autism experience in therapy. To get across an authentic flavor of what children experience, the author intersperses many case histories, excerpts from recorded sessions, and interviews with her narrative. The book examines three broad categories of therapeutic approaches—psychodynamic therapy, cognitive-behavioral therapy, and family systems therapy—any of which can be used in conjunction with medications. This is thought-provoking and informative reading for all parents who have, or are contemplating having, a child in therapy.

Rogers, Annie G. *A Shining Affliction: A Story of Harm and Healing in Psychotherapy.* New York, NY: Viking, 1995. 322 pp. $23.95. ISBN 0-670-85727.

When the book opens, Annie Rogers is beginning a one-year internship in clinical psychotherapy at a center for emotionally disturbed children. One of her first patients is Ben, a five-year-old diagnosed with "oppositional personality disorder" who was abandoned and abused by early foster parents. Rogers faithfully recounts what happens in play therapy sessions as Ben begins to trust her and open up to her. She also describes her own thoughts about what works and does not work with Ben and why. Midway through the book, Rogers has a breakdown and is hospitalized for weeks. Although she has previously received treatment for possible schizophrenia and manic depression, the breakdown appears to be triggered by a failed relationship with her own therapist, not her history of mental illness. With the help of a skilled therapist, Rogers eventually remembers incidents from her own abusive childhood. The book has much to say about harmful and helpful patient-therapist relationships.

First Person Perspectives

Duke, Patty and Gloria Hochman. *A Brilliant Madness: Living with Manic-Depressive Illness.* New York: Bantam Books, 1992. 285 pp. $22.50. ISBN 0-553-07256-0.

Actually two books in one, this book was written in alternating chapters by actress Patty Duke and medical writer Gloria Hochman. In her portion of the book, Duke recounts in painful detail how manic-depression has affected her life. Although her depression did not begin until she was sixteen, and her mania when she was eighteen, she recalls having panic attacks about dying from an early age. As a teenager, she began sleeping for days at a time, having uncontrollable crying bouts, abusing alcohol, and repeatedly attempting suicide. After fifteen years, she finally got the diagnosis that led to successful treatment with lithium. Co-author Gloria Hochman uses Duke's experiences as a springboard for chapters on types of manic-depressive illness and unipolar depression; the genetic basis of these disorders; treatments; and effects of manic-depression on family and friends. Hochman includes many case studies to show how manic-depression can vary from "classic" severe cases like Duke's to very mild cases, and everything in between.

Helfgott, Gillian, with Alissa Tanskaya. *Love You to Bits and Pieces: Life with David Helfgott.* New York, NY: Penguin Books, 1997. 337 pp. $11.95. ISBN 0-14-026644-5.

David Helfgott is the Australian pianist whose life was chronicled in the movie *Shine*. This biography, written by his wife, Gillian, alternates between scenes from his adult life and scenes from his childhood and young adulthood told to the author in his own words. The book traces David's development as a child prodigy, the emotional suffering he experienced at the hands of a fiercely protective and tyrannical father, and his eventual descent into a kind of mental "fog" which sometimes made him deaf even to his own playing. After years spent in and out of psychiatric hospitals, David is now attempting a professional comeback, but is still, according to the author, in a "near permanent state of elation and slight manic tendencies."

Kytle, Elizabeth. *The Voices of Robby Wilde.* Athens, GA: University of Georgia Press, 1995. 344 pp. $14.95. ISBN 0-8203-1715-2.

This is the attempt of a man with paranoid schizophrenia to "fully confide and express what it was like for him to exist as prey to hallucinations that ravaged his life though leaving his mind intact."

Although the book is written by a professional author, it is based on what the real "Robby Wilde," his friends, and family told her about Robby's experiences. For Robby, the voices first began in third grade. When he was not being tormented by voices, he felt himself torn between the contradictory needs to belong and to be as invisible as possible. His adulthood was spent in and out of institutions and in and out of work, striving for normalcy. The book includes many terrifying examples of what his voices said to him, eventually driving him to suicide.

Moorman, Margaret. ***My Sister's Keeper: Learning to Cope with a Sibling's Mental Illness.*** New York, NY: Viking Penguin, 1993. 320 pp. $11.00. ISBN 0-14-023121-8.

> This is the engrossing account of the complex relationship between two sisters—the author and her older sister, Sally, who has since grade school been troubled by manic and depressive episodes related to schizophrenia. The author writes eloquently about some of the differences in her childhood that she only later found out were not typical: the feelings that her mother felt she could do no wrong and her sister could do no right; the screaming fights between her mother and sister; her terror of becoming mentally ill herself; her efforts to convince herself that she was an only child after Sally was hospitalized at 18. It was only after her mother died that the author was forced to come to terms with Sally's mental illness and her long-neglected relationship with her sister. Her description of how she and her sister eventually forged some semblance of a normal sibling relationship is powerful and moving.

For Children

Clayton, Lawrence, and Sharon Carter. ***Coping with Depression.*** 3rd ed. New York, NY: Rosen, 1995. 158 pp. $15.95. ISBN 0-8239-1951-X.

> This well-written book for older children and teens explains depression in terms that are easy to understand. Causes of depression, the kinds of support that work, and treatment options are all discussed. Careful attention is paid to what can be done and how therapy and friends can help. A self-test and resources are provided.

Dinner, Sherry H. ***Nothing to Be Ashamed Of: Growing up with Mental Illness in Your Family.*** New York, NY: William Morrow, 1989. 160 pp. $7.95. ISBN 0-688-08493-1.

> The aim of this well-written book for middle school and high school readers is to help children deal with the stress of having a sibling or parent with mental illness. The author reassures readers that it is all right to feel emotions such as anxiety and sadness, and suggests practical strategies for coping. She also provides an overview of symptoms, causes, and treatments for the most common types of mental illnesses, including depression, anxiety disorders, schizophrenia, eating disorders, and Alzheimer's disease.

Foster, Constance H. ***Polly's Magic Games: A Child's View of Obsessive-Compulsive Disorder.*** Ellsworth, ME: Dilligaf Publishing, 1994. 20 pp. $12.95. ISBN 0-9639070-8-5.

> Polly, age ten, is starting to get worried about the "new, strange stuff" that she is starting to do: counting the steps as she walks up, flicking the light switch off and on exactly five times, washing her hands until they are red. Worse, her best friend, Annie, says that she is "crazy" and no fun to play with any more. After a trip to the doctor, Polly learns that she has obsessive-compulsive disorder, and that medical treatment may help. She also learns that she can still do all her favorite activities and have the same friends, despite being a little different now.

Gordon, Sol. *When Living Hurts.* New York, NY: UAHC Press, 1994. Revised ed. 127 pp. $10.00.
ISBN 0-8074-0505-1.

> The subtitle of this guide for teenagers and young adults is: "A lively what to do book for yourself
> or someone you care about who feels discouraged, sad, lonely, hopeless, angry or frustrated, un-
> happy or bored, depressed, sucidal." For young people in any of those categories, this is essentially
> a serious-minded pep talk in a book. The author focuses on helping readers to distinguish between
> rational and unrational unhappiness, and to take steps to help dispell unrational unhappiness. He
> emphasizes that to feel good about yourself, you need a sense of purpose in life, and suggests
> strategies for finding a purpose. Specific causes of unhappiness the book covers include issues
> related to sex, family, religion, the purpose of life, past experiences, attitudes about yourself and
> others, and more. A chapter about what to do if you or someone else is suicidal is included. The
> author stresses that his book is not meant to be the sole solution to depression, especially if it is
> due to a medical cause.

Kroll, Virgina L. *My Sister, Then and Now: A Book about Mental Illness.* Minneapolis:
Carolrhoda Books, 1992. 42 pp. $14.95. ISBN 0-87614-718-X.

> When Karen was a freshman in college, she began acting as if she was "living in a make-believe
> world." Her younger sister, Rachael, describes some of Karen's most frightening behaviors and
> explains how they make her feel. Conversations with her parents and a counselor help young
> readers and Rachael understand the nature of schizophrenia and what can and cannot be done to
> treat it. The book would be helpful for children in upper elementary grades who are struggling
> with feelings related to a behavior change in a sibling, regardless of cause.

Simpson, Carolyn, and Dwain Simpson. *Coping with Emotional Disorders.* New York, NY: Rosen,
1991. 146 pp. $15.95. ISBN 0-8239-1238-8.

> Although written for teenagers, this short book would also be valuable for parents looking for a
> quick overview of the issues. Information about mental illness is provided from two points of view:
> from the perspective of family members, and from the perspective of someone living with mental
> illness. The authors provide information about anxiety, depression, schizophrenia, and post trau-
> matic stress disorder. Several chapters are written specifically for the individual with mental ill-
> ness. The book is free of jargon, easy to understand, and very supportive.

Stawar, Terry L. *Fenwick the Fearful Frog.* Charlotte, NC: Kidsrights, 1996. 42 pp. $14.95.

> Fenwick was a happy frog until the day he slipped and fell off a lily pad. After that, he began to
> have many irrational fears. With the help of a friend, Fenwick learned that he cannot keep bad
> things from happening by worrying about them, and that his fears are just inside his head. This
> cheerfully illustrated book is appropriate for children up through about grade five.

■ ORGANIZATIONS

American Academy of Child and Adolescent Psychiatry
3615 Wisconsin Ave., NW
Washington, DC 20016
(202) 966-7300; (202) 966-2891 FAX
Web site: http//wwwpsych.med.umich.edu/web/aacap

> PURPOSE: A professional membership organization for child and adolescent psychiatrists.
> PUBLICATIONS: Fact sheet: *"Facts for Families."*

American Psychiatric Association
Division of Public Affairs
1400 K St., N.W.
Washington, DC 20005
(202) 682-6000

> PURPOSE: The Association is a not-for-profit medical specialty society representing more than 36,000 psychiatrists nationwide.
> SERVICES: Share information about mental health issues. Workshops.
> PUBLICATIONS: Catalog of materials (pamphlets; films; educational comic books; guides for educators, clergy, healthcare professionals, and the media) available from Public Affairs office.

Anxiety Disorders Association of America
6000 Executive Blvd., Ste. 513
Rockville, MD 20852
(303) 231-9350; (301) 231-7392.

> PURPOSE: To promote research into the prevention and treatment of anxiety disorders and to improve the lives of people with anxiety disorders.
> SERVICES: Coordinates national self-help group network; conducts public awareness campaigns; holds annual conference.
> PUBLICATIONS: Offers educational materials and a quarterly newsletter, *ADDA Reporter.*

Beach Center on Families and Disability
University of Kansas
3111 Haworth Hall
Lawrence, KS 66045
(785) 864-7600 voice & TTY; (785) 864-7605 FAX
E-mail: beach@dole.lsi.ukans.edu
Web site: http//www.lsi.ukans.edu/beach/beachhp.htm

> PURPOSE: Conducts research on training and disability issues affecting families, sponsors conferences, publishes and disseminates a wide range of publications on family issues.
> PUBLICATIONS: *"What You Need to Know about Your Child with an Emotional Disability and the IEP"* ($3.00); *"Crises That Threaten Out-of-Home Placement of Children with Severe Emotional and Behavioral Disorders"* ($4.40).

Canadian Mental Health Association
2160 Yonge, Floor 3
Toronto, Ontario M4S 2Z3
Canada
(416) 484-7750; (416) 484-4617

> PURPOSE: "A national voluntary association that exists to promote the mental health of all people."
> PUBLICATIONS: *"Families of People with Mental Illness"* ($7.50); *"Learning Diversity: Accommodations in Colleges and Universities for Students with Mental Illness"* ($8); *"Treating Depression"* ($1.25).

Depression and Related Affective Disorders Association
Johns Hopkins Hospital
Meyer 3-181, 600 N. Wolfe St.
Baltimore, MD 21287
(410) 955-4647; (410) 614-3241 FAX

> PURPOSE: A nonprofit organization that works to help people with depression and manic depression through education, self-help, and research.

SERVICES: Makes referrals to self-help support groups; sponsors research symposia; has outreach programs for educators, health care professionals, and others.

PUBLICATIONS: Publishes a quarterly newsletter, *Smooth Sailing,* and educational publications.

The Federation of Families for Children's Mental Health

1021 Prince St.
Alexandria, VA 22341-2971
(703) 684-7710; (703) 836-1040 fax

PURPOSE: To provide parent leadership in the field of mental health and ensure the rights of individuals with this disorder.

SERVICES: Support, information, advocacy. Has state-by-state listings of family networks.

PUBLICATION: Quarterly newsletter, *Claiming Children.*

Knowledge Exchange Network

Substance Abuse and Mental Health Services Administration
National Center for Mental Health Services
P.O. Box 42490
Washington, DC 20015
(800) 789-2647; (301) 984-8796 FAX; (301) 443-9006 TTY
Web site: http//www. mentalhealth.org

PURPOSE: "A national one-stop source of information and resources on prevention, treatment, and rehabilitation services for mental illness."

SERVICES: Information and referral, electronic bulletin board, publications.

PUBLICATIONS: Has a variety of print publications and videos on topics such as Children, Adolescents and Families; Community Support; Emergency and Disaster Assistance; and Mental Health Data and Statistical Information. Examples include: *"Mental, Emotional, and Behavioral Disorders in Children and Adolescents"; "Anxiety Disorders in Children and Adolescents"; "Conduct Disorder in Children and Adolescents"; "Providing Community Support for People with Severe Mental Illness"; "Teen Mental Health Problems: What Are the Warning Signs?"* Publications are available in print form free of charge, or may be read online.

National Alliance for the Mentally Ill (NAMI)

2101 Wilson Blvd., Suite 302
Arlington, VA 22201
(703) 524-7600; (703) 516-7991 (TTY)
(800) 950-NAMI (Helpline)

PURPOSE: Dedicated to improving the lives of people with severe mental illnesses.

SERVICES: Self-help, advocacy, support. Membership: $25.00 annual fee for supporting members.

PUBLICATIONS: Examples of NAMI's publications available include: *"Benzodiazepines"* ($.20); *"Depressive Disorders"* ($.20); *"Panic Disorder"* ($.20); *"Understanding Schizophrenia"* ($.20); *"Schizophrenia and Genetic Risks"* ($1.00); *"Patient Confidentiality and You"* ($1.00); *"Coping with Aggressive Behavior"* ($1.00). NAMI also sells books from a variety of publishers at a substantial discount to members. Request a publications catalog.

National Association for the Dually Diagnosed

132 Fair St.
Kingston, NY 12401-4802
(800) 331-5362; (914) 331-4569 FAX

PURPOSE: A nonprofit organization for parents and professionals designed to promote the interests of individuals who have both mental illness and mental retardation.

SERVICES: Provides information and referral, holds conferences, advocacy work.

PUBLICATIONS: Produces an extensive catalog of audio and video tapes, newsletters, and books on subjects such as diagnosis and assessment, drug therapy, residential services, social & sexual issues, family issues, and research.

National Clearinghouse on Family Support and Children's Mental Health

P.O. Box 751

Portland, OR 97207-0751

(800) 628-1696

Web site: http//www.adm.pdx.edu/user/rri/rtc

SERVICES: Provides a national toll-free telephone service with voice mail 24 hours a day. Response is typically a return phone call and a packet of information specific to your needs.

National Depressive and Manic Depressive Association

730 N. Franklin, #501

Chicago, IL 60610

(312) 642-0049; (312) 642-7243

PURPOSE: A nonprofit organization that strives to educate families, professionals and the public about depressive and manic-depressive illnesses; to advocate for research; to encourage self-help; and to improve access to care.

PUBLICATIONS: Newsletters, booklets, chapter directory of self-help groups; request a publications catalog.

National Foundation for Depressive Illness

P.O. Box 2257

New York, NY 10116

(800) 248-4344; (212) 268-4434 FAX

PURPOSE: To correct the myths surrounding depression and manic depression, and to improve the lives of affected individuals.

SERVICES: Information and referral.

PUBLICATIONS: Information packet.

National Institute of Mental Health

5600 Fishers Lane, Room 7C-02

Rockville, MD 20857

(301) 443-4513; (301) 443-0008 FAX

E-mail: NIMHPUBS@nih.gov

gopher.nimh.nih.gov

PURPOSE: This agency, part of the National Institutes of Health, conducts and supports research into mental health and mental and brain disorders.

SERVICES: Responds to public inquiries about mental health research and mental disorders; distributes information; sponsors public education campaigns.

PUBLICATIONS: Offers free booklets that provide lay people with general information on: Alzheimer's Disease, Anxiety Disorders, Bipolar Disorder, Depressive Illnesses, Eating Disorders, OCD, Schizophrenia, Paranoia, Sleep Disorders, Mental Health Services, Lithium, Medications. Also has publications on specific issues related to depression, panic disorder, and schizophrenia, and a variety of publications in Spanish. Request a publications catalog.

National Mental Health Association
1021 Prince St.
Alexandria, VA 22314-2971
(800) 969-6642; (703) 684-7722; (703) 684-5968 FAX
Web site: http//www.worldcorp.com/dc-online/nmha

> PURPOSE: A grassroots mental health advocacy organization that "seeks to achieve victory over mental illnesses and promote mental health."
> SERVICES: Information dissemination.
> PUBLICATIONS: NMHA publishes over 200 titles. Call or fax for a listing. Examples include *A Parent's Survival Guide to Childhood Depression; ADA and People with Mental Illness: A Resource Manual for Employers;* **The Bell** (quarterly newsletter). Offers discounts on publications for members.

Obsessive Compulsive Foundation
P.O. Box 70
New Haven, CT 06535
(203) 878-5669
Web site: http//pages.prodigy.com/alwillen/ocf.html

> PURPOSE: To provide support, education, and advocacy for people with OCD, their families, and the mental health community.
> PUBLICATIONS: Booklets and a newsletter.

Research and Training Center on Family Support and Children's Mental Health
Portland State University
P.O. Box 751
Portland, OR 97207-0751
(503) 725-4040; (503) 725-4180 FAX
Web site: http//www-adm.pdx.edu/user/rri/rtc/

> PURPOSE: The Center focuses on improving services to families whose children have mental, emotional, or behavioral disorders.
> PUBLICATIONS: Has an extensive publication list of books and article reprints published by the Center and by other publishers. Examples: **Taking Charge: A Handbook for Parents Whose Children Have Emotional Handicaps** ($7.50); **Glossary of Acronyms, Laws, and Terms for Parents When Children Have Emotional and/or Behavioral Disorders** ($3); **National Directory of Organizations Serving Parents of Children and Youth with Emotional and Behavioral Disorders** ($12).

30.

Mental Retardation

■ BOOKS

Basic Information

American Association on Mental Retardation. ***Mental Retardation: Definition, Classification, and Systems of Supports.*** 9th ed. Washington, DC: AAMR, 1992. 180 pp. $65.00. ISBN 0-9408980-30-6. (With workbook, plus 7 pages of worksheets, ISBN 0-040898-30-6.)

> This professional text explains the AAMR's "official" definition of mental retardation, as well as the AAMR's proposed system for doing away with the old classifications of mild, moderate, severe, and profound mental retardation. The book also discusses the three-step process recommended by the AAMR for diagnosing mental retardation, assessing strengths and weaknesses, and identifying supports needed. The worksheets can help parents/caretakers determine where their child is functioning and what supports he may need to be successful in his environment. Tear-out sheets are handy planning tools to use as the Individual Family Service Plan and the Individual Education Plan are being developed.

Dunbar, Robert E. ***Mental Retardation.*** New York, NY: Franklin Watts, 1991. 204 pp. $22.00. ISBN 0-531-12502-5.

> The author of this realistic, unbiased book begins by dispelling myths about mental retardation and then moves on to the facts. He explains the nature and characteristics of mental retardation, as well as the most common causes. A variety of options for educational and vocational planning are included. Resources and glossary are provided.

Fishly, Pat. ***I AM JOHN.*** Washington, DC: National Association of Social Workers Inc., 1992. $3.00. Code: 0360-7283/92.

> This paper was written to establish the need for advocacy for people with mental retardation over time. "John" represents treatment of the mentally retarded since the 1700s, offering a glimpse of

what it was like to have mental retardation and how it was treated in 1720, 1850, 1880, 1890, and into the twentieth century. This is sometimes heart-breaking reading, but it also shows how far we have come. This is a great tool to use for inservices for parent advocates and professionals working with parents.

Smith, Romayne, ed. ***Children with Mental Retardation: A Parents' Guide.*** Bethesda, MD: Woodbine House, 1993. 437 pp. $14.95. ISBN 0-933149-39-5.

When parents first learn that their child has mental retardation, life can seem completely out of control. This book was written to give families the information and support that will help them regain control. The book provides a thorough discussion of the nature and causes of mental retardation, as well as information on how the condition affects development. There is a first-rate look at the evaluation and diagnosis process, including an appendix of frequently used tests. At the heart of the book are several chapters that consider the emotional needs of families in dealing with the diagnosis and keeping family life on an even keel. Information is also provided on the legal rights and benefits of children with retardation, and on strategies for effective advocacy. Each chapter concludes with statements by parents about their experiences raising a child with mental retardation.

Education

Foxx, Richard M., and Ron G. Bittle. ***Thinking It Through: Teaching A Problem Solving Strategy for Community Living. Curriculum for Adolescents with Developmental Disabilities.*** Champaign, IL: Research Press, 1989. Not paginated. $14.95. ISBN 0-87822-298-7.

The focus of this curriculum is a structures approach for individuals with mental retardation as they face challenges such as emergencies and injuries. Stressful situations such as working with authority figures, safety issues, peer problems, accessing community resources, and self-advocacy are all addressed. This curriculum requires professional facilitation.

Hickson, Linda, Leonard S. Blackman, and Elizabeth M. Reis. ***Mental Retardation: Foundations of Educational Programming.*** Needham Heights, MA: Allyn and Bacon, 1995. 421 pp. $61.00. ISBN 0-205-14016-5.

This textbook was designed to introduce college students to the educational needs of children with mental retardation. For parents, it may be helpful in understanding the teacher's perspective on assessing and teaching students with mental retardation. Among topics covered are: different ways of defining and measuring intelligence; academic expectations for children with different degrees of mental retardation; formal and informal methods of assessing skills in the classroom; developing an IEP, from the teacher's perspective; instructional approaches; approaches to teaching different developmental and academic skills; early intervention. Case studies of students with different degrees of mental retardation, and how their needs can best be understood and met, are included.

First Person Perspectives

Buck, Pearl S. ***The Child Who Never Grew.*** 2nd ed. Bethesda, MD: Woodbine House, 1992. 107 pp. $14.95. ISBN 0-933149-49-2.

Pearl Buck's only natural child, Carol, appeared perfectly "normal" at birth. As she failed to walk, talk, and achieve other milestones at a typical age, however, her mother became increasingly uneasy. She trekked from doctor to doctor, and only after many years learned that her daughter's mental retardation was due to PKU, a metabolic disorder that researchers did not identify until Carol was an adult. Although Buck's journey to understanding began in 1920, the emotions she describes so eloquently will be very familiar to families of today. New material added to this edition—including an Afterword by Carol's sister, Janice—describe the many ways that Carol did, in fact, grow, despite the book's title. This book marked one of the earliest disclosures by a celebrity about a family member with disabilities.

Kaufman, Sandra Z. *Retarded Isn't Stupid, Mom!* Baltimore, MD: Paul H. Brookes, 1991. 256 pp. $18.00. ISBN 0-933716-96-6.

The Kaufman's daughter, Nicole, was not diagnosed with mental retardation until she was two and a half. As it was the 1960s, there was no formal educational help available until Nicole reached kindergarten age. In the meantime, Nicole's parents battled feelings of guilt, embarrassment, and inadequacy at not being able to cope better with their daughter's behavioral and emotional problems. Nicole was not a stellar student in school, and the family's experiences with the school system were not the best. With support and determination, however, Nicole eventually landed a job in a restaurant and married. The majority of the book is devoted to describing how Nicole and her husband, Edward, were successfully integrated into their community. This book offers a splendid example of how parents can learn from experience and use that information to plan and cope with raising a child with a disability.

Miller, Nancy B. *Nobody's Perfect: Living & Growing with Children Who Have Special Needs.* Baltimore: Paul H. Brookes, 1994. 307 pp. $21.00. ISBN 1-55766-143-X.

Parents of children with Prader–Willi syndrome may want to take special note of this book. The author wrote it in close consultation with four mothers of children with special needs, including the mother of a child with a genetic disorder similar to Prader–Willi syndrome. Many quotations from the parents about their experiences and feelings are used to illustrate the author's ideas about helping parents cope with the special challenges of raising a child with special needs.

Moise, Lotte. *Barbara and Fred - Grownups Now: Living Fully with Developmental Disabilities.* Fort Bragg, CA: Lost Coast Press, 1998. 211 pp. $16.95. ISBN 1-882897-08-0.

Part memoir, part report from the trenches of the disability movement, this thoughtful book has much to offer all readers who are committed to building a truly inclusive society. The author's third child, Barbara, was born with mental retardation at a time when parents were beginning to speak up for the right of their children with disabilities to become a part of their communities. After battling initial feelings of denial and shame, Moise plunged into the parent movement, founding and teaching in a school for children with disabilities when the local school system refused to serve them. Gradually, it became clear that Barbara, despite her label of "trainable mentally retarded," could achieve more than any of the "experts" had predicted. As Barbara learned and grew, so too did her family, and Moise shares many of the experiences that helped her family learn to support the independence and individuality of all its members. She also shares many of Barbara's own pointed insights and observations in her own words. By the end of the book, Barbara, now in her 40s, has found comfort in a stable, loving relationship with a man who has Down syndrome, but her financial future is not as secure. Moise uses her daughter's situation to reflect on how far society has come, and how far it still has to go before advocates for people with disabilities can rest easy.

O'Reilly, Diane. *Retard.* Macomb, IL: Glenbridge Publishing, 1989. 194 pp. $18.95. ISBN 0-944435-05-X.

In 1969, Diane O'Reilly was assigned to teach a class of lower income "educable mentally handicapped" children, ages 6-11. This plain-spoken book is her account of the changes in the children and herself over that year, as well as her views on the shortcomings of the system at the time. With little support from her colleagues, the administration, and the children's families, in some cases, Ms. O'Reilly was able to improve many of the students' behaviors, self-esteem, and academic achievements, but found others unreachable. The author offers a revealing glimpse of attitudes that may still be affecting the course of inclusive education today.

Perske, Robert. ***Deadly Innocence?*** Nashville, TN: Abingdon Press, 1995. 143 pp. $12.95.
ISBN 0-687-00615-5.

> This is the gripping, real-life story of Joe Arridy, a man with mental retardation who was sent to death row in the early 1900s. In prison, the warden became convinced of Arridy's innocence, but was ultimately unable to save him from the gas chamber. The book is sobering reading for anyone concerned with the way individuals with disabilities have historically been treated by society.

For Children

FICTION

Byars, Betsy. ***The Summer of the Swans.*** New York, NY: Viking, 1970. 142 pp. $15.99.
ISBN 670-68190-3.

> Sara, 14, is having a miserable summer. She feels awkward, ugly, and discontented. On top of everything else, she is irked by having to be a constant companion to her little brother Charlie, who has mental retardation. When Charlie gets lost in the woods, Sara discovers how she really feels about Charlie, and also learns that more people care about him than she ever knew. Several chapters are written from Charlie's viewpoint and convincingly capture his thought processes and feelings. Except for a few mentions of TV programs no longer on the air, this older book reads as if it were just written yesterday.

Carrick, Carol. ***Stay Away from Simon!*** New York, NY: Clarion Books/Houghton Mifflin, 1985.
63 pp. $5.95. ISBN 0-89919-343-9.

> This short chapter book set in nineteenth century Martha's Vineyard focuses on the stigma often associated with having a mind "too slow for schooling." Lucy, 11, and her little brother, Josiah, have grown up fearing Simon, the Miller's son. Simon has failed to learn to read or count at school, and seems odd because he likes to watch the younger children playing. When Lucy and Josiah get lost in a snow storm in the woods, however, Simon comes to their rescue and everyone learns that people are not always what they seem.

Lee, Harper. ***To Kill a Mockingbird.*** New York, NY: HarperCollins, 1995. 323 pp. $17.00.
ISBN 0-06-017322-X.

> Boo Radley, a young man with mental retardation, plays a small, but significant role in this classic tale of racial injustice. Radley, the young narrator's neighbor, is seen as mysterious and fearsome by the neighbor children, in part because he is never allowed to leave the house. Eventually, thanks to a moment of heroism, he is revealed to be a kind and thoughtful man who wants desperately to have friends. There are many editions of this book available; the one cited here is the 35th anniversary edition, and includes a new foreword by Harper Lee. Suitable for young adult and adult readers.

O'Shaughnessy, Ellen. ***Somebody Called Me a Retard Today . . . and My Heart Felt Sad.***
New York: Walker and Company, 1992. 20 pp. $14.85. ISBN 0-8027-8197-7.

> This very simply worded book is designed to help nondisabled children understand that children with disabilities have feelings too. Suitable for older preschool and elementary school children.

Saroyan, William. ***The Human Comedy.*** New York, NY: Dell, 1966. $5.50. ISBN 0-440-33933-2.

> In this coming-of-age story set during World War II, Homer McCauley learns firsthand about life and death while working as a telegram delivery boy for Western Union. His little brother, Ulysses, pals around with Lionel Cabot, an older boy with mental retardation. Lionel is depicted as always being on the outside looking in—longing to read the books in the library, but being unable to read, hoping in vain to be chosen to play games with the other boys in the neighborhood. An interesting read for thoughtful young adults and their parents.

Slepian, Jan. *The Alfred Summer.* New York: Macmillan, 1982. 119 pp. $15.00. ISBN 0-02-782920-0.
> When this story opens in the summer of 1937, Lester feels that he is an object of pity and derision. Although he can walk awkwardly and talk well enough to be understood if he takes his time, his cerebral palsy seems to scare every possible friend away. Then he meets Alfred, a happy-go-lucky boy with mental retardation and a limp. The two fall in with two other children who feel like misfits and spend the summer building a rowboat that they plan to use to get away from it all. Along the way, Lester learns that he is stronger both physically and emotionally than he ever knew and that some people, at least, are worth getting close to.

Slepian, Jan. *Risk N' Roses.* New York: Putnam & Grosset Book Group, 1990. 175 pp. $14.95. ISBN 0-399-22219-7.
> The Bronx, 1948. As the new kid on the block, eleven-year-old Skip is anxious to belong. She fears, though, that her older sister, Angela, will hold her back as usual. Angela has mental retardation, and tags along everywhere Skip goes. Eventually, Skip falls in with a group of street-wise girls who roam the neighborhood taking dares and looking for excitement. Angela makes friends with Kaminski, a lonely Holocaust survivor who raises prize roses. When Skip's friends turn to tormenting Kaminski, Skip is forced to decide whether it is more important for her to follow along with her friends or look out for her sister's best interests.

Thompson, Mary. *My Brother, Matthew.* Bethesda, MD: Woodbine House, 1992. 32 pp. $14.95 ISBN 0-933149-47-6
> Matthew was born prematurely. Now, as a little boy of about four or five, he moves and talks differently from other children and also has more trouble learning. His older brother, David, loves him, but also is bothered by the fact that his parents often seem to overlook his feelings and needs. Although the primary audience of this beautifully illustrated book is children in grades K-5, it will also help parents discover and validate sibs' special insight about their brother or sister with special needs.

NONFICTION

Bergman, Thomas. *We Laugh, We Love, We Cry: Children Living with Mental Retardation.* Milwaukee: Gareth Stevens, 1989. 48 pp. ISBN 1-55532-914-4. Out of print.
> Asa, 5, and Anna Karin, 6, are sisters who both have mental retardation. This book, illustrated with splendid black-and-white photos, traces some of their typical activities at home and at school. Anna Karin goes to a regular kindergarten but sometimes feels left out because her classmates cannot understand sign language, and she cannot speak. Both girls also go to physical and speech therapy, where they work hard to learn the skills their peers master easily. Both girls are shown as contributing and beloved members of their family. The book provides a good general understanding of some of the ways mental retardation can affect a child, but because the book was originally published in Sweden, some of the names and practices may seem unusual. In addition, in a question-and-answer section at the end, the author gives an IQ score cutoff that differs from that used in the United States.

McNey, Martha. *Leslie's Story: A Book about a Girl with Mental Retardation.* Minneapolis: Lerner Publications, 1996. 32 pp. $19.95. ISBN 0-8225-2576-3.
> In words and black-and-white photos, this book offers a glimpse of the life of Leslie Fish, 12. Leslie has mental retardation, hearing loss, and seizures due to a childhood bout with meningitis, but is very much a part of her family, her school, and her community. She is shown cooking with her mother, participating in a typical classroom, posing with friends, taking art lessons and ice skating, and celebrating her Bat Mitzvah. The text is careful to explain that some people prefer other labels to "mental retardation." Appropriate for children in early elementary grades.

Rosenberg, Maxine B. *My Friend Leslie: The Story of a Handicapped Child.* New York, NY: Lothrop, Lee & Shepard Books, 1983. ISBN 0-688-01690-1. Out of print.

> This is a simple and heartwarming story about two friends, one with physical and mental disabilities and one without. These friends care about and help each other. Leslie is fully included into a classroom at her school and that is where the relationship blossoms. The photographs by George Ancona capture beautifully the relationship between Leslie and her classmates. Suitable for children in early elementary grades.

■ ORGANIZATIONS

American Association on Mental Retardation
444 N. Capitol St., N.W., Ste. 846
Washington, DC 20001-1512
(800) 424-3688; (202) 387-1968
E-mail: AAMR@access.digex.net

> PURPOSE: To enhance life opportunities and choices of people with disabilities and their families by exchanging information that advances the skills and knowledge of individuals in this field.
> PUBLICATIONS: Publishes the *"Innovations"* series of monographs aimed at bridging the gap between research and practice. Also the newsletter, ***News and Notes,*** and the professional journals, ***Mental Retardation*** and ***AJMR.*** Various publications available with a request for a free packet.

The Arc of the United States
500 E. Border St., Ste. 300
Arlington, TX 76010
(817) 261-6003; (817) 277-0553 (TTY)
E-mail: thearc@metronet.com
http//TheArc.org/welcome.html

> PURPOSE: The Arc (formerly the Association for Retarded Citizens) works to improve the lives of all children and adults with mental retardation and their families.
> SERVICES: Information and referral about mental retardation, the Arc's programs, and local chapters. Advocates for inclusion of individuals with mental retardation in community life; fosters research and education regarding prevention of mental retardation.
> PUBLICATIONS: Has an extensive publications catalog, which includes many fact sheets (free with a self-addressed, stamped envelope) about specific topics related to mental retardation. Other publications include *"Toilet Training for Children with Mental Retardation"* ($2); *"Developmental Disabilities and Alzheimer's Disease"* ($5); *"Test Your School's IQ: Integration Quotient";* and publications for self-advocates. *"The Arc's Family Book for Parents of Children with Mental Retardation"* ($5) is intended to help families through the period following the diagnosis of mental retardation in a child. Some publications are available in Spanish as well as English.

Canadian Association for Community Living
Kinsmen Building, York University
4700 Keele St.
North York, Ontario M3J 1P3
Canada
(416) 661-9611; (416) 661-5701 (fax)
Web site: http//indie/ca/cacl/index.htm/

> PURPOSE: The CACL focuses on developing a welcoming, supportive community for all Canadians by working to ensure that people with mental handicaps become active members of their communities.

SERVICES: Advocates for people with mental handicaps and their families; and has a network of local chapters across Canada.

PUBLICATIONS: The CACL publishes a newsletter and other publications. Request a publications list.

The Children's Biomedical Research Institute

345 N. Smith Ave.

St. Paul, MN 55102-9912

PURPOSE: Conducts research to study the human immune system and how it responds to viruses.

SERVICES: Leading source of information about CMV (cytomegolovirus).

PUBLICATIONS: *"CMV: Diagnosis, Prevention and Treatment,"* a 20- page awareness booklet for parents, physicians, audiologists, nurses, and educators. Also, a periodic newletter about CMV, which can cause mental retardation.

Children's PKU Network

1520 State St., Ste. 240

San Diego, CA 92101

(619) 233-3202; (619) 233-0838

PURPOSE: Provides support and services to those involved in the treatment of Phenylketonuria.

SERVICES: Scale distribution; crisis intervention, regional coordinators council; scholarships; and Newborn Express Clearinghouse.

PUBLICATIONS: Newsletter, articles, resarch studies, and videos.

Cornelia de Lange Syndrome Foundation

60 Dyer Ave.

Collinsville, CT 06022-1273

(800) 223-8355; (203) 693-0159; (203) 693-6819 FAX

Web site: http//cdlsoutreach.org

PURPOSE: International non-profit family support group that strives for an early and accurate diagnosis of CdLS, and assists families in making informed decisions and plans for individuals with the syndrome.

SERVICES: Hotline, annual convention for parents and professionals, and support and funding of research into the cause and cure of CdLS.

PUBLICATIONS: Newsletter; Pamphlet *"What is CdLS?"*

Council for Exceptional Children

Division on Mental Retardation and Developmental Disabilities

1920 Association Dr.

Reston, VA 20191-1589

(703) 620-3660; (800) 845-6232; (703) 264-9494.

Web site: http//www.cec.sped.org

PURPOSE: "To foster public understanding, advocate, promote inclusion, promote effective instructional practices and provide a professional forum."

SERVICES: Information, training, referral.

PUBLICATIONS: Publishes the newsletter ***MRDD express*** three times a year; also the journals ***Exceptional Children*** and ***Teaching Exceptional Children.***

International Rett Syndrome Association

9121 Piscataway Rd.
Clinton, MD 20735
(300) 856-3334; (800) 818-RETT
Web site: http//www2.paltech.com/irsa/irsa/htm

> PURPOSE: "To support and encourage medical research to determine the cause and find a cure for Rett syndrome, to increase the public awareness of Rett syndrome, and to provide informational and emotional support to families of children with Rett syndrome." (Rett syndrome is a neurological disorder affecting only girls and causing impairments in language, hand function, and intellectual development.)
>
> SERVICES: Information and referral, advocacy, regional support groups.
>
> PUBLICATIONS: Newsletter, educational materials, fact sheets.

National Association for the Dually Diagnosed

132 Fair St.
Kingston, NY 12401-4802
(800) 331-5362; (914) 331-4569 FAX

> PURPOSE: A nonprofit organization for parents and professionals designed to promote the interests of individuals who have both mental illness and mental retardation.
>
> SERVICES: Provides information and referral, holds conferences, performs advocacy work.
>
> PUBLICATIONS: Produces an extensive catalog of audio and video tapes, newsletters, and books on subjects such as diagnosis and assessment, drug therapy, residential services, social & sexual issues, family issues, and research.

Prader-Willi Syndrome Association

2510 S. Brentwood Blvd., Ste. 220
St. Louis, MO 63144
(800) 926-4797; (314) 962-7869 FAX
Web site: http//www.athenet.net/~pwsa_usa/index.html

> PURPOSE: "to provide to parents and professionals a national and international network of information, support services, and research endeavors to expressly meet the needs of affected children and adults and their families."
>
> PUBLICATIONS: A bimonthly newsletter, **The Gathered View,** is included with membership. Publishes low-cost booklets and brochures, such as *"Prader-Willi Syndrome Weight & Behavior Management"* ($0.25); *"Speech and Language and Prader-Willi Syndrome"* ($0.25); *"What Every Parent of a Prader-Willi Child Should Know about Education"* ($0.25). The organization also sells (at reduced prices to members) other publishers' books, including **Management of Prader-Willi Syndrome** (L. Greensway and R. Alexander, eds.).

Rehabilitation Research and Training Center (RRTC) on Aging with Mental Retardation

Institute on Disability and Human Development
University of Illinois
1640 W. Roosevelt Rd.
Chicago, IL 60608
(800) 996-8845; (312) 996-6942 FAX
Web site: http//www.uic.edu/orgs/rrtcamr/index.html

> PURPOSE: "To promote the independence, productivity, community inclusion, and full citizenship of older adults with mental retardation through a coordinated program of research, training, technical assistance and dissemination activities."

SERVICES: Operates the Clearinghouse on Aging and Developmental Disabilities, a computerized database of publications.

PUBLICATIONS: Subscriptions to **A/DDVANTAGE** newsletter, published two times a year, are free. Also available: ***Information Directory on Aging and Developmental Disabilities*** ($10.00); ***Research Briefs*** on topics including age-related physical changes, funding for community living options, adjusting to changes in housing, and health and social supports among families.

The Roeher Institute

Kinsmen Building
York University
4700 Keele St.
North York, Ontario
Canada M3J 1P3
(416) 661-2023 V/TTY; (416) 661-5701 FAX
Web site: http//indie.ca/roeher/intro.html

PURPOSE: "Promotes the equality, participation, and self-determination of people with intellectual and other disabilities."

SERVICES: Information services include reference and referral information, customized responses to questions, the development of information packages on specific topics, and operation of an extensive library. Also conducts research and public policy analysis and social development and training.

PUBLICATIONS: Examples include: *Choosing an Inclusive Literacy Program: A Guide for People with an Intellectual Disability, Their Families, Friends and Support Workers; The Family Book: A Resource for Parents Who Have Learned Their Child Has a Mental Handicap; Keys to Understanding: An Orientation Manual on the History, Issues and Alternatives for People with Intellectual Disabilities.* **Entourage,** the Institute's quarterly magazine, promotes community living for people with intellectual or other disabilities ($20.00 in the U.S.; $19.26 in Canada).

Support Organization for Trisomy 18/13 (SOFT)

2982 S. Union St.
Rochester, NY 14624
(800) 716-SOFT; (716) 594-4621 FAX
Web site: http//pages.prodigy.com/NC/soft/soft.html

PURPOSE: To provide support for families of children with Trisomy 18, Trisomy 13, and other trisomies, and to promote public awareness.

SERVICES: Workshops, seminars, speakers' bureau.

PUBLICATIONS: ***The SOFT Touch,*** a bimonthly newsletter, plus a variety of books and pamphlets about Trisomy 18/13.

TASH

29 W. Susquehanna Ave., Ste. 210
Baltimore, MD 21204
(410) 828-6706
Web site: http//www.tash.org

PURPOSE: TASH advocates strongly for inclusion of all individuals in every aspect of life. Their membership is a blend of parents, self-advocates, and professionals. Among their goals: "building communities in which no one is segregated and everyone belongs"; "advocating for opportunities and rights"; "promoting inclusive education"; "disseminating knowledge and information."

PUBLICATIONS: Include a quarterly peer-reviewed journal *(**JASH**)* and a monthly newsletter. Information in the newsletter is pertinent to most parents, addressing current topics regarding inclusive schools, education methods, community living, and politics.

Turner's Syndrome Society of the U.S.
15500 Wayzata Blvd., #768-214
Wayzata, MN 55391
(612) 475-9944; (612) 475-9949 FAX

> PURPOSE: To provide family support and promote public awareness of the syndrome.
> SERVICES: A referral database is available.
> PUBLICATIONS: Quarterly newsletter and additional information about Turner Syndrome.

Visible Ink
40 Holly Lane
Roslyn Heights, NY 11577
(800) 358-0682; (516) 621-2445; (516) 484-7154 FAX

> PUBLICATIONS: Publishes two booklets: *"Physical Therapy Intervention for Individuals with Prader-Willi Syndrome"* ($5.00); and *"Children with Prader-Willi Syndrome: Information for School Staff"* ($5.00). Also a quarterly journal, ***Prader-Willi Perspectives,*** a nontechnical publication for families and professionals ($20.00 annually in the U.S.; $25.00 in Canada).

Williams Syndrome Association
P.O. Box 3297
Ballwin, MO 63022-3297
(248) 541-3630
Web site: http//www.williams-syndrome.org

> PURPOSE: To provide support and parent-professional networking.
> SERVICE: Computerized bibliography
> PUBLICATIONS: Semi-annual newsletter.

31.

Muscular Dystrophy and Other Neuromuscular Diseases

■ BOOKS AND PERIODICALS

Basic Information

Brown, Matthew. *Crying in the Night: An Autobiography.* Roswell, GA: Mission Publishing, 1995. $25.00. 264 pp.

> Matthew Brown, who has spinal muscular atrophy, was the 1977-78 Poster Child for the Muscular Dystrophy Association. In this upbeat autobiography, he describes his childhood battle to survive, how having SMA affected family life and his own behavior, and his lifetime association with the MDA, first as a camper and then as a fund-raiser. Although rough around the edges, this self-published book may give older children with SMA and their parents useful insights into what it is like to grow up with the disorder.

Corrick, James A. *Muscular Dystrophy.* New York, NY: Franklin Watts, 1992. 96 pp. $22.00. ISBN 0-531-12540-8.

> Via examples, pictures, and essays the author provides a basic understanding of the muscular dystrophies. In nontechnical language, he explains causes, treatments, and where research is and

has been going. A large portion of the text is devoted to providing real-life examples. A thumbnail sketch of the types of MD, a glossary, and list of resources is included.

Emery, Alan E. ***Muscular Dystrophy: The Facts.*** New York, NY: Oxford University Press, 1994. 108 pp. $18.95. ISBN 0-19-262449-0.
> Like the other books in Oxford University Press's "The Facts" series, this one provides a concise and readable, if somewhat detached, overview of the basics: diagnosis, symptoms, causes, treatment, and educational and daily care issues.

Quest. Muscular Dystrophy Association, 3300 E. Sunrise Dr., Tucson, AZ 85718-3208. (520) 529-2000.
> This glossy quarterly magazine includes articles about coping for and by parents and people with neuromuscular diseases; research; parenting issues; educational issues; and equipment; as well as information about useful resources. A subscription is free to anyone who has any of the 40 neuromuscular diseases in the MDA's program. Subscriptions are $10 for others within the U.S.; $20 elsewhere.

For Children

Hill, David. ***See Ya, Simon.*** New York, NY: Dutton, 1994. 120 pp. $14.99. ISBN 0-525-45247-8.
> The extraordinary friendship between two teenaged boys, Nathan and Simon, is the subject of this powerful novel set in New Zealand. Simon has muscular dystrophy but hates to be pitied, so Nathan tries his hardest to treat his friend like just another kid, in the process learning a great deal about human dignity and courage. Despite the subject matter, the book is more uplifting than dreary, with many humorous touches thrown in.

Osofsky, Audrey. ***My Buddy.*** New York, NY: Henry Holt, 1992. 30 pp. $5.95. ISBN 0-8050-3546-X.
> A young boy with muscular dystrophy talks about his service dog, Buddy. He describes how he and Buddy learned to be a team, and how Buddy enables him to be more independent by operating light switches, opening doors, accompanying him on shopping trips, and helping out at school. This illustrated book is suitable for older preschoolers and children in early elementary grades.

■ ORGANIZATIONS

Amyotrophic Lateral Sclerosis (ALS) Association
21021 Ventura Blvd., Ste. 321
Woodland Hills, CA 91364
(800) 782-4747; (818) 340-7500; (818) 340-2060 FAX
Web site: http//www.alsa.org
Web site: http//bro@huey.met.fsu.edu (Support group site)
> PURPOSE: Dedicated to finding the cause, prevention, and cure for ALS.
> SERVICES: Provides information and referral; funds research; conducts patient meetings for support and information exchange. Offers an info-bank, patient hotline (800-782-4747).
> PUBLICATIONS: Quarterly newspaper, ***Amyotrophic Lateral Sclerosis Association-Link;*** fact sheets; pamphlets.

Charcot-Marie-Tooth Association

601 Upland Ave.
Upland, PA 19015
(800) 606-2682; (610) 499-7487
Web site: http//www.charcot-marie-tooth.org

> PURPOSE: To educate and support people with CMT and their families and to support research.
> PUBLICATIONS: Quarterly newsletter; handbooks on CMT.

Charcot-Marie-Tooth International

1 Springbank Dr.
St. Catharines, ON, Canada L2S SKI
(905) 687-3630; (905) 687-8753 fax
e-mail: cmtint@vaxxine.com

> PURPOSE: Distributes information and supports research on an international level.
> SERVICES: Establishes networks for shared information; supports research.
> PUBLICATIONS: Bimonthly newsletter. Provides a resource list of shoemakers and helping aides.

Dystonia Medical Research Foundation

1 E. Wacker Dr., Ste. 2230
Chicago, IL 60601
(312) 755-0198
E-mail: dystfdtn@aol.com
Web site: http//www.iii.net/biz/dystonia.html

> PURPOSE: To support people with dystonia and their families; advance research into causes and treatments; increase public awareness.
> PUBLICATIONS: Quarterly newsletter; fact sheets and guidebooks for patients and medical professionals.

Families of Spinal Muscular Atrophy

P.O. Box 196
Libertyville, IL 60048-0196
(800) 886-1762
Web site: http//www.abacus96.com/fsma/

> PURPOSE: A volunteer, nonprofit organization that supports those with SMA (Werdnig-Hoffman, Kugalberg-Welander, adult spinal muscular atrophy) and their families, and promotes research into causes and cures of SMA.
> SERVICES: Information and referral.
> PUBLICATIONS: *Direction,* a quarterly newsletter provided by SMA, provides updates on research, information about new equipment, personal stories, and innovative creations made by parents for their children. Resources dot every page. Also offers a free booklet, *"Understanding Spinal Muscular Atrophy,"* available in English, Spanish, and French.

Muscular Dystrophy Association

3300 East Sunrise Dr.
Tuscon, AZ 85718
(520) 529-2000; (520) 529-5300
Web site: http//www.mdausa.org

> PURPOSE: "A voluntary health agency working to defeat 40 neuromuscular diseases through programs of worldwide research, comprehensive services, and far-reaching professional and public health education."

SERVICES: Information and referral; research.

PUBLICATIONS: *Quest* (described above); and *ALS Newsletter,* a bi-monthly sent free to anyone with ALS who is registered with MDA. Also pamphlets, including *"Friedreich's Ataxia,"* and *"Learning to Live with Neuromuscular Disease: A Message for Parents,"* free. Some publications available in Spanish.

National Ataxia Foundation

750 Twelve Oaks Center
15500 Wayzata Blvd.
Wyzata, MN 55391
(612) 473-7666; (612) 473-9289
E-mail: naf@mr.net
Web site: http//www.ataxia.org/

PURPOSE: To support people with hereditary ataxia and their families; educate the public and medical professionals; and support research.

PUBLICATIONS: A quarterly newsletter distributed to members; fact sheets and booklets on hereditary ataxia, Friedreich's ataxia, Charcot-Marie-Tooth, and spastic paraplegia.

NIH Neurology Institute

National Institute of Neurological Disorders and Stroke
P.O. Box 5801
Bethesda, MD 20824
(800) 352-9424; (301) 402-2186 FAX
Web site: http://www.ninds.nih.gov

PURPOSE: Supports research into brain and nervous system disorders.

PUBLICATIONS: Free publications include: *Neurological Disorders: Voluntary Health Agencies and Other Patient Resources* (a directory); *"Know Your Brain"* (fact sheet on anatomy and function); fact sheets on a variety of neurological disorders, including the dystonias, Friedreich's ataxia, Guillain-Barre syndrome, progressive supranuclear palsy, reflex sympathetic dystrophy syndrome, and syringomyelia.

Society for Muscular Dystrophy Information International

P.O. Box 479
Bridgewater, Nova Scotia B4V 2X6
Canada
(902) 682-3086; (902) 682-3142 FAX

PURPOSE: To encourage people with neuromuscular diseases and organizations to help themselves by sharing information.

PUBLICATIONS: Publishes two quarterly newsletters: *SMDI International Newsletter,* by and for individuals with neuromuscular disease; and *ACCESS-ABLE INFORMATION,* which provides information about disability resources. Also publishes a directory of organizations that serves people with neuromuscular diseases.

32.

Physical Disabilities

■ BOOKS AND PERIODICALS

Basic Information

Albrecht, Donna G. *Raising a Child Who Has a Physical Disability.* New York, NY: John Wiley & Sons, 1995. 228 pp. $12.95. ISBN 0-471-04240-4.

> The author of this reader-friendly guide, the mother of two children with neuromuscular disease, subscribes to a very broad definition of "physical disability." The information provided is intended to be helpful to parents of children with any condition that restricts their physical activities, from cancer, cleft palate, and dwarfism to spina bifida, muscular dystrophy, and cerebral palsy. Because of this broad audience, some chapters may not be specific enough for parents who are looking for detailed information about their child's particular disability—for instance, the information on what to expect during the diagnosis process and educational options is rather generic. Chapters on medical issues (Choosing Medical Equipment and Suppliers, Handling Your Child's Hospitalizations) and self-help skills (Skin Care and Protection, Choosing Attractive, Functional Clothing) may be of more practical help. Also useful is the plentiful advice on coping emotionally, which is offered in an empathetic and upbeat manner.

Buchanan, R.J., and K. Lewis. *The Directory of Nursing Facilities for Younger Adults with Chronic Physical Disabilities.* Lakeville, CT: Gray House Publishing, 1994. 333 pp. $65.00. ISBN 0-9393000-57-5.

> This comprehensive directory provides information about facilities in 45 states that care for young adults. Included are special care units and facilities with special programs and services specifically

for young people. Each entry describes the admission criteria, staff and services, number of beds, whether the facility is private or not-for-profit, age group information, and payment options.

Hanson, Marci J., and S. Harris. ***Teaching the Young Child with Motor Delays: A Guide for Parents and Professionals.*** Austin, TX: Pro-Ed, 1985. 228 pp. $29.00. ISBN 0-936104-91-0.

This manual offers tips on teaching in general, as well as step-by-step instructions for teaching important developmental skills to young children with motor delays. A special focus is on explaining how motor delays can lead to delays in other areas of development.

Maddox, Sam, ed. ***Spinal Network: Total Wheelchair Resource Book.*** 2nd ed. Malibu, CA: Spinal Network, 1994. 568 pp. $39.95. ISBN 0-943489-03-2.

Resource does not even begin to describe this book. Information is included about medical advances, therapy, orthotics, and more (this particular edition had 28 different articles that focused on the medical aspects of physical disabilities). There are pages of personal profiles and inspirational messages from people with a variety of physical disabilities. A sports section is included. A large section of this book is dedicated to getting peer support and locating organizations that will help the person with the disability and his family. Lists of resources are included. Although the primary audience of this book is adult readers who have a physical disability, parents, too, can glean much useful information.

New Mobility: Disability Lifestyle, Culture & Resources. New Mobility, P.O. Box 15518, North Hollywood, CA 91615-5518. (800) 543-4116. Web site: http//www.newmobility.com

Adults with physical disabilities, congenital or acquired, are the primary audience for this glossy monthly magazine. Articles include profiles of individuals with disabilities, health and medical issues, opportunities and adaptations for recreation and daily living, and editorials. Parents of younger children with physical disabilities may find the reviews of books and products (wheelchairs, health and daily living aids, alternative communication, and adaptive computer technology) and advertisements the most helpful. A one-year subscription is $37.95 in the U.S.; $45.95 in Canada.

Accessibility and Mobility

A Consumer's Guide to Home Adaptation. Boston: Adaptive Environments, 1995. 52 pp. $12.00 (book or audio tape).

This is an illustrated guide to making a home more accessible or safer. It includes worksheets to assess possible problems and solutions; sketches of construction detail for common home adaptations; information on working with contractors; and information on costs and funding sources.

Garee, Betty, ed. ***Ideas for Making Your Home Accessible.*** 6th ed. Bloomington, IL: Cheever, Publications, 1992. 94 pp. $6.50. ISBN 0-915708-08-6.

This simple little guide provides a comprehensive resource for remodeling, creating, and adjusting the home environment. Practical solutions are provided regarding financing, location of remodeling, information about entrances.

Thacker, John, Stephen Sprigle, and Belinda Morris. ***Understanding the Technology When Selecting Wheelchairs.*** Arlington, VA: RESNA, 1993. 110 pp. $16.50.

This manual explains technical specifications for various features of wheelchairs (frames, wheels and tires, joysticks, batteries, etc.) in practical terms. It includes tips on using this information to select a wheelchair.

Wheelchair Information Packet. Silver Spring, MD: ABLEDATA. $7.00.

This packet consists of the following fact sheets: "Informed Consumer Guide to Wheelchair Selection"; "Manual Wheelchairs Fact Sheet"; "Powered Wheelchairs Fact Sheet"; "Wheelchairs for Children Fact Sheet"; "Funding Assistive Technology Fact Sheet"; and "Scooters Fact Sheet."

First Person Perspectives

Mairs, Nancy. *Waist-High in the World: A Life Among the Nondisabled.* Boston: Beacon Press, 1996. $20.00. 212 pp. ISBN 0-8070-7086-6.

The author, who began experiencing symptoms of multiple sclerosis in high school, wrote this remarkable collection of essays as a kind of travel guide "for a country to which no one travels willingly: the observations and responses of a single wayfarer who hopes, in sketching her own experiences, to make the terrain seem less alien, less perilous, and far more amusing than the myths and legends about it would suggest." Among the many topics the author eloquently considers are: language related to disabilities; handling public reactions to her disability; the multitude of adaptations she must make to daily life; how it feels to have an "imperfect" body; how having a disability has affected her marriage and her parenting; air travel; what society's views about abortion and assisted suicide say about the worth of people with disabilities. The book includes a chapter about what it is like to be young and disabled, with information drawn from essays written by hundreds of young people with congenital or acquired physical disabilities.

Pearpoint, Jack. *From Behind the Piano: The Building of Judith Snow's Unique Circle of Friends.* Toronto: Inclusion Press, 1990. 132 pp. $10.00. ISBN 1-895418-00-3.

Plan to spend an evening with this book because you will simply be unable to put it down. As you read how Judith Snow, a woman with severe disabilities, was enabled to become a member of her community, you will understand the true meaning of "circle of friends." You will understand how friendship can and has moved bureaucratic mountains. You will also understand the inadequate understanding that exists in the world regarding persons who are disabled. This book will give you strength to go on. As often said by the author, "If Judith can do it, anyone can. . . ."

WINGS: A Newsletter For, By, and about Physically Disabled United Methodists. Fallbrook United Methodist Church, 1844 Winterhaven Rd., Fallbrook, CA 92028.

This unique Christian newsletter is both informative and entertaining. Articles focus on making congregations disability-accessible. Articles and entries focus on ideas and suggestions from readers, original stories, poetry and cartoons, personal essays, and anecdotes. A year's subscription is $6.00.

For Children

FICTION

Foreman, Michael. *Seal Surfer.* New York, NY: Harcourt Brace, 1997. Unpaginated. $16.00. ISBN 0-15-201399-7.

On land, Ben uses a wheelchair or crutches to get around. But in the ocean near his home, he moves around easily on a surfboard. One day, while fishing with his grandfather, Ben sees a baby seal born. This is the story of how Ben and the seal come to a special understanding of each other and the world around them over the course of three years. This picture book is illustrated with glowing watercolors and suitable for children ages 6 to 10.

Harshman, Marc. *The Storm.* New York, NY: Dutton, 1995. 32 pp. $14.95. ISBN 0-525-65150-0.

Jonathan is home alone on the family farm when he suddenly sees a tornado approaching. Although his legs are paralyzed as the result of an accident, he manages to lead several panicked horses to safety, and stays with them while the storm rages outside. After the storm passes, he is proud of himself and hopes that his friends might start seeing him for himself now, rather than as someone who uses a wheelchair. Children in upper elementary grades can read this book to themselves; younger children will enjoy looking at the striking, full-page watercolor illustrations while the book is read to them.

Mayer, Gina, and Mercer Mayer. *A Very Special Critter.* Racine, WI: Western Publishing Co., 1992. $2.99. ISBN 0-307-12763-X.

When Alex, a "Little Critter" who uses a wheelchair, joins the class, everyone initially worries about how they will get along with someone so different. They quickly learn that Alex is a cool little critter who is good at sports and designing Halloween costumes. In the end, they realize that Alex does need a little help now and then, but so does everyone else. The recommended grade level is preschool through third grade.

Muldoon, Kathleen. *Princess Pooh.* Morton Grove, IL: Albert Whitman, 1989. Not paginated. $14.95. ISBN 0-8075-6627-6.

Patty Jean is pretty sure that her older sister, the one in the wheelchair, the one on the throne, has the best life in the world—that is, until the day Patty Jean has an adventure that changes her mind about her sister's life. A great book for siblings aged 7-10 about awareness.

Walker, John C. *In Other Words.* Willowdale, Ontario: Annick Press, 1993. Not paginated. $4.95. ISBN 1-55037-310-2.

John is in a wheelchair. He has so much to say, but can't talk. When he tries, people do not understand him. Then he meets a new girl, and they begin to communicate in a unique way. As this fantasy unfolds, the reader will delight in the art of Connie Steiner and feel the warmth of the story these two children share. This is a gentle awareness book. Children will enjoy the story and will be encouraged to talk about physical and communicative challenges.

NONFICTION

Karolides, Nicholas. *Focus on Physical Impairments: A Reference Handbook.* Santa Barbara, CA: ABC-CLIO, 1990. 332 pp. $39.50. ISBN 0-87436-428-0.

This book was designed to provide young readers with information and resources about nine physical conditions, chosen because of their prevalence in childhood and adolescence. The conditions discussed are: visual impairment, hearing impairment, communication impairment, cerebral palsy, spina bifida, muscular dystrophy, multiple sclerosis, spinal cord injury, and epilepsy. For each disability, the author provides a definition and statistics about the incidence, then discusses developmental factors, social factors, management or treatment, recent developments, and tips on interacting with someone with the disability. Each chapter concludes with descriptions of both fiction and nonfiction books suitable for junior high or high school readers, nonprint materials such as films and videos, and organizations. Although the book is part of the Teenage Perspective series, it would be equally useful to parents and teachers looking for a nontechnical overview of the major issues related to these disabilities. The descriptions provided are quite meaty and offer a great deal of information aimed at helping readers understand the range of impairment that young people with a given disability may have.

Krementz, Jill. *How It Feels to Fight for Your Life.* Boston: Little, Brown, 1989. 132 pp. ISBN 0-316-50364-9. Out of print.

Fourteen children and teenagers with chronic illnesses or disabilities describe their daily lives and struggle for independence. Included is an essay about a fourteen-year-old boy with a spinal cord injury who plays wheelchair sports competitively. The book is illustrated with excellent black-and-white photos of the children.

Kriegsman, Kay Harris, Elinor L. Zaslow, Jennifer D'Zmura-Rechsteiner. *Taking Charge: Teenagers Talk about Life and Physical Disabilities.* Bethesda, MD: Woodbine House, 1992. 164 pp. $14.95. ISBN 0-933149-46-8.

> If you can get your pre-teen or teen to read this book, the whole family will very likely survive the teenage years. *Taking Charge* is organized by caring adults--two of whom have disabilities--but the substance of the book is drawn from the words of teens and young adults. Fifteen young people with spina bifida, cerebral palsy, muscular dystrophy, osteogenesis imperfecta, and other disorders answer questions such as: "How do you feel most of the time?" and "How independent are you?" Information is organized into three major sections: who you are; how you relate to others; and how you can be as independent as you can be. Each section begins with a short introduction to an individual with a disability. The resources section provides a helpful list of organizations and publications.

Ratto, Linda Lee. *Coping with Being Physically Challenged.* New York, NY: Rosen, 1991. 103 pp. $15.95. ISBN 0-8239-1344-9.

> This book was written for young readers with a physical disability to help them understand, cope, and look at the challenges they face with hope. Children describe their physical challenges and talk about what they have faced and how they worked through their emotions. The author suggests strategies for working through the anger, the hurt, and the fear. This is a simply written yet powerful book for older children and teens. A resource and reading list is provided.

Rosenberg, Maxine B. *My Friend Leslie: The Story of a Handicapped Child.* New York, NY: Lothrop, Lee & Shepard Books, 1983. ISBN 0-688-01690-1. Out of print.

> The story is a simple and heartwarming one about two friends, one with physical and mental disabilities and one without. While the title uses the currently politically incorrect term "handicapped," there is nothing inappropriate about how these two friends care for and help each other. Leslie is fully included into a classroom situation. The photographs by George clearly depict the girls' relationship and Leslie's activities. For ages 5-8.

Roy, Ron. *Move Over, Wheelchairs Coming Through!* New York, NY: Clarion, 1985. 83 pp. $15.95. ISBN 0-89919-249-1.

> Seven children who use a wheelchair were interviewed for this book for older elementary grades. Each chapter is devoted to a different child and the story of his/her life in a wheelchair. The book reveals how these children live from day-to-day, and their strategies for coping with a physical disability. This book is important because it provides a picture of the typical side of children with physical disabilities. This is a fine awareness book for children, as well as their parents.

Sirof, Harriet. *The Road Back: Living with a Physical Disability.* New York, NY: Macmillan, 1993. 160 pp. $13.95. ISBN 0-02-782885-9.

> This book is for teenagers or young adults who have recently acquired a disability through an accident or illness. It follows three fictitious teenagers—one with multiple sclerosis, one with a spinal cord injury, and one with temporary physical disabilities—from the moment they become disabled, through the rehabilitation process, to the day when they feel ready to get on with their lives. Along the way, the author explores the thoughts and emotions that are common at every stage of coping.

Winston, Lynn. *Ideas for Kids on the Go.* Bloomington, IL: Cheever, 1984. 69 pp. $6.95. ISBN 0-915708-17-5.

> This is a dual purpose book. First there are suggestions for parents as they manage the challenges of raising a child with a disability. Then, kids talk about having a disability, about developing coping skills, and about increasing self-esteem. This little book provides a support system, an awareness program, and a resource for recreation, all in one! An extensive resource list is included.

■ ORGANIZATIONS

American Chronic Pain Association
P.O. Box 850
Rocklin, CA 95677
(916) 632-0922

> PURPOSE: Mutual support
> SERVICES: Disseminates guidelines for selecting pain management facilities.
> PUBLICATIONS: Ask for their *Family Manual* and the *ACPA Chronicle,* a quarterly newsletter.

The Center for Universal Design
North Carolina State University
School of Design
Box 8613
Raleigh, NC 27695-8613

> PUBLICATIONS: Include *"Financing Home Accessibility Modifications"* ($20); *"Accessible Housing Design and Modifications"* ($2.50); *"Accessibility Standards and Regulations"* ($1.50); *"Grab Bars"* ($3); *"Universal Design for Decks, Patios, Porches, and Balconies"* ($5).

National Easter Seal Society
230 W. Monroe St., Ste. 1800
Chicago, IL 60606-4802
(312) 726-6200; (312) 726-1494 FAX
Web site: http//www.seals.com

> PURPOSE: To help people with disabilities achieve independence.
> Services: Operates nearly 500 direct service sites providing therapy and other needed services for children and adults with disabilities throughout the U.S. and Puerto Rico. Also sponsors public education campaigns, advocates for needed legislation and programs, and promotes use of assistive technology.
> PUBLICATIONS: *"Easy Access Housing Design Awards"* ($10.00) depicts winning designs of houses for people with disabilities. *"Making Life Better: A Catalog of Catalogs"* ($5.00) lists suppliers of assistive and adaptive equipment designed to make daily living easier.

National Information Center for Children and Youth with Disabilities (NICHCY)
P.O. Box 1492
Washington, DC 20013-1492
(800) 695-0285; (202) 884-8441 FAX
E-mail: nichcy@aed.org
Web site: http//www.nichcy.org

> PURPOSE: A clearinghouse that provides information on disabilities and disability-related issues, with an emphasis on children and young people birth to age 22.
> SERVICES: Personal responses to questions on disability issues; referrals to other organizations and agencies; database searches; technical assistance to parent and professional groups. Information and referral for parents of children with special needs.
> PUBLICATIONS: Fact sheets on physical and multiple disabilities in general, as well as on specific physical disabilities. There is a small charge for most print items, or they can be downloaded free of charge from the Internet.

National Scoliosis Foundation
5 Cabot Place
Stoughton, MA 02072
(800) 673-6922; (617) 341-8333 FAX
E-mail: scoliosis@aol.com

> PURPOSE: A nonprofit group providing information and referral. No membership fees, but donations are gladly accepted.
>
> SERVICES: Books, pamphlets, newsletters, doctor referral service.
>
> PUBLICATIONS: *Spinal Connection,* published twice a year.

Osteogenesis Imperfecta Foundation
5005 Laurel St., Ste. 210
Tampa, FL 33607
(800) 981-2663; (813) 287-8214 FAX
Web site: http//www.oif.org

> PURPOSE: To improve the quality of life for people with O.I. through research, education, and support.
>
> SERVICES: Information, referral, and support.
>
> PUBLICATIONS: Quarterly newsletter, *Breakthrough;* booklets include *"The Care of a Baby and Child with Osteogenesis Imperfecta"* and *"How to Distinguish Between Child Abuse and O.I."*

United Cerebral Palsy (UCP)
1660 L. St., N.W., Ste. 700
Washington, DC 20036
(800) 872-5827; (202) 776-0414 FAX; (202) 973-7197 TTY
Web site: http//www.ucpa.org

> PURPOSE: "To advance the independence, productivity and full citizenship of people with cerebral palsy and other disabilities, through our commitment to the principles of independence, inclusion, and self-determination."
>
> SERVICES: Information and referral; legislative advocacy; research. Local affiliates provide direct services to people with disabilities and their families, including therapy, assistive technology training, advocacy, and employment assistance.
>
> PUBLICATIONS: *Washington Watch,* a bimonthly newsletter, is described in the Advocacy section of this book. Also has a catalog of publications of interest to parents and advocates published by a variety of companies and organizations. Many publications can be downloaded from the web site.

33.

Rare Disorders

■ BOOKS AND PERIODICALS

Catalog of Multilingual Patient Education Materials on Genetic and Related Maternal/ Child Health Topics. Newark, NJ: Center for Human and Molecular Genetics, New Jersey Medical School, 1995. 245 pp. No charge.

> Included in this useful directory are listings of free or low-cost publications on a variety of common and uncommon disorders with a genetic component. The directory lists titles of the publications, reading levels, and addresses and phone numbers of the distributors of the materials. The bulk of the publications listed are published in English, but there are also many publications in Spanish and a smattering of publications in 30 other languages. One copy of the directory is available free from the National Maternal and Child Health Clearinghouse listed under "Organizations" below.

Exceptional Parent. P.O. Box 3000, Dept. EP, Denville, NJ 07834. (800) 562-1973. Web site: http//www.familyeducation.com

> This glossy monthly magazine is for parents of children and young adults with any disability. In a monthly column called "Search and Respond," readers can ask for help from other readers--including information about their child's rare or undiagnosed condition.

Gilbert, Patricia. ***The A-Z Reference Book of Syndromes and Inherited Disorders.*** 2nd ed. San Diego: Singular Publishing, 1996. 394 pp. $49.95. ISBN 1-56593-611-6.

> In nontechnical language, this practical guide covers 90 syndromes and inherited disorders, many of them considered rare. In one to four pages, the author describes each condition and how it affects children and adults, and discusses treatment options and issues related to daily living.

NARIC. *Directory of National Information Sources on Disabilities.* Silver Spring, MD: NARIC, 1994. 719 pp. $15.00.

> The two volumes in this set list hundreds of organizations and databases in the United States that provide information, referral, and direct services on a nationwide basis. The entries for each organization cover disabilities served, users served, description of the organization, and information services, including publications. Included are many organizations serving individuals with low-incidence disorders.

Pickett, Olivia K., Eileen M. Clark, and Laura D. Kavanagh, eds. *Reaching Out: A Directory of National Organizations Related to Maternal and Child Health.* Arlington, VA: National Center for Education in Maternal and Child Health, 1994. 190 pp. Free. ISBN 1-57285-001-9.

> This user-friendly directory lists nonprofit organizations that provide information and respond to questions from the public and health care professionals; national information centers funded by the Maternal and Child Health Bureau; and professional organizations that provide training to health professionals. It includes approximately 50 pages of listings devoted to organizations that focus on specific chronic illnesses and disabilities. Included are many organizations dealing with rare disorders, including connective tissue disorders, craniofacial disorders, metabolic disorders, neurologic disorders, neuromuscular disorders, skin disorders, and developmental disorders. One copy of the directory is available free of charge from the National Maternal and Child Health Clearinghouse, listed under "Organizations" below.

Thoene, Jesse G., ed. *Physician's Guide to Rare Diseases.* 2nd ed. Montvale, NJ: Dowden Publishing Co., 1995. 1200 pp. $129.99. ISBN 0-9628716-1-3.

> This text provides information on approximately 900 rare disorders. The following information is given for each disorder: description, synonyms, signs and symptoms, etiology (cause), epidemiology (prevalence), standard and investigational treatments, and resources for more information. It includes an index that allows the reader to look up symptoms and match them with conditions listed in the book. Although written primarily as a diagnostic tool for medical professionals, the book would be understandable to an interested lay person. The book is updated bimonthly by the publication of the **Journal of Rare Diseases,** also published by Dowden Publishing Company.

■ ORGANIZATIONS

Chromosome Deletion Outreach
P.O. Box 724
Boca Raton, FL 33429-0724
E-mail: cdo@worldnet.att.net
Web site: http//members.aol.com/cdousa/cdo.htm

> PURPOSE: A nonprofit support organization for individuals, families, and professionals seeking information on chromosome disorders involving deletions, additions, inversions, translocations, and rings.
> SERVICES: Helps to link up families with similar diagnoses for information sharing and support.
> PUBLICATIONS: Publishes a quarterly newsletter with information provided by members of the organization.

National Maternal and Child Health Clearinghouse

2070 Chain Bridge Rd., Ste. 450

Vienna, VA 22182-2536

(703) 356-1964; (703) 821-2098 FAX

E-mail: nmchc@circsol.com

Web site: http//www.circsol.com/mch

> PURPOSE: "Disseminates state-of-the-art information about maternal and child health." Most of the publications distributed were developed through programs funded by grants from the Maternal and Child Health Bureau.
>
> SERVICES: Clearinghouse staff respond to requests for information or refer callers to other information agencies and sources.
>
> PUBLICATIONS: Include *Understanding DNA Testing: A Basic Guide for Families* (#D088, no charge); *National Survey of Treatment Programs for PKU and Selected Other Inherited Metabolic Diseases* (#C049, no charge); *State Treatment Centers for Metabolic Disorders* (#B258, no charge).

National Organization for Rare Disorders (NORD)

P.O. Box 8923

New Fairfield, CT 06182-8923

(203) 746-6518; (203) 746-6481 FAX

E-mail: orphan@nord-rdb.com

Web site: http//www.NORD-RDB.com/~orphan

> PURPOSE: "A unique federation of voluntary health organizations dedicated to helping people with rare 'orphan' diseases and assisting the organizations that serve them." A rare or orphan disorder is one that affects fewer than 200,000 people in the U.S.
>
> SERVICES: Acts as the "primary non-governmental clearinghouse for information on over 5,000 rare disorders." Provides referrals to other sources of information and assistance. Helps families make contact with other families with similar diagnoses. Maintains a web page with many links to other sources of information. NORD's database can be accessed from the web page, as well.
>
> PUBLICATIONS: Publishes *NORD Resource Guide,* which includes detailed information on over 440 groups and organizations that serve people with rare disorders and disabilities ($25.00). The newsletter *Orphan Disease Update* is published three times a year and covers issues such as health insurance, relevant legislation, research into rare disorders, new medications and treatments, resources, and upcoming events of interest to families of people with rare disorders. The newsletter is sent to members of NORD and can also be read on NORD's web page. Membership is $30.00 for individuals.

Office of Rare Diseases

National Institutes of Health

Federal Building, Room 618

7550 Wisconsin Ave.

Bethesda, MD 20892-9120

(301) 402-4336; (301) 402-0420.

Web site: http//cancernet.nci.nih.gov/ord/

> PURPOSE: Conducts research and clinical trials regarding rare disorders and disseminates information to the public, health care providers, and research investigators.
>
> SERVICES: ORD's webpage offers information about more than 6,000 rare diseases, as well as about support groups and research and clinical trials. Also offers links to helpful databases such as MEDLINE and to other information resources about rare disorders.

34.
Sensory Integration Disorders

■ BOOKS

Anderson, Elizabeth, and Pauline Emmons. *Unlocking the Mysteries of Sensory Dysfunction.* Arlington, TX: Future Horizons, 1996. 91 pp. $19.95. ISBN 1-885477-25-5.

> Written by parents for parents, this book offers a nontechnical look at some of the major issues that concern parents of children with sensory integrative dysfunctions. The authors explain what sensory dysfuction is, and list many possible signs of it. They also address ways of reducing stresses at home (meals, baths, dressing, discipline, sibling interactions) and at school. Stories about the authors' children with sensory problems are included.

Ayres, A. Jean. *Sensory Integration and the Child.* Los Angeles, CA: Western Psychological Services, 1970. 191 pp. ISBN 0-87424-158-8. Out of print.

> This is the classic parent's guide to sensory integration (S.I.) issues. It is designed to help parents recognize S.I. problems in their child, to understand what is causing those problems, and to find out how sensory integration therapy may be able to help their child. There are chapters on normal S.I. development, as well as on a variety of different types of S.I. problems (vestibular system problems, motor planning problems, tactile defensiveness, visual perception and auditory processing problems, and difficulties related to autism). A useful chapter explains strategies that parents can use at home to help their child feel good about himself, feel comfortable in his environment, and enjoy play. The writing is very clear and parent friendly.

■ ORGANIZATIONS

Sensory Integration International
1602 Cabrillo Ave.
Torrance, CA 90501
(310) 320-9986; (310) 320-9934 FAX

> PURPOSE: "To develop awareness, knowledge, skills and services in Sensory Integration."
>
> SERVICES: Educational training programs, information and educational materials, evaluation and treatment services, research affiliated programs.
>
> PUBLICATIONS: Quarterly newsletter, *Sensory Integration.* Has a wide variety of publications such as: *"A Parents Guide to Understanding Sensory Integration"; "Movement Is Fun"; "Sensory Motor Handbook";* and reviews of research in Sensory Integration.

35.
Speech and Language Disorders

■ BOOKS AND PERIODICALS

Basic Information

Communicating Partners. Children's Hospital Foundation, c/o The Family Child Learning Center, 143 Northwest Ave., Building A, Tallmadge, OH 44278. (330) 633-2055; (330) 633-2658 FAX.

> This quarterly newsletter is designed for parents and professionals who work with children who do not yet talk, have language or speech delays, or have problems with conversations. The emphasis is on teaching parents to help their children play and to increase their desire to communicate. Topics covered include social play, turn taking, nonverbal communication, preverbal literacy, and specific problems related to diagnoses such as Down syndrome, autism, and deafness. One year's subscription costs $15.00.

Eisenson, Jon. ***Is My Child's Speech Normal?*** 2nd ed. Austin, TX: PRO-ED, 1997. 162 pp. $16.00. ISBN 0-89079-704-8.

> The author wrote this guide for parents and professionals who are concerned that a child's speech is delayed or who simply want to understand more about speech development in children. The book covers normal speech development through age 4, going into detail about problems with articulation, fluency, and voice. It also includes information about what parents can do to enhance their child's speech development at every developmental stage. The emphasis is on speech disorders that are unrelated to another disability, although there is one chapter on how "minimal brain dysfunction" (meaning ADD and several types of learning disabilities) can contribute to difficulties or delays in speaking.

Hamaguchi, Patricia M. *Childhood Speech, Language & Listening Problems: What Every Parent Should Know.* New York, NY: John Wiley & Sons, 1995. 213 pp. $14.95. ISBN 0-471-03413-4.

> This first-rate, reader-friendly guide is a boon both to parents of children whose sole difficulty is a communication disorder and to parents of children who have communication problems in conjunction with another disability. The book begins by explaining how to determine whether a child might need help with communication development, and provides a useful explanation of what the different types of scores mean (percentiles, age equivalents, standard scores, stanines, standard deviations). The heart of the book focuses on describing different types of speech, language, and listening problems, with information on how they can be recognized and treated. The author also offers helpful suggestions for helping a child with a specific difficulty improve his communication skills at home. Throughout the book are interesting case studies of children with different types of communication problems, with information on how their problems were recognized and treated.

Martin, Katherine L. *Does My Child Have a Speech Problem?* Chicago: Chicago Review Press, 1997. 160 pp. $16.95. ISBN 1-55652-315-7.

> This short guide is designed to help parents determine whether their child might have a speech or language problem requiring therapy. The author, a speech-language pathologist, answers parents' top 50 questions about stuttering and fluency, articulation, listening and auditory processing skills, language development, and voice problems. Included is a useful table showing milestones of receptive and expressive language usually attained by children from birth to five years.

Sowell, Thomas. *Late-Talking Children.* New York, NY: Basic Books/HarperCollins, 1997. 180 pp. $20.00. ISBN 0-465-03834-4.

> The author here presents his research into the phenomenon of "late-talking children"—children who have average or above average intelligence and normal receptive language, but significant delays in acquiring expressive language. According to the author, a significant number of children are misdiagnosed with autism, pervasive developmental disorders, or other disabilities, when in reality they are simply late talkers (typically beginning to speak around four years of age or later). The book identifies a number of personality traits and other characteristics (such as delayed toilet training) often associated with late talking, and shares numerous case studies of late talkers who eventually learned to speak normally.

Activities for Home and School

Gibbs, Betsy, and Ann Springer. *Early Use of Total Communication: An Introductory Guide for Parents.* Baltimore: Paul H. Brookes, 1995. 40 pp. $20.00 (for packet of three). ISBN 1-55766-183-9.

> Using a question-and-answer format and many quotations from parents, this manual explains how to use total communication (the simultaneous use of speech and sign) within the family. The emphasis is on children with significant expressive language delays due to Down syndrome, autism, etc., but who are not necessarily hard of hearing. A video with the same title complements the printed manual and is available for $40.00.

MacDonald, James D., and Paula Rabidoux. *Before Your Child Talks: A Curriculum for Building Social Habits that Prepare Children for Language.* Columbus, OH: Communicating Partners, 1997. (Available from: Children's Hospital Foundation, c/o The Family Child Learning Center, 143 Northeast Ave., Building A, Tallmadge, OH 44278.) 154 pp. $15.00.

> This manual is intended for parents or professionals working with children who have either not yet begun to talk or who have not yet developed functional conversational skills. It is based on the premise that children need to have certain social skills (such as the ability to imitate and take

turns) before they can become effective communicators. The authors include many examples of how and how not to interact with children who are developing communication skills, as well as checklists to evaluate both the child's and the parents' behaviors that may be contributing to delays in communication. Especially useful are the many examples of writing social and communication goals for IEPs or IFSPs of children with speech delays.

Manolson, Ayala. ***It Takes Two to Talk: A Parent's Guide to Helping Children Communicate.*** 3rd ed. Toronto, Ontario: Hanen Centre, 1992. 151 pp. $25.00. ISBN 0-921145-02-0.

> This practical manual describes strategies that parents can use to encourage shy and/or language delayed children to communicate as often and as clearly as they can. The approach focuses not only on changing the child's abilities and attitudes toward communication, but also the family's. The crux of the Hanen method is to encourage communication through the "3A Way": *allowing* the child to lead; *adapting* to "share the moment"; and *adding* langague and experience. The book also includes chapters devoted to ideas for enriching experiences using games, music, and art. The book is appropriate for parents of children who have not progressed beyond using two-word phrases, regardless of age.

Penning, Marge. ***A Language/Communication Curriculum for Students with Autism and Other Language Impairments.*** Lansing, MI: CAUSE, 1992. $90.00. No ISBN.

> This impressive work, originally written for children with autism, has been updated and expanded to provide a structured, ecological approach to language intervention for all children. This is a *complete curriculum,* with information provided in developmental sequence. Assessments and guidelines for inclusion of augmentative communication are included. It is a massive work, but worth the effort to read, digest, and use. While the author strongly recommends the consultation of a speech and language pathologist, the material is easily adaptable for use by teachers, aides, and childcare workers.

Schreiber, Linda R., and Nancy L. McKinley. ***Daily Communication: Strategies for Adolescents with Language Disorders.*** 2nd ed. Eau Claire, WI: Thinking Publications, 1995. 449 pp. $39.00. ISBN 0-930599-35-7.

> The authors describe this text as "an attempt to fuse language intervention and counseling for adolescents who have language disorders." By "counseling," the authors mean "discussing why a particular strategy will improve the adolescent's well-being and how it can be applied in daily communication." The book was designed for use in a group therapy session for students between the ages of ten and twenty. It includes many suggested activities to help students improve their skills in the areas of problem solving, listening, conversational speech, question asking, nonverbal communication, study skills, and survival language. Although written for professionals, the writing is exceptionally clear and jargon-free.

Schwartz, Sue, and Joan E. Heller Miller. ***The New Language of Toys: Teaching Communication Skills to Children with Special Needs.*** 2nd ed. Bethesda, MD: Woodbine House, 1996. 279 pp. $16.95 ISBN 0-933149-08.

> The focus of this friendly guide is on using toys and games to promote language acquisition in an entertaining way. The authors provide numerous examples of specific play strategies, games, and toys that are helpful for children at different developmental ages, from birth through age six. Adaptations for children with specific types of disabilities are included, as appropriate. Homemade alternatives to store-bought toys are suggested at each age level, since not all parents can afford to purchase a load of toys. The authors also describe many books that are useful for teaching speech and language concepts to children of different ages.

Advanced Reading

Jung, Jack H. *Genetic Syndromes in Communication Disorders.* Austin, TX: PRO-ED, 1989. 285 pp. $38.00. ISBN 0-89079-280-1.

> Written primarily for speech, language, and hearing professionals and students, this semi-technical text covers genetic syndromes that involve communication disorders. The first chapter provides a clear overview of medical genetics, explaining terminology, how chromosomal and single gene disorders occur, how family pedigrees are taken, and determining recurrence risks. The book then examines individual disorders with a genetic component, discussing causes, effects on hearing and speech, treatment of communication difficulties, and prognosis for people with the disorder. Conditions covered include: Chromosomal syndromes (Down syndrome, fragile X syndrome, Turner syndrome); Single Gene Syndromes (including a variety of syndromes that result in clefting, facial differences, and/or hearing loss); Polygenetic-multifactorial syndromes (cleft lip and palate, Pierre-Robin sequence, stuttering); Sporadic syndromes (including Cornelia de Lange and Prader-Willi syndromes); and Environmental syndromes (FAS, fetal cytomegalovirus syndrome, fetal rubella syndrome). Chapters on specific syndromes are 4-10 pages long and include references.

Schoenbrodt, Lisa, and Romayne A. Smith. *Communication Disorders and Interventions in Low Incidence Pediatric Populations.* San Diego: Singular Publishing Group, 1995. 250 pp. $39.95. ISBN 1-56593-220-X.

> This text provides information on the specific communication problems commonly associated with the the following disorders: traumatic brain injury, attention deficit disorder, Tourette syndrome, fragile X syndrome, neglect and abuse, prenatal drug exposure, autism and pervasive developmental disorders. Although intended primarily for speech-language pathologists, the information should also be valuable for parents seeking to understand the nature of, and treatment for, their child's communication delays.

Reference

Directory: Resources for Human Communication Disorders 1996. Bethesda, MD: NIDCD Information Clearinghouse, 1996. 102 pp. Free.

> This is a directory of 129 associations and organizations in the United States that have an interest in deafness and other communication disorders. Most of the organizations listed are national in scope and focus on health issues relating to hearing, balance, smell, taste, voice, speech, and language. Descriptions include contact information, including e-mail and Internet addresses, descriptions of the organizations, and information about publications and meetings.

Nicolosi, Lucille, Elizabeth Harryman, and Janet Kresheck. *Terminology of Communication Disorders: Speech-Language-Hearing.* 4th Ed. Baltimore, MD: Williams & Wilkins, 1996. 373 pp. $33.00. ISBN 0-683-06505-X.

> This useful and readable text offers definitions for hundreds of terms related to communication disorders. Cross references, illustrations, and information about language and audiometric and psychological tests and procedures are provided.

Stuttering

Fraser, Jane, and William H. Perkins, eds. *Do You Stutter: A Guide for Teens.* Memphis, TN: Speech Foundation of America, 1992. 80 pp. $1.00. ISBN 0-933388-27-6. (Publication #21)

> This helpful little book provides teens who stutter with information, suggestions, strategies, and counseling. Professionals in the area of speech and language pathology have written the chapters. With the help of sensitive cartoons, the teen is offered real help and guidance.

Perkins, William H. ***Stuttering Prevented.*** San Diego, CA: Singular Publishing Group, 1991.
204 pp. $32.50. ISBN 1-879105-50-0.

> The author explains strategies to restore fluency that are appropriate for different individuals. He
> also gives guidelines suggesting when professional help may be needed. Strategies are innovative
> and practical.

For Children

Kline, Suzy. ***Mary Marony and the Snake.*** New York, NY: G.P. Putnam's Sons, 1992. 64 pp. $12.95.
ISBN 0-399-22044-5.

> Mary, a second grader, always dreads speaking in class because of her stutter. Worse, a classmate
> named Melvin torments her by mimicking her stutter. Although initially reluctant to see the school
> speech therapist, she discovers that therapy is fun and really helps. By the end of the book, she is able
> to speak up when it matters the most, gaining the admiration of all of her classmates, even Melvin.

Patterson, Nancy Ruth. ***The Shiniest Rock of All.*** New York, NY: Farrar/Strauss/Giroux, 1991. 72
pp. $13.00. ISBN 0-374-36805-8.

> Fourth-grader Robert Morris Reynold hates his name, as his "r's" always come out sounding like "w's."
> When straight-A student Ashley Alston ridicules his speech problems in the school lunchroom, he's had
> enough. He smashes a peanutbutter and jelly sandwich into her face, and then finally agrees to see a speech
> therapist. The understanding therapist starts him on the road to better articulation and self-esteem.

■ ORGANIZATIONS

American Speech Language Hearing Association (ASHA)
10801 Rockville Pike
Rockville, MD 20822
(800) 638-8255 (V/TTY); (301) 571-0457 FAX
Web site: http//www.asha.org

> PURPOSE: A certifying body for speech, hearing, and language professionals and an accrediting
> agency for college and university programs and hospitals in speech-language pathology and audi-
> ology. ASHA also conducts research.
> SERVICES: Toll-free information and referral HELPLINE.
> PUBLICATIONS: Offers public information brochures about communication difficulties. Examples
> include: *"Answers [to] Questions about Child Language"; "American Speech-Language-Hearing As-
> sociation Answers Questions about Aphasia"; "Answers [to] Questions about Articulation Problems";
> "Answers [to] Questions about Otitus Media, Hearing and Language Development";
> "Answers [to] Questions about Voice Problems"; "Do Your Health Benefits Cover Audiology and Speech-
> Language Services?"; "Speech and Language Disorders and the Speech-Language Pathologist."*

National Information Center for Children and Youth with Disabilities (NICHCY)
P.O. Box 1492
Washington, DC 20013-1492
(800) 695-0285; (202) 884-8441 FAX
E-mail: nichcy@aed.org
Web site: http//www.nichcy.org

> PURPOSE: A clearinghouse that provides information on disabilities and disability-related issues,
> with an emphasis on children and young people birth to age 22.

SERVICES: personal responses to questions on disability issues; referrals to other organizations and agencies; database searches; technical assistance to parent and professional groups. Information and referral for parents of children with special needs.

PUBLICATIONS: Fact sheet on Speech and Language Disorders, as well as fact sheets on disabilities that can be associated with speech and language disorders. There is a small charge for most print items, or they can be downloaded free of charge from the Internet.

National Institute on Deafness and Other Communication Disorders (NIDCD) Information Clearinghouse

1 Communication Ave.
Bethesda, MD 20892-3456
(800) 241-1044; (800) 241-1055 TTY; (301) 907-8830 FAX
E-mail: nidcd@aerie.com
Web site: http//www.nih.gov/nidcd/

PURPOSE: "Collects, produces, and disseminates information on normal and disordered processes of human communication."

SERVICES: Provides information and resource materials on hearing, balance, smell, taste, voice, speech, and language. Operates a database with materials on these subjects. Information specialists respond to professional and public inquiries by phone.

PUBLICATIONS: Include the **Directory** described above; *"Update on Developmental Speech and Language Disorders"; "Information Resources for Consumers: Voice Disorders"; "Information Resources for Consumers: Language Disorders"; "Ear Infections Information Packet"; "Update on Stuttering."* Publications are free.

Stuttering Foundation of America

P.O. Box 11749
Memphis, TN 38111-0749
(800) 992-9392; (901) 452-7343; (901) 452-3931 FAX

PURPOSE: A nonprofit organization dedicated to the prevention and treatment of stuttering.

SERVICES: Toll-free hotline, listed above.

PUBLICATIONS: Newsletter, brochures, and books. Examples, which cost about $2 each, include: ***Stuttering Words*** (a glossary of terms commonly used by speech and language professionals who write about stuttering); ***If Your Child Stutters: A Guide for Parents; Treating the School Age Stutterer;*** and ***Stuttering: Treatment of the Young Stutterer in the School.***

Trace Research & Development Center

University of Wisconsin-Madison
S-151 Waisman Center
1500 Highland Ave.
Madison, WI 53705-2280
(608) 262-6966;(608) 262-8848 FAX; (608) 263-5408 TTY
E-mail: info@trace.wisc.edu
Web site: http//trace.wisc.edu

PURPOSE: "To advance the ability of people with disabilities to achieve their life objectives through the use of communication, computer and information technologies."

PUBLICATIONS: Offers a variety of publications for users and developers of technology. Examples include: *"Activities Using Headsticks and Optical Pointers"; "Beyond Yes/No in the Early Childhood Classroom"; "Construction Notes of Laptrays, Portable Communication Boards, and Adaptive Pointers";* and ***The Trace Resourcebook.***

36.

Spina Bifida

■ BOOKS

Basic Information

Bloom, Beth-Ann, and Edward Seljeskog. *A Parent's Guide to Spina Bifida.* Minneapolis: University of Minnesota Press, 1988. 92 pp. $16.95. ISBN 0-8166-1486-5.

> This book addresses the many concerns related to having a child with spina bifida. The authors describe the different types of spina bifida, causes, treatment, and terminology. A great deal of attention is paid to medical problems that may occur: hydrocephalus, orthopedic problems, bladder and bowel problems, skin sensitivity problems, obesity, and seizures. Less attention is given to developmental and emotional issues. The authors emphasize that each baby is an individual and that decisions must be made looking at the perspectives of the family and the child. Photographs are included.

Leibold, Susan, Pat Brown, Jeane Cole, and Paula Peterson. *Bowel Continence and Spina Bifida.* Washington, DC: Spina Bifida Association of America, 1995. 53 pp. $7.95.

> With special attention paid to developmental issues, this book provides an overview of bowel continence programs and bowel management techniques. Sample menus, bowel tracking sheet, and glossary are included.

Rauen, Karen. *Guidelines for Spina Bifida Health Care Services Throughout Life.* Washington, DC: Spina Bifida Association, 1995. 62 pp. $16.50.

> This book covers health care issues from birth through the adult years. Discussion about multidisciplinary health teams and the implications of appropriate and adequate health care is included. References are provided.

Rowley-Kelly, Fern L., and Donald H. Reigel. ***Teaching the Student with Spina Bifida.***
Baltimore, MD: Paul H. Brookes, 1993. 470 pp. $40.00. ISBN 1-55766-064-6.

> Each section of this professionally oriented text addresses a different aspect of spina bifida as it relates to
> the educational experience: health and related services; individualized education; intervention; social, emo-
> tional, and family support systems. Chapters are complete with glossary, references, and resources. This is
> an excellent guide and reference book with practical ideas and tips that make it a useful collaboration tool.

First Person Perspectives

Gaul, Gilbert M. ***Giant Steps: The Story of One Boy's Struggle to Walk.*** New York, NY:
St. Martin's Press, 1993. 182 pp. ISBN 0-312-08729-2. Out of print.

> Cary Gaul was born with spina bifida and club feet, and developed hydrocephalus when just a few
> days old. In ***Giant Steps,*** his father, a Pulitzer Prize-winning journalist, describes how the whole
> family struggled to maintain a sense of normalcy in the face of these disabilities: grappling with
> emotions related to the diagnosis, undergoing tricky operations, discovering that Cary had more
> sensation than originally suspected, and watching Cary's slow, but steady progress toward inde-
> pendent walking. Gaul also stops to philosophize about issues that confront all families of children
> with disabilities: living life in the spotlight; fighting insurance companies for adequate coverage;
> finding professionals who respect and listen to families' concerns.

Miller, Nancy B. ***Nobody's Perfect: Living & Growing with Children Who Have Special
Needs.*** Baltimore: Paul H. Brookes, 1994. 307 pp. $21.00. ISBN 1-55766-143-X.

> Parents of children with spina bifida may want to take special note of this book. The author wrote it in close
> consultation with four mothers of children with special needs, including the mother of a child with spina
> bifida. Many quotations from the parents about their experiences and feelings are used to illustrate the
> author's ideas about helping parents cope with the special challenges of raising a child with special needs.

For Children

Krementz, Jill. ***How It Feels to Fight for Your Life.*** Boston: Little, Brown and Co., 1989. 132 pp.
ISBN 0-316-50364-9. Out of print.

> Fourteen children and teenagers with chronic illnesses or disabilities describe their daily lives and
> struggle for independence. One of the essays is about an eight-year-old girl with spina bifida who
> plays the violin and attends her neighborhood school. The book is illustrated with excellent black-
> and-white photos of the children.

Lutkenhoff, Marlene, and Sonya Oppenheimer, eds. ***SPINAbilities: A Young Person's Guide to
Spina Bifida.*** Bethesda, MD: Woodbine House, 1997. 138 pp. $16.95. ISBN 0-933149-86-7.

> In sensitive, easy-to-understand language, this guidebook sets out to give young people with spina
> bifida the information and tools they need to become as independent as possible. It covers topics in
> four broad subject areas: medical issues and personal care (including skin care, mobility, and
> bowel and bladder care); relationships (with peers and family members); growing up (school and
> career issues); and healthy practices. Thanks to its thoroughness and readability, the book is also
> a splendid introduction to adolescent and young adult issues for parents and professionals.

Rabe, Berniece. ***The Balancing Girl.*** New York, NY: NAL-Dutton, 1993. 32 pp. $4.99.
ISBN 0-14-054876-9.

> Although Margaret has some difficulty getting around due to spina bifida, she has a special talent
> for balancing things. This illustrated story for children in preschool and early elementary grades
> shows how Margaret uses her talent to help make the school carnival a success. The sequel to this

book, **Margaret's Moves,** follows now nine-year-old Margaret's attempts to earn enough money for a speedy sports-model wheelchair. The book is out of print, but check your library for a copy.

■ ORGANIZATIONS

March of Dimes

Resource Center
1275 Mamaroneck Ave.
White Plains, NY 10605
(888) MODIMES; (914) 997-4764 TTY; (914) 997-4763 FAX
Web site: http//www.modimes.org

> PURPOSE: The Resource Center of the March of Dimes provides information to the public about birth defects, pregnancy, and children's health issues.
>
> PUBLICATION: Free fact sheet on spina bifida.

National Information Center for Children and Youth with Disabilities (NICHCY)

P.O. Box 1492
Washington, DC 20013-1492
(800) 695-0285; (202) 884-8441 FAX
E-mail: nichcy@aed.org
Web site: http//www.nichcy.org

> PURPOSE: A clearinghouse that provides information on disabilities and disability-related issues, with an emphasis on children and young people birth to age 22.
>
> PUBLICATION: Fact sheet: *"General Information about Spina Bifida."*

National Maternal and Child Health Clearinghouse

2070 Chain Bridge Rd., Ste. 450
Vienna, VA 22182-2536
(703) 356-1964; (703) 821-2098 FAX
E-mail: nmchc@circsol.com
Web site: http//www.circsol.com/mch

> PURPOSE: "Disseminates state-of-the-art information about maternal and child health." Most of the publications distributed were developed through programs funded by grants from the Maternal and Child Health Bureau.
>
> SERVICES: Clearinghouse staff respond to requests for information or refer callers to other information agencies and sources.
>
> PUBLICATION: One copy of *"What You Should Know about Folic Acid: For parents who have lost a pregnancy or had a child with spina bifida, anencephaly, or encephalocele"* (pub. #J107) is free.

NIH Neurology Institute

National Institute of Neurological Disorders and Stroke
P.O. Box 5801
Bethesda, MD 20824
(800) 352-9424; (301) 402-2186 FAX
Web site: http://www.ninds.nih.gov

> PURPOSE: Supports research into brain and nervous system disorders.
>
> PUBLICATIONS: Free publications include: **Neurological Disorders: Voluntary Health Agencies and Other Patient Resources** (a directory); *"Know Your Brain"* (fact sheet on anatomy and function); *"Hope Through Research"* brochure on spina bifida.

Spina Bifida Association of America

4590 MacArthur Blvd., NW, Ste. 250
Washington, DC 20007-4226
(800) 621-3141; (202) 944-3285; (202) 944-3295 FAX

> PURPOSE: To provide information on spina bifida, including progress in medicine, education, and legislation; to support research; and to encourage training of professionals.
> SERVICES: Toll-free information and referral number; liason to other organizations; professional advisory council; and annual national conference.
> PUBLICATIONS: In addition to publications described in section above, offers *"Spotlights"* ($0.75 each) on topics such as *"The Chiari Malformation," "Hip Function and Ambulation,"* and *"Urologic Care of the Child with Spina Bifida"*; ***Confronting the Challenges of Spina Bifida*** ($18.00), a curriculum for teaching self-care, self-esteem, and social skills; ***Parent/Teacher Packet*** ($12.00); ***A Guide to Hydrocephalus*** ($5.95); and ***Sexuality and the Person with Spina Bifida*** ($9.95). Also publishes ***Insight,*** a bimonthly newsletter. SBAA members receive a discount when purchasing publications.

Spina Bifida Association of Canada

220-388 Donald St.
Winnipeg, Manitoba R3B 2J4
Canada
(204) 957-1784; (204) 957-1794 FAX
E-mail: spinab@mts.net

> PURPOSE: "To improve the quality of life of all individuals with spina bifida and/or hydrocephalus and their families, through awareness, education and research."
> PUBLICATIONS: Offers free brochures on hydrocephalus, catheterization, and spina bifida, and several free coloring books for children. Other publications include: ***Kit for Parents*** ($10); ***Kit for Teens*** ($10); ***Learning Disabilities and the Person with Spina Bifida*** ($5.25). Some publications also available in French.

37.

Spinal Cord Injury

■ BOOKS

Basic Information

Maddox, Sam, ed. *Spinal Network: Total Wheelchair Resource Book.* 2nd ed. Malibu, CA: Spinal Network, 1994. 568 pp. $39.95. ISBN 0-943489-03-2.

> The primary audience of this book is adult readers who are paralyzed due to spinal cord injury, spina bifida, multiple sclerosis, or another physical disability. Parents, however, can also glean much useful information. Information is included about medical advances, therapy, orthotics, and more (this particular edition had 28 different articles that focused on the medical aspects of physical disabilities). There are pages of personal profiles and inspirational messages from people with a variety of physical disabilities. A sports section is included. A large section of this book is dedicated to getting peer support and locating organizations that will help the person with the disability and his family. Lists of resources are included.

Resources for People with SCI. Silver Spring, MD: ABLEDATA. $6.00.

> This information packet consists of the following fact sheets: "Informed Consumer Guide to Technology for People with Spinal Cord Injury"; "Informed Consumer Guide to Wheelchair Selection"; "Funding Assistive Technology Fact Sheet"; "Computer Access"; "Scooters Fact Sheet."

First Person Perspectives

Hockenberry, John. *Moving Violations: War Zones, Wheelchairs, and Declarations of Independence.* New York, NY: Hyperion, 1995. $14.95. ISBN 0-7868-8162-3.

> At 19, Hockenberry's spinal cord was severed in a car accident. In this, his memoir of his life as a paraplegic, he takes an unflinchingly honest look at how his injury changed his life and his views

of society. He explains how he manages to keep up with reporting assignments in wartorn Beirut, Somalia, Jerusalem, and New York City, and also how he copes on a day to day basis with discrimination and with small humiliations such as being trapped under his own bed. His words are often humorous, sometimes biting, and well worth the attention of all readers, whether or not they have a personal reason for caring about people with spinal cord injuries.

For Children

Kachur, Wanda Gilberts. *The Nautilus.* Minnetonka, MN: Peytral Publications, 1997. 172 pp. $7.95. ISBN 0-9644271-5-X.

> Kathryn, the heroine of this young adult novel, sustains a spinal cord injury in a car accident while visiting her grandmother. The story, which follows her through emergency treatment at a hospital and a stint at a rehabilitation center, includes a great deal of detail about medical procedures and therapies used in treating spinal cord injuries.

Krementz, Jill. *How It Feels to Fight for Your Life.* Boston: Little, Brown and Co., 1989. 132 pp. ISBN 0-316-50364-9. Out of print.

> Fourteen children and teenagers with chronic illnesses or disabilities describe their daily lives and struggle for independence. Included is an essay about a fourteen-year-old boy with a spinal cord injury who plays wheelchair sports competitively. The book is illustrated with excellent black-and-white photos of the children.

Panzarino, Connie. *Follow Your Dreams.* Silver Spring, MD: National Spinal Cord Injury Association, 1995. 29 pp.

> This is a children's book about wheelchairs, races, magic shoes, and courage. Kids teach kids about spinal cord injuries—each telling a little bit of their story within a child's fantasy.

Panzarino, Connie. *Rebecca Finds a New Way: How Kids Learn, Play and Live with Spinal Cord Injuries and Illnesses.* Silver, Spring, MD: National Spinal Cord Injury Association, 1994. 56 pp. $20.00.

> Rebecca and her mom were in a car accident. When Rebecca woke up, she was in the hospital and her whole life had changed. Learn all about wheelchairs, respirators, occupational and physical therapy, and adjusting to life with a spinal cord injury. Terry Terrific, Rebecca's best friend, asks all the hard questions and gathers information for all of us.

Powers, Mary Ellen. *Our Teacher's in a Wheelchair.* Morton Grove, IL: Albert Whitman & Co., 1986. Not paginated. $12.95. ISBN 0-8075-6240-8.

> Brian loves kids, enjoys his life as a teacher, and is young and handsome. Brian is in a wheelchair because he has a spinal cord injury. The reader meets Brian through a series of photographs. We get a glimpse of him at his job, in his home, and in the community he lives in. This is a simple, easy read and a catalyst for discussion.

Sirof, Harriet. *The Road Back: Living with a Physical Disability.* New York, NY: Macmillan, 1993. 160 pp. $13.95. ISBN 0-02-782885-9.

> This book is for teenagers or young adults who have recently acquired a disability through an accident or illness. It follows three fictitious teenagers—one with multiple sclerosis, one with a spinal cord injury, and one with temporary physical disabilities—from the moment they become disabled, through the rehabilitation process, to the day when they feel ready to get on with their lives. Along the way, the author explores the thoughts and emotions that are common at every stage of coping.

■ ORGANIZATIONS

American Paralysis Association

500 Morris Ave.
Springfield, NJ 07081
(800) 225-0292; (201) 912-9433 FAX
Web site: http//www.apa.uci.edu/paralysis

> PURPOSE: A nonprofit agency which encourages research to find a cure for paralysis caused by spinal cord injury and central nervous system disorders.
> SERVICES: 24-hour information and referral hotline.
> PUBLICATIONS: Publishes two newsletters and other materials.

National Spinal Cord Injury Association

8300 Colesville Rd., Ste. 551
Silver Spring, MD 20910
(800) 962-9629 Hotline; (301) 588-6959; (301) 588-9414 FAX
Web site: http//www.trader.com/users/5010/1020/nscia.htm

> PURPOSE: Improving care, producing results in research, and addressing everyday living issues of wheelchair users. The organization serves not only people with spinal cord injuries, but also persons with diseases or conditions similar to spinal cord injuries.
> SERVICES: Information and referral; provides care consultation services, implementing programs on prevention of SCI and abilities of individuals with SCI.
> PUBLICATIONS: Newsletter, pamphlets, fact sheets, and other publications such as those listed above. Request a catalog.

National Spinal Cord Injury Hotline

2201 Argonne Dr.
Baltimore, MD 21218
(800) 526-3456

> PURPOSE: Provides toll-free information and referral service for individuals and families with a spinal cord injury.
> SERVICES: Support and resources, referrals to peer-volunteers or professionals with expertise in SCI, referral to rehabilitation facilities and other spinal cord organizations and literature.

NIH Neurology Institute

National Institute of Neurological Disorders and Stroke
P.O. Box 5801
Bethesda, MD 20824
(800) 352-9424; (301) 402-2186 FAX
Web site: http://www.ninds.nih.gov

> PURPOSE: Supports research into brain and nervous system disorders.
> PUBLICATIONS: Free publications include: **Neurological Disorders: Voluntary Health Agencies and Other Patient Resources** (a directory); *"Know Your Brain"* (fact sheet on anatomy and function); *"Hope Through Research"* brochure on spinal cord injury.

Spinal Network

23815 Stuart Ranch Rd.
Malibu, CA 90265
(800) 543-4116

> PURPOSE: To provide a central source of information for people who use wheelchairs to find answers, connections, and resources.
>
> PUBLICATIONS: Sells books by a variety of publishers on all aspects of disability; request a publications catalog. Also publishes *New Mobility* magazine, listed in the Physical Disabilities section.

38.

Tourette Syndrome

■ BOOKS

Basic Information

Comings, David E. *Tourette Syndrome and Human Behavior.* Duarte, CA: Hope Press, 1990. 828 pp. $49.95. ISBN 1-878267-27-2.

>   This is the definitive source for information about Tourette syndrome. The book thoroughly explains the genetics, cause, behaviors, and treatment associated with this disorder. It also covers a number of disorders that may be associated with Tourette syndrome, including ADD and eating disorders. Resources are included, as is a child/adult behavior questionnaire to help determine whether Tourette syndrome may be present. For ease of reading and understanding, the book was written in "lay" terms; however, the professional will find it as helpful as the parent.

Haerle, Tracy, ed. *Children with Tourette Syndrome: A Parents' Guide.* Bethesda, MD: Woodbine House, 1992. 340 pp. $14.95. ISBN 0-933149-44-1.

>   This is a compassionate guide to understanding and living with a child or adolescent who has Tourette syndrome. A comprehensive explanation of the nature and causes of the disorder is provided in the first chapter. After that, chapter authors suggest options for treatment, medication, education, and behavior management. Care is taken to address the effects of TS on the entire family, and on the parents' marriage. In addition, there are chapters about how TS can affect a child's development, and on legal rights and benefits. At the end of each chapter are comments from other parents about their experiences and feelings. There is also a chapter written by an adult with TS about how it feels to have Tourette syndrome. This is a book to help parents cope, make decisions, and face the challenges ahead.

Hallowell, Edward. *When You Worry about the Child You Love.* New York, NY: Simon & Schuster, 1996. 281 pp. $23.00. ISBN 0-684-80090-X.

> For parents who suspect, or have just learned, that their child has an emotional or learning problem, this book provides an excellent overview of disorders that may make children mad, sad, afraid, or confused. The book explains when parents should worry about their children's behavior and seek professional help; discusses steps parents can take to help children manage their emotions and learn, no matter what the disorder; and discusses treatment options, including medication. Information on a number of disorders with a biologic or genetic basis is included: ADD, obsessive-compulsive disorder, conduct disorder, oppositional defiant disorder, overanxious disorder, panic attacks, learning disability, and Tourette syndrome. The author's conversational style and numerous anecdotes make this an easy read.

Koplewicz, Harold S. *It's Nobody's Fault: New Hope and Help for Difficult Children and Their Parents.* New York, NY: Times Books/Random House, 1996. 305 pp. $25.00. ISBN 0-8129-2473-8.

> This book focuses on what the author calls "no fault brain disorders"—emotional and behavioral disorders that are known or presumed to be caused by brain chemical abnormalities, rather than environmental causes such as bad parenting. Conditions covered include attention deficit hyperactivity disorder, obsessive compulsive disorder, separation anxiety disorder, social phobia, generalized anxiety disorder, enuresis, and Tourette syndrome. For each disorder, the author discusses symptoms, diagnosis, brain chemistry, treatment (with an emphasis on medications that can improve brain chemical functioning), and issues involved in parenting a child with the disorder. The book is very readable and filled with examples of children treated by the author.

Sacks, Oliver. *The Man Who Mistook His Wife for a Hat and Other Clinical Tales.* New York, NY: HarperCollins, 1987. 256 pp. $13.00. ISBN 0-06-097079-0.

> In this collection of stories about Dr. Sacks's many patients, there are two interesting, if short, chapters that explore some of the psychological and philosophical issues surrounding Tourette syndrome, its impact on the lives and identities of people with the condition, and society's perception of people with Tourette syndrome. There is not much basic information in these chapters, but Dr. Sacks's perspective on the condition is fascinating.

Shimberg, Elaine Fantle. *Living with Tourette Syndrome.* New York, NY: Simon & Schuster, 1994. 256 pp. $12.00. ISBN 0-684-81160-X.

> As the mother of three children with Tourette syndrome, Elaine Fantle Shimberg has considerable insight into the support and information needs of other parents. Perhaps because her children are now grown, the sections on adult issues in her book are especially strong, covering topics such as dating and social interaction, intimate relationships, finding and keeping a job, and housing. In comparison, the sections on educational issues seem sketchier, in particular when considering the laws under which children with Tourette syndrome can qualify for special education and classroom accomodations. The book also provides a useful overview of the causes, diagnosis, and treatment of Tourette syndrome, as well as strategies for dealing with the practical and emotional effects of Tourette syndrome on all members of the family.

First Person Perspectives

Hughes, Susan. *Ryan: A Mother's Story of Her Hyperactive/Tourette Syndrome Child.* Duarte, CA: Hope Press, 1990. 153 pp. $9.95. ISBN 1-878267-26-4.

> In this compelling autobiography, the author explains vividly what it was like to live those first years not knowing what was wrong with her child. She describe's her son's hyperactive escapades, his other troubling behaviors, and her own and her family's endless support. In the end, there is a

wealth of insight about dealing with the medical community, medications, hyperactivity, and especially the importance of family support and personal strength. The book concludes with a brief list of books to read and national organizations.

Seligman, Adam Ward, and John S. Hilkevich, eds. ***Don't Think about Monkeys.*** Duarte, CA: Hope Press, 1992. 206 pp. $12.95. ISBN 1-878267-33-7.

 This is a collection of essays written by people who have Tourette syndrome. Mincing no words, they describe what it is like to live with this syndrome, sharing their feelings of despair, their loneliness, and their successes. This is a real book about real people who live day-to-day with extraordinary challenges. It is also about the faith and love of friends and family.

For Children

Buehrens, Adam, and Carol Buehrens. ***Adam and the Magic Marble.*** Duarte, CA: Hope Press, 1991. 108 pp. $6.95. ISBN 1-878267-30-2.

 Adam has Tourette syndrome and has written a fun-filled story that introduces the reader to Tourette and provides some insight into what it is like to live with it. Adam weaves a delightful adventure story that is complete with bullies, magic, special friendships, and real heroes. Children will love reading this book. Adults will find that it serves as the perfect tool to lead discussions about differences, friendships, and challenging social situations.

Buehrens, Adam. ***Hi, I'm Adam: A Child's Story of Tourette Syndrome.*** Duarte, CA: Hope Press, 1993. 35 pp. $4.95. ISBN 1-878267-29-9.

 With a great deal of sensitivity, ten-year-old Adam explains what it is like to have TS and how he has progressed with it over his short life span. He discusses what it is like to have a body that does things he does not want it to. His frustration is evident, but he writes about it without the anger you might expect. This is a fine book to share with parents and children. It is open and honest and will help to develop a dialog about Tourette syndrome and special needs in general. The illustrations are ready to color. The author even leaves blank pages so other young authors can write their own stories.

■ ORGANIZATIONS

Tourette Syndrome Association
42-40 Bell Blvd.
Bayside, NY 11361-2820
(718) 224-2999; (718) 279-9596 FAX
E-mail: tourette@ix.netcom.com
http//TSA.mgh.harvard.edu/

 PURPOSE: To educate people with TS and their families, professionals, and the general public about Tourette syndrome; to provide moral support to people with Tourette syndrome; and to advance research into causes and cure of TS.

 SERVICES: Information and referral; sponsors local chapters.

 PUBLICATIONS: A quarterly newsletter provides information about national concerns and advances regarding Tourette syndrome. Each edition offers new books, papers and research information. The TSA also offers a variety of low-cost brochures and booklets for people with Tourette syndrome, family members, educators, and medical professionals. Titles include: *"An Educator's Guide to Tourette Syndrome"; "The Genetics of Tourette Syndrome"; "Discipline and the TS Child: A Guide for Parents and Teachers"; "Understanding Copralalia."* Some publications available in Spanish. Request a publications catalog.

Tourette Syndrome Foundation of Canada
238 Davenport Rd., Box 343
Toronto, Ontario M5R 1J6
Canada
(416) 636-2800; (416) 636-1688 FAX

> SERVICES: Information and referral; sponsors local chapters.
> PUBLICATIONS: Publishes a newsletter and other informational materials. Some publications available in French.

39.

Traumatic Brain Injury (TBI)

■ BOOKS

Basic Information

Deaton, Ann V. *Pediatric Head Trauma: Guide for Families.* New Kent, VA: Cumberland Hospital, 1987. 36 pp. $2.00. No ISBN.

> This brief guide is one of the few that focuses on pediatric head trauma. The author explains briefly and simply how the brain is injured. By following several children from the initial head injury through rehabilitation, the reader learns about the assessment and decision-making processes that occur. The author also explains levels of cognitive functioning. There is basic information about the activities that should accompany each stage of recovery.

Foxx, Richard M., and Ron G. Bittle. *Thinking It Through: Teaching a Problem Solving Strategy for Community Living. Curriculum for Individuals with Brain Injuries.* Champaign, IL: Research Press, 1989. Not paginated. $14.95. ISBN 0-87822-300-2.

> This manual offers a structured approach to help individuals with brain injuries regain cognitive skills. Situations that cause stress such as dealing with authority figures, peer issues, and self advocacy are addressed.

McMahon, Brian T., and Randall W. Evans, eds. *The Shortest Distance: The Pursuit of Independence for Persons with Acquired Brain Injury.* Winter Park, FL: G.R. Press, 1994. 156 pp. $32.50. ISBN 1-878205-68-4.

> Although this is a technical manual for rehabilitation specialists, the final three chapters may be useful to parents. They offer special information about empowerment, case management, and

promoting independence for the individual with traumatic brain injury. Information about the technological aspects of support is included. Resources from IBM are the focus for augmentative equipment.

Orton, Arthur E., Dell Power, and Paul W. Power. *Head Injury and the Family.* Winter Park, FL: G.R. Press, Inc., 1994. 246 pp. $29.95. ISBN 1-878205-61-7.

> This book provides a starting point for families and professionals as they begin to understand the enormous stresses and strains of living and coping with a family member with a head injury. Personal statements by family members offer a variety of coping strategies. They talk about challenges and life experiences that they have faced. Topics covered include family considerations, assessment, counseling, and support groups. The book includes an extensive list of publications, resources, videos, and organizations.

Schoenbrodt, Lisa, and Romayne A. Smith. *Communication Disorders and Interventions in Low Incidence Pediatric Populations.* San Diego: Singular Publishing Group, 1995. 250 pp. $39.95. ISBN 1-56593-220-X.

> One chapter of this manual is devoted to children with TBI. The information is intended to give speech-language pathologists the background they need to work with children with TBI, and covers such information as variability of outcome in TBI, typical learning difficulties, treatment, classroom modifications, and family issues.

Senelick, Richard C., and Cathy E. Ryan. *Living with Head Injury: A Guide for Families.* San Antonio, TX: Rehabilitation Institute of San Antonio, 1991. 149 pp. ISBN 0-929162-28-5.

> This book is suggested reading by the Brain Injury Association. It is a comprehensive guide that helps families understand how the brain works and what happens to it when it is injured. The authors explain the role of doctors and the team of professionals during the diagnosis and treatment period. Symptoms of TBI are described at great length. In addition, the family is acknowledged as the center of support for the injured individual. Several chapters focus on coping strategies and questions that families ask. A complete resource guide is included.

First Person Perspectives

Rife, Janet Miller. *Injured Mind, Shattered Dreams: Brian's Journey from Severe Head Injury to a New Dream.* Cambridge, MA: Brookline, 1994. $17.95. ISBN 0-914797-95-6.

> Janet Rife writes this book for families and survivors who have experienced the nightmare of head injury. She uses her personal journal as a way to tell her son Brian's story. She recounts the family's horror as they learn of Brian's accident and then the long wait for him to "wake up." Brian's return is to a new life, one neither he nor his family had expected. This story underscores the importance of friends, family, and support.

For Children

Aaseng, Nathan, and Jay Aaseng. *Head Injuries.* New York, NY: Franklin Watts, 1996. 112 pp. $22.00. ISBN 0-531-11267-5.

> This introduction to traumatic brain injuries for young adults would be an excellent first book for adults as well. In clear, simple language, the book explains the causes, prevalence, risk factors, warning signs, diagnosis, types and ranges of severity, long-term complications, and treatment of TBI. Jay Aaseng, who sustained a mild head injury when he was thirteen, contributes his first-hand experiences, and the head injuries of many celebrities are also discussed. The book is illustrated with black and white photographs and sketches.

■ ORGANIZATIONS

Brain Injury Association
1776 Massachusetts Ave., N.W., Ste. 100
Washington, DC 20036-1904
(202) 296-6443; (202) 296-8850 FAX
(800) 440-6443 FAMILY HELPLINE
Web site: http//www.biausa.org
> PURPOSE: Dedicated to improving the quality of life for people with traumatic brain injury and their families, and to promoting the prevention of head injury.
> SERVICES: Clearinghouse for information. Provides legislative information, educational programs, and awareness programs.
> PUBLICATIONS: Offers booklets, books, information packets, and videos on a wide variety of topics, including guides for families, first person accounts, educational materials, and the *National Directory of Brain Injury Rehabilitation Services.*

National Maternal and Child Health Clearinghouse
2070 Chain Bridge Rd., Ste. 450
Vienna, VA 22182-2536
(703) 356-1964; (703) 821-2098 FAX
E-mail: nmchc@circsol.com
Web site: http//www.circsol.com/mch
> PURPOSE: "Disseminates state-of-the-art information about maternal and child health."
> SERVICES: Clearinghouse staff respond to requests for information or refer callers to other information agencies and sources.
> PUBLICATION: One copy of *"Mild Head Injury: Care of the Child at Home"* (pub. #E032) is free.

NIH Neurology Institute
National Institute of Neurological Disorders and Stroke
P.O. Box 5801
Bethesda, MD 20824
(800) 352-9424; (301) 402-2186 FAX
Web site: http://www.ninds.nih.gov
> PURPOSE: Supports research into brain and nervous system disorders.
> PUBLICATIONS: Free publications include: *Neurological Disorders: Voluntary Health Agencies and Other Patient Resources* (a directory); *"Know Your Brain"* (fact sheet on anatomy and function); *"Hope Through Research"* brochure on head injury.

RRTC on Rehabilitation Interventions in TBI
Attn: Linda Herson
TIRR-Division of Education, B-107
133 Moursund
Houston, TX 77030
(713) 797-5945; (713) 797-5982
E-mail: lherson@bcm.tmc.edu
> PUBLICATIONS: TIRR operates a national database describing more than 350 print and audiovisual resources on TBI. A printed compendium of the entire database costs $55; printouts of up to two topic areas are free.

40.

Visual Impairments and Blindness

■ BOOKS

Basic Information

Greenblatt, Susan, ed. ***Meeting the Needs of People with Vision Loss.*** Lexington, MA: Resources for Rehabilitation, 1991. 136 pp. $24.95. ISBN 0-929718-07-0.

> Although written primarily for professionals, this is a great educational tool for parents as well. Many aspects of life with a visual impairment are covered, including effects on the family and the family's role. Special issues highlighted include diabetes, children, and adolescents. In the case study section, the author explains how professionals and families can work together to advocate for the child. A sample letter from a professional outlining adaptations for the school environment is reproduced.

Greenblatt, Susan L., ed. ***Providing Services for People with Vision Loss.*** Lexington, MA: Resources for Rehabilitation, 1989. 129 pp. $19.95. ISBN 0-929718-02-X.

> This professionally oriented publication discusses the "pieces" that are needed to provide appropriate services to families and individuals. Topics discussed include making referrals, coordinating care, the need to refer to mental health services, and self-help resources. A great reference section on aides and organizations is included.

Holbrook, M. Cay. ***Children with Visual Impairments: A Parent's Guide.*** Bethesda, MD: Woodbine House, 1996. 394 pp. $16.95. ISBN 0-933149-36-0.

> Written by parents and professionals, this guide provides important facts, instruction, tips, and insight about raising a child who has a visual impairment or is blind. Among the many issues

addressed are: the nature, causes, and degrees of visual impairment; medical concerns and treatments; coping emotionally with the diagnosis; how development is affected; daily life; family life; self-esteem; early intervention and special education; legal rights and benefits; literacy; orientation and mobility; and children with multiple disabilities. The book focuses on the concerns of parents of children from birth to about age six, but also contains a chapter that discusses educational, vocational, and social issues of older children and adults. Each chapter concludes with quotations from parents about their experiences and emotions, and the book includes many pages of resources and reading suggestions.

Tuttle, Dean, and Naomi Tuttle. *Self-esteem and Adjusting with Blindness: The Process of Responding to Life's Demands.* 2nd ed. Springfield, IL: Charles C. Thomas, 1996. 308 pp. $37.95. ISBN 0-398-06598-5.

This book traces the stages that children and adults go through in learning to cope with blindness. Many interesting excerpts from the works of blind authors are used to illustrate the emotional stages that individuals with blindness experience.

Education

Dominguez, Betty, and Joe Dominguez. *Building Blocks: Foundations for Learning for Young Blind and Visually Impaired Children.* New York, NY: AFB Press, 1991. 160 pp. $24.95. ISBN 0-89128-187-8.

This illustrated guide emphasizes the importance of the family in the development of preschoolers with visual impairments. Written in English and Spanish, it covers background information on visual impairments, education, and development, and suggests specific home activities to foster learning.

Sacks, Sharon Zell, Linda S. Kekelis, and Robert J. Gaylord-Ross. *The Development of Social Skills by Blind and Visually Impaired Students: Exploratory Studies and Strategies.* New York, NY: AFB Press, 1992. 232 pp. $39.95. ISBN 0-89128-217-3.

This text offers research on the social skills of blind and visually impaired children, as well as practical strategies to help families, educators, and others help children develop appropriate social skills. Information on how blind and visually impaired children tend to interact in integrated settings at school and in the community underscores the need for instruction in social skills from an early age.

Willoughby, Doris M., and Sharon L.M. Duffy. *Handbook for Itinerant and Resource Teachers of Blind and Visually Impaired Students.* Baltimore: National Federation of the Blind, 1989. 533 pp. $23.00 (print). ISBN 0-9624122-0-1.

The authors of this truly comprehensive volume wrote it with the purpose of analyzing the causes for educational problems in blind children and then giving appropriate solutions. Although it is intended primarily for teachers, it offers much of value to parents as well. There is information: on daily living with a young child (eating, sleeping, toilet training); explaining different degrees of blindness to classmates and families; medical issues; orientation and mobility issues; computers and keyboarding; as well as detailed information on adapting every academic subject for blind children. The information on literacy skills, including braille, is especially exhaustive. The writing throughout is very clear and jargon-free.

Literacy

Croft, Diane, Deborah Kendrick, and Albert Gayzaigian. *The CD-ROM Advantage: For Blind Users.* Boston: National Braille Press, 1994. 61 pp. $16.95. ISBN 0-939173-02-6.

"CD-ROM is a breakthrough publishing medium for blind people who have never had equal access to standard print publications and most notable reference works." People who are blind can benefit immeasurably from the technological advances in the computer world, and this little book explains how and why. Cookbooks, encyclopedias, magazines, and reference libraries are all available for the blind on CD-ROM. Find out how to access them by reading this book. Personal accounts of CD-ROM users are included.

Curran, Eileen. *Just Enough to Know Better: Braille Primer.* 4th ed. Boston: National Braille Press, 1994. $12.00. ISBN 0-939173-15-8.

This wonderful book will provide parents with "just enough" information about braille to be helpful to a child who is learning to read and write in braille. It covers the braille alphabet, punctuation, contractions, and numbers. Included is a story written by the mother of a child who is blind, and a story by a blind student about the things that were important to her when she was a student. Each page of the exercise sections is written in both print and braille. The tutoring pages for learning braille are simply written and explained.

Espinola, Olga, and Diane Croft. *Solutions: Access Technologies for People Who Are Blind.* Boston: National Braille Press, 1992. $21.95 ISBN 0-939173-21-2 (print). ISBN 0-939173-22-0 (Braille). ISBN 0-939173-23-9 (cassette). ISBN 0-939173-24-7 (disk).

This is a real tool for understanding the basics of computers and how to access them. Many aspects of participating in the computer age are addressed in simple, understandable terms, from using speech access systems and braille embossers to adapting work stations at your job or home. Special attention is placed on identifying what you will need to know, which is especially helpful for readers who do not know enough about computer systems to know what they want to ask! Lists of resources are provided.

Koenig, Alan J., and M. Cay Holbrook. *The Braille Enthusiast's Dictionary.* Nashville, TN: SCALARS Publishing, 1995. 548 pp. $45.00.

This comprehensive dictionary lists about 30,000 words in print and contracted braille forms. It is intended as a resource for teachers and parents making braille transcriptions.

Deaf-Blindness

Everson, Jane M., ed. *Supporting Young Adults Who Are Deaf-Blind in Their Communities: A Transition Planning Guide for Service Providers, Families, and Friends.* Baltimore: Paul H. Brookes, 1995. 384 pp. $39.00. ISBN 1-55766-161-8.

Helping young adults who are deaf-blind make a successful transition from school to community life is the goal of this text. The author explains the transition process, how to establish support systems, and strategies for expanding lifestyles for greater independence and satisfaction. Also addressed is how to identify barriers to transition after high school and utilize them for success. The book includes many case studies that illustrate how to use supports to achieve successful community integration.

Haring, Norris G., and Lyle T. Romer, eds. ***Welcoming Students Who Are Deaf-Blind into Typical Classrooms: Facilitating School Participation, Learning, and Friendships.*** Baltimore: Paul H. Brookes, 1995. 480 pp. $35.00. ISBN 1-55766-144-8.

> Although written for education professionals, this text offers helpful information for parents about what does and does not work when including deaf-blind students in typical classrooms, as well as the rationale for doing so.

Huebner, Kathleen Mary, Jeanne Glidden Prickett, Therese Rafalowski Welch, and Elga Joffee, eds. ***Hand in Hand: Essentials of Communication and Orientation and Mobility for Your Students Who Are Deaf-Blind.*** New York, NY: American Foundation for the Blind Press, 1995. 687 pp. (Vol. I), 136 pp. (Vol. II). $60.00 for set. ISBN 0-89128-937-2.

> This hefty two-volume set was developed to provide self-study and inservice training materials for teachers about deaf-blindness in children ages birth through 21. The books' nontechnical, reader-friendly language make them valuable for family members as well. Volume I covers basic information about how deaf-blindness affects a child's abilities to learn; general strategies for teaching and interacting with deaf-blind students; and specific strategies for teaching communication and orientation and mobility skills. Throughout, the focus is on helping students maximize their independence so that they can become included as fully as possible in their communities. Volume II includes appendixes covering medical information about vision and hearing loss, amplification, assessment instruments, and federal funding; a glossary; resources, including books and sources of information and equipment; and an index.

First Person Perspectives

Alexander, Sally Hobart. ***On My Own: The Journey Continues.*** New York, NY: Farrar Straus Giroux, 1997. 165 pp. $16.00. ISBN 0-374-35641-6.

> Sally Hobart began gradually losing her vision in her mid-20s. In this book, she chronicles her first steps toward regaining independence—adjusting to living in apartment alone, becoming a teacher of people who had recently become blind, learning to take public transportation, re-entering the dating scene, and attending graduate school. Her narrative gives a good feel for the practical differences between being blind and sighted, as well as a blind person's perspective of the sighted world. The author has previously written about her life in *Taking Hold: My Journey Into Blindness.*

Hull, John M. ***Touching the Rock: An Experience of Blindness.*** New York, NY: Random House, 1991. 240 pp. $10.00. ISBN 0-679-73547-X.

> At thirteen, John Hull lost the sight in one eye due to cataracts. Several years later, the sight in his other eye began to deteriorate, and he became completely blind in his late 30s. This book, written in journal form, begins at the point when he begins to think of himself as completely blind. In a number of short, thoughtful entries, he reflects on a myriad of differences between being blind and sighted: how dreams differ, the need to smile, how the passage of time is perceived, the importance placed on appearance, the types of interactions he has with others. Particularly fascinating are his experiences in helping his young children understand the nature of blindness.

Mehta, Ved. ***Sound-Shadows of the New World.*** New York, NY: W.W. Norton Co., 1985. 430 pp. $8.95. ISBN 0-393-30437-X.

> Blinded at four by meningitis, at fifteen Ved Mehta left his native India to continue his education at the Arkansas School for the Blind. In Little Rock, Mehta not only had to struggle to catch up academically with his classmates, but also to adapt to a strange new culture. After his initial homesickness, Ved began to make friends, date, and excel academically, eventually graduating as class saluta-

torian in 1952. Lively dialog and insightful observations make this account of Mehta's time in Arkansas a fascinating read. This is the fifth in a series of autobiographical books about Mehta's life.

Vermeij, Geerat. ***Privileged Hands: A Scientific Life.*** New York, NY: W.H. Freeman, 1996. 297 pp. $23.95. 297 pp. ISBN 0-7167-2954-7.

> Vermeij, a Dutch-born marine biologist, has been totally blind since birth. Here he recounts how he has been able to use his other senses to help him become a world-renowned expert on mollusks. His very readable biography touches not only upon his professional experiences trekking after mollusks, teaching, writing, and researching, but also upon the many obstacles he has had to surmount in order to succeed in school and in his chosen career.

For Children

Adler, David A. ***A Picture Book of Helen Keller.*** New York, NY: Holiday House, 1992. 32 pp. $5.95. ISBN 0-8234-0950-3.

> One of many biographies of Helen Keller available for young readers, this one is intended for children in grades 1-3. The book is well illustrated and focuses on Keller's childhood, including how she learned to communicate with Annie Sullivan's help. Interesting accomplishments in adulthood are also touched on.

Adler, David A. ***A Picture Book of Louis Braille.*** New York, NY: Holiday House, 1997. 34 pp. $16.95. ISBN 0-8234-1291-1.

> The Frenchman who developed the raised letter alphabet used by blind readers is profiled for children in grades 1-3 in this illustrated book. Highlights of Braille's childhood and adult life are discussed, along with some historical background about reading methods used by people who are blind.

Bernstein, Joanne E., and Bryna J. Fireside. ***Special Parents, Special Children.*** Morton Grove, IL: Albert Whitman and Co., 1991. 63 pp. $11.65. ISBN 0-8075-7557-3.

> This book provides an understanding of what it is like to grow up with a parent who is blind. Lisa, a sixth grader, teaches us how to handle sensitive situations such as using "seeing words" when talking to her dad, or any other person who has a visual impairment. Pictures provide the foundation for the text.

Eyerly, Jeannette. ***The Seeing Summer.*** New York: J.B. Lippincott, 1981. 153 pp. ISBN 0-397-31965-7. Out of print.

> When the new girl in her neighborhood turns out to be blind, ten-year-old Carey is initially disappointed. As time goes on, though, she learns that Jenny is more like her than different, and the two become best friends. When the girls are kidnapped by two bumbling men hoping for ransom money from Jenny's father, the two pool their skills and abilities to escape. The book includes an unobtrusive smattering of information on braille, orientation and mobility techniques, and do's and don't's of interacting with blind people.

Kroll, Virginia L. ***Naomi Knows It's Springtime.*** Honesdale, PA: Boyds Mill Press, 1993. 32 pp. $14.95. ISBN 1-56397-006-6.

> Naomi is blind, but enjoys the coming of spring with all of her other senses. She feels the changes in temperature, hears baby birds squeaking and the gentle breeze blowing, enjoys spinning on the tire swing, smells the flowers in bloom. . . . Although she cannot see the blue sky, she feels as if there is a rainbow in her mind. The vivid, slightly blurry illustrations help to emphasize the message that you don't have to see clearly to enjoy what is going on around you.

Litchfield, Ada B. *A Cane in Her Hand.* Morton Grove, IL: Albert Whitman and Co., 1977. 32 pp. $14.95. ISBN 0-8075-1056-4.

> Valerie is not blind, but sees "in a fog." Her sight deteriorates to the point where she must learn to use a cane or take too many lumps and bumps. This book for readers in early elementary grades shows how Valerie's teacher helps her by adapting lessons, how her friends accept her, and how her cane helps her. This book is great for awareness and acceptance.

Martin, Bill Jr., and John Archambault. *Knots on a Counting Rope.* New York, NY: Henry Holt, 1987. 32 pp. $15.95. ISBN 0-8050-0571-4.

> Sitting around the campfire with his grandfather, Boy-Strength-of-Blue-Horses begs to hear the story about who he is one more time. With frequent interruptions from his grandson, the old man recounts how Boy-Strength-of-Blue-Horses was born with "a dark curtain" in front of his eyes, yet learned to keep up with the other children in all respects—to ride like the wind and to cross some of the dark mountains. With its dramatic color illustrations, the book would be suitable to read aloud to younger elementary school children; older elementary school students (through grade 4) may enjoy reading the story to themselves.

McMahon, Patricia. *Listen for the Bus: David's Story.* Honesdale, PA: Boyds Mill Press, 1995. 48 pp. $15.95. ISBN 1-56397-368-5.

> Through words and color photos, this book presents a portrait of David, a kindergartner who is blind and has a hearing loss. David is depicted with parents, friends, and teachers, at school and in the community. He is shown as a capable, happy child who can ride a horse, use a hammer, and participate fully in life like other children his age. For children in lower elementary grades.

Radin, Ruth Yaffe. *Carver.* New York, NY: Random House, 1994. 70 pp. $2.99. ISBN 0-02-775651-3.

> When Jon was two years old, he was blinded in an accident that killed his father. Now 10, he yearns to learn to carve decoys as his father did. As Jon pursues his dream, he also finds friendship and self-confidence. For children 8-12.

Wright, Christine. *My Sister Katie: How She Sees God's World.* Minneapolis: Augsburg, 1990. 15 pp. $7.99. ISBN 0-8066-2497-3.

> This is a special day for Katie because her friend Sam and his dog Bowler are coming for a visit. From the time Katie gets up to the end of the day, the reader learns about coping with blindness. The book explains some of the adaptations that Katie, her family, and friends must make throughout the day. It was written to be a catalyst for discussion about disabilities, and includes suggestions for questions and leading discussions. This is one of Augsburg's *Talkabout* books.

■ ORGANIZATIONS

American Action Fund for Blind Children and Adults
18440 Oxnard St.
Tarzana, CA 91356

> SERVICES: Lends twin vision books for children (preschool through fourth grade) through the mail, at no cost to the borrower.

American Association of the Deaf-Blind

814 Thayer Ave.
Silver Spring, MD 20910
(301) 587-6545 TTY; (301) 588-8705 FAX

> PURPOSE: A national membership organization of people who are deaf-blind and others that promotes better opportunities and services for people who are deaf-blind.
> SERVICES: Legislative advocacy, deaf-blind awareness, technology development.
> PUBLICATION: Publishes a quarterly magazine, *The Deaf-Blind American.*

American Council of the Blind

1155 15th St., NW, Ste. 720
Washington, DC 20005
(202) 467-5081; (800) 424-8666; (202) 467-5085 FAX
E-mail: ncrabb@acb.org
Web site: http//www.acb.org

> PURPOSE: To promote the independence, dignity, and well-being of all blind and visually impaired people.
> SERVICES: Information and advisory services, scholarships for post secondary students who are blind, advocacy, public awareness and education campaigns, legal advice and assistance.
> PUBLICATIONS: Publishes *The Braille Forum*, a free monthly magazine with information on legislation, education, technology, recreation. Available in a variety of formats.

American Foundation for the Blind

11 Penn Plaza, Ste. 300
New York, NY 10001
(404) 525-2303
(800) AFB-LINE (232-5462)
Web site: http//www.afb.org/afb/
E-mail: afbinfo@afb.org

> PURPOSE: "To enable people who are blind or visually impaired to attain equality of access and opportunity that will ensure freedom of choice in their lives."
> SERVICES: Information and referral; advocacy; records and duplicates talking books; maintains Careers & Technology Information Bank (network of blind people who use assistive technology at home/work/school and are willing to advise others). Also maintains Helen Keller Archives (personal material donated by Helen Keller) and M.C. Migel Memorial Library (one of the world's largest collections of print material on blindness).
> PUBLICATIONS: *DOTS Newsletter,* a free quarterly publication on teaching and using braille; *Journal of Visual Impairment & Blindness; Directory of Services for Blind and Visually Impaired Persons in the United States and Canada; Dimensions: Visually Impaired Persons with Multiple Disabilities* ($22.95); *How to Thrive, Not Just Survive: A Guide to Developing Independent Life Skills for Blind and Visually Impaired Children and Youths* ($19.95); *An Orientation and Mobility Primer for Families and Young Children* ($12.95); *"Guide to Toys for Children Who Are Blind or Visually Impaired"* (free); many other publications. Call and request a catalog.

American Printing House for the Blind
1839 Frankfort Ave.
Louisville, KY 40206
(800) 223-1839; (502) 895-1509 FAX

PURPOSE: The world's oldest and largest publishing house for people who are blind.

SERVICES: Publishes talking books, books and periodicals in braille, and educational aids and tools. Has a database of volunteer- and commercially-produced books available in braille or other special media.

PUBLICATIONS: Has catalogs of braille publications, large-type books, educational aids, and print books for parents and professionals.

Blind Children's Center
4120 Marathon St.
Los Angeles, CA 90029
(213) 664-2153 (in LA); (800) 222-3567 (in CA); (800) 222-3566 (elsewhere in U.S.); (213) 665-3828 FAX
Web site: http//www.blindcntr.org/bcc
E-mail: info@blindcntr.org

PURPOSE: To provide services that meet the special needs of blind and partially sighted infants and young children.

SERVICES: Operates early intervention and preschool programs; funds and conducts research; toll-free hotline; publications program.

PUBLICATIONS: All of the following booklets are very parent-friendly and illustrated with photos of children and their families: *Let's Eat: Feeding a Child with a Visual Impairment* ($4.00); *Heart-to-Heart,* parents sharing their personal feelings about having a child who is blind or visually impaired ($2.00); *Talk To Me* ($2.00); *Dancing Cheek to Cheek* ($4.00).

California Deaf-Blind Services
650 Howe Ave., Ste. 300
Sacramento, CA 95824
(916) 641-5855

PUBLICATIONS: This organization will send free fact sheets about a variety of topics as related to persons who are deaf-blind. Some topics include: *Communication, What Is He Trying to Tell Me?*; *Light Sensitivity*; *Awareness of Medical Issues in Relation to Changes in Behavior*; *Ideas for Recreation and Leisure Activities*; *Alphabet Soup*; *Supported Education*; *Relaxation Strategies*; *Strategies for Successful Medical Appointments for Individuals with Deaf-Blindness*; *Innovative Living Options*; *Touch Cues*; *How to Interact with Individuals with Dual Sensory Impairments.*

The Carroll Center for the Blind
770 Centre St.
Newton, MA 02158
(617) 696-6200; (800) 852-3131

PUBLICATIONS: This school distributes a series of journal articles, including: *Computer Access Evaluation for Persons with Low Vision, Large Print Computer Access.* Also a resource guide which covers topics such as Character Enlarging Programs, Dedicated Word Processors, Selective Magnification, and Computer Accessories, and includes an extensive product review and bibliography. Request a publications list.

DB-LINK

345 N. Monmouth Ave.
Monmouth, OR 97361
(800) 438-9376; 503-838-8821 TTY; 503-838-8150 FAX
E-mail: dblink@tr.wosc.osshe.edu
Web site: http://www.tr.wosc.osshe.edu/dblink/

> PURPOSE: DB-LINK (The National Information Clearinghouse on Children Who Are Deaf-Blind) is a federally funded information service that gathers and disseminates information about children and adolescents who are deaf-blind.
>
> PUBLICATIONS: Free fact sheets are available online or in print, large print, braille, or ASCII on topics including: *"Communication"; "Early Interactions with Children Who Are Deaf-Blind"; "Psychological Evaluation of Children Who Are Deaf-Blind"; "Recreation and Leisure."*

The Hadley School for the Blind

700 Elm Street
P.O. Box 299
Winnetka, IL 60093-0299
(708) 446-8111; (708) 446-8153 FAX

> PUBLICATIONS: The Hadley School provides "an individualized distance [parent/child] education program." This free home study program provides the family with information that will help them acknowledge their child's strengths, become aware of his/her challenges, and develop an array of strategies that will set the stage for success. Courses include, ***Reach Out and Teach, Child Development I and II, Learning, Play and Toys, Braille Reading for Family Members, Hope for Parents of Blind Children,*** and ***Knowing the Systems.*** Correspondence courses in braille or on tape for students who are deaf or deaf-blind are also available in academic subjects, for vocational or technical education, and for personal enrichment. The school newsletter offers support, resources, and practical ideas for enriching the lives of the child who is visually impaired and his family. Write or call for an information packet.

Helen Keller National Center

111 Middle Neck Rd.
Sands Point, NY 11050-1299
(516) 944-8900 (voice/TDD); (516) 944-7302 FAX

> PURPOSE: To assist young people who are deaf-blind make the transition from school to adult services.
>
> SERVICES: Conducts research; provides technical assistance to those who work with deaf-blind people; operates regional offices that assist people who are deaf-blind in finding appropriate services.
>
> PUBLICATIONS: Pamphlets; fact sheets (such as *"Guidelines for Helping People Who Are Deaf-Blind," "Without Sight and Sound: Facts about Deaf-Blindness"*); a newsletter; and the ***Directory of Agencies Serving the Deaf-Blind.***

John Tracy Clinic

806 W. Adams Blvd.
Los Angeles, CA 90007
(800) 522-4582 (voice/TTY); (213) 749-1651 FAX

> PURPOSE: Supports and trains parents of children who are deaf or deaf-blind.
>
> PUBLICATIONS: Offers two correspondence courses for parents of children with hearing losses (for ages birth to 18 months, and 18 months through 5 years); and one correspondence course for

parents of children who are deaf-blind. The courses focus on communication needs, child development, and family relationships. Courses are offered in English and Spanish. Parents receive the correspondence courses free of charge; professionals pay a small fee.

National Association for Parents of the Visually Impaired
P.O. Box 317
Watertown, MA 02272-0317
(800) 562-6265; (617) 972-7444 FAX

> PURPOSE: "A national organization that helps parents to find information and resources for their blind and visually impaired children including those with additional disabilities. NAPVI provides leadership, support, and training to assist parents in helping children reach their potential."
> SERVICES: Parent to parent network on rare eye conditions; provides updated information on legislation that affects the education of children with visual impairments; holds local, regional, and national conferences.
> PUBLICATIONS: Quarterly newsletter *Awareness; Legislative Handbook for Parents; Mainstreaming the Visually Impaired Child; Preschool Learning Activities for the Visually Impaired; The Student with Albinism in the Regular Classroom.* Discount for members.

National Association for Visually Handicapped
22 West 21st St.
New York, NY 10010
(212) 889-3141; (212) 727-2931 FAX
Web site: http//www.navh.org

> PURPOSE: To provide information, referral, and services to people with partial vision and the professionals who work with them.
> SERVICES: Lends large print books by mail (free); acts as a clearinghouse of information about services available; provides information on large-print reading material and visual aids.
> PUBLICATIONS: Catalog of Large Print Loan Library (free). Also publishes two newsletters in larger print—one for children and one for adults—and booklets such as *"About Children's Vision: A Guide for Parents."*

National Braille Press
88 Saint Stephen St.
Boston, MA 02115
(617) 266-6160; (617) 437-0456
E-mail: orders@nbp.org
Web site: http://www.nbp.org

> SERVICES: Adult and children's books in braille. Children's books are also sold in twin vision format. The Press also offers a braille book club for children. Request a catalog of publications.

National Eye Institute Information Center
Publications Distribution Center
2020 Vision Place
Bethesda, MD 20892-3655
(800) 869-2020

> PURPOSE: A division of the National Institutes of Health, the NEI funds and conducts research on the eye and vision impairments.
> PUBLICATIONS: Offers fact sheets on subjects such as *"Cornea and Corneal Diseases"; "Selected National Eye Health-Related Organizations";* and *"Selected Resources for People with Low Vi-*

sion." Also has information packets, including *"Amblyopia and Strabismus"; "Cataract Surgery"; "Kertoconus"; and "Retinitis Pigmentosa."* Provides database searches—information on publications and AV materials available from other sources on selected topics such as *"Childhood Disorders"; "Inherited Disorders";* and *"Materials for Parents of Visually Impaired Children."* Has a school educational program about the eye, common eye problems, and eye safety, recommended for grades 4-8. All materials from the NEI are free of charge.

National Family Association for Deaf-Blind

c/o Helen Keller National Center
111 Middle Neck Rd.
Sands Point, NY 11050-1299
(516) 944-8900 (V/TTY); (516) 944-7302 FAX

> PURPOSE: A support network for families of people who are deaf-blind.
> PUBLICATION: Publishes *NFADB Newsletter.*

National Federation of the Blind

1800 Johnson St.
Baltimore, MD 21230
(410) 659-9314

> PURPOSE: A national membership organization of and for the blind which works to improve social and economic conditions of blind persons.
> PUBLICATIONS: Has an extensive catalog of literature and materials, including many free items, in many formats: inkprint, braille, talking book disk, cassette, and computer disk. Some of the topics covered include Blind Children/Blind Parents, Braille, Careers, Daily Living, Discrimination, Education, and General Interest. Also publishes a monthly newsletter, *Braille Monitor.* Please note that the organization prefers to receive orders by mail, rather than over the phone.

National Library Service for the Blind and Physically Handicapped

Library of Congress
1291 Taylor St., NW
Washington, DC 20542
(800) 424-8567
E-mail: nls@loc.gov
Web site: http//lcweb.loc.gov/nls

> PURPOSE: Provides a free library service to people who are blind or have a physical impairment or learning disability that prevents them from using standard printed materials.
> SERVICES: Lends books and magazines in braille or talking book format free of charge to eligible readers via postage-paid mail. Also lends cassette players for talking books.
> PUBLICATIONS: Two bimonthly publications, *Braille Book Review* and *Talking Book Topics,* list new books added to the collection. Reference circulars on topics of interest to people with disabilities and service providers are also available. Twin-vision books can be borrowed from the Library of Congress's regional libraries.

Parents of Blind Children

National Federation of the Blind
1800 Johnson St.
Baltimore, MD 21230
(410) 659-9314; (410) 685-5653 FAX

> PURPOSE: "A national membership organization of parents and friends of blind children reaching out to each other to give vital support, encouragement, and information."

SERVICES: Braille pen-pal service (Slate-Mates); national networking services for parents; workshops for parents.

PUBLICATIONS: Newsletter *(Future Reflections)* for members. Free publications: *"Braille Storybook Resources"; "Selected NFB Literature for Blind Youth"; "Art Lesson Plans for the Blind."* Please note that the organization prefers to receive orders by mail, rather than over the phone.

Recording for the Blind & Dyslexic
20 Roszel Rd.
Princeton, NJ 08540
(800) 221-4792; (609) 520-7990 FAX

SERVICES: For a one-time membership fee, people who are blind or who cannot use printed materials due to physical or perceptual disabilities can borrow educational books on cassette tape. Taped books include textbooks, computer manuals, and research materials, as well as fiction, drama, and poetry. A print catalog of materials on tape is available for a small fee, or borrowers can call the toll-free number to ask about specific titles.

Appendix
Publishers' Addresses

Note: Publishers' names consisting of a first and last name are alphabetized under the last name.

A

ABC-CLIO, 130 Cremona Dr., P.O. Box 1911, Santa Barbara, CA 93116-1911.

Ability Workshop Press, 1601 Old Bayshore Hwy., #260B, Burlingame, CA 94010. (800) 897-9001; (415) 692-8997 FAX.

Abingdon Press, 201 Eight Ave., South, Nashville, TN 47577. 812-357-8011.

ABLEDATA, 8455 Colesville Rd., Ste. 935, Silver Spring, MD 20910. 800-227-0216; 301-608-8912 TTY; 301-608-8958 FAX.

Academic Therapy Publications, 20 Commercial Blvd., Novato, CA 94949. 415-883-3314.

Academy Chicago Publishers, 363 West Erie, 7th Floor East, Chicago, IL 60610. 312-751-7300.

Adaptive Environments, 374 Congress St., Ste. 301, Boston, MA 02210. 617-695-1225 V/TDD; 617-482-8099 FAX.

A.D.D. WareHouse, 300 NW 70th Ave., Ste. 102, Plantation, FL 33317. 800-233-9273; 954-792-8545 FAX.

Addison-Wesley, Rte. 128, Reading, MA 01867. 800-447-2226.

AGS, Inc., P.O. Box 99, Publishers Bldg., Circle Pines, MN 55014-1796. 612-786-4343; 800-328-2560.

Allyn & Bacon, 160 Gould St., Needham Heights, MA 02194-2315. 800-852-8024; 617-455-7024.

Allyn & Bacon Canada, 1870 Birchmount Rd., Scarborough, Ontario M1P 2J7.

AFB, American Foundation for the Blind-Press, 11 Penn Plaza, New York, NY 10001.

American Association on Mental Retardation, 444 North Capitol St. NW, Washington, DC 20001. 202-387-1968.

American Library Association, Publishing Services, 50 E. Huron St., Chicago, IL 60611. 312-944-6780; 800-545-2433.

American Publishing Co., P.O. Box 988, Evanston, IL 60204-0988.

Annick Press, 15 Patricia Ave., Willowdale, Ontario M2M 1H9 Canada. 416-221-4802.

The Arc of New Jersey, 985 Livingston Ave., North Brunswick, NJ 08902. 908-246-2525; 908-214-1834 FAX.

The Arc of the United States, 500 E. Border St., Ste. 300, Arlington, TX 76010. 817-261-6003; 817-277-0553 TDD.

Archon Books, Div. of Shoe String Press, Box 657, 2 Linsley St., North Haven, CT 06473. 203-239-2702.

Association for the Care of Children's Health, 7910 Woodmont Ave., Ste. 300, Bethesda, MD 20814-3015. 301-654-6549.

Augsburg, P.O. Box 1209, 426 S. Fifth St., Minneapolis, MN 55440. 800-328-4648.

Autism Research Review, 4182 Adams Ave., San Diego, CA 92116. 714-281-7165.

Autism Society of North Carolina, 2216 Sanderford Rd., Raleigh, NC 27610. 919-821-4138.

Avon, 105 Madison Ave., New York, NY 10016. 800-654-5888.

B

Bakersfield ARC/Hearts Connection, 3200 North Sillect, Bakersfield, CA 93308. 805-327-8531.

Ballantine, 210 E. 50th., New York, NY 10022. 212-751-2600.

Bantam, 666 Fifth Ave., New York, NY 10103. 800-223-6834.

Barron, 250 Wireless Blvd., Hauppaugh, NY 11788-3917. 516-434-3311; 800-800-645-3476.

Beach Center, University of Kansas, 3111 Haworth Hall, Lawrence, KS 66045. 913-864-7600.

Beacon Press, 25 Beacon St., Boston, MA 02108-2892. 617-742-2110.

Betterway Books, P.O. Box 219, Crozet, VT 22932. 804-823-5661.

Birch Lane Press, 120 Enterprise Ave., Secaucus, NJ 07094. 201-866-0490; 201-866-8159.

Blackwell Publishers, 350 Main St., Malden, MA 02148. 617-388-8200.

Blackwell Science, Inc., 350 Main St., Malden, MA 02148. 617-388-8250.

John F. Blair, 1406 Plaza Dr., Winston-Salem, NC 27103. 910-768-1374; 800-222-9796.

Blind Childrens Center, 4120 Marathon St., Los Angeles, CA 90029. 213-664-2153.

Books Beyond Borders, Inc., 3640 Walnut St., Ste. A, Boulder, CO 80301. 303-449-6440.

Bradford Publications, 5805 Fox Chapel Dr., Austin, TX 78746-6209. 512-328-8316; 800-354-2760.

Branden Books, 17 Station St., Box 843, Brookline Village, MA 02147. 617-734-2045.

Paul H. Brookes Publishing, P.O. Box 10624, Baltimore, MD 21285. 800-638-3775; 410-337-8539 FAX.

Paul H. Brookes, Canadian distributor. Order from: Copp Clark Professional, 200 Adelaide St, West, Toronto, Ontario M5H 1W7. 800-815-9417; 416-597-1617 FAX.

Brookline Books, P.O. Box 1047, Cambridge, MA 02238. 617-868-0360; 800-666-BOOK.

Brown County ARC, P.O. Box 12770, Green Bay, WI 54307-2770. 414-498-2599.

Brunner/Mazel, Magination Press. Contact American Psychological Association, c/o APA Books, 750 1st St. NE, Washington, DC 20002. (202) 336-5500; (202) 336-5630 FAX.

Buffalo River Press, 2274 S. 1300 W., Ste. G8-300, Salt Lake City, UT 84106. 801-582-1155.

Bull Publishing, P.O. Box 208, Palo Alto, CA 94302. 800-676-2855; 415-327-3300.

Butterworth-Heinemann, 313 Washington St., Newton, MA 02158. 800-366-2665; 800-446-6520 FAX.

C

Calliope, 211 S. Chadbourne Ave., Madison, WI 53705. 608-238-9258.

Cambridge University Press, 32 E. 57th St., New York, NY 10022. 800-221-4512.

Captus Press, c/o York University Campus, 4700 Keele St., North York, Ontario M3J 1P3 Canada.

CAUSE, 313 S. Washington Square, Ste. 040, Lansing, MI 48944-2122.

The Center for Applied Research in Education, c/o Prentice-Hall Direct, 240 Frisch Ct., Paramus, NY 07652. 201-909-6200.

Center for Law and Education, Larsen Hall, 6th Floor, 14 Appian Way, Cambridge, MA 02138.

Center on Human Policy, Syracuse University, School of Education, 805 S. Crouse Ave., Syracuse, NY 13244-2280. 800-894-0826; 315-443-4355 TTY; 315-443-4338 FAX.

Channing L. Bete Co. Inc., 200 State Road, South Deerfield, MA 01373. 800-628-7733.

Checkerboard Press, 30 Vesey St., New York, NY 10007.

Cheever Publications, P.O. Box 700, Bloomington, IL 61702. 309-378-2961.

Chicago Review Press, 814 N. Franklin St., Chicago, IL 60610.

Children's Press, Div. of Grolier, Inc., Sherman Turnpike, Danbury, CT 06816. 203-797-3500; 203-797-3197 FAX.

Clarion Books, c/o Houghton Mifflin Trade Books, Wayside Rd., Burling, MA 01803. 800-225-3362.

Communication Skill Builders, 555 Academic Ct., San Antonio, TX 78204. 800-211-8378; 800-232-1223 FAX.

Council on Exceptional Children, 1920 Association Drive, Reston, VA 22091. 703-620-3660.

Creative Arts Books Co., 833 Bancroft Way, Berkeley, CA 94710. 415-848-4777.

Crossroad Publishing Company, 370 Lexington Ave., Ste. 2600, New York, NY 10017. 212-532-3650; 212-532-4922 FAX.

Cumberland Hospital, P.O. Box 150, 9407 Cumberland Rd., New Kent, VA 23124. 800-368-3472.

Current, Inc., P.O. Box 2559, Colorado Springs, CO 80901. 719-594-4100.

D

Dell Publishing, 666 5th Ave., New York, NY 10103. 800-223-6834.

Demos Vermande, 386 Park Ave. S., Suite 201, New York, NY 10016. 800-532-8663.

Devinjer House, P.O. Box 130, Sparta, Ontario, Canada N0L 2H0.

Dilligaf Publishing, 64 Court St., Ellsworth, ME 04605. 207-667-5031.

DO-IT, College of Engineering/Computing & Communications, University of Washington, 4545 15th Ave. NE, Room 206, Seattle, WA 98105-4527. 206-685-DOIT; 206-685-4054 FAX.

Doubleday, 666 5th Ave., New York, NY 10103. 800-223-6834.

Dowden Publishing Company, 110 Summit Ave., Montvale, NJ 0764f5. 201-391-2778; 800-707-7040; 201-391-9100 FAX.

Duke University Medical Center, Box 90660, Durham, NC 27708-0660. 919-687-3600.

Dunn and Hargitt, 22 N. 2nd St., Lafayette, IN 47902. (317) 423-2624.

E

Educational Systems Association, P.O. Box 96, Kearney, NE 68848-0096. 303-234-6261.

Educators Publishing Service, 31 Smith Place, Cambridge, MA 02138-1000. 617-547-6706.

ETR Associates, P.O. Box 1830, Santa Cruz, CA 95061-1830.

M. Evans, 216 E. 49th. St., New York, NY 10017. 212-688-2810.

F

Faber & Faber, 53 Shore Rd., Winchester, MA 01890. 781-721-1427.

Family Resource Center on Disabilities, 200 S. Michigan Ave, Ste. 1520, Chicago, IL 60604. 312-341-0900.

Family Support Institute Press, 30 E. 6th Ave., Ste. 300, Vancouver, British Columbia, Canada V5T 4P4. 604-875-1119; 604-875-6744 FAX.

Fawcett, c/o Random House, 201 E. 50 St., New York, NY 10022. 212-751-2600; 800-726-0600.

Fetal Alcohol Educational Program, 1975 Main St., Concord, MA 01742. 617-739-1424.

Fithian Press, P.O. Box 1525, Santa Barbara, CA 93102. 800-662-8351.

Four Leaf Press, 2020 Garfield St., Eugene, OR 97405. 541-485-4938.

Four Winds Press, 265 Tenafly Rd., Tenafly, NJ 07670. 201-569-3586

Free Press, Division of Simon and Schuster, 866 Third Ave., New York, NY 10022. 800-223-2336.

Free Spirit Publishing, 400 First Ave, N., Ste. 616, Minneapolis, MN 55401-1730. 800-735-7323; 612-337-5050 FAX.

Friendship Press, 475 Riverside Dr., New York, NY 10115. 212-870-2586.

G

G.R. Press, Inc., 100 E. Linton Blvd, Suite 403B, Delray Beach, FL 33483. 407-274-9906.

Gallaudet University Press, 800 Florida Ave., NE, Washington, DC 20002. 888-630-9347; 800-621-8476 FAX.

Gemma B. Publishing, Box 713-740 Corydon Ave., Winnipeg, Manitoba, Canada R3M 0YI.

Georgiana Organization, P.O. Box 2607, Westport, CT 06880. 203-454-1221; 203-454-3788 FAX.

Gillette Childrens Hospital, 200 E. University Ave., St. Paul, MN 55101. 612-291-2848.

Glenbridge Publishing Ltd., 6010 Jewell Ave., Lakewood, CO 80232. 800-986-4135; 303-987-9037 FAX.

Gospel Publishing House, 1445 Boonville Ave., Springfield, MO.

Grey House Publishing, Pocket Knife Square, Lakeview, CT 06039. 860-435-0868; 800-562-2139.

GSI, P.O. Box 746, DeWitt, NY 13214. 315-446-4849.

Guilford Press, 72 Spring St., New York, NY 10012. 800-221-3966.

H

The Hanen Program (U.S. address), P.O. Box 1213, Buffalo, NY 14240-1213. 416-921-1073; 800-380-3355 FAX only.

The Hanen Centre (Canadian address), 252 Bloor St. West, Ste. 3-390, Toronto, Ontario M5S 1V5. 416-921-1073; 800-380-3355 FAX only.

Harcourt Brace Co., 6277 Sea Harbor Dr., Orlando, FL 32887-6777. 407-345-2000; 800-225-5425.

HarperCollins, 10 E. 53rd St., New York, NY 10022. 800-242-7737.

Harris Communications, Inc., 15159 Technology Dr., Eden Prairie, MN 55344-7714. 800-825-6758; 800-825-9187 TTY; 612-906-1099 FAX.

Hartley & Marks, Box 147, Point Roberts, WA 98281. 800-277-5887.

Harvard Common Press, 535 Albany St., Boston, MA 02118. 617-423-5803.

Harvard University Press, 79 Garden St., Cambridge, MA 02138. 800-448-2242; 800-962-4983 FAX.

Herald Press, 616 Walnut Ave., Scottdale, PA 15683. 800-245-7894.

Hill and Wang, 19 Union Square West, New York, NY 10003. 800-631-8571.

Hometown Press, Box 154, Carbondale, CO 81623. 303-963-1268.

Hope Press, P.O. Box 188, Duarte, CA 91009-0188. 818-303-0644; 800-321-4039.

Human Kinetics, P.O. Box 5076, Champaign, IL 61820. 800-747-4457.

Human Services Institute, c/o Sulzburger & Graham Publishing, 505 8th Ave., New York, NY 10018. 800-366-7086; 212-947-0360 FAX.

Hunter House, P.O. Box 2914, Alameda, CA 94501-0914. 800-266-5592; 510-865-4295 FAX.

Hyperion, 114 Fifth Ave., New York, NY 10011. 800-343-9204; 212-633-4811.

I

Illinois State Board of Education, 100 N. First St., Springfield, IL 62777-0001. 217-782-6601.

Impact Publishers, P.O. Box 1094, San Luis Obispo, CA 93406. 800-246-7228.

Inclusion Press International, 24 Thome Crescent, Toronto, Ontario M6H 2S5 Canada. 416-658-5363; 416-658-5067 FAX.

Institute on Community Integration, 109 Pattee Hall, 150 Pillsbury Dr. SE, Minneapolis, MN 554355. 612-624-4512.

Institute on Disability/UAP, University of New Hampshire, 7 Leavitt Lane, Ste. 101, Durham, NH 03824-3522. 603-862-4320; 603-862-0555 FAX.

J

Jason and Nordic, P.O. Box 441, Hollidaysburg, PA 16648. 814-696-2920; 814-696-2920 FAX.

Johns Hopkins University Press, 2715 N. Charles St., Baltimore, MD 21218-4363. 410-516-6900; 800-537-5487.

Johnson Institute, 7205 OHMS Lane, Edina, MN 55439-2159. 800-231-5165.

Journal on Autism and Developmental Disorders, c/o Plenum Publishing Corp. 233 Spring St., New York, NY 10013. 800-221-9369.

K

Kidsrights, 10100 Park Cedar Dr., Charlotte, NC 28210. 704-541-0100; 704-541-0113.

KSF, 630 Ninth Ave., Suite 901, New York, NY 10036. 212-582-5600.

L

Landmark, 12160 Killbrook Dr., Florissant, MO 63037-5025.

Learner Designs, Inc., P.O. Box 747, Lawrence, KS 66044-0747. 913-842-9088.

Lerner Publications Company, 241 First Ave. North, Minneapolis, MN 55401. 800-328-4929.

Learning Disabilities Association of Canada, 200-323 Chapel, Ottawa, Ontario K1N 7Z2. 613-238-5721; 613-245-5391 FAX.

The Learning Works, P.O. Box 6187, Santa Barbara, CA 93160. 800- 235-5767; (805) 964-1466.

Let's Face It, P.O. Box 29972, Bellingham, WA 98228-1972.

Little Brown, 34 Beacon St., Boston, MA 02108. 800-343-9204.

Lothrop, Lee & Shepard, 105 Madison Ave., New York, NY 10016. 800-631-1199.

Love Publishing Company, P.O. Box 22353, Denver, CO 80222. 303-757-2579; 303-782-5683.

Lowell House, 2020 Ave. of the Stars, Los Angeles, CA 90067. 310-552-7555; 310-552-7573 FAX.

LRP Publications, 747 Dresher Rd., P.O. Box 980, Horsham, PA 19044-0980. 800-341-7874, ext. 275; 215-784-9639 FAX; 215-658-0938.

M

Macmillan Publishing Co., 1633 Broadway, New York, NY 10019. 212-654-8500.

Magination Press. Contact American Psychological Association, c/o APA Books, 750 1st St. NE, Washington, DC 20002. (202) 336-5500; (202) 336-5630 FAX.

Media Publishing, 2440 O St., Ste. 202, Lincoln, NE 68510-1125. 800-36-MEDIA.

Julian Messner, 299 Jefferson Rd., Parsippanny, NJ 07054. 201-739-8000; 614-771-7398.

Midgard Press, Division of Westport Publications, 1102 Grand, Ste. 2300, Kansas City, MO 64106.

Minnesota Department of Health, Services for Children with Handicaps, 717 Delaware SE, Minneapolis, MN 55414. 612-623-5000.

Mission Publishing, P.O. Box 1176, Roswell, GA 30077.

MMB Music, 3526 Washington Ave., St. Louis, MO 63103. 800-543-3771; (314) 531-8384.

Modern Signs Press, 10443 Los Alamitos Blvd, Los Alamitos, CA 90720. 310-596-8545.

Montana University Affiliated Rural Institute on Disabilities, 52 Corbin, University of Montana, Missoula, MT 59812. 406-243-5467; 406-243-2349.

The Thomas More Press, c/o RCL, 200 E. Bethany, Allen, TX 75002. 800-527-5030; 800-688-8356.

John Muir Publications, P.O. Box 613, Santa Fe, NM 87504-0613. 505-982-4078; 800-888-754.

N

Nancibell, 1720 Filbert St., Paso Robles, CA 93446. 805-541-3836; 800-223-1819.

National Association for the Education of Young Children, 1834 Connecticut Ave., NW, Washington, DC 20009-5786.

National Association of Social Workers, Inc., 750 First St. NE, Ste. 700, Washington DC 20002-4241. 800-227-3590.

National Cued Speech Association, Nazareth College, 4245 East Ave., Rochester, NY 14618. 800-459-3529.

National Braille Press, 88 Saint Stephen St., Boston, MA 02115. 617-266-6160.

National Center for Clinical Infant Programs, 733 Fifteenth St., NW, Washington, DC 20005. 202-347-0308.

National Centr for Law and Learning Disabilities, P.O. Box 368, Cabin John, MD 20818. 301-469-8308.

National Fragile X Foundation, 1441 York St., Suite 215, Denver, CO 80206. 303-333-6155; 800-688-8765; 303-333-4369 FAX.

National Institute of Mental Health, 5600 Fishers Lane, Room 7C-02, Rockville, MD 20857. 301-443-4513; 301-443-0008 FAX.

National Maternal and Child Health Clearinghouse, 2070 Chain Bridge Rd., Ste. 450, Vienna, VA 22182-2536. 703-356-1964; 703-821-2098 FAX.

National Professional Resources, 25 S. Regent St., Port Chester, NY 10573. 800-453-7461; 914-937-9327 FAX.

National Spinal Cord Injury Association, 8300 Colesville Rd., Ste. 551, Silver Spring, MD 20910. (301) 588-6959; (301) 588-9414 FAX.

New Harbinger Publications, 5674 Shattuck Ave., Oakland, CA 94609. 800-748-6273.

Newmarket Press, 18 E. 48th St., New York, NY 10017. 212-832-3575; 800-669-3903.

NIDCD Information Clearinghouse, 1 Communication Ave., Bethesda, MD 20892-3456. 800-241-1044; 800-241-1055 TTY; 301-907-8830 FAX.

O

Orchard Books, 95 Madison Ave., New York, NY 10016. 800-433-3411; 212-213-6435 FAX.

Oxford University Press, 198 Madison Ave, New York, NY 10016-4314. 800-451-7556.

P

PACER Center, 4826 Chicago Ave. South, Minneapolis, MN 55417-1098. 612-827-2966.

Pantheon, 210 E. 50th St., New York, NY 10022. 800-638-6460.

Park Nicollet Medical Foundation, 5000 W. 39th St., Minneapolis, MN 55416. 612-993-8000.

Peachtree Publishers, 494 Armour Circle, NE, Atlanta, GA 30324.

PEAK Parent Center, Lehman Dr., Ste. 101, Colorado Springs, CO 80918. 800-282-0251.

Penguin Books Canada, 10 Alcorn Ave., Ste. 300, Toronto, Ontario M4V 3B2 Canada. 416-925-2249; 416-925-0068 FAX.

Penguin Books USA, 375 Hudson St., New York, NY 10014. 212-366-2000; 212-366-2666 FAX.

Tim Peters and Company, 87 Main St., Peapack, NJ 07977. 800-543-2230; 908-234-1961 FAX.

Peterson's, Box 2123, Princeton, NJ 08543. 800-338-3282; 609-243-9150 FAX.

Peytral Publications, P.O. Box 1162, Minnetonka, MN 55345. 612-949-8707.

Phonic Ear, 3880 Cypress Dr., Petaluma, CA 94954-7600. 707-769-1110; 707; 769-9624 FAX.

Plenum, 233 Spring St., New York, NY 10013. 800-221-9369.

Pocket Books, c/o Simon & Schuster Consumer Group, 1230 Avenue of the Americas, New York, NY 10020. 800-223-2336.

Prentice-Hall, c/o Simon & Schuster, One Lake St., Upper Saddle River, NJ 07458. 201-236-7000.

Pro-Ed, 8700 Shoal Creek Blvd, Austin, TX 78758. 800-897-3202; 512-451-8542 FAX.

Putnam Berkley Group, 200 Madison Ave., New York NY 10016. 212-951-840; 800-631-8571.

R

Raven Press, Lippincott-Ravin Publishers, 227 E. Washington Square, Philadelphia, PA 19106. 800-638-3030.

Rayve Productions, P.O. Box 726, Windsor, CA 95492. 800-852-4890; 707-838-2220 FAX.

Real Life Story Books, 19430 Business Center Dr., Northridge, CA 91324.

Rehabilitation Institute of San Antonio, 9119 Cinammon Hill, San Antonio, TX 78240. 210-691-0737.

Research Press, 2612 N. Mattis Ave., Champaign, IL 61821. 800-519-2707; (217) 352-1221 FAX.

RESNA, 1700 N. Moore St., Ste. 1540, Arlington, VA 22209-1903. 703-524-6686.

Resources for Rehabilitation, 33 Bedford St., No. 19A, Lexington, MA 02173. 617-862-6455.

Rodale Press, 33 E. Minor St., Emmaus, PA 18098. 610-967-5171; 800-527-8200.

G. Allan Roeher Inst., York University, Kinsmen Bldg., 4700 Keele St., Downsview, Ontario M3J 1P3 Canada.

Rosen Publishing Group, 29 E. 21st St., New York, NY 10010. 800-237-9932; 212-777-0277 FAX.

S

Sage Publications, 2455 Teller Rd, Thousand Oaks, CA 91320. 805- 499-0721.

St. Martin's Press, 175 Fifth Ave., New York, NY 10010. 800-221-7945; 212-420-9314 FAX.

SCALARS Publishing, P.O. Box 158123, Nashville, TN 37215.

Schoolsearch, 127 Marsh St., Belmont, MA 02178. 617-489-5785; 617-489-5641 FAX.

Science and Behavior Books, Box 60519, Palo Alto, CA 94306. 415-965-0954; 800-547-9982.

Second Story Press, 30 Commerce Pk. Rd., Milford, CT 06460. 203-878-6417.

Harold Shaw Publishers, Box 567, 388 Gundersen Dr., Wheaton, IL 60189. 800-SHAW-PUB; 708-665-6793 FAX.

SIECUS, Publications Dept., 130 W. 42nd St., Ste. 350, New York, NY 10036-7802. 212-819-9770.

Sierra Books, P.O. Box 5853, Pasadena, CA 91117-0853. 818-355-0181.

Simon and Schuster, 1230 Avenue of the Americas, New York, NY 10020 800-223-2336; 212-698-7007.

Singular Publishing, 401 West A St., Suite 325, San Diego, CA 92101-7904. 800-521-8545; 619-238-6789 FAX.

Sopris West, 1140 Boston Ave., Longmont, CO 80501. 800-547-6747; 303-776-5934 FAX.

Southern Illinois University Press, P.O. Box 3647, Carbondale, IL 62902-3697. 618-453-2281; 800-346-2680.

Speciality Press, 300 NW 70th Ave., Plantation, FL 33317. 954-792-8944.

Speech Foundation of America. *See* Stuttering Foundation.

Spinal Network, P.O. Box 8987, Malibu, CA 90265. 800-543-4116.

James Stanfield Co., P.O. Box 41058, Santa Barbara, CA 93140. 805-897-1185.

State of Conneticut Board of Education, 110 Myrtle Ave, Westport, CT 06880. 203-341-1015.

Gareth Stevens Publishing, 1555 N. River Center Drive, Ste. 201, Milwaukee, WI 53212. 800-341-3569; 414-225-0377 FAX.

Stuttering Foundation of America, P.O. Box 11749, Memphis, TN 38111-0749. 800-992-9392; 901-452-7343; 901-452-3931 FAX.

T
Teachers College Press, Columbia University, 1234 Amsterdam Ave., New York, NY 10027. 212-678-3929; 212-678-4149.

Therapy Skill Builders, c/o Communication Skill Builders, 555 Academic Ct., San Antonio, TX 78204. 800-211-8378; 800-232-1223 FAX.

Thinking Publications, P.O. Box 163, 424 Galloway St., Eau Claire, WI 54702-0163. 715-832-2488; 715-832-9082 FAX.

Charles C. Thomas, 2600 S. First St., Springfield, IL 62794. 800-258-8980; 217-789-9130 FAX.

Time Warner, Time Life Inc., 2000 Duke St., Alexandria, VA 22314. 800-621-7026.

Times Books, 201 E. 50th St., New York, NY 10022. 800-733-3000; 212-572-4949 FAX.

TJ Publishers, 817 Silver Spring Ave., Silver Spring, MD 20910.

Trace Research & Development Center, University of Wisconsin-Madison, S-151 Waisman Center, 1500 Highland Ave., Madison, WI 53705-2280. 608-262-6966; 608-263-5408 TDD; 608-262-8848 FAX.

U
U.S. Dept. of Education, 400 Maryland Ave. SW, Washington, DC. 202-401-2000.

U.S. Dept. of Education, Office of Special Education and Rehabilitative Services, 330 C St., SW, Room 3132, Washington, DC 20202-2524. 202-205-8241 voice/TTY.

Underwood Books, P.O. Box 1609, Grass Valley, CA 95945. 916-274-7997; 916-274-7179.

University of Alaska Press, P.O. Box 756240, Gruening Bldg., Fairbanks, AK 99775. 888-252-6657; 907-474-5502.

University of California Press, 2120 Berkeley Way, Berkeley, CA 94720. 800-822-6657; 510-643-7127.

University of Georgia Press, 330 Research Dr., Athens, GA 30602. 800-266-5842; 706-369-6131.

University of Minnesota Press, 111 Third Ave. South, Ste. 290, Minneapolis, MN 55401. 612-627-1970; 612-627-1980.

University of North Carolina Press, P.O. Box 3400, Chapel Hill, NC 27515. 800-848-6224; 919-966-3829 FAX.

University of Washington Press, P.O. Box 50096, Seattle, WA 98145-5096. 800-441-4115; 206-543-3932 FAX.

University Press of Colorado, P.O. Box 849, Niwot, CO 80544.

Ups and Downs, Calgary Down Syndrome Association, 1001 17th St. NW, Calgary, Alberta T2N 2E5 Canada. 403-289-4394; 403-289-4339.

V

Vantage, 516 W. 34th St., New York, NY 10001. 212-736-1767.

Verbal Images Press, 19 Fox Dr., Fairport, NY 14450. 716-377-3807; 716-377-5401 FAX.

Villard Books, c/o Random House, 201 E. 50th St., New York, NY 10022. 212-572-2211; 212-572-6026 FAX.

Visible Ink Incorporated, 40 Holly Lane, Roslyn Heights, NY 11577. 516-621-2445.

W

Walker and Company, 435 Hudson St., New York, NY 10014. 800-AT-WALKER; 212-727-0984 FAX.

Waterfront Books, 85 Crescent Rd., Burlington, VT 05401-4126. 800-639-6063.

Franklin Watts, c/o Grolier, Inc., Sherman Turnpike, Danbury, CT 06816. 203-797-3500; 203-797-3197 FAX.

Western Psychological Services, 12031 Wilshire Blvd., Los Angeles, CA 90025. 800-648-8857; 310-478-7838 FAX.

Albert Whitman and Co., 6340 Oakton St., Morton Grove, IL 60053. 800-255-7675; 847-581-0039.

Windswept House Publishers, P.O. Box 159, Mt. Desert, ME 04660.

Woodbine House, 6510 Bells Mill Rd, Bethesda, MD 20817. 800-843-7323; 301-897-5838 FAX.

Woodbine House, Canadian distributor. Order from: Monarch Books, 5000 Dufferin St., Downsview, Ontario M3H 5T5. 800-404-7404; 416-736-1702 FAX.

Writer's Press, 5278 Chinden Blvd., Boise, ID 83714. 800-574-1715; 208-327-0566.

Y

York Press, P.O. Box 504, Timonium, MD 21094. 800-962-2763; 410-560-6758 FAX.

Index

of Organizations

Index

of Authors

Index

of Titles

Index

of Subjects

◆ **Notes** ◆

◆ **Notes** ◆

■ ABOUT THE AUTHOR

A specialist in Early Childhood Special Education, Wilma K. Sweeney teaches for Tehachapi Unified School District in California. She is also an adjunct professor at Bakersfield College, and a consultant for Kern County Early Start Services, an infant and toddler program. The mother of three sons, two with fragile X syndrome, Sweeney and her family live in Tehachapi, California.